ACCLAIM FOR
ONE DAY OF THE CIVIL WAR

"Absorbing. . . . This is a cleverly conceived and
consistently engrossing look at the Civil War."
—*Publishers Weekly*

"This unique work effectively captures the scope and rich
variety of the Civil War experience by focusing on the events
of one day—the war's midpoint. Here the reader will find fierce
combat, adventure, routine, executions, boredom, and all manner
of human experience played out on a worldwide stage.
Bob Willett is a first-class storyteller."
—Curt Johnson, author of *Civil War Battles* and
Artillery Hell: The Employment of Artillery at Antietam

"Drawing on official documents, diaries, personal
letters, and reminiscences, Robert Willett has painted a
dramatic portrait of the 'everyday war' Billy Yank and
Johnny Reb endured. It's all here: terror, boredom, complaints,
praise, heroics, incompetence, reward, and punishment.
Readers will be fascinated by it and, after reading it, will
appreciate what 'real war' is between the headline-making
battles. This is a fine book, thoroughly researched and
thoughtfully presented—and enjoyable reading."
—William Riley Booksher, author of
Bloody Hill: The Civil War Battle of Wilson's Creek

ROBERT L. WILLETT, JR., an international banking consultant, is a lifelong student of the Civil War and a contributor to *Civil War Times,
Illustrated*. He lives in Cocoa Beach, Florida

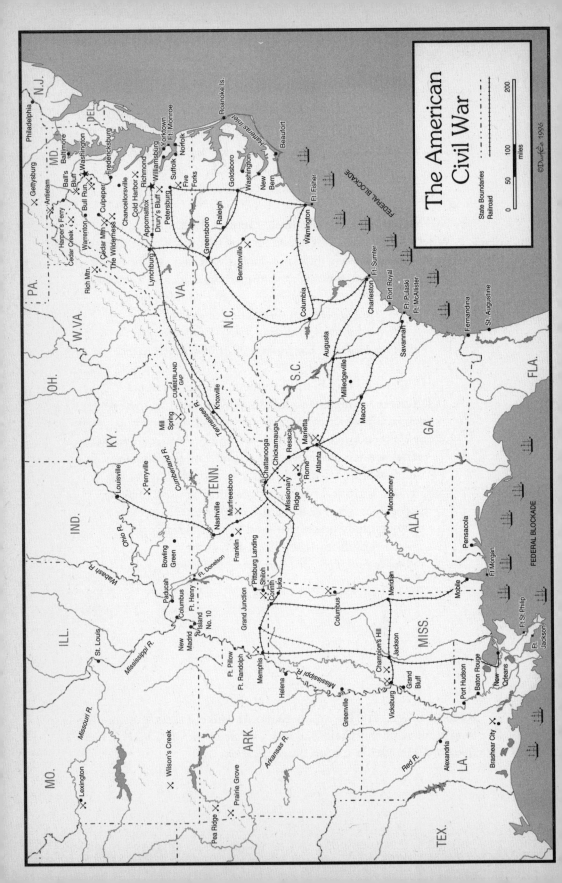

The American Civil War

State Boundaries
Railroad

miles
0   50   100   200

©Durlée 1996

ONE DAY OF THE
CIVIL WAR

America in Conflict
April 10, 1863

★

Robert L. Willett, Jr.

A PLUME BOOK

PLUME
Published by the Penguin Group
Penguin Putnam Inc., 375 Hudson Street, New York, New York 10014, U.S.A.
Penguin Books Ltd, 27 Wrights Lane, London W8 5TZ, England
Penguin Books Australia Ltd, Ringwood, Victoria, Australia
Penguin Books Canada Ltd, 10 Alcorn Avenue, Toronto, Ontario, Canada M4V 3B2
Penguin Books (N.Z.) Ltd, 182–190 Wairau Road, Auckland 10, New Zealand

Penguin Books Ltd, Registered Offices: Harmondsworth, Middlesex, England

Published by Plume, an imprint of Dutton NAL, a member of Penguin Putnam Inc.
This is an authorized reprint of a hardcover edition published by Brassey's Inc.
For information address Brassey's Inc., 8000 Westpark Drive, First Floor, McLean, VA 22102.

First Plume Printing, August, 1998
10 9 8 7 6 5 4 3 2 1

Grateful acknowledgment is made to the following for permission to reprint previously
published material:

Photo of Elisha Rhodes in *All for the Union* by Robert Hunt Rhodes copyright © 1991
by Robert Hunt Rhodes, permission of Crown Publishers, Inc.

Photo of Corydon Foote in *With Sherman to the Sea* by Olive Deane Hormel and
Corydon Edward Foote copyright © 1960 by Olive Deane Hormel, permission of
HarperCollins Publishers, Inc.

 REGISTERED TRADEMARK—MARCA REGISTRADA

LIBRARY OF CONGRESS CATALOGING-IN-PUBLICATION DATA:
Willett, Robert L.
One day of the Civil War : America in conflict, April 10, 1863 /
Robert L. Willett, Jr.
p.   cm.
Originally published: Washington [D.C.] : Brassey's, c1997.
Includes bibliographical references (p.   ) and index.
ISBN: 0-452-27977-1
1. United States—History—Civil War, 1861–1865.   I. Title.
E468.9.W55   1998
973.7—dc21   98–6226
                                                                                                    CIP

Original hardcover design by Oksana Kushnir
Printed in the United States of America

To Donna for not only participating in all phases of the book, but for her continued encouragement through good times and bad—and to three wonderful kids, Leslie, Tom, and Barb for their tolerance of Dad's obsession and their hours of help.

They have proved once again that family is more than sharing a last name.

CONTENTS

LIST OF MAPS

PREFACE

It is well that war is so terrible—we should grow too fond of it.
Robert E. Lee at Fredericksburg

The history of the American Civil War has held a fascination for Americans exceeding that of any other war. It has been studied from every perspective imaginable: strategic, tactical, organizational, logistical, social, psychological, medical, geographical, and political. Biographies and autobiographies of the principals abound. The great battles—Manassas, Shiloh, Antietam, Fredericksburg, Chancellorsville, Gettysburg, and the others—have all been analyzed over and over by talented military historians.

The battlefields where these bloody affairs took place have been preserved and enshrined. Important anniversaries are celebrated by legions of men re-creating the high drama played out on these fields more than a century earlier, the reenactments complete in every detail: uniforms, weapons, sounds, and tactics. All of this may be taken as evidence that we indeed have become too fond of this war, that we have ignored the key point General Lee made: War is terrible.

The terror of war peaks in the climax of battle. But major battles, about which so much has been written, consumed only some 120 days of the war's four years. What of the other 1,338 days? What was the Civil War *usually* like for the people who lived it? By focusing on the experiences of soldiers, sailors, and noncombatants on a single day at the virtual midpoint—April 10, 1863—I hope to provide a typical cross section of the war. Unfortunately, the records of this "normal" day suggest that the terror of war and all its other bitter emotions—grief, boredom, anger, loneliness, depression—were present in varying degrees throughout our nation's great ordeal. Sadly, on this day the war was only half over.

No single day can be extracted in its entirety without overlapping into days preceding and following. Some of the events of April 10 require some preliminary explanations, just as some require additional comments about the days following. The focal point, however, is on this Friday and its events, told as much as possible by those who were there—using their letters, diaries, and memoirs, as well as newspapers and official records.

The book is divided into sections covering the East, the West (including one chapter on the Far West), and the navies. The division between East and West is primarily the chain of the Allegheny Mountains. It seems easiest to keep track of the various bodies of troops by using these two regions, East and West, but that choice was purely arbitrary.

The East and West were different in some ways, partly because of the mountain ranges that kept them separated and partly by the nature of the people. While most characteristics of warfare were the same, the war in the West was more mobile, more fluid than the war in the East. The important border states were in the West, and there were more incidents of brother against brother in the West because loyalties were so divided. One historian summarizes that the Virginia campaigns were more conventional, and the Western campaigns were less so, more in keeping with frontier fighting of the West itself.

A brief word about some military terms might be helpful. In both North and South the terms "department" and "district" referred to a geographic organization, while the designations of "army," "corps," "division," and "regiment" referred to operational units. Sometimes an army carried the same name as the department.

Quotes from various sources throughout the book reflect both spelling and punctuation peculiarities of the era, as well as the education and ability of the writers.

After years of research, it is understandably impossible to acknowledge all the people who contributed to the research effort. But it is safe to say that without the help of my wife, Donna, there would be no book. She was co-researcher, critic, editor, and proofreader from beginning to end. Her contribution is immeasurable. Others who gave special assistance were Leise Von Oettingen, librarian at Loutit Library, Grand Haven, Michigan, who helped us begin our research. Dr. Richard Sommers, archivist at the U.S. Army Military Institute in Carlisle, Pennsylvania; Michael Meier, at the National Archives in Washington, D.C.; Derris Raper, a researcher at the University of North Carolina, who fastidiously scoured the manuscripts of the Southern Historical Collections; Milton Weller, who prepared maps for the better understanding of the reader; and Don Engel, who photographed and researched in

Washington and New Bern, North Carolina. I am grateful to John Divine and Peg Holter of Waterford, Virginia, for their continued encouragement; Colonel Harold Fleming for his initial edit; Ingrid and Norton Pereira for unstinting hospitality in Washington, D.C.; Brassey's editors Don McKeon and Kathleen Graham for patience and professionalism; Leona Schecter for her many contacts and experience as a literary agent; Tom and Nadene Willett and Leslie Mitchell for computer expertise and assistance; Curt Johnson for sharing his knowledge of the Civil War; and Earle and Judy Kittleman for help at the National Park Service and Library of Congress. To the countless others who helped, knowingly or unknowingly, over the years—thank you!

INTRODUCTION

★

AT THE MIDPOINT

The United States was far from united on Friday, April 10, 1863, and the two governments, Union and Confederate, were doing their best to govern citizens in the frenzied passions of a civil war. A letter dated April 10, 1863, to President Abraham Lincoln offers a clue to the agony of the times:

> Sir:
>
> . . . I have two sons; one of them Sylvan my oldest aged 28 years is in the Federal army a volunteer in the 1st Regiment of the Excelsior Brigade Co. K and the other James my youngest son unfortunately went to Louisiana a few months before this war commenced, and, before I could extricate him from those mad people he had enlisted in the rebel army, a boy then less than 18 years old. I assure you nothing could be more painful, both to my wife and myself.
>
> My son Sylvan is a true and loyal man, and was in the battle of Fredericksburg. He is an educated man; was admitted to practice law at the Bar of New York, write a good hand, and is intelligent and amiable, I think that he can serve you & the country more advantageously with the pen and head than with the musket.
>
> Our prayer to you is that you may give him employment . . . so that he may not come in contact in battle with his Brother, and perhaps kill him.
>
> [Sylvan] is a private in the ranks of the army of the Rappahannock, and capable of performing duties of a much higher grade. No other consideration than patriotism induced him to enlist in the Federal army, and will do his duty faithfully there or wherever he may be placed.
>
> I am Sir, etc.
>
> Delphy Carlin[1]

The events that had shaped the last two years had been fast-moving and dramatic; although the battles and loss of life had made little change in the original territorial lines, the country, and the lives of the citizens, would be changed forever.

A look at the two sections of the country, North and South, provides the backdrop for the events of April 10.

THE NORTH

For the North, up to April 10, 1863, there had been mostly bad news. The previous two years of war offered little comfort for those who supported Lincoln's cause, and prospects were gloomy. There was the recent navy setback at Charleston Harbor, where the Union "iron-clads," supposedly invincible, had been turned back as they moved into the harbor, ending the attempt to occupy Charleston. Then there was the December fiasco at Fredericksburg, Virginia, where 12,353 Union soldiers were killed, wounded, or missing,[2] and the rest of the army had fallen back across the Rappahannock River with nothing gained. Near Vicksburg, Grant was still trying various means to get at the town. He had tried digging canals, assault, river expeditions, and naval blockade, but nothing had worked. Union victories had been few and far between, and those usually were followed by a reversal of some sort.

The only good news was that most of the fighting was taking place in the South rather than in Union territory. While this was a blessing, it also kept the war from being as real to the North as it might have been, except for the losses. The South had heard the cannons, had felt the panic of being in the path of approaching armies, had seen the litter of wounded and dead. The North had not. The early battlegrounds had been south of the Mason-Dixon line, except for a brief Maryland incursion at Antietam, which produced the bloodiest day of the war. The Union casualties to date, killed, wounded, and captured, were more than 113,000.[3] While daily life for most in the North had been untouched, many Northern families had been affected in the worst way possible, by the loss or suffering of a loved one . . . and the war was just half over.

According to later figures, disease was the biggest killer. In the tables of losses for the whole war, 93,000 Union men were killed in battle or died of battle wounds, but 186,000 died of disease.[4] Confederate figures were not available, but an assumption could be made that the same ratio applied to Southern troops. Union figures show that in April

1863, 3,871 men died in hospitals of non-battle-related causes, principally of typhoid, chronic diarrhea and lung disease.[5] On April 10, 137 men died of disease in Union hospitals. No consolidated records exist for Confederate hospitals, so no count can be made of their hospital deaths on that day.

The politics of the time were brutal. Lincoln, although revered today, was scorned, vilified, ridiculed, and slandered by his fellow politicians, the press, and many of the military. Author Richard Henry Dana wrote in March 1863, ". . . as to the politics of Washington, the most striking thing is the absence of personal loyalty to the President. It does not exist. He has no admirers, no enthusiastic supporters . . . This is felt by all, and has got down through all the layers of society."[6]

In July 1862, Lincoln had selected Henry Halleck, a relatively unknown major general, to be the ranking general of the Northern armies. George Templeton Strong, a prominent Northern attorney, commented after his first encounter with Halleck, "Halleck is not the man for his place. He is certainly—clearly—weak, shallow, commonplace, vulgar."[7] He was also indecisive, and would offer little help to the Union armies in coming campaigns. He had the distinction of being labeled the most unpopular man in Washington.[8]

The cabinet consisted of Secretary of War Edwin M. Stanton, Secretary of State William H. Seward, Secretary of the Treasury Salmon P. Chase, and Secretary of the Navy Gideon Welles. Edward Bates was the attorney general and Montgomery Blair was the postmaster general. There was an invisible vice president then, too, named Hannibal Hamlin. In no way could any of them be considered Lincoln supporters. In the first years of Lincoln's administration, Stanton had been almost contemptuous of the president, although by April 1863 he had begun to find fewer faults and more wisdom in Lincoln than he had expected. Both Chase and Seward were frequently outspokenly antagonistic toward the president.

In addition, the elections of November 1862 had been a setback for the president. Peace Democrats (Copperheads) and War Democrats had come close to taking control of the House of Representatives from the Republicans, principally because of the failure of the Northern armies to win on the battlefield and the mounting deaths in these unsuccessful military clashes.[9] A negotiated peace was not a possibility; an offer had been made by the French to mediate a settlement, and it was rejected out of hand.[10] Great Britain was still considered a potential ally of the Confederacy, and each Union loss caused more concern about possible European intervention. The Northern worry was still there, but by

April 1863 there was a decreasing likelihood of Britain's aiding the South. Some of the reasons were summarized by George Templeton Strong in his April 14 diary entry:

> We drift fast toward war with England, but I think we shall not reach that point. The shop-keepers who own England want to do us all the harm they can and to give all possible aid and comfort to our slave-breeding, woman-flogging adversary, for England has degenerated into a trader, manufacturer, and banker, and has lost all the instincts and sympathies her name suggests. She would declare war against us fast enough if she dared follow her sordid impulses, but there are dirty, selfish considerations on the other side. She cannot ally herself with slavery, as she inclines to do, without closing a profitable market, exposing her commerce to privateers and diminishing the supply of breadstuffs on which her operatives depend for life.[11]

Legislation setting up the machinery for the draft had passed on March 3, 1863, and conscription would begin in July. Volunteering in the North had almost ended; there were too many good jobs to be had, too much money to be made, and the disfigured veterans coming back by the trainload were discouragement enough. The summer of 1863 would see draft riots tear Northern cities apart as the draft began in earnest.

Lincoln's Emancipation Proclamation, announced in September 1862, was also a cause of Northern unrest. It was not overwhelmingly popular in the North, and in some quarters, a shift from "Save the Union" to "Free the Slaves" went against the grain for both social and economic reasons. The stated purpose of the war originally had been to restore the Union, but after September 22, 1862, it was also to free the slaves. The proclamation freeing the slaves was a less-than-popular move, but shrewd politician that Lincoln was, he knew it was inevitable. This also meant that blacks would have to become part of the solution. By April 1863, black regiments were being formed in the East, although a number of isolated units had already been formed in South Carolina and in the West. The new policy of the government was to raise as many black regiments as possible and to send these regiments into battle. Although blacks were paid less than whites and could be led only by white officers, they had arrived at an equality that had never been possible before.

The exact military strength on Friday, April 10, is almost impossible to reconstruct. A muster of Union troops in all areas had been ordered by President Lincoln in connection with an amnesty granted to all deserters who returned by April 1.[12] Unfortunately, those figures were never compiled, but the best estimate is that 552,000 men were actually present for duty. The muster did, however, play a significant part in the daily routines of the many units scattered throughout the land.

There were still recruiting drives such as one advertised in the *Nashville Union* for a light artillery battery: "Inducements; no marching, no picket or guard duty; transportation superior to cavalry or infantry." There is no evidence that the battery was raised.[13] But recruiting had become increasingly difficult throughout the Union as the war went on.

Desertion was a factor; after two years of fighting, men needed to go home for a variety of reasons. More than 200,000 men deserted during the four years of the war, and during the early spring of 1863 desertions were averaging 4,650 a month.[14] It was hard to keep track of everybody.

On the day that concerns us here, a new unit, the 27th Michigan Volunteer Infantry Regiment, was being formed in Port Huron, Michigan; it saw service until April 1865. (A typical Union regiment, at its formation, had ten companies of 100 men each, or 1,000 total; however, few regiments in the field would number that many, and frequently would have fewer than 400 men.)[15] By war's end the 27th counted 432 dead of battle and disease. Two other units, the 109th Illinois Infantry Regiment and the New York Marine Artillery Battalion, were disbanded that same week. The 109th was disbanded by General Grant, "having lost 237 men principally by desertion, and the Officers (except those of Co. K) having proved themselves utterly incompetent."[16] The Marine Artillerymen were mostly seamen recruited for use on army ships, but the members were unhappy with land assignments. The War Department did admit that their recruitment was unfair and disbanded the unit.[17]

By April 10, 1863, the Union had passed through its second winter, but the people shuddered at the prospects of spring and the struggles that were to come. The civilians at home were sheltered from the agony and the destruction of the battlefield felt by the people of the South, but their anguish—inflicted by the endless casualty lists from places such as Fredericksburg, Shiloh, Manassas, and the Peninsula—was just as real.

The words of a little-known, unnamed, camp song of that time sum up the feeling of the soldiers:

> *Our comrades fill many a grave, boys*
> *Our brothers are crippled and maimed,*

Of those who fall as they fell, boys,
Their country need not be ashamed;
We sigh for the blessings of peace, boys,
We tire of the war-bugle's blast,
We'll conquer before we go home, boys,
We'll fight for our flag till the last.[18]

THE SOUTH

Jefferson Davis, president of the Confederate States of America, had governed his country for almost two years. But it was a nation unlike its Northern counterpart. The eleven states within its borders were united by reason of disunity. Davis was leading separate, testy governments in their search for a future. "The Union" was the rallying cry in the North; "States Rights" was the cry of the South. Southern states were economically and socially dependent on the slave. Although only a small minority of Southerners owned slaves, the political power and economic success of the South as a whole depended on the low-cost labor of slavery for the production of cotton. Estimates in the 1860 census put the total population of the eleven sceding states at 9 million, including 3 million slaves.[19]

The mood of the South was upbeat and confident on this bright spring day, even though losses in the first two years of the war had been staggering; total casualties were more than 125,000.[20] Even with the disadvantages of fewer men under arms, less production, a smaller population base, and no navy, the South had staved off virtually every Yankee effort to invade; with the exception of northern Tennessee, the Mississippi Valley, and some Atlantic coastal seaports, its land remained intact. The Southern army numbered roughly 286,000 present for duty,[21] and its leadership was superb. In the East, West Point graduates Robert E. Lee, Thomas J. Jackson, J.E.B. Stuart, James Longstreet, and others had stymied the Union army in almost every encounter. The leadership so desperately sought by Lincoln seemed to abound in Virginia.

But that didn't mean that all was well in the South or that happiness prevailed everywhere. In the 1861 secession fever that swept the Southern states, the populace plainly felt that one Southern fighting man was the equal of ten Yankees. Two years later, there was more than a little doubt about that fact. On April 10, President Davis worried the confident populace with a speech that said plainly that the war would last a great deal longer. Davis said that the planters should plant some corn to eat instead of cotton to sell:

Let fields be devoted exclusively to the production of corn, oats, beans, peas, potatoes, and other food for man and beast. . . . Alone, unaided, we have met and overthrown the most formidable combination of naval and military armaments . . . ever gathered together. . . . We must not forget, however, that the war is not yet ended, and that we are still confronted by powerful armies and threatened by numerous fleets.[22]

A major concern was the nearly complete blockade around the Confederacy. There was only one open link, the Mississippi River between Port Hudson, Louisiana, and Vicksburg, Mississippi. The Northern navy controlled the waters of the Atlantic and the Gulf of Mexico, and occupied such places as Roanoke Island, Virginia; New Bern and Washington, North Carolina; some harbor islands outside Charleston, South Carolina; Port Royal, South Carolina; Pensacola, Florida; and New Orleans and on up the Mississippi to Baton Rouge, Louisiana.[23] These Northern successes of the first two years were not as dramatic as the Southern battlefield accomplishments, but they were a vital part of the Northern blockade strategy.

The railroads in the South were not in good shape and were not meeting the needs of either the military or the civilian distribution systems. On April 14 a report was sent from assistant adjutant-general William Wadley, to Secretary of War James A. Seddon, setting out the needs of the various railroad lines. The report listed a need for twenty-three engines and more than seven hundred cars in order for the roads to become effective means of transportation. He closed by saying: ". . . for the last two years the railroads of the country have been unable to meet promptly the requirements of Government. Can we expect any better result in the future without some change in their condition? I think not."[24] In his Corn versus Cotton speech, President Davis also spoke about the lack of transportation, which contributed to the scarcity of resources. A rainy winter and the lack of a central authority to control the railroads had speeded the railroads' decline, which in turn had isolated many areas and created regional shortages.

With the blockade in place and inadequate railroads, food supplies began to dwindle; that the strategy was effective was demonstrated by the bread riots in Richmond, Virginia. On April 3, a mob, led by women who were angry over rising food prices and food shortages, roamed through Richmond. President Davis confronted the mob, pulled the change from his pocket, and flung the coins to the mob, ordering them to go home or he would have troops fire on them. The mob dispersed.[25] This incident showed that there was unrest and concern about provisions for the coming months. The blockade was proving effective, and that was part of the reason for Davis's speech on April 10.

The *Weekly Jr. Register* of Franklin, Louisiana, reflected these concerns. In one of the newspaper's unique editions printed on wallpaper due to paper shortages, its April 9 issue reported:

> When shall we have PEACE! Everybody is asking the question, "when shall we have peace and when shall the blockade be raised?" There seems to be in the minds of the people a sanguine feeling in the matter which doubtless owes its existence to the recent publications about the disposition of the French Emperor to intervene . . . As for Great Britain, we have no more hope of the interference of that nation to stop the war than we have of China doing the same thing. The British Queen (metaphorically speaking) would give one of her ears if America should eat itself up in civil war . . . We shall have peace when the North, either by reason of exhaustion, or of internal dissensions, can no longer make war on us.[26]

Conscription had been a part of the Confederate scene since March 1862, but it was an individual program in each state, not a uniform, centrally administered plan. Volunteering had dwindled by spring 1863, and only the draft produced more recruits for the battles ahead. The hiring of a substitute was allowed by all conscription regulations, but this was not an option for the poorer farmers of the South—an ad in a Richmond paper for a substitute showed an asking price of $2,500.[27]

In the spring of 1863, desertions plagued the Southern military even more than its Northern counterpart.[28] There were several reasons why: soldiers were never too far from home; what few rations they were given were pretty bad; and many had not volunteered but been drafted (the Union's draft did not become effective until later in the year), and as the war dragged on, they questioned their need to fight to keep slaves, which few of them owned. Indeed, one of the principal reasons for the average Confederate soldier's sometimes bitter attitude toward the "Cause" was the clause in the Conscription Act that allowed anyone with twenty or more slaves to avoid the draft and required at least one white man on every slaveholding plantation. It was the age-old "Rich man's war, Poor man's fight!"[29] The desertion rate was a constant drain, even though it was understandable, and was a significant problem for both sides. Although the Union had begun solving the problem, in the South it just kept getting worse.

Spring was a bad time; the farmers needed to get crops in, and there was no one at home to do it. There was a much more informal attitude toward perfect attendance in the Confederate ranks; some of the men reasoned that they could go home and be back in time for the next fight. That's what they were there for, fighting; they felt the rest was all pretty useless. Some of them actually were sick or recovering from wounds; there was no breakdown of the figures, but it is fairly safe to say that the vast majority had simply "gone home."

In some cases the ploys were ingenious. The Richmond paper reported on the eleventh: "On Friday morning a soldier was arrested by the train guard of the Fredericksburg Road (Lt. Heppay) for deserting from his company near Fredericksburg. He was dressed in a full suit of a women's clothing, hoop skirts, etc. He hoped by this device to be able to spend some time at home. The would-be woman was divested of his toggery and sent to Gen. Lee for disposal."[30]

It has been the aura of the Confederate army that honor, chivalry, and duty were ingrained in all its members, and they obviously were in many. However, the frequent pleas that came from wives and family asking for help on the troubled home front often took priority over the more distant commitment to secession. The draft, the twenty-slave rule, lack of food, bad weather, and home problems were always in the back of a soldier's mind; any small change would tip the scale and send him home.

There were some executions of deserters, but they were infrequent. Surprisingly, President Davis, the cool, aloof, dispassionate politician, frequently was the source of clemency.

Perhaps the words of a Confederate private, Franklin Lafayette Riley, explained the Confederate perspective: "March 30–31, 1863 near U. S. Ford, Bad weather. Bill Jones and Isaac Alexander, Co B are listed as deserters but probably are just taking care of business at home. Probably this is true of most of our 'deserters.' Since Jan. the regiment has received 6 recruits but has lost 24 men, 10 by desertion, 8 by death, 6 by discharge."[31]

The spring of 1863 was in many ways the high mark of the Confederacy; the lives of its people would become increasingly difficult from this time forward. The specters of desertion and the blockade would affect the lives of all those confident citizens who proudly proclaimed the eventual triumph of their cause. But the feeling of the day was confidently put forth in the *Rockingham Register and Virginia Advertiser* on April 24: "The situation at present: Nothing could be more auspicious than the present situation of the Confederacy. In every quarter the designs of the enemy appear to be baffled: Port Hudson, Vicksburg, Opening Mississippi, Charleston. Only the blockade is effective."[32]

★

General Halleck was reduced to chief of staff under Lieutenant General Ulysses S. Grant in March 1864.

Jefferson Davis was captured May 10, 1865, after Appomattox, and was held for two years before he was released without prosecution.

PART ONE

★

THE DAY IN THE EAST

The East was divided in its outlook on April 10: the North had its doubts as to the future; the South was convinced of its ultimate victory. The military situation in the East involved almost exclusively only two players, the Union Army of the Potomac and the Confederate Army of Northern Virginia. The original Union plan was to capture Richmond, but that was thwarted in 1862. Now it seemed the goal was to destroy the Southern army. The North-South line ran almost where it had two years before, and in spite of a Northern move that came within the outskirts of Richmond in 1862, the two opposing eastern armies now faced each other closer to Washington than to Richmond. Southern victories on the Peninsula, both Bull Runs, Fredericksburg, and a bloody draw at Antietam all reinforced Southern confidence. Their leadership—Lee, Jackson, Stuart, and Longstreet—had proved their ability on every occasion.

The North was gloomy and despondent: still looking for an effective general, still looking for a victory, and still looking for hope.

1

★

THE CAPITALS

WASHINGTON, D.C.

The weather had been wet and cold but was warm and sunny in Washington this Friday. The last snow, which had fallen on April 5, was now gone. The mood might have brightened slightly because of the weather, but it remained gloomy for most Washingtonians. The recent Union defeat at Fredericksburg, with its enormous slaughter and lack of leadership, still clouded the outlook for the coming months. The most recent setback, the navy's defeat at Charleston on April 7, increased the frustration level for government officials, military, and civilians alike.

Washington, as a southern city, was open to Confederate attack; since the first days of the war one of the principal concerns of the Union army's military strategy had been the protection of the capital. Lincoln had kept some 30,000 troops in Washington when McClellan made his assault toward Richmond in early 1862, and he had denied the reinforcement of McClellan by Pope when Jackson roamed loose in the Shenandoah. (McClellan didn't really need reinforcements; his army was twice the size of Lee's.)

So Washington had its share of concerns. And now Lee was in Fredericksburg, only sixty-five miles away. But the city still had 45,000 men under Major General Samuel P. Heintzelman in and around town, and newly appointed Major General Joseph Hooker and his Army of the Potomac, with more than 130,000 men, were between General Lee and Washington, which was of some consolation to the Washingtonians.

The Washington of 1863 was so different from the prewar city that it was hard to remember what it had been like before 1860; even the Capitol dome had finally been finished. In keeping with the concerns of the government, fortifications, barricades, guards, sentries, and various installations ringed the south section of town and beyond. Willard's Hotel was one of the centers of activity, busier and sometimes more productive than the White House or the Capitol.[1] The importance of Willard's was described by novelist Nathaniel Hawthorne: "Among the crowd were office hunters, wire pullers, editors, army correspondents, inventors, artists and railroad directors, mostly waiting for some favor, and meanwhile consuming whiskey skins, gin cocktails, brandy smashes and rum cobblers in an atmosphere of cigar smoke."[2]

Horsecars were hurrying along on a double track that stretched six miles from the navy yard to Georgetown. If you didn't choose to take the trolley, and could afford it, there was always a "hack" to take you anywhere in the city. Peddlers lined most of the city streets hawking soaps, candy, clothing—all kinds of products. In contrast to the bustle of the city, Lafayette Square was a place of peace and quiet, boasting large mansions, beautiful and exotic gardens, and shady trees. "In cold weather the square was deserted, but on warm and pleasant days children romped on the grass, ladies in crinoline walked around the flower pots and pointed their parasols at exotics new to them. On benches sat rows of soldiers who had limped in and sat with their crutches and empty sleeves. . . ."[3]

Farther to the southwest, over in Virginia, a circle of Union camps closed around Washington. The 7th Michigan Cavalry Regiment was part of the circle, camped about fifteen miles southwest of Fairfax Courthouse in Virginia. The unit had just been assigned to thirty days of picket duty. On April 10 200 men of the 7th were sent south to an area near Manassas to scout for their brigade. Sergeant Edwin Havens wrote home on April 12:

> We left camp that afternoon about 3 o'clock and reached here at six. We are about 15 miles from Fairfax [Courthouse] near the junction of Wolf Run with the Occoquan Creek. We pass it in a southern direction from Fairfax C.H. over fields through grubs, woods, following no direct road but picking our way as best we could, until we reached Fairfax Station on the R.R. (Orange & Alexandria) when we came onto the "corduroy" leading here. Near the station a part of the Penn. Bucktails were encamped and as we passed their camp a company was just moving off for picket on the chain of fortifications around there, which extend nearly a mile in this direction. The country is hilly, almost mountainous, all the distance from Fairfax C.H. here and right here it is all hills from 50 to 200 feet in height . . . The lines extend in a westerly direction along the bank of the Occoquan to the mouth of Bull Run and then along the Run to Centerville . . . We are on the extreme front as the Creek, about 40 feet in width, is all that separates us from the Rebel country.[4]

Also part of the defenses in Virginia protecting Washington were the camps of the 6th Michigan Cavalry. Private James Harvey Kidd recalled:

> A semi-circular line of pickets was established in front of Washington, the right and left resting on the Potomac, above and below the city respectively. Our detachment guarded the extreme right of the line. Colonel Gray was five miles to the left, with the remainder of the Sixth, and the Fifth still farther away in that direction.[5]

The troops who had been in and around Washington for two years had left some signs of their presence. On April 10 artilleryman Levi Baker of the 9th Massachusetts Battery was at Fort Ramsay, just off the Leesburg Pike near Falls Church. He wrote, "As the weather grew warmer, our commander found our camp was so bad that it would be dangerous to the health of the company." Then he explained, "Our park was an old cavalry camp, and was never cleaned out. We commenced finding the earth, which had from 4–6 inches of manure on it, and had made good progress in casting it off when orders came to break camp & go to Centreville. The centre section returned to camp about the 12th of April."[6]

Within these lines was a series of forts in and south of Alexandria, Virginia. One of these forts was Fort Lyon, just south of the city of Alexandria. The 34th Massachusetts Infantry Regiment was in the fort on the tenth, according to Charles H. Moulton, a former newspaperman from Worcester, Massachusetts. The regiment had received its orders on the tenth, but didn't know where it would be going. He wrote that feelings were running high:

> Even now heavy salutes can be distinctly heard from Washington denoting the return of President Lincoln from his visit to the Army of the Potomac. In the course of a few days you will hear some stirring news from "Fighting Joe." The regiments all around have also got orders to march and are cheering as I write. Instead of regretting to leave their comfortable quarters the brave boys are anxious to go ahead and close up this treacherous rebellion. Our own boys of the 34th are well aware of the fact that it is hard to leave such a familiar home as has been Camp Lyon, but nevertheless, they all prefer the change after remaining in garrison for so long a period.[7]

On April 10, General Heintzelman received a summons from Halleck, the military's senior general, who had said he needed 20,000 men from Heintzelman to get ready to march to Suffolk, Virginia, or to Washington, North Carolina. Both places were under pressure and might need help soon.[8]

One of the troopers who would go to Suffolk was Private Harry F. Jackson, who was still in camp north of the Potomac, parading for the general muster called on the tenth. Parades were a big part of the camp routine, and many Union army units in camps all over the country were parading to count their people—and maybe show off a little. Jackson reported: "It was a big thing to see our battalion paraded yesterday for muster. Those who hadn't previously drawn new clothing drew it this week. Every man's boots, belts and boxes were well blacked, and every man had white gloves. Each company tried its best to excel the others in the movements. The results was that they were all perfect and there was no choice."[9]

Inside the city, there were numbers of qualified, even great men, yet they remained as divided and fractious as any group at any given period of American history. One of the many discontented souls who heaped hatred on the president was an Ohio congressman, Clement L. Vallandigham, a Copperhead or Peace Democrat. As a spokesman for the Copperheads he had become a vicious opponent of Lincoln and the war, advocating a negotiated peace allowing for slavery and a separate South. On this date, he was back in his home district stirring up all the trouble he could.

There had been any number of rumors about assassinating Lincoln, but Lincoln seemingly remained untroubled. He voiced concern about only one man, Count Adam Gurowski, a European revolutionary who lived in Washington.[10] Gurowski's diary for the tenth stated: "Agitated as my existence has been, I never fell among so much littleness, meanness, servility as here. To avoid it and not despair, or rage, or despond, several times a day, it is necessary to avoid contact with all politicians, and reduce to a few, very few, all intercourse with them."[11]

His diary revealed a pathological hatred of Lincoln and Seward; his erratic behavior probably gave Lincoln good cause for concern.

Lincoln's relations with Congress were not always cordial, so it was fortunate for the president that Congress had adjourned March 4 and was not in session on April 10. Lincoln, too, was away, reviewing the Army of the Potomac.

The international scene was reasonably quiet this day. Seward noted, "This government has heard with surprise and regret that a loan has been made, in London, to the insurgents, with conditions of security and payment, openly hostile to the United States."[12] In spite of this,

England's feelings toward the South were turning cold, and England, as well as the rest of Europe, was increasingly negative toward involvement on either side.

The French were having troubles of their own in Mexico, and the British people were supporting the Union blockade by doing without cotton, a staple requirement of the garment industry. The working class of Great Britain was paying a steep price but would not ever consider supporting the South and its unholy slavery. That feeling was captured in the poem "John Brown's Body" by Stephen Vincent Benét:

> And yet the slow root-thought works
> Gradually through men's minds.
> The Lancashire spinners,
> Thrown out of work because no cotton can come
> To feed their mills through the choking Union blockade,
> Yet hold starvation meetings and praise the Union.[13]

Through it all Washington kept on its busy pace. It was reminded of the war by the torrent of wounded brought to the city after battles, and saw on its streets the crutches, slings, and bandages of the wounded, but it also saw citizens coming from all parts of the nation: freed slaves, blockade-runners, gamblers, manufacturers, inventors, office seekers, ship captains, and others looking to become a part of the action—for profit or patriotism. For all its sophistication, the capital still showed signs of a frontier flavor. In March 1863 there were some 10,000 cattle grazing at the foot of the unfinished Washington Monument.[14]

The war sparked invention, and various new weapons had been developed by a variety of inventors who appeared daily to promote their gadgets: boots for walking on water, machine guns, aerial torpedoes, and other devices both practical and impractical. The president was intrigued with many of these inventions and was patient with their developers. On April 10, tests were conducted on two devices at Lincoln's request. The first was an incendiary artillery shell, the second a sort of rudimentary flamethrower. Tests were made in Alexandria, and a twelve-page report reconstructed the tests for the president. The flamethrower was a go, but the artillery shell had some problems. The report was signed by Stephen Vincent Benét (grandfather of the poet).[15] Whatever happened to these many inventions, including the never-used flamethrower, they had no effect on the war's outcome.

Although the outskirts of Washington had been stripped clean of lumber and fortifications, the capital area had come back from its 1861 era of mud and sleaze, and presented a more positive scene. The city had improved its outward appearance, but its moral level had suffered. Prostitution was prevalent in Washington, according to the descriptions of entertainment available to visitors, military and civilian alike. The *Washington Star* had tried in vain to pressure changes in attitude, but "in 1863, the women of the town were as much a feature of the Washington scene as the soldiers themselves."[16]

From other reports, it seemed that the behavior of the nation's defenders was a considerable problem to the staid and circumspect natives.

> The *Star* was wont to treat the wenches with a roguish masculine indulgence; called them by euphemistic names—Cyprians, fallen angels, daughters of Eve, the g'hals, gay young ducks. When it used harsher epithets, it had been provoked, like the rest of Washington, to righteous anger by the irresponsible volunteer officers who lost all sense of decency in their freedom from family restrictions . . . Washington had always been noted for its prostitutes; but the *Star* estimated that, before the war, there had been not more than five hundred in the entire District of Columbia. The fallen angels of wartime had been recruited, like the soldiers, from the States. . . . In 1863 the *Star,* after an investigation, made the considered statement that the city had about five thousand prostitutes, while there were half as many more in Georgetown and Alexandria.[17]

In other activity, a few plays were advertised in the *Washington Evening Star*. Grover's Theatre, on Pennsylvania Avenue near Willard's Hotel, on April 10 presented *Heart of Mid-Lothian* with Susan Denis, J. M. Ward, and Annette Ince. The paper also announced the first Washington appearance of John Wilkes Booth, who was playing the Duke of Gloucester in *Richard III* (admission was twenty-five, fifty, or seventy-five cents).[18] In just over two years, he would make his most infamous appearance at Ford's Theater. The Washington Theater had a real value on the next day, April 11, a double feature—*Pocahontas* with Mrs. John Wood and *Slasher and Crasher*.[19]

Life went on in the big city.

RICHMOND

In Richmond the weather was bright and sunny; since spring had been a long time in coming, it was a welcome change.

Richmond had gone through a difficult two years. Union Major

General George B. McClellan's Army of the Potomac had marched almost to the gates of the city in the spring of 1862, close enough so his Union soldiers could hear the church bells tolling in the city. That was past, but not forgotten by the people of Richmond. McClellan's campaign had been well planned but disastrously executed.

This fact built confidence in Richmonders; that confidence had been recently increased by the movement of Major General John B. (Sam) Hood's and Major General George Pickett's divisions to bottle up the bothersome Union forces in Suffolk and some other coastal areas. Their presence near Richmond was certainly reassuring. So the mood was upbeat; in spite of the trenches and barricades almost encircling the city, there seemed to be little immediate threat.

In one sense the city and the South were more united than ever, in spite of the everlasting squabbles among the states. Lincoln's Emancipation Proclamation, which took effect January 1, 1863, removed almost any chance for a peaceful compromise. The fact that the proclamation applied only to slaveholders and their slaves meant it affected very few Southerners on a day-to-day basis. The Southern slaves were supposedly free; however, the proclamation was issued by a government that no longer represented or controlled them. Slave auctions were still taking place as usual. An ad in the April 10 *Charleston Daily Courier* announced:

Auctions: Estates, slaves (By Masters in Equity)
Private sales: Negroes, estates

In Richmond, slaves still had many roles to play. Major General Richard Ewell's family owned a slave named Emmeline. She was in Spring Hill, Tennessee, overseeing some of Ewell's property. Ewell had been badly wounded at the battle of Groveton, Virginia, and lost one leg. While recuperating in Richmond he had been a difficult patient, refusing to take medication and treatment and totally upsetting his wife, Lizinka. Finally, she told Ewell she was sending for Emmeline to take over Ewell's recovery program. Emmeline was known as a no-nonsense lady who usually got her way; the threat of bringing Emmeline to nurse Ewell back to health was enough to change his attitude, and he then became as docile as a lamb.[20]

Life had changed dramatically for the citizens of Richmond, now the capital of the Confederacy. The city's population had risen to 140,000, up from a prewar total of 40,000. The new hospitals, although the best in the South, were overcrowded, and wounded Confederates wandered the streets of the city at all hours. Every day their presence brought home the real price of war.

The increased population caused great demand for food, clothing, and other supplies; shortages, caused by the condition of the railroads and the Union blockade, gave rise to inflation: flour increased in price from $7 to $28 a barrel; bacon from $.20 to $1.20 a pound; firewood from $3 to $15 a cord; and whiskey, if you could find any, from $.25 to $35 per gallon.[21] Even when there was no shortage of an item, the price kept going up. The wartime journal of Confederate government official Josiah Gorgas noted, "Meal is $16 per bushel, yet there is not positive scarcity. I cannot fathom this state of things. I suppose the fear of scarcity combined with the plethora of money induces people to 'lay up' a stock, and thus they enhance the price of provisions."[22] Food shortages were the cause of the so-called bread riots of early April, but the newspaper played down the riots, insisting that rioters had been prompted more by looters than by hunger.[23] The whole episode, though, prompted concern about future city unrest.

Davis's speech in Richmond on April 10 and its underlying message—preparation for troubles ahead and a long war—were in sharp contrast to the optimistic speech he gave in Richmond just ninety days earlier, in January, when he had said, "If the war continues we shall only grow stronger as each year rolls on . . . we see in the future nothing to disturb the prospect of independence for which we are struggling."[24] His April 10 speech did prompt some action on the part of planters. On April 12 one patriotic planter, David Crenshaw Barrows, wrote to his overseer, "I write to you in reference to the cotton crop. I want you to plant *not* more than two hundred fifty acres in cotton. If you have planted more than that, . . . plow it up, and plant the land in corn and peas . . . Let there be no mistake about this. There is great excitement through the country about this."[25]

As Lincoln dealt with unpopularity and an unsupportive cabinet, Davis faced many of the same problems. The Confederate president was constantly at odds with his own Congress, the Southern states, and his cabinet. The South had its heroes—Lee, Jackson, Stuart, and others—but they did not include Davis. Early in the war he had borne responsibility for most of the decisions necessary to conduct the war. Writ of habeas corpus was gone, and conscription was a year old, but the expansion of the draft in the fall of 1862 to include men eighteen to forty-five (it would be expanded again, in 1864, to include men from seventeen to fifty) had raised the Davis opposition to new heights. Mary Chesnut of Charleston, wife of Confederate General James Chesnut and a friend of Davis's, wrote in her diary, "There is a perfect magazine of discord and discontent in that Cabinet, . . . He was criticized for not being more aggressive, for promoting his relatives to military commands beyond their competence, and for engaging in vendettas against generals whom he disliked."[26] In Charleston, the newspaper *Mercury* was one of Davis's chief critics, but it was supported by many other papers, and impeachment rumblings had been heard from South Carolina. That summer, Representative James L. Alcorn of Mississippi would be quoted as calling Davis a "miserable, stupid, one-eyed, dyspeptic, arrogant tyrant."[27] In all, Davis was about as popular in the South as Lincoln was in the North.

This Friday, April 10, 1863, Congress was in session; it was not one of its stormier meetings, and little was accomplished. In previous months there had been a number of instances of fights, duels, and near duels between the members, a good indicator of the depth of States Rights passion. The Senate passed four bills on April 10, none of which was to have much impact on the war or the South's citizens. In secret session there was discussion of a bill to appropriate $10 million to pay for the construction, armament, and equipment of ten ironclad warships to be built in Europe. The bill was postponed.[28]

President Davis's cabinet consisted of Secretary of War James A. Seddon, Secretary of State Judah P. Benjamin, Secretary of the Treasury Christopher G. Memminger, Secretary of the Navy Stephen R. Mallory, Postmaster General John H. Reagan, and Attorney General Thomas H. Watts. On the whole, his cabinet was fully as cantankerous as the cabinet of Lincoln, but its members also left much of the leadership to Davis, adding to his exhausting job.[29] On this date Memminger succeeded in closing a loan from England in the amount of £10 million.

By April 1863, a host of new businesses flourished in Richmond. Soldiers on furlough, convalescing, or stationed there demanded entertainment, so in addition to theaters, concerts, and balls, the city saw gambling and prostitution flaunted and prospering, even in the middle of the city.

The natives looked for their own brand of entertainment and showed some genuine concern for others battered by the war. On April 10, the *Richmond Dispatch* announced a "Grand Military and Civic Ball for destitute wives of the soldiers of Richmond."[30] The cost was $3 for one man and two ladies. The *Dispatch* also announced the opening of a new exhibit at Metropolitan Hall of "War Illustrations, pictures and paintings." As might be expected, war dominated the life of the city. But the mood included much gaiety—and a bright confidence that might be shaken but was still intact. The people accepted the mounting number of wounded brought in and the hosts of new graves, the gambling, the whores, the shortages, and the corruption, trying to maintain a lifestyle that absorbed all these changes.

On any given day, some soldiers would be coming home on furlough and some would be going back to the fight. On the ninth, Buddy Mercer was home, and his sister's diary made this poignant entry: "How much like the good old times to have Buddy to drive and talk with me. When will we drive together again? God only knows."[31] On July 20 would come the dreaded word that Buddy had been killed at Gettysburg.

One thing did not change in the South; this was a white man's war. At no time were blacks allowed to enlist as Confederate soldiers. Individual slaves would follow their white masters to war on occasion, but having them armed made the Southerners nervous, and only incidental occurrences were recorded of blacks actually in battle. This in spite of a black population that approached 3 million at the start of the war.

White women were above blacks, yet far below white men. A letter from B. N. Clemens, chief of the Appointments Bureau in Richmond, dated April 10, 1863, responded to a request from Mississippi to fire a postmaster and appoint a certain Mrs. Willbanks in his place. The reply: "I have to inform you that married ladies are not eligible to appointment as postmasters as they cannot legally execute an official bond." The letter further states that Clemens would be receptive to a *suitable* person's recommendation for appointment.[32]

THE EXECUTION OF CAPTAIN WEBSTER

A sign of the turbulent times was the execution that Friday in Richmond of a young Union officer, Captain Alphonso Charles Webster. Webster appears to be the only Union officer executed for the crime of parole violation. The practice of paroling captured soldiers was common in the early war years. There were few prisons on either side, so captured men were paroled until they could be exchanged for a like soldier of the opposite army. The parole was given when a soldier promised not to fight again until he had been exchanged.

Webster was a Maine man who had been in a Pennsylvania unit briefly but was court-martialed and resigned. He then apparently served briefly as a Confederate runner in Virginia. In June 1862, Captain Samuel Means of the Independent Loudoun Virginia Rangers was in Waterford, Virginia, near Leesburg, recruiting a company of Union cavalry. Means came across Webster (now a civilian) in the border town, recruited him, and because of his military manner, made him drillmaster.[33] This unit was involved with the Confederate 35th Virginia Cavalry Battalion in a brief battle in Waterford on August 27, 1862. In that battle, Webster was wounded, captured, and paroled.

Then, in December, Webster was captured again by the 35th Cavalry and was sent to Richmond for disposition. The night of his capture, he sat by the campfire with the Confederates telling anecdotes from his life to the officers of the battalion, and he impressed them, to say the least. Captain Frank Myers, one of the listeners that night, later wrote: "[We] . . . sat with him all night listening to the story of his life, which . . . was as full of romantic adventure as any depicted by Sir Walter; . . . by his own confession no sin in the decalogue had been untouched by him."[34] The next day Webster was sent south to Richmond under guard, and he was jailed in the political prison called Castle Thunder on December 18, 1862.

Webster made a number of unsuccessful escape attempts. Shortly after New Year's Day 1863, Webster's cellmate made a bone key to fit the Ranger's handcuffs and led him downstairs to hide in tobacco leaves left from the prison's earlier function as a tobacco warehouse. Webster was discovered shortly after he was hidden and was brought back to his cell. He was shackled with leg irons so he could move his feet only twelve inches at a time, and was put in a room by himself on the third floor. But that wasn't enough to keep him from yet another attempt: ". . . after dark [he] jumped from a third story window and fell in a pile of rubbish breaking both legs . . . he was found concealed in a pile of lumber, and he was again shackled and placed in a dungeon."[35]

In March 1863, three months after his capture, Webster's trial began. He was charged with killing a Captain Simpson, with killing one John Jones from Hillsboro, Virginia, and with violation of his parole. The witnesses duly appeared against Webster in the court-martial, and he was convicted "in the same kind of trial he might have been convicted if crucifying the saviour."[36] He was not allowed any witnesses or any defense, and the sentence was death by hanging, to be carried out on April 3. The sentence was for the crime of violation of parole, not for either of the murder charges.[37] Elizabeth Van Lew, a Union spy who lived in Richmond, wrote in her journal about the Union captain:

> . . . Webster, tried as a spy but they failed to find him guilty on this charge, and being determined that he should not escape, tried him upon the charge of having violated his parole upon this he was convicted . . . so seriously was he injured that he could not after-

wards turn over in his bed, yet in this situation he was kept with wrists and ankle irons until the surgeon finally ordered them to be taken off.[38]

It must have been clear to Webster at this time that he had lost his only two hopes: acquittal or escape. He was confined to a chair, his broken legs never having been set, so escape was not an option. He wrote, or had written for him, a strange but eloquent letter to President Davis. He claimed the trial had allowed him no defense against the charge of parole violation; although he had found witnesses to defend him on the murder charges, he had not expected the parole violation charge. Second, he claimed that he had, through his wife, furnished Confederate Brigadier General D. H. Hill information about Federal troop movements. Third, he protested that the Articles of War permitted him an appeal of the death penalty. Fourth, he begged to have a few additional days of life, if no executive clemency were to come from Davis. His letter ended with the plea:

> I am only twenty three years old and am the sole support of my sorrowful wife.
>
> In conclusion, I would humbly ask your Excellency to exercise that clemency of judgment that you on earth only have power to extend to me. I feel assured, Sir, that when the Angel of Peace returns to earth and shall again spread his white wings over the bleached land, the clash of arms shall be hushed, and the independence of your government secured, it will never be a cause of regret to your Excellency if in merciful exercise of your parogitive you grant me a further respite of my poor life, that I in the time still allowed you to live may render myself more fit to die and appear before the awful tribunal of my maker before whom the accused and the accuser must one day appear and when justice alone reigns, answer for these deeds of good and evil. Grant my request, Mr. President, and when death shuts out from my gaze the beautiful light, and my days on earth are numbered, your mercy shall be remembered in my dying moments and you shall share with my poor wife the last prayers of your humble servant.[39]

The plea was enough to grant him seven more days of life; the new execution date was April 10, 1863.[40] The week passed swiftly, and then it was time. As the cortege arrived to take him out to die, undoubtedly Webster hoped that something would keep him from his appointment.

He was composed as he was strapped into a straight-backed chair and manhandled into the waiting carriage.

Two thousand Confederates were lined up at Camp Lee, outside Richmond, to watch the sentence carried out. In the carriage, Webster's only recorded remarks were "This is a solemn occasion" and, as they neared the scaffold, "I never thought it would come to this." He maintained complete composure as he was hauled awkwardly up the thirteen stairs of the scaffold and was put on the trapdoor. He was dressed in his best, a Federal captain's uniform, although his epaulettes had been given to the prison commander, Captain Alexander, to be sent to his wife, Alice, in Point of Rocks, Maryland. Several minutes were spent with the minister as they secured the noose and foot straps. Then Webster made his last request: he wished to give the signal himself by dropping his hat, and in the hushed, pleasant springtime afternoon at 12:45 P.M., viewed by the military formations and hundreds of morbid curiosity seekers, the young Federal officer slowly lifted his hat from his head, glanced toward the sky, dropped his hat, and died.[41]

The execution, the bread riots, the wounded, the funerals, and the president's speech, all were accepted by the people of Richmond with the adaptability gained over two years of war. Even though Davis warned of a longer war, he closed his April 10 speech with these words:

> Let us all unite in the performance of our duty, each in his sphere, and with concerted, persistent, and well-directed effort, there seems little reason to doubt that under the blessing of Him to whom we look for guidance, and who has been to us our shield and our strength, we shall maintain the sovereignty and independence of these Confederate States, and transmit to our posterity the heritage bequeathed to us by our fathers.[42]

2

MR. LINCOLN'S ARMY

The weather up until April 7 had been cold and snowy, but April 10 turned out to be beautiful, with light southwest winds. Fruit trees were in full bloom, and there was a profusion of flowers. President Lincoln decided to get out of Washington and see "his" army, the Army of the Potomac, headquartered in Falmouth, Virginia.

The Army of the Potomac was the center of attention for most of the war, but in the spring of 1863 it was the least successful of all the Union formations. This army had yet to win a decisive victory, and its battleground was Virginia, virtually on the doorstep of Washington. The bad luck was mostly due to two simple facts: Confederate commanding general Robert E. Lee was the best military mind of his time, and the Northern generals were mediocre at their best.

The first of the army's leaders was Major General George B. McClellan, a terrific administrator but a victim of what Lincoln called the "slows," a reluctance to engage the enemy in battle. Next was Major General Ambrose Burnside, who didn't want the job and who had led the army in the disastrous Fredericksburg battle, losing over 12,000 men. On April 10, 1863, the job belonged to Major General Joseph Hooker.

Hooker was brash and confident—to a fault. He had been chosen over the protests of some cabinet members, but Lincoln thought he was the best at hand and, after considering Major General John Reynolds (who wouldn't have taken the job anyway) and Major General George Meade (who would get it next), he turned to "Fighting Joe" Hooker.[1]

Lincoln needed a general who believed in himself but knew his own limitations. The president's concern was Hooker's overconfidence. Hooker also had a reputation with the ladies and was known to overuse alcohol from time to time. The staid Union statesman Charles Francis Adams wrote that Hooker's headquarters was something between a barroom and a brothel, and it was said that one version of the word *hooker* began to be applied to professional ladies because of a train car of camp followers that often showed up near the general's headquarters.[2]

During the three months since Hooker had taken charge, the Army of the Potomac had indeed made a substantial turnaround. Prior to Hooker's appointment, desertion and disease had taken their toll, and after a muddy January march in a brief and abortive campaign following Fredericksburg, morale was at low ebb. Hooker set out to clean up the camps, improve the food, start a furlough program, and secure proper equipment for his men.

He was a surprisingly good administrator, just like McClellan, and soon he was almost as popular as "Little Mac" had been. The furlough plan worked best; he set up a system whereby furloughs were given first to units with the best efficiency ratings. This was incentive enough to get everybody motivated; soon every regiment was looking sharp and sending its boys home on furlough. The troops knew when a leader worked for them, and Hooker, with all his other faults, was a good camp commander. In fact, Major General Oliver O. Howard, one of Hooker's corps commanders, mentioned, "In truth, during February, March and April, the old cheerful, hopeful, trustful spirit which had carried us through so many dark days, through so many bloody fields and trying defeats, returned to the Army of the Potomac."[3]

Hooker's organizational changes were most visible in his consolidation of the cavalry. His reorganization resulted in the massive Cavalry Corps, about 11,000 strong, which he assigned to Major General George Stoneman. As a result, Union cavalry could be used as Confederate cavalry had been used since the beginning of the war—as a separate arm of the army. Before this, Union cavalry had been made up of a series of regiments operating mostly as mounted infantry. After the reorganization it could be consolidated and used for offensive purposes.[4]

As close as anyone could come to an actual count, the Army of the Potomac had 137,000 men with 410 pieces of artillery, broken down as 115,000 infantry, 11,000 cavalry, and 9,000 artillerymen, with 2,000 other troops all spread out along the north side of the Rappahannock, across the river from Fredericksburg.[5] The army was in good shape. It had rested for three months, and even crusty old George Meade reported: ". . . the morale of our army is better than it ever was so you may look for tough fighting next time."[6]

LINCOLN'S VISIT

On April 3, Lincoln informed Hooker that he was going to pay a visit to the army: "Our plan is to pass Saturday night on the boat; go over to your camp Sunday morning; remain with you till Tuesday morning, and then return. Our party will probably not exceed six persons of all sorts."[7] Hooker replied that he was happy to have the president visit, "only regret that your party is not as large as our hospitality."[8]

A grand review was important to the president; it would give him personal insight into the army, insight he felt he needed to make the critical decisions that were coming. His purpose in visiting the army was not only to see Hooker but also to see firsthand the poor luckless soldiers who had fought so superbly and been led so poorly. He wanted to look his men in the eye; in that brief week he looked into 130,000 pairs of eyes, trying to see the future of this army and, perhaps, the Union.

Lincoln's party took the little steamer *Carrie Martin* down the Potomac on Saturday, April 4, but a bad snowstorm kept them anchored overnight on the river and kept them from landing on schedule. In the Lincoln party were Mrs. Lincoln; Thomas "Tad" Lincoln, the president's youngest son; Attorney General Bates; Dr. Anson G. Henry; and newspaper reporter Noah Brooks. Compared to current presidential forays outside the capital, Lincoln's trip was as casual as a Sunday stroll in the garden. Noah Brooks mentioned, "If the rebels made a raid on the Potomac at that time the capture of the chief magistrate of the United States would have been a very simple matter. So far as I could see there were no guards on board the boat, and no precautions were taken against a surprise."[9]

Since the reviews of the troops had been delayed by the weather, Lincoln decided to extend his visit; instead of going home on Tuesday, the seventh, he stayed until Friday, the tenth. The review that snowy Monday was not canceled completely; the president managed to review the newly formed Cavalry Corps.

Ten-year-old Tad Lincoln had found an army man to escort him during his many trips and adventures. Tad's young companion was a happy participant in the various parades, being most impressed by Monday's cavalry review. This young soldier recalled, "Never can I forget the beautiful, benign expression of Lincoln in meeting the enthusiasm of not less than one hundred thirty thousand willing soldiers."[10]

On Tuesday there was no review, and Lincoln almost got himself in trouble with Mrs. Lincoln for something that wasn't his fault. At Major General Daniel E. Sickles's III Corps headquarters, beautiful Princess Salm-Salm, the wife of a Prussian count who was a colonel in a New York regiment, made a bet with some ladies that she could kiss the president. Sickles gave his blessing, and Lincoln was soon deluged with kisses from a bevy of belles. Mrs. Lincoln found out about it later, and no matter how strongly the president protested his innocence, his good wife would not be quieted. "But, Mother, hear me," the president pleaded. "Don't mother me," rejoined his indignant spouse; "And as for General Sickles, he will hear what I think of him and his lady guests. It was well for him that I was not there at the time."[11] To get Sickles back into some semblance of Mrs. Lincoln's good graces, the president invited Sickles and Brigadier General Carl Schurz to take the steamer back to Washington with them when they left on Friday.[12]

On Wednesday, April 8, the biggest review took place: four corps, the II, III, V, and VI—a total of over 75,000 men—passed in front of the president. Lincoln's review, and his consequent closeness to the soldiers, brought from the rank and file of the army emotional reactions showing their affection and concern for their president. In the ringing prose of the day, Sergeant Ira Seymour Dodd, 2nd Division, VI Corps, after his part in the review on April 8, wrote:

> The scene was more impressive because there were no idle spectators. This was no gala day for curious, gazing, merry-making crowds . . . but solemnly, silently save for the measured tramp of battalions and the rolling of the drums a nation's strength was massing as if to weigh itself and ask its own soul if it were fit for the mighty work and the awful sacrifices awaiting it . . .
>
> But now our moment has come. We take our place in the moving ranks. We march in close column with double company front so that each regiment took up small space. As we neared the reviewing stand the tall figure of Lincoln loomed up. He was on horseback and his severely plain, black citizen's dress set him in bold relief against the crowd of generals in full uniform grouped behind him. Distinguished men were among them; but we had no eyes save for our revered President, the Commander in Chief of the Army . . . great leader of a nation in its hour of trial. There is no time save for a marching salute; the occasion called for no cheers . . . but we passed close to him so that he could look into our faces and we into his.
>
> None of us to our dying day can forget that countenance! From its presence we marched directly onward toward our camp and as soon as "route step" was ordered and the men were free to talk they spoke thus to each other: "Did you ever see such a look on any man's face?" "He is bearing the burdens of the nation." "It is an awful load; it is killing him." "Yes, this is so; he is not long for this world!"
>
> Concentrated in that one great, strong yet tender face, the agony of the life and death struggle of the hour was revealed as we had

never seen it before. With new understanding we knew why we
were soldiers.[13]

Hooker's chief of staff, Brigadier General Dan Butterfield, was at
Lincoln's side through most of the week. He later recalled:

> Bands were playing and the President passed through the
> camps. The men cheered to the echo again and again. Thousands of
> them crowded around his horse, hoping to touch his hand or hear his
> voice or look into his eyes—those deep, fathomless eyes, half closed,
> as if to hide their sadness . . . The soldiers showed their affection
> for Lincoln, and gave expression to it in many ways. They were
> allowed their own way that day.[14]

Later Lincoln wandered through the hospital tents where the sick
and wounded from Fredericksburg were being cared for. There he
found a similar show of affection. He made an effort to stop and say
something to each of the men, shaking hands, patting shoulders, and
showing his deep and genuine concern. Correspondent Noah Brooks
reported, "More than once as I followed the President down the long
rows of weary sufferers, I noticed tears of gladness stealing down their
pale faces; for they were made happy by looking into Lincoln's sympa-
thetic countenance, touching his hand and hearing his gentle voice."[15]
One of the ladies in the crowd of dignitaries was the same Princess
Salm-Salm. "I could not look into [his face] without feeling kindly
towards him," she wrote, "and without tears starting to my eyes, for
over the whole face was spread a melancholy tinge, which some will
have noticed in many who are fated to die a violent death."[16]

The review brought moments of pride and pleasure for many of
the troops marching for their president. In spite of all their setbacks and
losses, their pride remained the strength of the Army of the Potomac.
Private Arthur Van Vleck expressed his pride in his unit and the army
when he wrote, "The whole scene was delightful to any lover of order,
beauty and music . . . I cannot describe what I felt but I vowed to be
true to that flag while it waved where I was."[17]

On Thursday, April 9, there was a review of I Corps, under the
very capable Major General John F. Reynolds, and an impressive
massed artillery review. Finally, on the tenth, the last two corps were
scheduled—the XI Corps, under Major General Oliver O. Howard, and
the XII Corps, under Major General Henry W. Slocum. The ceremony
took place at Stafford Courthouse, at the northern edge of the army's
encampment. Alonzo Quint, chaplain of the 2d Massachusetts, described

Lincoln and the review after a three-and-one-half-hour wait on the parade ground:

> He is a good rider. Mounted on a horse with a general's caparison, he dashed on through mud, swamp and ditches, without the slightest hesitation; evidently to the disadvantage of some of his followers. The 21 guns saluted him, and he rode very rapidly along the lines (if lines they were) while the escort of lancers, with their gayly fluttering red, formed 3 sides of a square around the spot occupied by the President's wife and the chief military dignitaries, and in which the President soon stationed himself. He was dressed in black, with a curious article on his head, the upright part being cylindrical, very much like the section of a stove pipe, with a flat roof and a horizontal and circular rim at the lower part. It must be quite stiff, and, I judge, painful to the head. I have heard it intimated, however, that such absurd things are quite common in the North. . . .
>
> Suddenly the bugle gave the order, and at once each regiment, moving at the double quick, changed front. The effect was indescribably beautiful. Then the marching, each regiment still formed by divisions, moving at quick step around the fields. The ground was rolling, and the sight of regiments disappearing in hollows, or emerging was picturesque. As the consolidated drum corps of each brigade reached the President they wheeled to the left and there remained to give the "ruffles" as the flag of each regiment was successively bowed in honor of the chief executive.[18]

Private Rice Bull of the 123d New York Infantry remembered that it was "the final and last [review] by the 12th Corps, that was now through its period of training and was ready to take the field."[19]

The day made many impressions on the men of the army. Henry Henney, a bandsman with the 55th Ohio Regiment, related his disappointment at not being able to perform for his president. But as a spectator, he was able to get a good look at the First Lady. He observed: "There were several good looking ladies present. The president's wife, though, in my judgment, is not so good looking."[20]

A Maine private, John W. Haley, part of an honor guard, wrote in his diary:

> Mr. Lincoln is one of the plainest of men, while his wife is quite the reverse. . . . as Mr. Lincoln rode by, I noticed he was weeping. Why he wept I know not—whether he was thinking how many had fallen, or how many will soon fall. It might be neither. But this I do

know: under that homely exterior is as tender a heart as ever throbbed, one that is easily moved toward the side of the poor and downtrodden. He is probably aware that a battle cannot long be deferred.

I can guess as much as this. A review of this entire army means something of more important character than just to please the president. And so, as I wended my way to camp, a feeling of uneasiness and horrible uncertainty possessed me.[21]

The reviews had gone extremely well, the troops were inspired, and the president was reassured and even slightly rested. Possibly one of the reasons the army showed so well was that not everyone participated. Hooker was doing everything possible to make himself and his army appear in a favorable light for the president, and tattered, worn uniforms were not likely to make the required impression. Private Edwin O. Wentworth, a Massachusetts private, explained to his family that his cap didn't fit, so he wasn't allowed to march. That caused him no problem, he said, since ". . . it is hard work to go on such a review as will be held today. Quite a number are left in camp because their clothes are not good enough."[22]

In all the diaries, letters, and reminiscences, there were few entries that had any overtones of complaint about the reviews. The closest was an April 9 entry in the diary of the provost marshal of the army, Brigadier General Marsena R. Patrick, who complained, "I had to go over to court at Gen. Sickles' HQ and lost an hour, in consequence of the non-arrival of members of the court, and it was finally postponed, until next Saturday, to enable the officers to attend the Review of the 1' Corps today and of the 11' Corps tomorrow. I hope the President will soon get off so that we can once more get to work."[23]

The parades had some uninvited spectators as well. Most of the reviews were held in plain sight of Lee's army, just across the Rappahannock River, and the activity gave some entertainment to Lee's 60,000 Southerners, who had already bested this army every time they had met. One Union private, Jacob H. Cole, recalled waiting for his unit to pass in review:

As we thus prepared for the final ceremony, I could see on the heights beyond Fredericksburg, which a few weeks before we had been trying to win, long brown lines. It was the Confederate Army of Northern Virginia, gazing at its opponents in the field. There, no doubt, were the eyes of Lee, of Longstreet and Jackson all fixed upon us.[24]

For either side, it must have been a strange sensation to be able to see the enemy and know he was looking back. Both sides were taking the measure of the troops who would soon be trying to kill them.

But politics could not be forgotten for long. Some saw personal opportunities in Lincoln's visit. The taciturn George G. Meade was not the typical political figure, and he was not beloved by his troops; one soldier's description of him was that he was "a Goddamned, goggle-eyed old snapping turtle."[25] But Meade saw an opening to cozy up to the president, and he did so. He wrote a letter to his wife, saying, "In view of the vacant Brigadiership in the regular army, I have ventured to tell the President one or two stories, and I think I have made decided progress in his affections."[26]

The week had not been all work and no relaxation, and in his brief visit the president had added to the growing collection of Lincoln anecdotes. One day shortly after they arrived, Tad persuaded his father to show him a real "grayback," a live Confederate soldier. The Lincolns, father and son, were escorted to the picket line opposite Fredericksburg, and sure enough, they could clearly see the stars and bars of the Rebel flag floating over a building on the south side of the river. Two Confederate pickets (guards) could be seen across the river, and they shouted that the Yanks had been beaten in Charleston. A Rebel officer heard the exchange, came down to the river's edge, and looked at the presidential party through his field glasses. Perhaps he made out the tall figure on the north bank as Lincoln, but in any event he doffed his hat, made a long courteous bow, and retired.[27]

While the president was riding out to a parade, passing through a black settlement where large groups of children crowded around to see their emancipator, Mrs. Lincoln asked him how many of "those pica-ninnies" were named Abraham Lincoln. He replied, "Let's see, this is April 1863. I should say that of all those babies under two years of age perhaps two thirds have been named for me."[28]

Another Lincoln moment took place in an ambulance taking the president, Brooks, Hooker, and a group of army officers out to review the I Corps on April 9. The driver, a typical teamster, shouted volley after volley of oaths. Lincoln finally touched the driver's shoulder and asked, "Excuse me, my friend, are you an Episcopalian?" No, the driver replied, he was a Methodist. "Well," Lincoln said, "I thought you must be an Episcopalian, because you swear just like Mr. Seward, who is a church warden."[29]

In spite of the fact that Lincoln was riding almost fifty miles a day, going to reviews and camps that covered hundreds of square miles from Aquia Creek to Falmouth to Stafford Courthouse and then over to

VI Corps southeast of Fredericksburg, he seemed more relaxed than he had for some time. Noah Brooks mentioned that to the president, who mused that it was a great relief to get away from Washington and the politicians, "but nothing touches the tired spot."[30] A New York regimental surgeon, Dr. George T. Stevens, was amazed at Lincoln's endurance during the course of the many reviews: "How one unaccustomed to such physical fatigues could endure such labor, commencing early in the morning and only resting at dark, was a wonder. It seemed as if the president's physical, like his mental constitution, could bear up under the most trying and continued labors."[31]

Finally it was over; the reviews ended and the president could postpone his journey back to Washington no longer. General Butterfield remembered, "The sounds of those manly cheers of the soldiers, and the touch of so many hands and the fire of so many brave eyes awakened fresh life in his pale and anxious face. It was something to feel, even for a moment, the burden of that heavy heart had been lightened."[32]

Late in the afternoon of April 10, the president's party left Aquia Creek Landing on the *Carrie Martin* for the trip back to Washington, with the out-of-favor Sickles and General Schurz. Lincoln was acutely conscious of Mary Lincoln's icy reserve toward General Sickles and her unhappiness with the president for his part in the matter. He teased Sickles about the princess:

> "I never knew until last night that you were a very pious man."
> Sickles replied in some confusion that he felt the President had been misinformed. "Not at all," said the president, "Mother says you are the greatest Psalmist in the army. She says you are more than a Psalmist, you are a Salm-Salmist."[33]

This broke the tension and Sickles was forgiven.

In Washington, Lincoln was reviled and ridiculed by the press and his fellow Republicans, cabinet members, and Congress. But in the company of 130,000 men who had endured the bloodbaths of two years of fighting and who were still prepared to suffer and die for their president—there he found the friendship and adoration that sustained him in the coming years.

While the officers and soldiers went back to their preparation for more war, Lincoln went back to fight his own battles in Washington. But the experience in early April on the northern bank of the Rappahannock had put new determination in all who were there—determination they would need in the months to come.

LIFE IN THE CAMPS

After Lincoln's departure, life returned to what could pass for normal: picketing, drilling, and writing letters home.

Camp life in the Army of the Potomac had settled into a fairly comfortable routine, but there were stirrings now as the weather warmed and the roads began to dry up. Hooker had about 40,000 men whose enlistments were due to expire in May, and he wanted to get in one more fight before they left him. Soon after Lincoln's visit, Hooker ordered current maps of the city of Richmond, lots of them.[34]

Hooker's improvements had made a difference. Brigadier General John Gibbon had just returned from the hospital, where he had been recovering from wounds received at Fredericksburg. He wrote:

> Gen. Hooker did a great deal to improve the condition of the men, and by a wise system of granting furloughs in moderate number added to the contentment of the men and checked the desertions which just before had increased to an alarming extent. The truth was that not sufficient attention had been paid to the fact that our men were entirely cut off from their homes and families, and many of them suffered from homesickness and became discouraged with the hard and dangerous work they had to do and the inadequate results flowing therefrom.[35]

Some of the soldiers took their own furloughs, with sometimes tragic consequences. An item from the *New York Times* of April 10 reported that Charles Node of the 8th New York Infantry had been on furlough in New York City but had decided not to go back to his unit, since he was convinced he would be discovered and shot as a deserter. Instead he took poison and gave some to his fiancée, Mary Strube. He died, but she did not.[36]

Another innovation of Hooker's was the creation of a series of corps patches to wear on the shoulder, identifying units. Corps were identified by design, and division by color. It was another morale builder for the units and their members, and is still used in today's army for the same purpose.

These factors helped to raise spirits; the relative comfort of their quarters, created with the ingenuity of the campaigners, made the quiet life along the Rappahannock almost bearable. Captain Samuel Fiske of the 14th Connecticut Infantry wrote a tongue-in-cheek description of his "house":

I have a house myself I would like to show you, with a brown mud front, water in every part of it, at this present writing, and all the modern (army) improvements, including a real door on hinges, with a latch to it; a chimney that never smokes (unless the wind is very strong from the northeast); fireplace . . . our patent army transparent water proof roofing; and everything about the whole building so convenient that I may say I can put my hand upon it; sitting here by the fire, as I am, with my feet upon the mantel (not marble; that proves too cold for comfort), in true Yankee style. The parlor, sitting room, dining room and library are so arranged as to be easily thrown together in one apartment. The sleeping rooms are well ventilated; and to be brief, the whole forms a snug tenement for a family of suitable size, such as is rarely to be found and I might add . . . could be rented on easy terms, with a limited amount of furniture, as the owner is thinking of moving to Richmond.

There is a good deal of variety in the style of architecture. My own building is a severe classic, without ornament, rather low and heavy, inclining to the Doric, or perhaps even to the Egyptian order. But we have specimens of the airiest, most fantastic Gothics, of the tasteful Corinthian capitals . . . One of my neighbors is nearly on the model of the Athenian Parthenon . . . Some model after a heathen temple, some after a Yankee wood-shed, some after an Indian wigwam, and some after a woodchuck's hole.[37]

Fiske was not only an infantry captain but also a correspondent for a hometown newspaper, the *Republican*; he wrote a number of articles covering the activities of a fictional soldier, Dunn Browne.

The army had been in the same area of Virginia since December 1862. After the battle of Fredericksburg, it retreated back across the river and moved into almost the same quarters it had left, minus the 12,000 casualties of the fight. As a result, there were camp embellishments that were not the norm. Log huts with canvas roofs were one innovation, particularly those that had log chimneys, "which presented a most incendiary appearance, as it seemed as if very ample arrangements had been made to fire the whole camp. Notwithstanding the seemingly incongruity, however, these apparently inflammable structures were the chimneys of the camp, and plastered well inside with Virginia mud as they were, served their purpose admirably."[38]

This took vast quantities of wood, for the huts and for firewood, and it wasn't long before the whole area was denuded of trees. As an old rail-splitter, Lincoln had been fascinated by the stumps; as he went from ceremony to ceremony in his April visit, he remarked that this

stump was really ragged and that stump was done by a pro.[39] Sam
Fiske wrote about the disappearing trees when he looked back on his
stay along the Rappahannock: "It was early in December when we
bivouacked among these forest-covered hills and ravines: it is late in
April now that we are gathering up our traps to leave. The forests have
disappeared. The whole country is intersected with roads leading from
one city, of ten or five thousand inhabitants to another."[40]

Because the army had been in quarters so long, there were even
some attempts to get gardens started. Lieutenant J. N. Favill had his
own garden, which he described philosophically:

> The weather is most extraordinary throughout February, March
> & up to today April 10th, it has been just like spring. Many of the
> men have laid out flower gardens, and some have even planted seeds
> and beguiled themselves into believing it possible they may remain to
> see them grow. The fields and adjacent woods are full of wild flow-
> ers and many of them have been transferred to the soldier's plots,
> especially the bluet, a tiny modest flower which here covers with its
> beauty the banks and shady nooks of woods.[41]

The activities of the men in ranks ranged from required roles in
drill and in picketing to the more passive roles of gardening, writing
home, or, a favorite in any war, napping. Probably for fear of sharpshooters, fishing had been prohibited in the Rappahannock, although
there were many men who ignored the order.

Captain Fiske, writing as Dunn Browne, aptly described the activities of idle days such as April 10:

> Meantime, while we are waiting, what are we doing with our-
> selves? When a great army is doing nothing, how is it employed?
> Well, you know that idlers always have the hardest kind of a life to
> live. However it may be in other things, certainly soldiers have to be
> pretty busy even doing nothing. An army, lying still, is always on the
> move. Its ordinary functions of respirations and nutrition keep in
> motion a good many active agencies. It eats and drinks through the
> toils of a host of busy commissaries and teamsters, and details of men
> by night and by day. It doesn't put on its clothes but by the labor of
> many hands, and the thoughts of many brains. "To keep its pot
> boiling" requires the rumbling of many fuel wagons, and uses the
> limbs of braying mules. It doesn't sleep at night but with its eyes
> wide open; and every officer and every soldier has to take his turn,
> about one in three or four days, as eye for his regiment or camp. It

keeps its long arms stretched out in all directions, feeling for danger, and avoiding surprise; and all, in turn, must take their share of this active duty; each serving his turn as a finger, so to speak.[42]

On April 13, Private Wilbur Fisk (no relation to Captain Sam) of the 2d Vermont Infantry wrote his own version:

> Of course you know that we are still idle here, and if I should tell you that all "was quiet along the lines," I don't think it would cause any one a very deep sensation of relief. Yes, we are fairly surfeited with idleness and indolence. To be sure we have our regular routines of duties—guarding, "fatigueing," besides drills occasionally, and roll calls regularly. To go "on fatigue" as probably everyone knows, means to go to *work*. Generally it consists of either shoveling or chopping. But we have no rifle-pits to dig, as last year, nor breastworks to throw up. We have had, as yet, no Chickahominy swamps to bridge over and corduroy, nor acres of timber to fell, but it is not too late for these things to happen yet.[43]

In camp, certainly the pickets had a most important role—protecting the Union army from unpleasant surprises; picket duty could often be hazardous. A brigade or other unit would be assigned a section of the front lines to "picket." The chief duties were to watch for surprise movements and to stay alert. This duty often meant hours of boredom broken by minutes of terror. Any strange noise, movement, or activity could mean danger, and every man knew it. Along the brigade's line, smaller units would be sent out: the closer the line was to the enemy, the smaller the unit. Captain Henry Blake of the 11th Massachusetts added that it wasn't unusual to find the brigade commander back in camp, enjoying its safety and comfort while his men took their turn on the picket line.[44]

During the early spring there had been an understanding that pickets on the two sides of the river would refrain from shooting at each other. This private truce happened sometimes when opposing camps were close to each other, and pickets made their own rules. As Captain Blake put it:

> Thus month after month passed quietly away. The grass began to sprout in the sods of the barracks, and the rumors of an advance daily thickened. No shots were exchanged between the pickets, who pushed their bayonets into the ground, and made waterwheels or ornaments of bone and laurel-wood to occupy the weary hours, and

floated across the river boats and sticks, to which newspapers were fastened for sails.[45]

One of the most perceptive Civil War diarists was First Lieutenant Elisha Hunt Rhodes, of the 2d Rhode Island Volunteers. He was in the VI Corps near Franklin's Crossing on April 10, just back from a short leave in Rhode Island. He was on picket duty; on April 14 he made these observations about picketing:

> We are on picket again, and I am occupying a house owned by a Mr. Pollock. A young man, a nephew of Mr. Pollock, is here on a visit. He has but one leg, having lost the other while serving in the Rebel Cavalry. He is on parole and so has the liberty of the plantation. Across the river and only a few yards distant I can see fifty Rebels gazing at the Yankees. Just beyond them is a large fort with long lines of rifle pits on each side. The Rebels are very anxious to get northern papers. A few minutes ago I saw one of their little boats made of a board with a paper sail and a tin can nailed upon the board come sailing across the river. I received the boat and took out of the can a late Richmond paper. The Rebel called out, "Send me a New York paper." but I declined as it is against orders. In accordance with orders I broke the boat in pieces, although a rebel shouted that he would shoot me if I did not stop. But I broke the board notwithstanding, and he did not shoot.
>
> Gen. Thomas J. [Stonewall] Jackson came down to the river bank today with a party of ladies and officers. We raised our hats to the party, and strange to say the ladies waved their handkerchiefs in reply. Several Rebel sentinels told us that it was Gen. Jackson. He took his field glasses and cooly surveyed our party. We could have shot him with a revolver, but we have an agreement that neither side will fire, as it does no good, and in fact is simply murder. We shall go back to camp tomorrow, as other troops will take our place on out-post duty. I am very well and try to enjoy myself.[46]

Such restraint seems strange when compared to the vicious fighting that took place when battles actually started. But on days such as April 10, 1863, proximity and boredom often made the fighting men curious about their opposite numbers.

One of the men's other duties was parading. Lincoln's review was hardly a novelty, except for the chief executive's presence, since most of the units had had parades for muster, for inspection, or for training all through the previous months. It seemed as if they had a parade whenever any officer had nothing else planned. Private Wentworth wrote his wife, "We've been kept busy about everyday for the past month drilling, inspecting, and undergoing reviews. We have been reviewed, nine times in the past two weeks."[47]

Drilling, parades, and picketing kept most of the men busy. But the drilling wasn't always as demanding as it seemed. A 5th New Jersey Infantry Regiment sergeant, William K. Haines, wrote in his diary on the tenth: "Company drill today. I asked (Cap't) Kelly to go to his quarters and let me drill the company. When he left I doublequicked them down into the timber, stacked arms, and we plaid cards until the drums beat recall."[48]

Sam Fiske briefed his readers about camp life:

> And so, with guard and picket, inspections, parades and reviews, with all the little and great, necessary and unnecessary, matters of camp life, rubbing-up of guns and distributing rations, writing letters and attending courtsmartial, bringing wood and water and plastering walls, reading newspapers and pitching quoits, we manage to fill up pretty easily all the working-hours of the twenty-four . . . a dull, monotonous, stupid, indifferent, make-shift of a life, soon to be broken in upon by the excitement of a great and eventful campaign.[49]

Fiske closed with a melancholy synopsis that probably reflected the thoughts of most of the men:

> There is nothing very attractive about this locality. It is bare, bleak and desolate; muddy, dusty and in ruins; all the beauty trampled out long ago under the ruthless tread of a great army. And there are no visions of glory to endear it to our memory; no successes gained, no wreaths and laurels, to crown it in our recollections: and yet it is somehow a little hard to pull up our stakes and tear down our walls for departure, after all. We have something of a home feeling for our poor little mud-built cities. Our streets are not Broadways; but a part of our life has grown round those little log-huts and chimneys of plastered sticks.[50]

Private Wilbur Fisk tried to summarize the Yankee soldier's attitude; on April 6 he wrote:

> The Lord knows we are anxious to finish this job as soon as possible, and return to our heart-loved homes. Notwithstanding the

discouragements, rough dealing and bad management we have been subjected to, there is scarcely a man who shrinks from the coming contests. Of course there are some who are always finding fault, but in this regiment they are a piteous minority. The grumblers are pretty well sifted out. Account for it as you may, those who came here from mere love of adventure, with no heart for the work, who were always grumbling at every measure the Government adopted, and found fault when the best was done for them that could be done, these were the first to get broken down and sent home. The staunch patriots, who love their country and are willing to fight for it, are here yet, and will remain here till the regiment is sent home, if not absolutely compelled to do otherwise. The health of the regiment was never better, and when the word comes, we are ready and willing to go forward and do our duty but we may not go until the word does come. Yes, we are *willing* to go forward—not anxious for mere love of excitement, but like men in earnest, who know they have a great and important work to do, and can comprehend its magnitude. We have seen too much of war to desire its novelty, and we have seen too much of it to shrink from its horrors.[51]

One evening, a Federal band played for both sides of the river. "Dixie" brought cheers from the Southerners. The next song, "Yankee Doodle," brought down the house on the Northerners' shore. But the plaintive melody the band played next was different:

> *And yet once more the bugle sang*
> *Above the stormy riot;*
> *No shout upon the evening rang,*
> *There reigned a holy quiet.*
> *The sad, lone stream its noiseless tread*
> *Spread o'er the glistening pebbles;*
> *All silent now the Yankees stood;*
> *All silent stood the Rebels:*
> *For each responsive soul had heard*
> *That plaintive note's appealing,*
> *So deeply "Home, Sweet Home" had stirred*
> *The hidden founts of feeling.*[52]

★

The Army of the Potomac and the Confederate Army of Northern Virginia next met in battle at Chancellorsville, Virginia, on May 1, 1863. The first move came when Hooker, on April 10, ordered Gen-

eral Stoneman to cross the Rappahannock and move around the flank of Lee's army. There were 30,000 casualties. It was a decisive Confederate victory.

General Hooker was demoted after Chancellorsville and replaced by Major General George G. Meade.

Major General John Reynolds was killed at Gettysburg July 1, 1863.

President Abraham Lincoln was shot in Washington on April 14, 1865, and died the next day.

Tad Lincoln died of complications of pleurisy July 15, 1871, at age eighteen.

Private Van Vleck died in Libby Prison on December 21, 1863, after his capture in August.

Private Edwin Wentworth was killed at Brandy Station on May 12, 1864.

Colonel (Count) Salm-Salm was killed in 1870 while in the Prussian army.

Captain Samuel Fiske was killed in the Wilderness in May 1864.

3

★

GENERAL LEE'S ARMY

Just across the Rappahannock River, the Army of Northern Virginia's Berry Benson, one of Stonewall Jackson's II Corps, the "Foot Cavalry," heard the same band and remembered somewhat differently: "Once a federal band came down to the river and played 'Dixie.' We cheered them vociferously, of course. Then it played 'Yankee Doodle.' Then it played 'Home Sweet Home' and the cheer went up loud and long from both sides of the river."[1] Whether it met with cheers or silence, "Home Sweet Home" touched a responsive chord in both armies.

The pride of the South, the soldiers of the Army of Northern Virginia, sat and watched all the activity on the northern bank of the Rappahannock during Lincoln's visit: his reviews, the preparations, and the ceremonies. Although most of the action took place in full view of the ragged soldiers of the South, it didn't impress them greatly. They had beaten these same Yankee soldiers in almost every battle, and knew that they had an ace card that the Union couldn't match: Robert E. Lee, general, commanding. The ground they occupied was the same ground they had held when they beat back the Union's General Burnside in December.

Jedediah Hotchkiss, mapmaker for Stonewall Jackson, described on April 10 the fields scarred by the December slaughter at the battle of Fredericksburg:

> After dinner Brown and I went to . . . the Marye House,—looking at the many evidences of the hard fought field that were visible; torn trees, battered walls, broken houses. The day was very pleasant and spring-like and the grass and grain are just brightening up, the peaches reddening to blossom and the birds enlivening the scene, but the evidences of grim visaged war hang as clouds amid the brightness.[2]

The sunny spring day spread over the acres of the old battlefield, and the men rested peacefully, waiting for coming operations. But on April 10 there were concerns about two problems that plagued the Confederate Army of Northern Virginia. The first was Lee's health. For the first time since he took command of "his" army, fifty-six-year-old General Lee had been taken ill. In March he had contracted a serious throat infection, then developed acute pains that affected his back, arms, and chest.[3] It was suggested that those symptoms indicated more serious and more permanent problems, but the general was more concerned about his army than about his own well-being; shortly after April 6 he went back to full duty as army commander. From then on, though, he would have occasional spasms that continued to affect his health.[4]

The second problem was food, both for the troops and, almost more important, for the horses and mules. Lee's subsistence problems were staggering. As he sat in his headquarters on March 27, 1863, on Lee's Hill in Fredericksburg, he wrote a letter to Secretary of War Seddon expressing concern over the welfare of his men and asking for more and better rations:

> The troops of this portion of the army have for some time been confined to reduced rations, consisting of 18 ounces of flour, 4 ounces of bacon of indifferent quality, with occasional supplies of rice, sugar or molasses. The men are cheerful, and I receive but few complaints; still I do not think it is enough to continue them in health and vigor, and I fear they will be unable to endure the hardships of the approaching campaign.[5]

Seddon referred Lee's request to the commissary, who referred it to the transportation officer, who begged off by saying he could not deliver rations, even if they were available.

As for the horses, Lee telegraphed to his artillery chief, Brigadier General William Pendleton, some distance in the rear of Fredericksburg: "To bring them up now would but add to our difficulties and might destroy the animals . . . It is impossible to get any more forage except such as the railroad can bring and what you can bring and what you can get in the neighborhood."[6]

Major General Samuel Jones, in Dublin, Virginia, advised Seddon on April 2: "If the horses are brought into Virginia now they will probably starve. If they are sent further south they would probably have to go to Georgia before forage could be found in abundance."[7] Again on April 16, Lee informed Davis that he anticipated resuming his aggressive campaign by May 1, but added: "My only anxiety arises from the present immobility of the army, owing to the condition of our horses and the scarcity of forage and provisions."[8]

To solve this problem, Lee sent his I Corps commander, Lieutenant General James Longstreet, to search for provisions with two divisions, Major General George Pickett's and Major General John B. (Sam) Hood's. This left Lee in Fredericksburg with Stonewall Jackson and his II Corps; two divisions, Major General Lafayette McLaws's and Major General Richard Anderson's, left over from Longstreet's corps; plus Major General J.E.B. Stuart's cavalry. Altogether, 60,298 men[9] faced Hooker's 136,724 men, odds of more than two to one against Lee.[10] As of March 31, 1863, Lee was supported by 96 artillery pieces; Hooker had 410.

While the troop strengths of the two armies differed by more than two to one in men and four to one in guns, the key ingredient, leadership, was the balancing factor for the South. Lee and Jackson functioned beautifully as a team, Lee using Jackson's corps to cover more ground marching than the Union believed possible. They were supported by the dependable James Longstreet and one of the finest cavalry officers, J.E.B. Stuart, whose total understanding of the many uses of that branch of service was at that time unmatched by any Union cavalryman. Lee the strategist, Longstreet and Jackson the field commanders, and Stuart the scout decidedly outmatched the Union leadership on every count.

Jackson was probably one of the strangest, most difficult leaders on either side. He was a religious zealot, a hypochondriac who was forever concerned with his "blood balance," and he sucked on lemons continually. On April 10, his four divisions made up the only full corps in Lee's army. The Confederate line along the Rappahannock stretched thin over twenty-five miles of river, with Stuart's cavalry holding either end of the line.

On April 9, part of Stuart's cavalry had moved as far east as the Culpeper Court House.[11] In Fredericksburg, Jackson was well entrenched behind the same fortifications that had bloodied Burnsides's attacks in December and had been improved by months of work since then. Although he was in a magnificent defensive position, Lee had no intention of staying around Fredericksburg; he was waiting only for the spring weather to dry out the roads to get at the Army of the Potomac. He had corresponded frequently with Seddon; on April 9 he answered Seddon's request to furnish some of Lee's troops to Johnston in Mississippi:

Should General Hooker's army assume the defensive, the readiest method of relieving General Johnston [in the west] and General

Beauregard [at Charleston, South Carolina], would be for this army to cross over into Maryland. This cannot be done, however, in the present condition of the roads, nor unless I can obtain a certain amount of provisions and transportation. But this is what I would recommend, if practicable.[12]

The South was beginning to feel the pinch, and was learning that gallantry on the field still needed to be reinforced by some nourishment and transport.

IN THE CAMPS

The officers' planning and their politics were important, but not necessarily to the Rebel soldiers. Their concerns in April 1863 were the same as those of the Yankees just across the river: food, a roof, and some wood for a fire—but mostly food. Some of the troops found that fresh fish could help the situation. Edward Moore, a Virginia artilleryman, wrote how easy it was to catch fish:

Our fare here was greatly improved by the addition of fresh fish, so abundant at that season of the year in the Rappahannock and the adjacent creeks. To a mountaineer familiar with the habits of the wary trout and other fish that are caught with hook and line, the manner of fishing here was very novel. Of the herring and shad left by the hundreds in the grass and the shallows as the tide receded, the soldiers had only to wade in and with stick or bare hand to secure all they could carry.[13]

Fish was one fresh food; another was rat. Berry Benson noted that there was some sport in chasing rats, and some, including Blackwood, Berry's sixteen-year-old brother, sampled them: "They gave it as their opinion that rats tasted like young squirrel and the rest of us took their word for it."[14]

Scurvy was always a concern, although the coming of spring brought some hope for relief, according to Doctor James McFadden Gaston, a soldier from South Carolina: "Our troops are in very good health, excepting cases of scurvy from sameness of diet without vegitables, and that will soon be remedied by the vegetation of fields and gardens of the country."[15]

The families at home tried to help, sending their loved ones packages wherever and however they could. Thomas Ruffin bemoaned the fate of a parcel from home: "Charlie Hester could not get the cake and wine through. Someone stole the wine, and the cake became damaged, they ate it."[16] Maybe it sustained some other gray-clad soldier.

Some soldiers went home because they were sick or because they were needed to plant crops or to take care of family, but the reverse was true as well. Some soldiers who could have gone home stayed with their regiments. Charles Chewning of the 9th Virginia had been wounded in the leg in late 1862, and he reported back to his unit on April 9, only to be sent home the next day: "I have returned to my beloved Ninth to see Colonel Lee in answer to my letter. He received me with great courtesy but my pleas are to be unrewarded. I am told to go home to heal properly. I head home with a heavy heart in the morning."[17]

There was another solution for some, since furloughs were almost nonexistent. On April 10 Doctor Gaston wrote his wife repeating his request that she come to Fredericksburg to see him. If he couldn't come home, maybe she could get to him. He and a friend urged their spouses, suggesting, "As to any difficulties in the way of accommodations for you and Sallie in camp, all is obviated by an arrangement today, to get a house between our camps and remote from any body of troops. This place was abandoned by a Yankee family, on approach of our army, and has furniture that will be useful to us in keeping house."[18]

The Confederates turned out to be fully as creative as their Northern foes when it came to housing. Over the months they, too, had designed and built some cozy retreats from rain and snow. But they weren't all perfect. They used wood when it was available, dug holes for basements, sometimes used barrels for chimneys, then topped the whole thing off with sod roofs. Some of the efforts aroused literary descriptions of their retreats such as that by Ohioan Edmund DeWitt Patterson, now with the 9th Alabama:

> Instead of April showers with sunshine between them making raindrops sparkle like diamonds, the rain falls ceaselessly and my tent gives back a hollow rumbling sound. The damp north wind comes sighing around my frail tenement, chasing the smoke down the chimney to seek room within, as if afraid to come in contact with the cold cheerless air without. But the day's duties are done, the fire burns brightly and my tallow candle set in a genuine soldier candlestick, a bayonet, adds to the light and comfort-like appearance. Without darkness—within light.[19]

The Rebel soldiers suffered from lack of wood just as did their opposites on the northern banks. According to North Carolina's Leonidas A. Torrence, "It begins to look like Spring. but I don't think the

Farmers can do much on their farms for their fenses are all burnt and the timber is all burn till they can get nothing to fense there farms with . . . you have no idea how the Army reads out things where they go."[20]

Private Franklin L. Riley of the 16th Mississippi Infantry sounded reasonably cheerful about his little home: "We have been here long enough to have quite comfortable quarters. Some have tents with dug out basements, chimneys, and fireplaces. Most of us (including me) have huts made of poles, chinked and daubed, floored with pinetops, roofed with pieces of tent cloth, heated with chimneys."[21] Berry Benson, on the other hand, described a dismal camp: "So the whole country presented a dreary scene of hills covered over with huts, tents 'Merrimacs,' flies, all kinds of soldier habitations, and no tree nor bush for shelter, and no grass, all dusty and gray beneath. A deserted camp of this kind presents a scene of utter desolation."[22]

In the few days before April 10, the snow had finally melted, and the ground, stripped as it was of forest, was bare and drying out. However, earlier in April, the army had completed the latest of a series of tactical maneuvers, practices for military movement, but in a new and very novel way. Private William Andrew Fletcher took part:

> At this place, I guess the greatest snowball battle of the age was fought. It started near where we were quartered, by two companies, and they were reinforced from time to time, spreading from company to company, to regiment from regiment, to brigade from brigade, to division by opposing forces consolidating as they passed from one point to others; officers soon joined in, both line and mounted field and somewhat brought about order. Couriers could be seen going to and from, same as in battle, with horses at speed, so the word was passed to the front as there was one encampment after another charged, the excitement was grand; regiment after regiment, brigade after brigade and division after division joined in, until it was said that the whole of Longstreet's corps had snow-battled.[23]

John Worsham, another of Jackson's men, remembered, "When the snow was on the ground I have seen several times more than twenty-five hundred men engaged in a game of snowballing!"[24] The snowballing, which started out informally at the first snowfall, had progressed to a full-scale drill by the time of the heavy snow the first week of April.

But on April 10 the snow was gone, and the day was fresh and beautiful. The routines of the Southerners mirrored the routines of their

Yankee adversaries: drill, picket, inspections, parades, drill, picket, inspections, and on and on. As was true in the Union lines, picket duty was the toughest and the most hazardous of the camp routines. Usually a brigade was posted to a sector, staying up to a week. Then the smallest army units, squads, would find their picket posts, as close to the enemy as possible, and settle in to pass their allotted time.

There were tacit agreements between opposing pickets directly across from each other on the banks of the Rappahannock to stack arms and not fire on each other, but the men never knew if everyone was in full accord. Picket duty was frequent—and always nerve-racking. Worsham wrote:

> While they were on this outpost picket duty, a soldier's nerves, too, were tried! Far to the front he stood on his lonely beat, only occasionally moving because he feared he might attract the attention of the enemy's sentinel on similar duty, who might shoot him from a distance, or creep up later and shoot him! . . . Knowledge of this created an uneasy feeling that could not be gotten rid of, and the man on outpost guard was uneasy until he was again in camp with his comrades.[25]

There were some bright moments on picket, according to Captain Elias Davis, who wrote home, "We go on picket tomorrow to our old Post 2½ miles from camp. I hope the weather will continue as warm as it is now, if it does I shall catch some fish. When on picket last time I caught a fish ten inches long."[26] An officer of the 37th Virginia, Captain James H. Wood, wrote of the comradeship between opposing pickets as they sat on opposite sides of the river:

> A tacit armistice was maintained by the soldiers themselves. This was done neither by pen or tongue, but simply by acts, developing into such a kindly feeling that frequently in the absence of officers interchange of visits were made by crossing the river on improvised rafts for the exchange of tobacco from the Confederates for coffee from the Federals. This occurred daily . . . In passing down the river along this line I discovered a small improvised craft of bark provided with paper sails gliding to the Federal side with its plainly seen lading. My duty was to investigate and have arrested the violators of this plain breach of discipline . . . I could not find it in my heart to do this . . . I simply failed to see or know of the little craft.[27]

John Worsham recalled his picketing days: "Occasionally some of the men went down to the river's edge, and had a talk with the Yanks on the other side."[28] When it became necessary, both sides were equally ready to kill each other on command, but lacking that requirement they were all perfectly content to share their boring lives. After the brigade came in from picket duty, Worsham explained:

> The brigade had its daily drills, camp guard duty, inspections, etc. The daily roll calls and cooking left very little idle time for the Confederate soldier. Notwithstanding this, one could always hear someone singing, laughing, whistling, or in some way indicating that the camp was not dead. We indulged in games of all kinds, ball, marbles, drafts, chess, cards, etc.[29]

If camp life seemed much the same on both sides of the Rappahannock, there was one difference on the Southerners' side. In Lee's army, religious fever had swept the camp and was having a marked effect on the men. This wasn't too surprising when a comparison is made between Lee's headquarters and Hooker's. Lee, Jackson, and artillery general Pendleton were all devout Christians; Pendleton was an ordained Episcopal minister, and Jackson was a faithful church member, as was Lee. With their encouragement, religion sprouted the way flowers sprouted in the April weather. Across the river, Hooker's personal headquarters was less religious in its behavior, which might have set the tone for his troops. Given the rumors about Hooker's personal life, it is probably safe to say that he was not as devout in his religious convictions as Lee or Jackson.

On April 9, John Paris, a chaplain in General Jackson's corps, wrote home pleading for more chaplains. Jackson wanted a chaplain for every regiment in his corps, but Paris was the only one in his brigade. Paris reported: "Upward of 200 have professed religion in the town and a fine work is progressing in Lanton's Brigade."[30] Samuel Firebaugh's diary entry for April 9 recounted, "Evening organized our Soldiers Christian Society. Meeting very interesting and I pray God that we through his Divine ade May be the Means of doing Much good. May God bless and guide us in this our attempt to put down Camp immoralization."[31] Private Franklin L. Riley went to church for different reasons:

> Many of our men have attended—some partly to avoid boredom, others, including myself, both to keep ourselves occupied *and* from interest. The Services are worthwhile but I am not ready to

become a church member as yet. I am afraid I will not be able to live up to my profession, but I agree with what the chaplains are doing. . . . Almost all of the officers of the 16th Miss. are professing Christians and attend Services regularly (when they are not on duty).[32]

Many of the Confederates were concerned about their mortality; as the time approached for the renewed campaigns, they wanted to take every opportunity to prepare themselves for the coming battles. Private Edgar Allan Jackson, Company F, 1st North Carolina Infantry, was in Lee's camp near Guinney Station on the Richmond, Fredericksburg, and Potomac rail line. His nostalgic letter to his mother on April 15 said:

As I sit in my tent this morning and listen to the fall of rain upon my cloth house pleasing recollections of by-gone times crowd thick and fast upon my imagination; the many happy hours spent in indolent pleasure in turn file by me, some of them, it is true, tinged with sorrow, but such would, compared to those I now pass through, be considered almost happy. I am reminded of the times when lying down and listening to the patter of the rain upon the shingles, the sweet restorer of tired nature, sleep, soon wrapped me into unconsciousness.

I guess you had begun to think I had forgotten you; such, however, is not, nor never will be, the case. "Brass may corrode, marble monuments moulder into dust," but my recollections of you will never moulder as long as there is breath in this poor earthly frame. I should prove recreant to your early attentions and would deserve to be shunned by all who knew me.[33]

It was Edgar's last letter. The next letter his father received was from Sergeant Lyman Foster, dated May 11, 1863:

Sir, I send you by this boy, Warren, Edgar's Bible and hymnbook which I took from his person after he was killed, supposing you would like to have them as a keepsake.

The dear boy died bravely at his post with his face toward the foe. I found nothing else upon his person. He was buried on Monday last, I think, near the "Wilderness" where he fell. I was wounded soon after he was killed, the evening of the same day. Our company suffered very severely during the day, having 9 killed and some 15 wounded.

Sympathizing deeply with you in your affliction, I remain, yours etc.[34]

Edgar was just seventeen and a half; he had enlisted in July 1861. From the time he enlisted until his death he never went home on a furlough. He was killed instantly when he was hit above the right eye by a bullet in the opening moments of the battle of Chancellorsville on May 1, 1863.

Always, the men in the army were concerned about their families at home. Sickness was present everywhere on the home front, and epidemics appeared frequently. Lieutenant Joel Blake was a Florida soldier in Lee's army near Fredericksburg; he wrote his wife, Laura, on April 10:

I have just been relieved from a good deal of anxiety & uneasiness by the arrival of your long and interesting letter of the 1st. I do humbly thank God that he has so mercifully preserved my dear family from that disease & death which seemed to be sweeping over the whole country. My uneasiness for the last three or four days has rendered me almost entirely unfit for duty. Lt. Peeler got a letter from Simadosia Peeler, who stated that cousin Tom had just been to see her & that he said the scarlet fever was raging on the Lake in an aggravated and malignant form. I was almost certain I would hear that it was in my family & not getting a letter quite as soon as I expected, my imagination has troubled me no little. . . .[35]

By this time, the soldier of the Army of Northern Virginia had lost much of his innocence about the war, about himself, and about the army. He was now a professional soldier; he had learned the soldier's most important lesson, never volunteer; he had retained his sense of humor and his initiative as he had learned to support himself by living off the land; and he had learned to supply himself from the enemy dead. Franklin Riley wrote in his journal on April 10:

Orders issued by the Union army threaten that any Confederate soldier who wears Union clothing or equipment may be charged and shot as a spy if he is taken within Union lines. Guess I better not be taken. I'm not a spy, but some of my equipment is Federal issue. In fact, this is true of most of us. Although inclined to be cantankerous, the Federal Quartermaster has furnished us with supplies for a long time. No, we can't allow him to be ungracious. It would hurt his character. . . . For his own good, we must continue to accept his hospitality.[36]

In all manners he was a far different soldier than the April 1861 volunteer; yet he was realistic about the future. James Robertson reflected his uncertainty in a letter to his wife on April 13, 1863: "Though sound in health and strength, I feel that life to many of us hangs upon a slender thread."[37]

Edmund D. Patterson, in a letter home on April 10, said: "It would not do for a soldier to look on the dark side, and the present would be hard to bear were it not for the faith in the future, though I must confess that mine is composed more largely of hope than of belief. Still it is a faith for that."[38]

★

Exactly two years later, April 10, 1865, General Robert E. Lee made his farewell address to his troops at Appomattox.

General Stonewall Jackson was wounded on May 3 at Chancellorsville and died on May 10.

General J.E.B. Stuart was killed at Yellow Tavern on May 11, 1864.

Corporal Leonidas Torrence was mortally wounded at Gettysburg on July 2, 1863.

Private Edgar Allan Jackson was killed at Chancellorsville on May 1, 1863.

Lieutenant Joel Blake was killed at Gettysburg on the first, second, or third of July 1863, but his body was never recovered.

4
★
LONGSTREET'S
INDEPENDENT COMMAND

While the two eastern armies warily faced each other across the Rappahannock River near Fredericksburg, another army was roaming the countryside of eastern Virginia and North Carolina under the command of one of Lee's corps commanders.

"Old Pete" was his nickname, but he was neither old nor named Peter. He was Lieutenant General James Longstreet, the forty-two-year-old I Corps commander in the Army of Northern Virginia. On April 10, he was leading an independent command in eastern Virginia and down into North Carolina. He had three missions: first, to gather food and forage; second, to protect Richmond; and third, to get back to Lee when needed.

Longstreet had been under General Lee's command since 1862, when Lee took over the defense of Richmond, and Longstreet sometimes chafed under the restrictions of a corps commander. But when Longstreet was detached from the Army of Northern Virginia, he was given free reign to gather forage, bottle up Union forces, and attack, if necessary, using his own judgment. Lee wrote Longstreet, giving him carte blanche to do as he saw fit: "I leave the whole matter to your good judgment."[1] This was something Longstreet had yearned for: an independent command.

Longstreet had the most difficult task of any military commander, North or South, on April 10. The two main eastern armies were quiet, but Old Pete's forces, split as they were, were all engaged in some action on the tenth.

In his autobiography, Longstreet's chief of staff, Colonel G. Moxley Sorrell, recalled: "Meantime, our army was in want of all supplies. The subsistence Department lacked fresh meat. In southern Virginia and eastern North Carolina there were said to be large quantities of small cattle which, fattened on the good Virginia pasture lands would greatly help the subsistence officers. There were also there large stores of bacon and corn."[2]

Longstreet took Hood's and Pickett's divisions on his expedition, and intended to join Ransom's brigade, detached earlier, leaving McLaws's and Anderson's divisions with Lee in Fredericksburg. Besides these two divisions, Longstreet also controlled the Department of Richmond, the Department of South Virginia, the Division of North Carolina, and the District of Cape Fear as well, adding up to about 43,500 troops. Old Pete's current assignment suited him just fine, and he wanted to make the most of his chance. His plan, as he reported to Lee, was to place troops around several of the coastal cities occupied by Northern forces and keep them busy while he scavenged the countryside for supplies. The plan was simple and sensible; however, events would impress Longstreet with the complexities of independent command. Trying to juggle troops in scattered locations and soothe the egos of all his commanders was a new experience for the somewhat unimaginative South Carolinian.[3]

One of the forces in North Carolina and Virginia then under Longstreet consisted of troops in the Department of North Carolina, commanded by Major General D. H. Hill. Down in Wilmington, Brigadier General William H. Whiting commanded the District of Cape Fear, also under Longstreet. When Hill ordered Ransom's brigade out from under the Cape Fear command, Whiting howled in protest. It didn't matter that the brigade had been given to Whiting less than a month before; it was his, and he protested to Longstreet that a Union land move on Charleston would require his troops, not Hill's, so he could not spare the men.

Another of Longstreet's department commanders, Major General Sam French of the Department of South Virginia, was just as upset when Longstreet took part of his command. French explained:

> The next thing I knew, April 9, he [Longstreet] put his command in motion and took from me a division and a number of batteries and was on his way to Suffolk without informing me in any way of his designs, or of his wishes. The next day I put a staff officer in charge of the department headquarters and with my other staff officers rode to Suffolk and took command of my own troops there that had been removed without sending the order through my office which courtesy required . . . I found Gen. Longstreet down near the front, where there was considerable artillery firing and skirmishing on the advanced line. Longstreet asked me to accept the com-

mand of all the artillery which I refused to do. I told him I did not intend to give up the command of my division to anyone, but was willing to give all the assistance I could.[4]

Longstreet had set his plan in motion in March 1863. He detached Pickett and Hood with their divisions down the James River to begin a siege of Suffolk, Virginia. He also sent General D. H. Hill with his 11,000 men to harass the Union camp in Washington, North Carolina. Longstreet had tried to get troops of Major General Arnold Elzey's Department of Richmond to use with his divisions, but Elzey committed himself only to provide some troops to demonstrate against Williamsburg, Virginia. These three moves—Suffolk; Williamsburg; and Washington, North Carolina—would contain the Yankees, leaving the fertile backwater areas of the Blackwater and the Tar rivers for the raiding commissaries of Longstreet. The moves were never meant to capture or attack, they were meant to contain and distract, and that they did.

SUFFOLK, VIRGINIA

The Union troops that held many coastal towns in the South were spread out in a number of isolated concentrations. The Union VII Army Corps was led by Major General John A. Dix, who had his headquarters at Fort Monroe, Virginia. His troops were in or near the Virginia towns of Hampton, Norfolk, Yorktown, and Suffolk, with 15,000 troops under Major General John J. Peck in Suffolk alone. With Longstreet's 20,000 men under Hood, Pickett, and French, the odds at Suffolk on April 10 were in favor of the Confederates. Union reinforcements were being sent from General Heintzeleman in Washington, D.C., so it was difficult to know exactly how many Union troops were in Suffolk on the tenth, but it was probably only slightly more than 15,000.[5]

At one point, Longstreet hoped to attack Suffolk, but Lee felt such a move could accomplish little.[6] For whatever reason, no serious attack was ever launched during the siege. It was a valuable Union outpost for Norfolk, a railhead and buffer to the port area that served the naval forces in the blockading fleets. Suffolk's strategic importance was emphasized in a *Philadelphia Enquirer* article summarizing the campaign in its April 24 issue:

It must be remembered that the military authorities charged with the occupation of Norfolk established an important post at a considerable distance to the southwest of that city—at Suffolk, where the Petersburg and Norfolk Railroad intersects the Seaboard and Roanoke Railroad, leading to Weldon, N.C. Suffolk is also at the head of navigation on the Nansemond River, which empties into the James River near its mouth.[7]

Some of the soldiers in Longstreet's ranks, even on the tenth, had guessed the real purpose of the movement: Private J. Thomas Petty, 17th Virginia Infantry, commented on April 10, "Suffolk, by common consent, is our destination: a fight seems inevitable though many believe we are only on a gigantic foraging expedition to cover which an attack on Suffolk will be threatened, a very nice little ruse de guerre which 'Old Pete' knows how to hoodwink Yankee Peck with."[8]

On April 10, Longstreet's Rebels were moving swiftly down from Petersburg using five pontoon bridges to cross the Blackwater River and head toward the Union fort at Suffolk. "On the 8th of this month we started from Petersburg to this point. We marched five days in succession, marched from 18 to 23 miles a day," wrote Confederate H. C. Kendrick to his family from a "camp near Suffolk."[9] This was home country to many of Pickett's men; Virginia regiments made up most of his division, while Hood's men were mostly from Texas. One of Pickett's men, John Henry Lewis, mused, "I was in Pickett's division at this time, and we had quite a number of men belonging to that section of country, all near our homes; and here was again tested the manhood of our boys. They had been away from home for a year, and were in a position to leave the army and go home. The temptation was great; yet there were no desertions. Every man did his duty."[10] This must have been a most unusual unit.

By the night of April 10, the Confederates had placed themselves in line, covering three sides of the Union Suffolk encampment. There still was the Union railroad link to Norfolk, and swamp, to the east, but Rebels to the north, south, and west. The Confederate movement had been swift.

One of the Federal signal towers was in the top of a trimmed-off pine tree, and it had been abandoned by the Union as the Rebels pressed in on Suffolk. A curious Confederate climbed to the top for a leisurely study of the enemy. A Federal artillerist gave him a little time to satisfy his curiosity, then threw a shell at the tower to scare its occupant. The Confederate was shaken but not panicked. However, a second shell put him into motion, and "his legs, to the amusement of men on both sides, soon brought him to safe cover."[11] But that night this same Rebel decided to get back at the Yanks. He dressed and equipped a full-size dummy in butternut clothes, named him "Julius Caesar," put him on the platform, and waited. Soon the artillery opened on this casual spotter, but in spite of many near misses, he never moved. The Confederates couldn't hold back their secret for long, and soon called for three cheers for Julius Caesar. The Yanks realized they had been fooled, but took it in good nature and added their cheers to the Confederate praise for the old hero.[12]

New regiments, both Northern and Southern, were being sent to Suffolk. Dr. James R. Boulware of the 6th South Carolina Infantry recorded his march on April 10:

We lay down last night feeling like we would be aroused before morning but were agreeably surprised to learn that no orders had come to march. A little before noon orders came to move at 1 o'clock precisely. We went to Franklin—passed Genl. Hood on the roadside—the boys heartily gave him cheer after cheer for we all took a great liking to him while we were in his Division. After stopping nearly an hour we went to South Quays—having gone eight miles when we camped that night we left our camp guarded by sick men and took every available man with us. We hardly left enough to guard around camp—it speaks well for the health of our Regt.[13]

David E. Johnston of the 7th Virginia Infantry recounted two unhappy incidents during the troop movements. The 7th left Kinston on April 9, took railcars to Goldsboro and Weldon, North Carolina, marched through the Blackwater region to near Suffolk, and met Hood's division. On the way, two Southerners were killed, a man named Adams, in a fight in Goldsboro, and Manley Reece of the 24th Virginia, who was swept to his death between Kinston and Goldsboro from the top of one of the railcars.[14]

Private W. H. Morgan of the 28th Virginia Infantry was on the move and had his own ideas about the expedition's real purpose:

About the 4th of April, 1863, the brigade left North Carolina by train for Franklin Station, Va., south of Petersburg, on Blackwater River and marched down near Suffolk and had several skirmishes with the Yankees, who occupied the town. No attempt was made to capture the place. I think the object of the expedition was to give the Confederates an opportunity of gathering supplies along the Blackwater River and beyond, and by threatening Suffolk, prevent the Yankees sending reenforcements to Hooker, whom Lee was confronting on the Rappahannock.[15]

The Confederates were moving swiftly and silently down the peninsula, and the siege of Suffolk was about to begin.

THE UNION CAMP

While the Confederate troops were shifting into position on April 10, most of the Union troops were continuing life as usual inside their picket lines. General Peck was taken by surprise when the Confederate siege began. Pickets from the 1st New York Mounted Rifle Regiment were on the west side of the Nansemond River that day when General Peck ordered bridges across the river blown up. A New York captain, David E. Cronin, observed, "The advance of General Longstreet upon Suffolk was so swift as to be almost a surprise to our commanding general, who, in his excitement, ordered the bridge across the Nansemond to be blown up before our pickets at Provident Church were notified and withdrawn."[16]

It was estimated by Peck that some 40,000 to 60,000 men faced his forces on April 10, although the actual number was closer to 20,000.[17] General Halleck, in Washington, D.C., had telegraphed Peck, in Suffolk, to send 3,000 men to Major General John G. Foster, then being confronted by Confederate General Hill in Washington, North Carolina. Peck loaded trains with the requested men on the tenth, but when he learned that Hood, Pickett, and French were all infesting his own territory in Suffolk, he recalled the troops. Everyone was expecting the Rebels to attack Suffolk and reclaim their territories, not realizing that the intent of the Confederates was to create a diversion to keep the Yankees inside their perimeters.

There had been plenty of opportunity for the Union troops to fortify their positions in Suffolk since General Peck had arrived in September 1862, and the fortifications were strong and impressive.

Even with all the Southern activity outside the Union lines, a reasonably normal form of life went on inside; supplies were at hand, brought in by railroad from Norfolk. The railroad was critical to supplying the Union forces in Suffolk, but it was prone to accidents as well as being highly vulnerable to Rebel raiders. On April 10, a train loaded with ammunition was on its way to Suffolk from Norfolk, when the engineer missed a signal and the train plunged from an open drawbridge into the shallow waters of the south fork of the Elizabeth River, killing the engineer and Captain Isaac B. Bowditch of Vermont, a commissary captain stationed in Suffolk. The accident also wrecked the engine and four freight cars.

This unfortunate event might partially have been caused by the fact that in July 1862 the Norfolk and Petersburg had been taken over by the Union's Military Railroad, which had reduced the gauge from five feet to four feet, eight and a half inches. Most equipment had been adjusted to that width, but there had been problems prior to April 10. The N & P repair shops were all in Confederate hands in Petersburg, so Yankee equipment repairs and replacements had to be made in Portsmouth, Virginia, at the Seaboard and Roanoke shops.[18]

Another train wreck happened not in Suffolk but near Lynchburg, in western Virginia. The train left Lynchburg the morning of April 10 on the Virginia and Tennessee Railroad with 400 exchanged Confederate prisoners aboard and ran off the track near a place called Touris Crossing, injuring eleven soldiers, five seriously.[19]

Even with the railroad problems, new Union regiments were being transferred in. Private Charles F. Johnson described the unexpected transfer of his 9th New York Infantry to Suffolk:

> On the Tenth of this month I was on guard at Camp Hamilton [near Fortress Monroe, Virginia] dreaming of no other move before the final one for home, and on the evening of the next day, we were in Suffolk, Virginia in front of the foe again. We started from Camp Hamilton about eight o'clock in the evening, and before daybreak the next morning we were in Norfolk. Here a bit of news reached us that was not overly pleasant. A train of cars had run through a drawbridge on the Suffolk railroad, and instead of going to the front in cars, we were expected to foot it.[20]

On its first full day in Suffolk, a tragedy befell that same regiment:

> And now a sad and melancholy duty awaits this pen of mine. I will write it boldly, however, or my hand might falter. Here is the note. "Sunday, April 12th. Lieutenant-Colonel Kimball was shot dead this morning, by General Corcoran. It was a useless murder. I have just seen the body and could not control my feelings at all."[21]

The colonel was near his tent, close to that of Brigadier General Michael Corcoran, the brigade commander. In the pitch-black night, Kimball challenged a group of approaching horsemen that included the general. They refused to identify themselves, so Kimball drew his sword and Corcoran shot him. A routine event, challenging an unknown presence, and not so routine, dying in the process. No formal charges were made against Corcoran.

There were some skirmishes during the siege, but there is no record of any on the tenth. There was picketing, guard duty, and even a payday for Massachusetts Private Charles Spencer, but he got only four months' pay instead of the six months' he expected.[22]

The camp itself was apparently comfortable for some. Captain David Cronin of New York reminisced:

> Our regimental camp at Suffolk was largely and handsomely planned. It was laid out in the form of a parallelogram and the spacious quarters for men and officers, constructed of pine logs, inclosed a level parade ground. Some of the officers' quarters were tastefully and even elegantly furnished the deserted houses in the neighborhood affording an abundant assortment of comforts and even luxuries which it was claimed if not used, would have been destroyed.[23]

IN THE CONFEDERATE CAMPS

The area was home country for Major General George Pickett, and he was in love. On April 15 he wrote a long letter to his future wife, Sallie, from his camp near Suffolk:

> Now, my Sallie, may angels guide my pen and help me to write—help me to voice this longing desire of my heart and to intercede for me with you for a speedy fulfillment of your promise to be my wife. As you know, it is imperative that I should remain at my post and absolutely impossible for me to come for you. So you will have to come to me. Will you, dear? Will you come? Can't your beautiful eyes see beyond the mist of my eagerness and anxiety that in the bewilderment of my worship—worshiping as I do, one so divinely right, and feeling that my love is returned—how hard it is for me to ask you to overlook old-time customs, remembering only that you are to be a soldier's wife? A week, a day, an hour, as your husband, would engulf in its great joy all my past woes and ameliorate all future fears.[24]

The familiar story of peaceful picketing was told again here in Suffolk. After the war, Confederate veteran M. J. Clark of North Carolina remembered:

> While our army was around Suffolk, Va., two companies, A and F, of the 11th Mississippi Infantry Regiment, were placed on picket (outpost) in trenches in sight of Suffolk and the Federal forces.

I was a member of Company F. Early in the day one of our boys called "Yank!" and, receiving a prompt answer, acquiesced in the request that there be no firing on the line during the day. One of the boys in Company A, Jerry Gage, who soon after fell in battle, proposed to exchange papers, holding one up in his hands. Mr. Yank said all right and started toward our line with one in his hand. Jerry Gage went to meet him, and another friend and another, and so on until our whole picket force had left the pits. There was a lake, or something of the kind, about halfway between us; and when we got there, and the other Yanks, who had left their pits, we found a Yank with a skiff, who invited us to go over to their camp, which was in sight. We accepted the invitation, and he put us all across.

By this time a big crowd of Yanks were around us, some proposing to make peace, some swapping buttons and the other things; and the proposition was made to some of the boys to go up town and have a game of poker. We were having a big time until a Yankee officer came rushing down, very much excited, and yelled out: "What does all this mean?" He said the like was never heard of; and if the crowd did not disperse immediately, the batteries would be opened on it. He refused to allow the skiff to cross the lake, and I thought we were going up sure; but another officer standing near us, remarked, "Boys, don't pay any attention to that d—— fool. They know better than to fire into their own men. We will see that none of you are harmed and are put back safe on your side of the lake."

So we all shook hands, with a good-by and good luck, and were put safely across. Not a gun was fired during the whole day. We went back into our pits, and after dark were called in, and marched the whole night, evacuating the area.[25]

April 10 was a cold and rainy day in Suffolk, but the forage activity kept most of the Confederates busy. The diary of Mrs. Virginia Clay, a Macon, Georgia, belle, quotes a letter she had just received from a suitor stationed near Franklin, Virginia, a few miles west of Suffolk:

In the meantime, large foraging parties and immense wagontrains have been sent out for provisions. So that this of forage may be the grand design after all, and instead of living that we may fight, are fighting that we may live, the latter being a very desperate situation, but the more laudable endeavor of the two, perilling our lives not only for the vitality of our principles as patriots, but for the very sustenance of our lives as men, seeking corn and bacon as well as the "bubble reputation at the cannon's mouth."[26]

One of Pickett's men, Walter Harrison, wrote, "Thus . . . Suffolk was threatened in front, and its garrison kept pretty well confined within their strong works, while the successful operation of gathering and hauling off corn and bacon from the surrounding country was carried on, without serious opposition, for six or seven weeks."[27]

During the siege the Confederates went about their normal routines, which included such things as election of officers—a Civil War system for providing leadership. It was not always a simple process, as John Dooley of 1st Virginia Infantry detailed:

April 10—today I am on extra tour of Guard duty for absence from roll call when at Jack Keiley's [a friend] the other night. But about 9 A.M. I am relieved by Company C electing me a Lieut. in their company.

And here I will take occasion to explain the Cause of my election. In the first place, Capt. H., Co. C. had signified to the Col. his desire of having me as one of his Lieuts. It being decided by some authority that the Col. or Brigadier could not appoint a 1st Lieut., an election was held. A large majority of the members of Co. C were conscripts, new men in the Regt.; the old members were only 5 or 6. The new members, greatly in the majority, desired to elect one of their own number; and the old members, together with the Capt. and Col. of the Regt. were somewhat predisposed in my favor.

It has been maliciously said that the new men or conscripts were bullied into electing me by threats from the minority. But that, I was told, was not the Case, and the only intimidation held out to them was by our Col. presiding over the election, who told the Company in case any raw recruit was elected that he would instantly have him examined before the board. The party opposed to my election, thinking that their candidate could not stand the test of an examination, abandoned him and voted for Lieut. Kehoe of Company J. This vote was pretty equally divided, and on a second ballot I was told I was elected.

If there was any unfairness in the election I do not know of it, and would rather have remained all my life in the ranks than to have permitted myself to be elected by means the least unfair. . . .

Two or three days before the election I was promised the whole "conscript" vote . . . if I would only promise if elected to serve their interests. I told the person who waited on me that I should give no promise whatever . . . I had not even asked any one to propose me for a candidate. He said the new members would all vote against me unless I made this promise, and I responded 'Allright' (or its equivalent), so that today when my election was announced, I was a little surprised and asked an explanation from the Capt of the change in the men's votes. His explanation was that given above.[28]

And that's how he became Lieutenant, later Captain, Dooley.

Elizabeth Curtis Wallace, a young girl who lived nearby, was caught between the two armies just south of Norfolk on the Dismal Swamp canal. Her home, called Glencoe, was located between the Union troops and the Confederates, and it hosted soldiers of both sides, willingly or unwillingly. Her journal talks of health, hardships, and soldiers:

> Friday April 10
> Another white frost. Three frosts and a rain is the general rule of nature so now we may expect milder weather and rain. . . . Rachel and Charles, being sick, Tamar on the eve of confinement and no servant to call upon, we sent for Mrs. S. who always comes to lend a hand when she is wanting. Oh it is such a comfort to have a woman about the house that knows what to do and will do it.
> Saturday 11.
> A lovely spring day. . . . Mr. Wallace started to Norfolk but was stopped by the Yankee pickets. No one has been allowed to go in or come out of town today. Of course we could get no paper, but the news is flying that our Rebels are about to attack Suffolk from three points, that Washington, N.C. is surrounded by Confederates and that Yankees there, three brigades had capitulated.[29]

Those were indeed rumors. There were frequent sallies made by both sides to and from Suffolk, and there was a great deal of heavy skirmishing during this period, but no extended engagement was fought.

Although no real attempt was made to capture any of the Union ports, or to reoccupy any territory, the Union trumpeted the Confederate lack of success as meaningful victories. The *Philadelphia Enquirer* reported:

> Nevertheless, General Longstreet went at his plan with energy, and from April 11, when he first drove in our pickets, until Tuesday last, he kept up an incessant series of attacks of the most harassing and vexatious character to General Peck's troops. He rushed his squadrons of cavalry against our lines in one place and established batteries of field artillery to sweep the Nansemond River at others.

He maneuvered to overwhelm us here and flank us there, and in every way endeavored to penetrate our lines, but was baffled in every attempt by the watchfulness, activity, endurance, skill, and courage of General Peck and his brave companions in arms.[30]

It was a splendid testimonial for a defense that was never called upon to resist a convincing attack, at the same time allowing the Confederates to restock their larders and reprovision Lee for his next campaign. A biography of Gen. Hood unkindly characterizes the Suffolk campaign as "A Series of Poorly Executed and Unco-ordinated Military Maneuvers Carried On by a Motley Collection of Misfits and Malcontents."[31] But while these two forces sparred and danced and waited for some action in Suffolk, a little Union force was facing a more active enemy in North Carolina.

WASHINGTON, NORTH CAROLINA

While Hood, Pickett, and French were foraging on the Virginia peninsulas and creating minor panic in Union Major General Dix's installations, Confederate Major General D. H. Hill was on another Longstreet mission. Hill was a difficult but capable commander—and Stonewall Jackson's brother-in-law as well. In March he had set out from his headquarters in Goldsboro, North Carolina, with about 11,000 men, headed for the Union fortifications in Washington. He arrived outside Washington on March 30, almost two weeks before the Suffolk siege began. Hill's mission was to create a diversion to Longstreet's main thrust at Suffolk and thus to prevent the Union troops from reinforcing each other. Hill's forces had marched so fast, and arrived so unexpectedly, that there had been no chance to reinforce the 1,200-man Union garrison there.

Union Major General John G. Foster was in command of the Department of North Carolina, with 14,000 men in the XVIII Corps. He usually had his headquarters in New Bern; however, he had been caught in Washington when Hill arrived outside the town, and since he was unable to leave, he was still there on April 10. His 1,200 men belonged to the 44th Massachusetts Infantry, the 27th Massachusetts Infantry, three companies of loyal 1st North Carolina Volunteers, one company of the 3d New York Artillery, and 100 blacks. The North Carolinians were called "Buffaloes" and were for the most part deserters from the Confederate army. They were at some risk; if they were caught the chances were they would be treated as traitors and hanged.

Fort Washington was the name of the little installation that had been built by Union troops in 1862 as part of the coastal occupation controlling the Albemarle and Pamlico waters. The fort itself sat in the rear of the town, but it was supported by four blockhouses ringing the town and it was armed with various types of artillery pieces. The fort was a "strong, quadrangular, bastioned fort, surrounded by a ten foot ditch and heavy abattis."[32] John J. Wyeth of the 44th Massachusetts wrote this about the earthworks:

> It [the earthwork] is at right angles to the breastworks, thrown up to a height of about 15 feet. It is fully 60 feet long, about fifteen thick at the base, and six or seven feet at the top. We utilize the hole made by building this hill, by covering it with a strong roof, then covered that with sand a foot or two deep; and as the Johnnies don't seem to use mortars, we feel tolerably safe, in having a roof over our heads, in case of a sudden flight of meteors.[33]

Although it was not the fanciest U.S. fort, it apparently kept the troops out of the line of fire. The other parts of the town's defenses were the Union gunboats that blockaded the Pamlico and Tar rivers, three of which were caught upriver with the army in Washington when Hill suddenly appeared.

April 10 was just one of the seventeen days of the siege, with bombardment by the Confederates almost constant. The Rebels had completely encircled Washington, leaving the Pamlico River as the only route in or out. The Confederates placed their forces on hilltops surrounding the town and, with their artillery and cavalry, had complete control.

Prior to April 10, two attempts had been made by the Union navy to run small boats past the Rebel guns; both had successfully carried messages to the Union fleet some eighteen miles downriver at the mouth of the Pamlico. The boats would come back by night, creeping past the quiet guns of Hill's North Carolina troops. Some supplies were being brought in this way, and they were badly needed by the tenth day of the siege.

Inside the fort, the townspeople and the Union troops were well protected from the effects of the Confederate shelling, but still the volume of shells hitting inside the town made for some confined living. The regimental history of the 44th Massachusetts recounted April 10 in Washington, North Carolina:

> On the morning of Friday, the 10th, my two comrades had come in from picket duty, and had turned in to make up their sleep;

about nine o'clock I was engaged in hanging out my blanket . . . a squad of men were at the well . . . some firing was going on as usual, but attracted no attention, until one shell seemed rather nearer than common, when I looked up just in time to see it burst, seemingly almost overhead; the group at the well stood not on the order of their going, but scattered with more haste than dignity, some of them making comical exhibitions in their endeavors to combine rapid locomotion with the completion of their interrupted toilet.[34]

Most of their friends had been in the shelters for some time, and they found the arrival of these new occupants to be most entertaining.

Confederate Private John L. Holt, 56th Virginia, wrote to his wife on the fourteenth: ". . . we have very heavy cannonading every day our men would shell the town to pieces I expect if it were not for women and children They [Federals] wont let them come out."[35] Holt's units were busily firing on the town on a daily basis and keeping pressure on the Union. Their intention was to avoid civilian casualties, but civilians took no chances and kept to their shelters.

Annie Blackwell Sparrow, whose father, Captain Thomas Sparrow, was commander of the old Confederate local militia company, was one of the cellar dwellers in Washington. She wrote:

At the beginning of the siege, Gen. Hill had asked the Commandant of the garrison that the women and children be allowed to leave the town, but this was refused . . . The firing began at dawn and ended at sunset, so we felt secure at night . . . As we could, the ladies of the two families cooked enough to last during the day, and as early as possible, we repaired to our underground retreat. Where, with rugs, chairs, books, and sewing, and dolls for the children, we managed to while away the days.[36]

She also wrote about her brother, who had been in bed when an artillery shell passed through his headboard while he was sleeping. He cried out, "Oh, Mommer, I'ze struck!" He was actually untouched, but later Annie Sparrow found out that her father was with a Confederate artillery unit that was firing on the town "at that very time." Signs of this shelling remain today. Two houses on the waterfront still have cannonballs embedded in their fronts, the balls themselves plainly visible.

After a day of shelling, on the night of April 10 an attempt was made to establish communications between the Union blockading fleet, downriver from Washington, and the forces in the town. Captain David

A. Taylor was ordered to take a small detachment from New Bern, find the gunboats below Washington, and go into town. On April 21, Taylor reported:

> On the morning of the 10th instant, in company with Lieut. J. B. Knox, acting signal officer, I started from New Bern and that evening met the gunboats 12 miles below Washington. I directed Lt. Knox to report to Captain McCann, commanding gunboat fleet in Pamlico River. . . .
>
> That night, in company with Lieutenant-Colonel McChesney, First North Carolina Infantry, and Lieutenant Josselyn of the Navy, and accompanied by my flagmen, Jacob A. Reed, Company I, 3rd New York Artillery, and Horace P. Baker, Company E, Third New York Artillery. I went to Washington in a row-boat and reported to Maj. Gen. J. G. Foster.[37]

One of the 27th Massachusetts volunteers explained: "These supplies were an imperative necessity, as there was not enough of ammunition to have withstood a desperate and persistent assault, while for three days our horses had only sufficient food to maintain life. The desperate attempt to sink these vessels had failed to harm them materially."[38]

The same Yankee also told of two incidents on April 10 that relieved the tedium of the siege:

> The top of the flagstaff of Fort Washington was shot away, when one of our men gallantly climbed the staff, and nailed the flag to the shivered top. As he was about to descend, a shot struck the staff below him, felling him to the ground. One of the most foolhardy acts of the siege occurred during this contest, when one of the garrison mounted the parapet with a rocking chair, and derisively rocked there during the hottest of the fire. It was a miracle that he escaped unhurt.[39]

The daring flagpole climber was Private David Myrick of Battery G, 3d New York Artillery, but it appears the rocker will forever be nameless.[40]

Tragedy was also part of the fort's day; the 44th Regiment's surgeon, Dr. Robert Ware, died at ten A.M. This twenty-nine-year-old Harvard graduate had worked for the Sanitary Commission, caring for the sick and wounded in the Peninsula campaign, before being appointed surgeon of the 44th Massachusetts. In his eulogy, it was said, "In the eloquent language of one of the officers of the Sanitary Commission, he was 'one who, through months of death and darkness, lived and worked in self abnegation; lived in and for the sufferings of others, and finally gave himself a sacrifice for them.' "[41]

As was very common, Dr. Ware had been taken ill suddenly; he had been the picture of health only one week prior to his death, but sickened and died in a matter of days. Zenas T. Haines, a Massachusetts corporal, wrote, "One week ago no event could have been more unexpected by us . . . Dr. Ware was the embodiment of physical health."[42]

Ware had written a letter home on April 2, saying: "The face of events has greatly changed since last I wrote and at present we are regularly besieged; cut off from the world outside and surrounded more or less by batteries, which boom away at intervals, to keep us constantly aware of their existence."[43] The doctor would be sorely missed. His old hospital, a residence called Elmwood, still stands.

In spite of Lincoln's Emancipation Proclamation, feelings about the role of blacks in the war were mixed. Many of the Northern soldiers had never had any contact with blacks, and their attitudes were a mixture of curiosity and superiority. But when blacks could help, attitudes changed. One of the men of the 3d New York Artillery made that point: "This was our first experience with armed negroes, and it was wonderful how quietly it was submitted to by many who had loudly declared, 'they never would fight side of a nigger!' Whitworth shots, exploding shells, and bullet tz-z-zps, were wonderfully persuasive arguments on such a question, and settled it once for all with the garrison of Washington."[44]

A 27th Massachusetts Yankee commented:

> The colored people were loyal and helpful, and had the most implicit confidence in our arms, apparently thinking we could withstand the world. Whatever we did, was all right and "like as we did it." When McKeever arrived with the schooners, one old woman rushed to the wharf, and seeing what had been done, straightened up, exclaiming, "Ise a proud woman dis da!" As to their opinion of us, as compared with their former masters, one said: "Seems dat uze hab different heads from dese year people."[45]

There were numbers of "contrabands"—slaves seeking escape— coming into the lines and bringing with them information, some good, some not so good. Corporal Haines remarked, "Contrabands who came in yesterday, report the rebels confident of having us in their power, and as saying that they can keep back any reinforcements which may be sent to us."[46]

Some of the old feelings were still evident. Union Lieutenant G. S. Williams wrote his parents, "We met their pickets and captured one of them and also a darky with orderly sergeant's stripes on (Think of that)."[47]

The basic duty of picketing took on the same characteristics it had at Fredericksburg, Suffolk, and other places. It was live and let live, and try to communicate about things important to the rank and file. In one particular case, the health of men recently taken prisoner was reported by John J. Wyeth, 44th Massachusetts: "Beyond the creek, about an eighth of a mile up the road, we could see the rebel picket quietly smoking a pipe; so we did the same . . . We were relieved at dark by three men of 'I' [company], who said they were here yesterday, and heard from the rebel picket that the prisoners were doing well."[48]

A volunteer from the 27th Massachusetts wrote, "The opposing pickets were near to each other, and being placed after dark, often trenched upon each other's lines, but when discovered, were peacefully withdrawn to their proper place." His explanation was: "The picket line was comparatively safe, for, the enemy being disposed to a truce, we had every reason to sustain it. They felt sure of us. As one put it, 'We are sure of you uns soon, and don't care to fight.' "[49]

Some of the pickets' experiences, if not dangerous, were at least unpleasant. On picket duty (again), Wyeth recalled:

April 10—We had a rough time last night, Patten and myself being the outpost victims. The water flooded the road knee-deep, wetting us through; but we knew no one could crawl upon our post without being heard, on account of the splashing they must make. We were bothered only twice during the night: once when the corporal of the guard (Mason) waded to us, found we were awake, and retreated in good order; and again as we sat on the old ammunition-box, soaked through, we were disturbed by something crawling over our feet. I struck at it with my gun but made no impression. We supposed it was a moccasin.[50]

Picket duty was no great pleasure, but conditions in the camp offered little improvement. The living conditions and rations in Washington were getting worse, but the trickle of food coming in the small boats was enough to keep the problem from being critical. In a letter home, Zenas T. Haines wrote, "We are living on three-quarters rations, but thus far have kept hunger at bay. Gen. Foster has taken possession of all provisions for sale in Washington, and says we can subsist on them thirty or forty days. We have despatched a few cattle, but the meat is poor stuff—lean and garlicy—barely fit to eat."[51]

The area around Washington still was a land of plenty, according to a letter from Lieutenant G. S. Williams, an officer who was on an expedition toward Washington: "The old man who owned the place was very well off and had a large supply of hams, smoked beef, tongue etc in a small house a little way from the one we occupy."[52] He goes on to say that his men liberated those tasty goods in spite of the old man's protests.

Private A. S. Webb of North Carolina reported that the Confederates weren't as lucky. Even as they foraged for food and supplies:

> An order was received from the War Department a week or so ago to reduce our rations to ¼ pound of bacon a day. But Gen'l Hill wouldn't allow—while we were on the other side of the River we only had ¼ of lb a day for several days. We can get along very well with half a pound a day. We haven't drawn but one or two days rations of flour since we left Magnolia. We drew some crackers on the Newbern campaign but haven't had any on this campaign. I never wanted some biscuits as bad in my life.[53]

Confederate R. A. Shotwell, who was one of the foragers, reported, "The fruits of our trip are now apparent here, as fully 20,000 barrels of bacon and large quantities of cornmeal and sweet potatoes await shipment. Potatoes sell here for $1 and in Richmond for $16."[54]

THE RESCUE EXPEDITION

With all the bombardment and pressure on Washington, North Carolina, Union headquarters in New Bern had tried desperately to send more troops north to help Foster hold off Hill's Confederates. Foster telegraphed Halleck in Washington, D.C., on the ninth; Halleck wired Major General Erasmus D. Keyes in Fortress Monroe, but all departments were hanging on to their troops, with pressure being felt from Longstreet at Williamsburg, Suffolk, and Washington, North Carolina.[55] General Keyes did agree to send Terry's brigade, about 3,000 men, to New Bern by steamer, but he was having trouble getting ships to make the transfer.[56] There simply weren't enough seaworthy transports available.

In New Bern, the chain of command was as follows: Major General John G. Foster, commanding, Department of North Carolina, primarily XVIII Corps; the First Division of that corps was commanded by

Brigadier General Innis N. Palmer; the Second and Third divisions were located in the Department of the South in Hilton Head, South Carolina; the Fourth Division was commanded by Colonel T. F. Lehmann; and the Fifth Division was commanded by Brigadier General Henry Prince. Under Prince in the Fifth Division was Brigadier General F. B. Spinola, who was commander of the First Brigade.

Since Foster was trapped in Washington, North Carolina, Palmer, as senior brigadier, was in charge at New Bern. He was ordered to send an expedition to relieve Foster. Over Spinola's strenuous objections, Palmer selected Spinola to lead the expedition. It was a hazardous undertaking, against a force that was considerably larger, and Spinola was a New York politician, not a combat commander. Both Palmer and Prince were West Pointers, had fought in the Mexican War, and had experienced battles in the past; Spinola was concerned about his own inexperience. Spinola's report later said he was requested to report to Prince's headquarters early on April 8, and did so. Prince was very concerned that the mission would be a great failure and that all involved would be captured:

> General Prince at this interview also invited me to volunteer to take the command of the expedition, which I declined in the most positive and unmistakable language. I was entirely willing to take my chances with others of either falling upon the field or being taken prisoner, but my own good sense promptly told me that the size of the expedition and the importance of its trust forbade one of my limited military experience from assuming its command, except under positive orders from my superior officers, and then, in obedience to a willing heart, could only promise to do the best I could to accomplish the object of the expedition.[57]

But Prince insisted, and Palmer, then in command, ordered Spinola to take the expedition and relieve Foster in Washington. Spinola expressed his "astonishment at it, and told General Palmer that I could not assume command unless I received a written order to that effect."[58]

With this inauspicious start, Spinola's task force set out for Washington with 7,407 men (actually, Spinola counted only 6,465)[59] and the requested written order from Palmer. The first test was at Blount's Creek, some twenty miles north of New Bern, where the Union troops encountered their first real opposition. There had been a few brushes with pickets, but on April 9, Hill's Confederate artillery opened on the task force, bringing the expedition to a halt. Spinola's sixteen guns were brought up on the south bank of Blount's Creek and traded shells with

Hill's artillery, on the north bank. Spinola's brigade faced a causeway, the only route open on the swampy route to Washington. The causeway led to the river, but the road was under heavy, and accurate, artillery fire.

Thomas Kirwan of the 17th Massachusetts described the scene as Spinola pondered his next move:

About this time, Adjutant Cheever of the Seventeenth came down the line, inquiring for Captain Splaine, and said "Captain, you are ordered to the right of the line. . . ."

"Cheever, what is it?"

Cheever glanced at the captain and lowered his head and said, "You charge the causeway."

Captain Splaine answered "We will charge it," and at once ordered his company to "Right dress! Front! Fix Bayonets!" and glanced along the line. His glances were answered by those of his unflinching men, ready to obey his next order with equal alacrity . . . and along they marched with heads erect, preserving the cadence of the march, reached the right of the line and reported to Colonel Fellows . . .

At this moment Colonel Amory [of the 3rd Massachusetts] rode up, looked at the company, and asked Colonel Fellows, "What is this company doing here?" On being answered that it was there to charge the causeway, he exclaimed, "What! Who ordered it?"

"General Spinola," was the answer, and then with a painful look on his face he actually scowled at Captain Splaine, and said,

"Don't dare to move, sir, until I return. . . ."

In a few minutes, Colonel Amory, accompanied by General Spinola, returned to where he had left the company in question, and then there was fun for the boys. Colonel Amory told the general that he protested against sending that company over the causeway, and added, "If you order it forward, I shall order it back and will take the responsibility!"

Colonel Amory was re-enforced by Colonel Fellows, and there was a lively time between them. The upshot of this colloquy was that this company of the Seventeenth was ordered back to its position in line. If it had charged over that causeway, not a man would have returned to tell the story.[60]

The difficulty was that the creek was not fordable; the only bridge had been disabled by the Rebels, and swamps and forest prevented any lateral movement. So Spinola headed back to New Bern, arriving on April 10.

The Confederates were used to driving off any numbers of Yankees; Spinola's brief attempt had only reinforced their contempt for Union forces. Private W. J. Baker, from a North Carolina regiment, wrote, "Since writing to you we have had near here—at Blount's Creek Mill, quite an interesting little battle—The Yankees came out to that point in large force and attempted to cross the creek but were driven back by our forces . . . They were severely punished and fell back very hastily—They will not fight on anything like fair terms."[61] Sergeant George Erwin of North Carolina wrote, "They, the Yanks, skedaddled that night for Newbern and all is now quiet."[62] George Wills, a Protestant minister fighting with the 43rd North Carolina Infantry, reported, "Had a little skirmish the other day with Gen. Pedigrew's Brig. and about 5,000 Yankees from Newberne. it only lasted a few minutes and then they run."[63] This episode gave even more hope to the Confederates that there might be a quick end to the war.

Wills wrote to his sister on April 12, after Spinola had been turned back, "There is still one thing that I love to think of, whether it is true or not I can't tell, it is this, last spring we had to fight hard, very hard and were defeated. This spring we hardly meet before they give way. That makes me think the war will end one of these days."[64] Wills could not know of the two years of war still left.

Lamotte Davendorf, a soldier with the 3d New York Artillery, was unimpressed with Spinola. He said, "Oh, I tell you Genl. Foster is the man for me if he had been with us instead of Spinola we would have went through."[65] Spinola was described by Tom Kirwan of Massachusetts as "a 'bully boy' who knew comparatively nothing about military matters. He certainly was not a great general."[66]

Union Lieutenant G. S. Williams gave his opinion about the selection of the rescue party:

> Although there were two other Generals at this place (Palmer and Prince) Gen. Spinola was ordered to take command. Now I do not mean to say anything against anyone but I positively think that the reason why neither of the ranking Generals took command was that they thought it was a most dangerous expedition and they were afraid of their military reputation being lost. . . . We got back on Friday and never in my life was I so done up.[67]

A brief, final word came from the absent Major General Foster, who sent a message on the tenth through his chief of staff to General

Palmer: "I am directed by the major general commanding to say that he could have wished that you had yourself come in command of the forces which moved yesterday from New Bern under General Spinola, notwithstanding the confidence you express in his activity and intelligence."[68]

There was a deep concern about the fate of Washington and the regiments boxed in there. This was expressed in a letter written by Private A. S. Bickmore of the 44th while he was on temporary duty in Beaufort, North Carolina. The letter was dated April 10, 1863:

Perhaps you may think I am somewhat blue this evening—possibly I am, for the conviction that my regiment will have to surrender comes home with no pleasant feelings. There is not certainly—and I would like to have you mark the fact, for our friends at home seemed to think that the '44th' would never march or fight much—a regiment of 9 months men in this Army Corps that has done as much marching and fighting as ours has, and members of other regiments will tell you the same thing.[69]

On this Friday, there would be no relief for the beleaguered forces of General Foster, either by boat or by land, and there would be some lingering doubts about the efforts to effect this relief.

THE NAVY'S ROLE

The U.S. Navy, too, played a part in Washington, although it was frustrated by the guns of the Confederates at Hill's Point and Rodman's Point, guns that commanded the river between Washington and the sea. Several ships of the Union North Atlantic Blockading Squadron were located at the mouth of the Pamlico River. A number of these Union gunboats could anchor upriver and shell Rebel emplacements to keep them from overwhelming the city. The navy was to work with the army, offering communications, troop transports, and gun support whenever possible.

Besides the ships already at Washington (the *Commodore Hull,* the *Ceres,* and the *Louisiana*), the *Hunchback,* located farther downriver toward the sea, was also a part of the gun support of the besieged Washington. With the Confederate encirclement of Washington and the placement of their artillery on the highest of the riverbanks, the only route for supplies was via the river, eighteen nautical miles from the nearest Union port.

One of the naval heroes of the Washington episode was Master's

Mate Edwin McKeever, who made one of the first runs past the Confederate blockade and repeated the deed several times. Stephen Blanding, a fellow crewman on board the *Louisiana,* recalled:

> At length, Master's Mate McKeever informed Commander Renshaw that if he would furnish him with four men he would run the blockade or sink in the attempt. It was a hazardous undertaking, but there was no other way to get dispatches to the fleet below or receive word from them. Our commander hesitated a moment, and then called for volunteers. Half the ship's company responded to the call. Renshaw informed them when in line, of the dangers and perhaps death in the undertaking, and asked them if they were willing to face it. "Yes, yes," exclaimed one and all.[70]

Later, Blanding proclaimed that McKeever's name was entered on the log as "the bravest of the brave." McKeever had several times before taken a little sailboat down the river and back up again; on April 10 he did it again, this time with two schooners loaded with ammunition and forage. Lieutenant Colonel McChesney of the 1st North Carolina Infantry was making a similar trip, this time with Captain Taylor, although he previously had come up with McKeever.[71]

Adequate supplies of ammunition were a concern for the navy. Although the schooners running the blockade had brought back ammunition on their return trips—as the skipper of the *Louisiana,* Commander R. T. Renshaw, had requested—the ammo they brought was sometimes not the kind that was needed. The navy felt that small ships, with bales of hay stacked on their decks to provide protection, could pass up and down the river with little problem, providing the necessary ammunition and supplies.[72] Renshaw wrote, "There are six 24-[pounder] howitzers on the boats now at this place, and it appears that there is no ammunition to be had for them." His frustration was showing as he continued, "This neglect I am at a loss to account for. If we had any other guns that shrapnel was furnished for, it would not be of so much importance, as we need them very much. Our position at this place at present is very critical and requires prompt action."[73]

The shortage of ammunition caused actions that puzzled Stephen Blanding:

> The rebs brought a thirty two pound Parrott rifle gun to bear on us [the *Louisiana*] from the roadside at the end of the bridge. The first shot they fired struck us, carrying away our mizzen gaff. It seemed an age before we got the order to fire, and in the meantime

the rebels peppered us well. At last Lt. Westervelt, who was reserving his order on account of the ammunition being short, gave us the order to fire. We brought three guns to bear on the rebels in the woods and the ball opened in earnest. We had fired five rounds when we received the order to cease firing. I looked at the lieutenant in amazement, what could he mean by such an order? Here the rebels were sending in their shot and shell as fast as they could load and fire, and the order came to cease firing on our side. It seemed Commander Renshaw was on shore when the fight began at the bridge conferring with General Foster, but as soon as he could make his hail heard on board, the lieutenant sent a boat ashore for him. He came on board, and, looking round upon the officers and crew, demanded of the lieutenant why he was firing away the ammunition. "Why, sir," said the lieutenant, "they will shoot us to pieces." "I don't care," replied Commander Renshaw, "if they shoot your heads off; send the men below; then I shall be sure there will be no more firing for the present on our part. Why, our ammunition is almost expended, and should the rebels make up their minds to charge in over that bridge, what resistance could we make? Boatswain, pipe the men below." And there we lay on the berth deck, while the rebs sent in their compliments, without the power to return them.[74]

The future of Washington, North Carolina, was very much in doubt on April 10.

GLOUCESTER POINT, VIRGINIA

The town of Gloucester Point is on a tip of land on the York River directly across from Yorktown, Virginia. It had been occupied by the North since 1862; however, just up the peninsula, Confederate forces held King and Queen Courthouse, and made frequent raids on Gloucester Point. Williamsburg, located on the south side of the York River, just above Yorktown, was also held by the Union. The troops in Williamsburg were not far from heavy Southern troop concentrations outside Petersburg.

Longstreet, already involved at Suffolk and Washington, initiated a third maneuver, a demonstration down the York River peninsulas on either side of the river using Elzey's Department of Richmond forces. The Confederates were trying to keep pressure on all the Virginia–North Carolina coastal Union forces and still keep the foraging, a program that was already in high gear, in motion.

Longstreet wanted to use part of General Elzey's command for his two other excursions, toward Suffolk and North Carolina, but Elzey demurred. He was recovering from a facial wound he had received at Gaines's Mill in the peninsula campaign, and was afflicted with what might today be called post-traumatic stress disorder, or combat fatigue. He was jumpy, despondent, and inclined toward the use of alcohol, and he declined to serve under Longstreet.[75] He did, however, agree to make a diversionary movement toward Williamsburg and Gloucester Point in the hope of drawing the attention of General Dix's Union troops at Yorktown, troops that might otherwise sail to the rescue of Suffolk and Washington, North Carolina.

Elzey gave the diversionary assignment to Brigadier General H. A. Wise, whose brigade numbered almost 2,000 men with two batteries of artillery. In a frequent Civil War circumstance—a man on one side being related to someone on the other—Confederate General Wise was the brother-in-law of Union General George Meade. Wise set out on April 8, sending a portion of his forces with Colonel Tabb's 59th Virginia to move in around Fort Magruder, about one and a half miles from Williamsburg. He was in place on the night of April 10, ready to attack.

One of the attackers, Benjamin Robert Fleet, wrote home on the twelfth:

> Notwithstanding our expecting to be engaged the next morning, I laid down on my blanket and with another over me, slept very soundly. We were up and ready to start by 3 o'clock, and after our chaplain had made a few remarks and prayed with the regiment, we started off. The night was cool and clear, and although everyone spoke in a whisper, all seemed cheerful and ready to do their duty.[76]

Meanwhile, across the river from Williamsburg, another Confederate force was moving from King and Queen Courthouse, Virginia, down the north side of the York River to Gloucester Point in yet another diversion. The Confederates, under Colonel D. J. Godwin, moved into position in front of the Union camp at Gloucester Point. His report told of the action:

> By daybreak on Friday morning [April 10] I appeared in front of his works, and remained there during the day, making demonstrations at several different points. I appeared alternately as infantry and cavalry, and so maneuvered my troops as to represent a heavy force. I drove in his pickets early on Friday morning, killing one,

wounding another, and captured two unhurt. I had 2 men wounded, 1 badly the other only slightly. I kept up these demonstrations Saturday, Sunday, Monday and Tuesday until 12 PM at which time I returned to my camp, leaving behind, however, two full companies to watch the enemy's movements. The enemy's force at the point consisted of two infantry regiments, one battalion of cavalry and two field batteries. I am satisfied that my demonstrations had the effect of diverting his force to the Peninsula. I found it utterly impossible to attack him behind his works with success, and therefore decided not to do so. His fortifications at the point are strong and thorough.[77]

Colonel Godwin added a postscript: "Capt. Robert Tomlin, a volunteer aide, who behaved with distinguished gallantry, I regret to say was severely wounded in the leg."[78] In spite of this report, Captain Tomlin is an unknown. There is no record indicating his service.

Colonel Godwin had a rather vague assignment. He was in command of the enlistment and conscription activities of the 2d Congressional District of Virginia, and reported only to Secretary Seddon. He had been a colonel in the 9th Virginia; for unspecified reasons he had resigned his commission, but was trying to regain his command.[79] On April 10 he was leading two companies of his conscripts against Gloucester Point, but was running for the Confederate Congress as well. The *Richmond Enquirer* printed this ad:

. . . Col. D. J. Goodwin [Godwin] as a candidate for Congress from the Norfolk (2nd.) Cong. district. He is the soldiers' and refugees choice and will serve if elected. We intend to give him our unqualified support believing him to be in every way qualified and competent.

[signed] Refugees[80]

The Union troops in the Gloucester Point camps were elements of the 169th Pennsylvania Infantry and the 2d Massachusetts Cavalry, plus one company of the 6th New York Cavalry, as well as the 4th Delaware Infantry. Colonel A. H. Grimshaw of the 4th Delaware was in command; he was incensed by the dashes made on his pickets and threatened to burn every residence of the Southern village in retaliation.[81]

The clash was duly reported in the official records. However, Lyman S. Foster, a member of the 169th Pennsylvania, made no reference to any action at Gloucester Point, although he did mention some activity in Williamsburg in his letter home on April 12:

We do have a little fun here once in awhile the rebs come down just enough to keep us waked up we burnt Williamsburg yesterday the rebels make a dash in there every few days the inhabitants are most all rebs they help them all they can they did fire from their house at our men they took us by surprise yesterday morning and drove us back from the town when we got ready we drove them back and burnt the town they done their best to take us prisoners but could not do it the general says the first picket they shoot he will burn all the houses in sight of the lines.[82]

Colonel Tevis of the 4th Delaware filed a report on the twelfth stating that on that day he found on a reconnaissance from Gloucester Point that Colonel Godwin and Major W. R. Vaughn with 200 cavalry had been down since Friday (April 10) but were returning to King and Queen Courthouse at six P.M. on the twelfth.[83] In both Gloucester Point and Williamsburg, casualties were inflicted both on the Confederates and on the Yankees, with little result.

The *Yorktown Cavalier* reported an eerie occurrence outside Williamsburg on the tenth:

On Friday last Mr. Allen Sissons of Gowanda, Cateraugus Co., NY disintered the body of his brother C. S. Sisson of the 72nd Regt NYSV Sickles Brigade and R R Doty, of the same regiment, from the graves on the battleground at Williamsburg, enclosed them in metalic coffins, and the next day proceeded to convey them to their former places of residence in Western New York. The bodies were far lighter than when buried, and the uniforms and blankets which were on them were not so much rotted but that they held together to raise them out of their graves.[84]

It should be noted that the battle of Williamsburg was fought on May 5, 1862, and that the 72d New York was a participant in that battle. The bodies had been in the ground almost a full year.

The prevailing Union feeling in the eastern seaboard area around Norfolk, Gloucester, Washington, and New Bern was one of confusion. Telegrams flying back and forth among these areas showed the pressure of Longstreet's three-pronged expedition and the frustration of the Union leaders in their troop placement.[85] Whatever else Longstreet accomplished, he acquitted himself well in his primary assignment, the resupplying of the Army of Northern Virginia. His foragers sent wagon train after wagon train back to the hungry and poorly mounted men of the army, waiting on the banks of the Rappahannock. His second mission, defending Richmond, was accomplished by his investitures of coastal Union forces. But, unfortunately, the third part of Longstreet's task was not fulfilled. When Lee called him back to the Rappahannock in late April, as the Army of the Potomac was making its move, Longstreet had committed himself to siege warfare and had lost his mobility. So Old Pete could not quite get into motion in time to make the battle of Chancellorsville. Lee and Jackson would have to make do with what they had, while Lieutenant General Longstreet sat this one out.

★

Union General Corcoran, who killed Colonel Kimball, was killed when his horse fell on him in December 1863.

The siege of Suffolk was lifted on May 4, 1863.

The siege at Washington, North Carolina, ended on April 15, 1863, when the 5th Rhode Island under Colonel Sisson passed the CSA batteries in the schooner Tempest.

General Pickett lost all three of his brigade commanders at Gettysburg: Generals Lewis Armistead and Richard Garnett of Pickett's division were killed, and General Kemper was severely wounded.

General Pickett did marry his Sallie, but not until September 18, 1863, after Gettysburg. He died in 1875; she lived until 1931.

Colonel Amory and his wife, Laura, had a daughter born in New Bern. Amory, his wife, and her mother died in Beaufort, South Carolina, on October 7, 1864, of disease.

George Wills was killed at Winchester, Virginia, on September 19, 1864.

5

★

WHERE IT ALL BEGAN

While Virginia had been fought over for two years, and North Carolina was under fire on April 10, 1863, South Carolina had remained relatively free of damage from the war that had started there in April 1861.

Immediately after the Fort Sumter attack almost two years before, Charleston had been euphoric as it saw the Federal forces defeated in Charleston Harbor, and the state of South Carolina became the pioneer in secession. The whole scene was one of unbridled joy, with bright uniforms, bands playing, and cannons roaring. The Yankee demons would bother them no more; the big game of war would soon be over, and life would settle back to its customary balls, parties, commerce, and trade.

Two years had passed, and the war was real; the costs were higher than expected, and it was hard to get back the war fever of the spring of 1861. But there was joy in Charleston on this April tenth; just three days earlier the invincible Yankee ironclads had tried to attack Charleston and had failed badly. There was a renewed hope that the South would win the war and life as before would resume. There was a feeling of déjà vu—as Pierre Beauregard was once again in command in Charleston, now a full general, blooded at First Manassas and Shiloh.

Charleston Harbor had a number of forts to protect it against an attack: Fort Sumter, which was still badly in need of repairs from the April 1861 bombardment; Castle Pinckney, with its smaller guns; Fort Moultrie, inside the harbor; Fort Johnson, on James Island; and Fort Wagner, at the mouth of the harbor.[1]

On Tuesday, April 7, the U.S. Navy had appeared in force to test its ironclads against the forts of Charleston; Union troops were positioned on the outer islands, ready to occupy the city if the navy could silence the forts.

Fourteen ships attacked the forts, and in less than two hours they were forced to break off the attack. Union casualties were fewer than Confederate casualties—only two killed and twenty wounded—however, the ironclad steamer *Keokuk* was sunk and several other ships were badly damaged. Most of the Union's wooden ships left Charleston shortly after the battle for a more friendly reception farther south at Union-held Port Royal, South Carolina. The damaged ships would be repaired and refitted there before moving on to other assignments.

The Union forces considered themselves lucky as far as the *New Ironsides* was concerned. A Confederate report later confirmed that it had been a close call:

The U.S. frigate *New Ironsides* narrowly escaped destruction during the bombardment in Charleston harbor, April 7th, 1863, when she laid for an hour directly over a boiler-iron torpedo containing 2,000 pounds of powder off Fort Wagner. It was designed to be exploded from an electric battery on shore, but every attempt to fire it failed, and the operator was suspected of treachery, until it was ascertained that one of the wires had been cut by an ordnance wagon passing over it.[2]

The cumbersome Union ironclad vessels were no match for these solid fortifications. According to one report, over 2,000 shells were fired by the Confederate forts, but only 139 shots were fired by the ironclads.[3] While these numbers were indicative of a one-sided fight, the Confederate commander was not pleased at his side's waste of ammunition. On April 10, Beauregard chastised Brigadier General Roswell S. Ripley, commander of the First Military District and in charge of harbor defenses, saying, "It is hoped that officers will not again throw away so much precious ammunition."[4]

According to Union reports, though, those shots had not been as wasted as Beauregard might have thought. The reports counted as many as 441 hits of the 2,000 shots fired at the Union navy, a remarkably accurate performance given the fact that these were moving targets, partially submerged, and some distance from many of the guns. The U.S. Navy did not level criticism about wasted ammunition; it would have preferred more gunfire from its fleet.

From the beginning, Lincoln had been pessimistic about the success of a Union fleet attack on Charleston. He had listened with interest as Secretary Welles and Assistant Secretary of the Navy Gustavus Fox lauded the invincibility of the ironclad battleships, but as the hour of attack drew closer, Rear Admiral Samuel F. Du Pont, commander of the South Atlantic Blockading Squadron, who would make the attack, grew more and more cautious. Welles himself, as evidenced by his diary, had become lukewarm to the idea of taking on the forts of Charleston Harbor. The unsuccessful April 7 assault was proof that the gunboats were too slow, awkward, and blind to deal with effective artillery from shore installations.

There was to have been a resumption of the attack on Wednesday, April 8, but a conference with the commanders of the ships convinced Du Pont that damage to the vessels had been too severe, and there would be no further attack. Welles's diary entry for April 9 spoke of his uneasy feeling about the attack:

A yearning, craving desire for tidings from Charleston, but the day has passed without a word.

A desperate stand will be made at Charleston, and their defenses are formidable. Delay has given them time and warning, and they have improved them. These great and long-delayed preparations weigh heavily upon me. As a general thing, such immense expeditions are failures. . . . For months my confidence has not increased, and now that the conflict is upon us, my disquietude is greater still. I have hope and trust in Du Pont, in the glorious band of officers that are with him, and in the iron bulwarks we have furnished, as well as in a righteous cause.

The President, who has often a sort of intuitive sagacity, has spoken discouragingly of operations at Charleston during the whole season. Du Pont's dispatches and movements have not inspired him with faith; they remind him, he says, of McClellan. . . . We must wait patiently but not without hope.[5]

Welles sounded even gloomier in his entry on the tenth, not just about Charleston, but about everything:

The President has not yet returned [from the Army of the Potomac]. The cabinet did not convene today. Affairs look uncomfortable in North Carolina. The army there needs reinforcing, and had we Charleston we would send more vessels into these waters.

Neither the War Department nor army men entertain an idea that the Rebels have withdrawn any of their forces from the Rappahannock to go into North Carolina, but I have apprehensions that such may be the case. From what quarter but that can they have collected the large force that is now pressing Foster?

Then came a hopeful entry, still on the tenth:

We have more definite yet not wholly reliable rumors from Charleston. A contest took place on the afternoon of the 7th, Tuesday, of three hours, from two till five. Two of our vessels are reported injured—the *Keokuk,* said to be sunk on Morris Island, and the *Ironsides,* disabled. Neither is a turret vessel. On the whole, this account, if not what we wish, is not very discouraging. The movement I judge to be merely a reconnaissance, to feel and pioneer the way for the grand assault.[6]

That hope was soon shattered when Du Pont reported that this had been the grand assault and his decision was to not renew the attack.

Union Major General David Hunter, commander of the Department of the South, was ready to supply the army troops to occupy Charleston after the navy had prepared the way. After the April 7 defeat, Du Pont sent a dispatch to Hunter, who was aboard the U.S. transport *Ben De Ford*: "I attempted to take the bull by the horns, but he was too much for us. These monitors are miserable failures where forts are concerned; the longest was one hour and the others forty five minutes under fire, and five of the eight were wholly or partially disabled."[7] On April 8, Du Pont admitted in a dispatch to Hunter, "I am now satisfied that that place cannot be taken by a purely naval attack."[8]

Often relations were not the best between army and navy, but in this case, Du Pont and Hunter had great respect for each other. On the eighth, after Du Pont's attack, Hunter, who had been on a ship in sight of the battle, signaled Du Pont:

Not knowing yet what have been the results of your attack of yesterday, so far as Fort Sumter is concerned, I cannot but congratulate you on the magnificent manner in which the vessels under your command were fought. A mere spectator, I could do nothing but pray for you, which, believe me, I did most heartily. The cumbersome Union ironclad vessels were no match for these solid fortifications.[9]

This must have been welcome praise for Du Pont, who was expecting the wrath of Washington to fall on him, and he responded the same day:

General: I am this moment in receipt of your most gratifying letter of this date. I did not, however, require this to satisfy me of your deep sympathy in our operations of yesterday, intensified by the fact that circumstances beyond your control prevented that which of all things you would most have desired—an immediate and active co-operation.[10]

By April 10, Hunter had kept only some 4,000 of his troops on Seabrook and Folly islands and sent the rest of his force back to Hilton Head.[11] For some of these troops, in crowded quarters on navy transports, these were bad days. M. H. Fitzgerald of the 81st New York Infantry, which had boarded the *Morton* on the sixth and was just leaving for Port Royal on the tenth, recorded in his diary: "Very pleasant but the wind blows poorty brisk and all quiet on board as yet about one oclock in the afternoon orders came aboard for to leave Edisto inlet so they weid anchor and set sail for Port Royal agane said all the afternoon and it was poorty rough I was sick as a horse." They arrived in Port Royal the next morning.[12]

Another private on board was B. S. De Forest, who recalled:

On the 10th of April, at noon, our division was ordered back to Port Royal. We weighed anchor and the whole fleet set out to sea. In crossing the bar, our vessel struck four times, and so hard as to throw her boilers out of place, which produced leakage. The pumps were set at work, and a flag of distress hoisted, which brought the *Key West* to our relief. She took us in tow, bringing us in safety to Hilton Head on the following morning.[13]

De Forest was impressed by Hilton Head, but after only two days his unit was sent up to New Bern to aid in the relief of General Foster.

The attack was now ended; it was the task of the Union leadership to break the bad news to the public in the best possible terms. The president's secretary, John Hay, who had been sent down to Charleston to assess the situation, telegraphed the president on April 10:

I had some conversation with Cap't Rodgers, Fleet Captain of the S.A.B. Squadron. He said that although the attack had been unsuccessful & the failure would of course produce a most unhappy effect upon the country, which had so far trusted implicitly in the invincibility of the monitors, all the officers of the Navy, without exception, united in the belief that what they had attempted was impossible, and that we had reason for congratulation that what is merely a failure had not been converted into a terrible disaster.[14]

And that was how it was presented: a simple failure from start to finish, but not to be compounded by repeated futile attempts.

General Hunter thought he could still accomplish the conquest of Charleston. On April 10 he sent Brigadier General Truman Seymour, his chief of staff, to Washington, D.C. His message introduced the general, stating that General Seymour had been in Fort Sumter when it was captured in 1861, and knew its capabilities. Hunter closed by saying, "I am still confident that the problem of reducing Charleston only needs for its execution that the necessary means be placed at my command, to this end, I cordially commend Gen. Seymour's representations to your consideration."[15]

The Confederates had fully expected the attack to be renewed on the eighth; the next week the *Southern Illustrated News* of Richmond sneered, "Yankee dates of the 13th say the fight at Charleston was only a reconnaissance in force. Pooh! So was their disaster at Fredericksburg."[16] Another article in the same paper reasoned, "The lying Yankees announced the capture of Charleston in order to influence the Connecticut elections and to delay any tendency on the part of European power to make a further move towards the recognition of the Confederate States."[17]

John B. Jones, a clerk in the Rebel war department, felt the report was issued for economic reasons: "We are not informed of a renewal of the attack on Charleston. . . . In New York they have been exulting over the capture of Charleston, and gold declined heavily. This report was circulated by some government officials, at Washington, for purposes of speculation."[18]

There were still many who wanted not to avoid the fighting but to be a part of it. Annie J. Jones wrote to her son Cadwallader about the excitement in Charleston:

You have seen by the papers on Wednesday that the long expected attack has been made at Charleston. We heard that the iron clads were there and your father went off next morning. M—— went with him, having received orders by the same papers to rendezvous at the Citadel in Charleston.

You knew he volunteered for the attack in Capt. Thomas's company of exempts. They were to stop a few hours in Columbia and reached the scene of action probably yesterday. He was very much delighted and went off with high spirits. You know he has so long and so eagerly desired to go.[19]

Pliny Brown, a civilian employee of the Confederate government, wrote from Charleston to his old boss, Colonel E. P. Alexander, in Richmond. He mentioned the principal issue of the day:

> The firing was principally at Ft. Sumter—the damage to the fort has been repaired, it was quite significant, of course. That must not be known—during the fight there was great excitement with all—it was an experiment—Mail Clad vessels against a powerful fort—from one of the forts a broadside was poured into the Iron Sides—she immediately left . . . it can't be possible that our guns could destroy such a vessel as the Keokuk nine hundred yards off (That is the distance reported) if so Iron Clads are humbugs. . . . The Yanks are landing some troops on the islands about the mouth of North Edisto River—but little attention is paid to them as yet—in we cant get at them—There are various rumors as to the number of the Enemy hereabout (From 35,000 to 60,000 men) . . . The City is full of officers, come on from different posts to see the coming fight—Gen. G. W. Smith, Gen. Wade Hampton and a host of others are here eager for the fray—Gen. Beauregard appears uneasy at times—he is looking very well. . . . I see by the papers you have had in your part of the country a bread riot—I hope the soldiers get enough to eat.[20]

The Confederate military minds were busy in Charleston after the brief engagement of April 7. Dispatches flew around, moving troops, keeping or transferring guns, preparing for a possible land attack from the forces outside the harbor, and, incidentally, intercepting all the signals being sent from the Union's *New Ironsides*.[21]

It seemed that life in Charleston had been relatively untouched by wartime conditions, but the sadness of the South shows profoundly in an undated entry in the diary of Mary Chesnut:

> Rose Freeland . . . was a beautiful girl . . . Rose was engaged to Captain Harrison. He was only to be in town three hours. She had been engaged to him ever so long, and now nothing would do him but he must be married and march away. So they hurried off to dress for this sudden and private wedding.

As they went off: "Oh, Mrs. Chesnut, his company has orders to march at three—he only has two hours more here."

"Tell that to the marines! After the ceremony is over, I'll make you a bet—Captain Harrison will invite his superior officer to the wedding. You will see him there. And they will cause his hard heart to relent. See if they don't. And he will grant Captain Harrison two or three weeks furlough."

They laughed me to scorn. Two weeks after or more, the beautiful bride, lovelier than ever, called with her splendid-looking husband—for there never was a handsomer pair. He was still to leave the next day!

This was in February, 1863. Today I write—October of the same year—Captain Harrison came home to die of his wounds. Poor Rose and her newborn baby died, too, with him, one might say—for it was so soon after.

All three lie buried in Hollywood Cemetery.

When Mr. Preston urged me to begin this journal and keep it regularly—during the year '63 I burned so much, lost so much—that there are few scraps left me—and I find it hard to arrange them.[22]

The Chesnut diary is one of the foremost documents of daily life in the South in those years, but her dates are not always accurate. Afraid they would fall into Union hands, Mrs. Chesnut destroyed many of her notes in 1863.

Emma Holmes wrote in her diary on the tenth that, while Charleston had changed little, sickness and death were never far away. "The girls shocked me beyond measure by announcing Alex Rose's death of pneumonia, after three days illness—so young and in the full flush of early manhood."[23]

Pliny Brown added a happier note in his letter: "We are faring very fine down here boarding at hotels and some doing perhaps better than before the war." Then he talked fashion:

Col. should you ever visit these parts go first to your tailor and order some very fine clothes—you cant imagine how fine the officers dress here—I was so shabby when I first came on that I was almost ashamed to walk in the streets except in the dark. Now you ought to see me (umph)

The ladies are not allowed to visit the city. Those that are here seem very reluctant to go. They have been requested to go—The weather has been very pleasant ever since I have been here—much cooler than I supposed.[24]

Emma Holmes's diary kept no social secrets: "Ann Frost broke off hers [engagement] to Duff Calhoun . . . What a sad feeling it gives to think that such a great man as John C. Calhoun should have for his eldest grandson a youth without brains or common sense."[25]

The economic scene, not the social one, was of interest to Josiah Gorgas, Southern chief of ordnance, who penned an optimistic diary entry on April 7. He felt the British loan to the Confederacy was ". . . undoubtedly the forerunner of recognition. It was subscribed at 90, and rose immediately to 5% premium . . . [repayment] depends entirely on our ability to bring the war to a successful close; and the avidity with which the loan is taken up shows that this is a foregone conclusion among capitalists—the most cautious, and sensitive portion of the thinking public."[26]

FOLLY ISLAND

A number of Union troops had recently arrived on the north end of Folly Island, located outside Charleston Harbor. Among these men were elements of the 100th New York Infantry and a battalion of New York artillery called the 1st Marine Artillery, about 300 in both units. They were under General Hunter's command and were to be a part of the occupation of Charleston when (and if) the ironclads could succeed in their mission. Since the fleet had been defeated, the New Yorkers were waiting for their next orders.

On the night of April 10, an attack was made by men of the 21st South Carolina Regiment (Confederate), under command of Lieutenant Colonel Alonzo T. Dargan. The regiment was camped on Morris Island, just across Lighthouse Inlet from Folly Island. According to the *Charleston Daily Courier,* there were about forty men in the raiding party, which came across Lighthouse Inlet and landed on Folly Island at about ten o'clock at night. They ran into Yankee pickets, wounding one and taking another one prisoner.[27] The wounded picket was Charles Sabine, a corporal in Company H, from Naples, New York. In a letter home on February 15, Sabine had cautioned his brother:

I want you to bee kind to Mother and when she wants you to do anything [for] her do it willingly and only think it a pleasure to wait on her—Mother is old my brother [she was fifty-six] and cannot live but a few years at the longest iff you are kind to her as she is to you

then you will have nothing to regret on that account in the future—
Bee a good boy and go to school and learn all you can you may bee a
good schollar just as well as not—Do not do as I have done shun all
evil sosciety drain not the drugs of the wine cup you may bee an
honor to socity as well as to bee a lofer walk not in the footsteps that
I have tread in iff you will do as i tell you to do you will thank me
for it . . . I look back with shame and regret on my past life but
what few years remaing there is left for to live I will try to make up
in the future for the past . . .[28]

John McDonald was the captured picket; he was taken to Charleston and jailed. He told his jailers that Folly Island had a force of some
4,000 to 5,000 infantry in addition to an artillery force of about 1,250
men,[29] which was a considerable exaggeration.

The commander of the Union 100th New York Infantry that night
on Folly Island was Colonel George B. Dandy; in his rather lengthy
report on the affair, he basically substantiated the article in the Charleston newspaper, with some additional comments about the marine artillery. The artillery force on the north point of the island at that time was
about sixty men:

Our lookouts and pickets were all instructed, in accordance
with Gen. Seymour's orders, to keep concealed, to watch carefully,
and each picket was instructed to communicate to me by one of their
number information of any movement of the enemy. Captain Mac-
Farland and myself had taken a position easily reached by any of the
pickets, with which and the route leading thereto they were all well
acquainted.

At about 11 p. m. an attack was made by a detachment of the
enemy, variously estimated by the pickets as 200 to 500 men. The
night was exceedingly dark. After having examined closely every
person who saw them, my own impression is that there were not less
than two companies, perhaps 120 men, composing the attacking
party [there were actually forty] . . . Having passed to the rear by
the edge of the woods skirting the long sand bar separating us from
the regiment they met and attacked our extreme left picket (numbering 3 men and a corporal), dispersing them and mortally wounding
the corporal, Charles Sabine, Co. H, and taking prisoner John Mc-
Donald, of Company H. No information was given me by any of the
pickets of the approach of the enemy. They were first perceived by
the detachment of Marine Artillery, who disgracefully abandoned
their pieces, leaving their officer, Lt. Sands, alone with them. Having

deserted their pieces this detachment ran over a picket of my regiment stationed near there, and they also abandoned their posts without giving any information of the approach of the enemy.

The enemy, having accomplished their object, retired before I could bring either my guns or men to bear upon them . . . After the attack was over 6 of the Marine Artillery men could not be found, and the same was the case in the morning ensuing.[30]

The 1st Marine Artillery was a unit of misfits, known for its malcontents and for its abusive recruiting methods. Its epitaph was found in a report from the adjutant general's office:

Men of this regiment were discharged from 1/10/63 to 3/10/63 as they arrived from gunboat and other service . . . Field and staff and commissioned officers were discharged per G.O. 91 H.Q. 18 A.C. dated 3/28/63 to date from 3/31/63.

AGO. This regiment was mustered out in consequence of its demoralized condition and as a favor to the enlisted men who appear to have been enlisted under false statements and promises. . . .[31]

The Confederate raiding party from the 21st South Carolina Infantry suffered no casualties that Friday night.

THE STONO SCOUTS OF EDISTO INLET

The U.S. bark *Kingfisher* was one of the ships of the South Atlantic Blockading Squadron, operating out of Port Royal, South Carolina. A report issued from the bark on April 10, 1863, told of an event that would take some months to resolve. Two contrabands who came on board the *Kingfisher* on April 9 told the skipper that a body of Confederate pickets was on Edisto Island, just south of Charleston, with orders to keep watch on navy traffic and report to their superiors. Acting Master's Mate John C. Dutch of the *Kingfisher* proceeded ashore to surprise the scouts:

Conceiving it to be a safe and easy matter to capture them, I left the ship at 6 P.M. with the launch, in charge of Acting Ensign Rhoades; first cutter in charge of Acting Masters' Mate Jordan, and my gig, taking with me Surgeon Wescott, having in all 35 men from the ship, well armed with rifles, having our howitzer in the launch; also allowed 10 contrabands to accompany us. Proceeded to Edisto, landed at Middletons' Estate, then proceeded by land about one mile to the estate of Mr. Whaley, where we surprised and captured Sgt. Townsend Mikell, R. E. Seabrook, J.J. Wescoat, A.C. Lee, W.S. Murray, W.B. Whaley, F.M. Bailey, Joseph Eddings and W.G. Baynard, privates belonging to 3rd South Carolina Regiment, with their arms and accoutrements consisting of 9 carbines, 2 sabres, 3 saddles and bridles and a small quantity of ammunition, all of which I herewith forward to you, the only casualty being a rifle shot in the left ankle of Mr. Rhoades, a report of which Surgeon Wescott herewith forwards. Although the expedition was unauthorized, I felt it to be my duty, and inasmuch as some of the prisoners had something to do with capturing two of your men from the *Fernandina* trust you will justify the act.[32]

An undated letter from Union navy Captain Percival Drayton told of a later visit to the captured South Carolina pickets:

We took prisoners the other day on Edisto Island a picket of seven young men, none over twenty, and as two of them are the nephews of Mr. Seabrook the only man besides my brother I ever cared for in the state, I went to see them. I found that 6 of them are the sons of very rich men. They are enlisted for the war overflowing with zeal, talk of their officers with almost veneration, evidently think their army is invincible and are quite satisfied to be common soldiers.[33]

The taking of the nine enlisted men even prompted a bulletin in the local paper: "9 of the 'Rebel Troop' or Stono Scouts, were surprised Friday morning by a party of the enemy, at the Point of Pines, North Edisto, and taken prisoners. The information was brought by two servants attached to the 'Rebel Troop,' who were out with the party when taken prisoners, but managed to make their escape."[34]

Six weeks later, correspondence indicates that the capture of these scouts still frustrated the Union officers. General Hunter wrote with indignation to his old friend Admiral Du Pont on May 25, 1863:

I have been already so much mortified with regard to the nine prisoners of war, the sons of leading secessionists—Seabrook &c. recently captured by the Navy, that I have concluded not to address His Excellency the President on the subject.

I must say, however, in view of all the facts and in justice to the

officers of my command who have all been condemned to death by
the rebel Congress that the delivering up of these aristocrats, the sons
of leaders in this rebellion, to be exchanged as ordinary prisoners of
war instead of being kept to be hanged for everyone of my officers
injured would be one of the grossest outrages ever committed on the
American people, and I think you will find that the people will so
decide.

I hope, Admiral, on a full review of the case you will think with
me and will decide at once to turn these prisoners over to me. The
recent release of some of our prisoners is only intended by the rebels
to induce us to release these pets of the aristocracy: they would then
commence their old game and laugh at us in our folly. I am thus
earnest feeling conscious if I were not so that all the bloodshed this
folly would inaugurate would be justly charged to me.[35]

The prisoners were being held on a naval vessel, the *Vermont,* but
Du Pont was at a loss to know what to do with them. The day after he
received Hunter's message, May 26, he replied, reassuring Hunter that,
although he had orders to send the prisoners to Fortress Monroe, he
would continue to hold them on the *Vermont.* In a message to Secretary
of the Navy Gideon Welles, Hunter made another passionate plea for
custody of these Rebels as hostages rather than as prisoners of war:

I have the honor to call your attention to certain prisoners now
on board the U.S.S. *Vermont,* captured at Edisto Island in April last
by an armed expedition from the U.S. bark *Kingfisher* and have most
respectfully to ask under the peculiar circumstances of the case that
these prisoners, nine in number, may be turned over to my custody.

From copies of the *Charleston Mercury,* regarded as a semi-
official paper, and from abstracts from the Richmond papers repro-
duced in the northern press, it appears that the late rebel Congress
passed an act condemning to death all white officers commanding or
acting in concert with colored troops, thus, in effect, condemning to
death all the white officers in this department, and further declaring
that colored soldiers if captured, should not be held subject to exchange as other prisoners of war.

Until this alleged act of the rebel Congress shall have been
disproved or disavowed by the rebel government I most respectfully
but earnestly urge that all prisoners captured in this department
whether by the Army or Navy shall be retained as hostages for the
safety of the officers and troops under my command if captured by

the enemy; the alleged act of the rebel Congress not declaring out-laws the officers of the Navy inasmuch as colored men in the Navy so far as I have any knowledge are not armed but are merely used as boat's crews and other laboring duties. On this point it is possible that I may be misinformed, but if so then the retaliation resolutions will then apply to the Navy as well as to the Army and will furnish an additional reason why those prisoners should not be exchanged, paroled or discharged from custody by this department.[36]

Hunter's fears may have been well founded. Only three weeks before this plea, on May 1, 1863, the Confederate Congress had autho-rized President Jefferson Davis to execute any white officer leading black troops. There is no evidence that this became policy in the South, but it was, of course, a matter of genuine concern to those white officers who could be affected. General Hunter was a leader in the use of black troops; he had already established two regiments and had used them in the capture and occupation of Jacksonville, Florida.[37]

Hunter was not successful in gaining custody of the nine Rebels on board the *Vermont*. Although there is no specific evidence to prove their exchange, most of the nine appear on the rolls of the 3d South Carolina Regiment as present in July and August, 1863 indicating that they were exchanged in the normal manner.[38]

Lincoln's new policy allowing blacks in the military was a turning point in the treatment of both ex-slaves and freemen in the North. Blacks were allowed to serve, but only in segregated black regiments. Led by white officers, and originally paid only $10 per month instead of the white soldier's $13, they would contribute numbers of regiments, as well as lives, to the Union cause. Eventually, back pay was given to most of the black troops, but they served for many months without the knowledge that this would be done. The inclusion of blacks was a major change for Lincoln's administration, and it was done with some trepida-tion.

Almost totally ignored in this major policy change were Hunter's previous efforts to include enlistment and training of black soldiers; he had been too far ahead of his time. One of Hunter's regiments formed before the change in "official" policy on blacks was the 1st South Carolina Infantry (African Descent). Records show that this regi-ment was sent on expeditions along the coast of Georgia and Florida in late fall 1862, but its members were not really sworn in until January 31, 1863.

The 1st South Carolina Infantry had been part of the Union force that took, then occupied, Jacksonville, Florida, in March 1863. On March 31, orders took them back to Beaufort, South Carolina. Around April 8 they were assigned picket duty at Port Royal Ferry, on the Coosaw River—not a bad assignment, they thought. Their colonel, Thomas Wentworth Higginson, wrote:

> It meant blackberries and oysters, wild roses and guerilla existence in place of the camp routine. To the colored soldiers especially, with their love of country life, and their extensive personal acquaintance on the plantations, it seemed quite like a Christmas festival. Besides, they would be in sight of the enemy, and who knew but there might be a raid or skirmish?[39]

Susie King Taylor, a young black girl who had been adopted by the regiment while at Port Royal, wrote in her memoirs of the relaxed atmosphere between the forces: "Some mornings I would go along the picket line and I could see the rebels on the opposite side of the river. Sometimes as they were changing pickets they would call over to our men, and ask for something to eat, or for tobacco, and our men would tell them to come."[40]

Hunter still hoped for broader powers in his department, powers to raise regiments of freed slaves in that area. He wrote to Lincoln, thanking him for his new policy and again asking for power to raise regiments in his department: "I have now to beg . . . that I may have liberty to organize colored regiments and commission their officers, and that I may have authority to deal promptly and finally with all officers who oppose a vigorous prosecution of the war or any of its necessary measures."[41] Lincoln did not respond.

The most famous black regiment was the 54th Massachusetts Volunteer Infantry, whose heroism was the subject of the movie *Glory*. On April 10, the 54th had not yet mustered enough men to become a recognized regiment; that would not happen until May 13. On the tenth the new recruits waiting for muster were in Readville, Massachusetts. Recruit Corporal James Henry Gooding, a budding reporter, wrote to the *Boston Mercury:* "We have received 315 recruits, making a total of 614, and more expected daily. The ground about the barracks has dried enough now to make walking quite a pleasure."[42]

THE EXECUTION OF PRIVATE KIENER

The day in the East witnessed a second execution. Michael Kiener died that Friday morning in front of a Confederate firing squad in Savannah,

Georgia. His was a common offense, desertion, but the death sentence was for firing at an officer sent to bring him back.

Kiener's real name was Michael La Voi. A Frenchman, he had lived in the South only a year when the war broke out. He enlisted in the 1st Georgia Sharpshooter Battalion, Company B, in January 1862; one year later, on January 22, 1863, he deserted. In a letter dated March 11, 1863, to General Beauregard, he pleaded:

> I take the liberty to address you and be pleased to accept my apology in so doing. I am a French man by birth and one year a resident of the south. I joined the army voluntarily and intended to serve during the war.
>
> An evil spirit came over me and I did that which I ought not to have done. But, sir, a vessel dashed to pieces cannot be repaired.
>
> In regard to my shooting at Maj. Anderson, permit me to say that my gun went off in the boat accidentally. Anderson [a fellow deserter, not the major] and myself had previously cocked our guns & talked of destroying himself rather than be taken prisoner. I disagreed to this proposition. At the time he shot himself I jumped round and my piece discharged. I never entertained any thought of killing Maj. Anderson.
>
> I am a poor stranger without a friend in the world and throw myself at your feet, and ask a Christian gentleman and officer for but 30 days only that I may make the proper arrangements for the future state.
>
> I indulge to hope that you will grant a dying man a little time. Man can kill my body but God alone knows I am innocent of the offense which has been charge against me. In conclusion I respect Maj. Anderson as an officer and gentleman.[43]

His plea went for naught, and the guns of his comrades at arms snuffed out his life on schedule.

★

Admiral Du Pont was relieved in June 1863 by Admiral Andrew Foote. Foote died of Bright's disease before he could take command, and Admiral John Dahlgren became squadron commander of the South Atlantic Blockading Squadron.
Charleston would remain in Confederate hands until February 1865.
Charles Sabine died of his wounds in Beaufort, South Carolina, on April 29, 1863.

John McDonald was taken to Libby Prison in Richmond, then exchanged at Camp Parole near Annapolis, where he died on March 27, 1864, of delirium tremens.

Corporal James Henry Gooding was killed at Olustee, Florida, on February 20, 1864.

PART TWO

★

THE DAY IN THE WEST

On April 10, 1863, the situation in the West was very different from that in the East. For our purposes, "the West" is the area from the Allegheny Mountains and their southern extension west to the Mississippi River. On the tenth the Union had forces on the west bank of the Mississippi moving toward Vicksburg and forces on the west side of the river in southern Louisiana. The actions of both these forces are included in this section.

The Confederacy had no Lee in the West, and while the North was still probing for Southern weaknesses, there had been some noticeable territorial gains in New Orleans, Tennessee, and the Mississippi Valley. The Union/Confederacy line had moved south to include almost all of Kentucky and Tennessee down to Nashville and Memphis, and it fingered down the Mississippi River on both sides. In the West there had been few outright Union defeats, as there had been in the East, so there was not the pall of gloom that seemed to follow the Army of the Potomac.

The Union had three large units in the West: Major General William S. Rosecrans led the Army of the Cumberland in Murfreesboro, Tennessee; Major General Ulysses S. Grant commanded the Army of the Tennessee in Milliken's Bend, Louisiana; and Major General Nathaniel Banks headed the Department of the Gulf in New Orleans. The Confederacy had three separate commands, too, but all were under the command of General Joseph E. Johnston, who was usually in Jackson, Mississippi. His three units were the Army of Tennessee in Tullahoma, Tennessee, under General Braxton Bragg; the Department of Mississippi and East Louisiana, led by Lieutenant General John C. Pemberton in Vicksburg; and the Department of East Tennessee, under Brigadier General W.G.M. Davis in Knoxville.

6

THE ARMY
OF THE CUMBERLAND

William Starke Rosecrans was the forty-four-year-old major general in command of the Union Army of the Cumberland. A graduate of West Point, class of 1842, he had his headquarters in Murfreesboro, Tennessee, just below Nashville on the road to Chattanooga.

The Army of the Cumberland had spent three months in camps near Murfreesboro, which gave them and the Confederates opposing them a lengthy breathing spell. In this spring of 1863 most of the public clamor concerned the Army of the Potomac's failures against Lee and Grant's continued frustrations in his attempts to capture Vicksburg. Maybe for this reason there was not as much attention paid to Rosecrans. The bulk of his army came from nearby Illinois, Indiana, and Ohio, with other Midwestern states—Michigan, Iowa, Wisconsin, Tennessee, Kentucky, and Kansas—supplying the rest.

The Army of the Cumberland was probably the least known of the Federal armies; it had fewer men than either Hooker's Army of the Potomac or Grant's Army of the Tennessee, and its mission was less well defined. A brief summary of the army's strategy was put forth by Rosecrans's chief of staff, Brigadier General (and future president) James A. Garfield, in a letter home dated April 10, 1863:

One thing was settled soon after my arrival, and that was that it is useless to advance into the rebel territory unless we are prepared to hold the ground we win in battle. This cannot be done until we make our supplies secure. We have therefore established a triangle of posts with Nashville as its northern apex and Franklin and Murfreesboro its base, facing south. These points we have strengthened by erecting by far the best fortification built during this war. At the same time we have used every available pound of transportation power to bring up supplies and store them in their several places, so that we now have rations to last till September and forage until July.

　　We have communicated with General Burnside (now in Cincinnati), who responds generously to all our requests and has promised to move forward and hold the lines of the Cumberland, thus securing our rear. At the same time he will push a column into East Tennessee, and put his New England troops abreast of us in line of battle. His forces are now in motion to take the place assigned to them. That done, it relieves four of our brigades, now doing garrison and railroad duty in the rear. The army will then be foot loose and will move. As we climb we can pull the ladder up behind us without danger. The enemy may then cut off our railroad if he can, and we will not be compelled to turn back.[1]

　　Rosecrans had not had great success in the field. From December 1862 to January 1863, he had been in command at the battle of Stones River, which in a sense was a Union victory—but something less than an unqualified success. The South had been holding Murfreesboro until the battle, but after the four-day struggle, Bragg's troops withdrew south toward Shelbyville, allowing the Union to occupy Murfreesboro. Later studies of the battle termed it a Confederate tactical victory, but Bragg still had too few men to hold back Rosecrans. At Stones River, Rosecrans had possession of the battlefield after the fighting stopped, a rare Union experience. Since that battle, the Army of the Cumberland had occupied itself just as the Army of the Potomac had: it entrenched, fortified, reinforced, resupplied, and rested, waiting for better weather and better roads.

　　Rosecrans had originally had a good relationship with General Halleck, the Washington, D.C., general in charge of all generals, but it was becoming strained. After Stones River, Rosecrans had been urged to make a move on Bragg's army. General Halleck wanted several things of the Union forces: to keep pressure on Pemberton at Vicksburg and on Lee in Virginia, and to show some positive signs of western Union progress to the people at home. He thought these requirements could be met if Rosecrans would initiate a campaign in Tennessee. Although Rosecrans was a very capable commander who had improved his army with drill, training, and better field conditions, he was, in Halleck's opinion, too cautious. In spite of Halleck's urgings, Rosecrans did nothing.

　　Thirty-two-year-old Major General Philip Sheridan was the commanding general of the 3d Division, XX Corps, Army of the Cumberland, with his camp in Murfreesboro. In his memoirs, he wrote of that spring:

In the meanwhile General Rosecrans had been materially reinforced by the return of sick and wounded men; his army had become well disciplined, and was tolerably supplied; and he was repeatedly pressed by the authorities at Washington to undertake offensive operations.

During the spring and early summer Rosecrans resisted, with a great deal of spirit and on various grounds, these frequent urgings, and out of this grew an acrimonious correspondence between him and General Halleck.[2]

There were stirrings in Rosecrans's camps, but no definite plans for immediate action on April 10, 1863.

If Washington was not happy with Rosecrans, his troops were. The general was held in high regard by his men, as evidenced by the song sung by the troops at their evening campfires, reported by a Union artilleryman, Captain Ephraim A. Wilson of the 10th Illinois:

> *Cheer up, cheer up, the night is past,*
> *the skies with light are glowing.*
> *Our ship moves proudly on, my boys,*
> *and favoring gales are blowing.*
> *Her flag is at the peak, my boys*
> *To meet the traitorous faction.*
> *We'll hasten to our several posts*
> *And immediately prepare for action.*
> CHORUS
> *Old Rosey is our man (repeat)*
> *We'll show our deeds where'er he leads*
> *Old Rosey is our man.*

The song, when once started would be taken up by thousands of voices, and when they came down to the chorus you would fairly be taken off your feet.[3]

John Beatty, a Union colonel who had just been promoted to brigadier general, spoke of Rosecrans's popularity in his diary on the tenth:

My parchment [promotion certificate] arrived today, and I have written the necessary letter of acceptance and taken the oath, and henceforth shall subscribe myself yours very respectfully, B.G., which in my case, will probably stand for big goose.

General Rosecrans halted a moment before my quarters this

evening, shook hands with me very cordially, and introduced me to his brother, the bishop, as a young general. The general asked me why I had not called. I replied I knew he must be busy and did not care to intrude. "True" said he, "I am busy, but always have time to say how d'ye do." . . . The general's popularity with the army is immense.[4]

Private A. S. Bloomfield, 1st Ohio Light Artillery, added his praise:

Old Rosey has sentenced three men in this army to be shot publicly. One for killing his orderly sergeant with a bayonet. One for deserting, another for deserting and going into the rebel lines and returning as a spy for them. One was shot yesterday, the other two are to be shot the fourteenth. Rosey is just the man for me and this government.[5]

The executions Private Bloomfield wrote about were probably those of James Welch, 40th Indiana, and Ezekiel Ennis, 6th Kentucky, both scheduled to be shot on the tenth for desertion.[6] Welch's sentence was suspended, according to the *Cincinnati Daily Commercial,* "in consequence of his disordered intelligence." Ennis was lucky, too. He had been court-martialed in October 1862 but wasn't sentenced until April 2, 1863. During the intervening months Ennis had stayed with the regiment and performed well in several actions. A letter from his commanding officer, also signed by virtually all the officers in the 6th Kentucky Regiment, was sent to General Garfield, and on April 9, President Lincoln reprieved Ennis, who survived the war.[7] None of the court-martial proceedings against Welsh or Ennis mention murder, only desertion. The spy might have been a man mentioned by General Beatty in a letter home:

A fellow claiming to have been sent here by the Governor of Maine to write songs for the army, and who wrote songs for quite a number of regiments, was arrested some days ago on the charge of being a spy. Last night [April 10] he attempted to get away from the guard and was shot. Drawings of our fortifications were found in his boots. He was quite well known throughout the army and for a long time unsuspected.[8]

Rosecrans was in constant motion throughout his camp. He required little sleep and was accustomed to putting in long days. James M. Sligh, quartermaster sergeant in Michigan's 1st Engineers and Mechanics Regiment, wrote, "Gen. Rosecrans is around every day seeing what is going on . . . He passed through our camp yesterday—seeing what condition our camp was in." He added with obvious pride, "I am happy stating that not any Regt. in the army of the Cumberland can beat us in keeping a clean camp."[9]

Rosecrans's aides could not keep up the pace he set, so he changed them frequently. He believed in drill and reviews, and these two activities were mentioned repeatedly in letters from his soldiers. The parading had been difficult during the winter but by April 10 the weather was fine. Late in March, Asbury Welsh of the 15th Ohio wrote to his father: "The weather is extremely hot here today for the time of the season and has an inclination to make one lazy, but we have plenty of duty to keep us straight."[10]

Conditions apparently stayed that way; on April 10 Captain James Montgomery, 33d Ohio reported: "Weather still fine."[11] Lieutenant Daniel W. Howe, 79th Indiana, agreed: "Weather pleasant with an indication of an approaching warm spell."[12] "Weather delightful," according to Charles Hood, a first lieutenant in the 31st Ohio.[13]

Physically, the area was very dry and dusty—even after a rather wet winter. Sergeant Eugene H. Bronson of the 4th Michigan Cavalry described his surroundings:

> The streams here are drying up. . . . they all run over a continued bed of limestone rocks and the soil generally is red clay and tis either mud to the knees or dust as deep but tis very fertile and where there is crops planted they look well . . . but for miles around this place the soldiers have burned up the fences and there is so much government stock horses and mules running around that tis impossible for vegetation to attain any growth . . . so you can see that we don't see much farming except when we go out on picket or scouts then we make vegetables suffer such as onions lettuce strawberries in fact anything we can eat fares slim in the hands of a soldier.[14]

The Army of the Cumberland had set up its camps in fortifications abandoned by the Confederates after the battle of Stones River, when the Union army had pushed Bragg's army south to Tullahoma. In a letter to his sister, Private A. S. Bloomfield enclosed a detailed drawing of the works with a two-page description of the fortifications and their intricacies:

> The space inside the forts is over one mile each way. I have not represented [in his drawing] one half of the creeps and turns in the

breastworks. There are over eight miles in length if straightened out. . . . The timber is all cut out for two miles each way. . . . There is about one tenth of the surface that nothing grows on being lime stone rock. There is a space here of six miles square that there is no more than rails enough to fence it. There are a few pens of an acre or so that we keep cattle and mules in. The government is running one of the steam mills here and we are using the rails for fuel. The rails are all cedar and would be worth fifty cents apiece in Cleveland.[15]

Because of the detailed drawings in the letter, even though it was to his sister, he was deeply concerned that the letter would fall into the wrong hands. He warned, "Please take care of these two sheets. This is a rebellious document but I trust it will get in no hands but those that are laboring for the same cause I am."[16]

Asbury Welsh also discussed the defenses, in a letter dated March 19: "Our men are still fortifying; five or six earthen forts are being fast completed. Our position will soon be the strongest in the west, and woe unto the rebels should they ever attempt to drive old Rosy and his legions out of it."[17]

The Southerners never did try to take back their old fortifications, and as the months passed, the Union soldiers began to feel at home. Captain Angus L. Waddle wrote:

For six months we enjoyed all the comforts which can fall to a soldier's lot. Our camps, located in and about Murfreesboro, were well chosen and soon became things of beauty. The cedar which grew so lavishly about the town was largely used in their adornment and the streets, on each side of which were planted stately evergreens, gave them the appearance of well laid out villages . . . At Gen. Rousseau's [Rousseau was the commanding general of the 1st Division, XIV Corps] headquarters a large building capable of seating several hundred persons was built entirely of cedar branches and used as a chapel, where nightly meetings were held . . . Commissary department was in good working order and sutler's tents well stocked with supplies of every description.[18]

The camps had taken on a look of their own, with dwellings not quite similar to those at Fredericksburg but comfortable enough for those resting up after the last battle. The men of the Army of the Cumberland were issued so-called dog tents. Here's what they looked like, according to Lieutenant Henry A. Buck:

Each tent is composed of two pieces of canvas, each about 5 feet square and exactly alike. On three of the edges are buttons or button holes like a double breasted coat. Each man carries one of the pieces and when we camp, two pieces are stretched over a ridge pole, raised upon a couple of stakes and the corners of the edges which have no buttons are pinned to the ground. This makes a tent for 2 men. By prolonging the ridgepole and buttoning on other pieces a tent can be extended indefinitely.

One end is closed . . . with whatever is convenient and before the other end is built a huge fire when it is cold enough to need one. We sleep with our feet to the fire . . . The boys call these domiciles "Dog Tents" and they really bear a striking resemblance to dog kennels.

We refused them at Camp Sheridan last Dec. but are now glad to get them.[19]

There were some problems with massing so many men, animals, and equipment in one area. General Beatty wrote a graphic description of a very unpleasant but common situation in Civil War camps:

Many frame houses, and very good ones, too, have been torn down, and the lumber and materials used in the construction of hospitals. There is a fearful stench in many places near here, arising from decaying horses and mules, which have not been properly buried, or probably not buried at all. The camps, as a rule are well policed and kept clean; but the country for miles around is strewn with dead animals, and the warm weather is beginning to tell on them.[20]

Some of the construction activity was made possible by the new sawmills that were being shipped, virtually intact, from Louisville. Private Bloomfield was impressed, and wrote to his sister:

Today there was another saw mill came down on the cars all ready to put up. It will be running in a few days. The one that is up runs day and night. The man that has the engineering to do at this place says the work has only fairly begun. I think the help at this place would be good if there were not so many dead horses and mules around. There are also several slaughter yards.[21]

As usual, no circumstances were identical for everyone, and officers tended to get better treatment than the men in the ranks, not an uncom-

mon occurrence in any army. But that was no guarantee that officers
lived in luxury. Alfred Lacey Hough, acting second in command of his
battalion, wrote to his wife on March 30, after he had just come back to
his battalion from leave in Detroit, describing two brand-new officers,
Lieutenants Morris and Hays, just assigned to Hough's command:

> Oh, you ought to see Morris after drill, Hays remarks to him
> are funny in the extreme. Morris is a fine officer, I was very fortunate
> in getting him.
>
> He and Hays afford me a great deal of amusement. They oc-
> cupy the tent next to me, and the contrast between theirs and mine is
> marked, mine is fixed up with a great deal of comfort about it, to
> accomplish which took a deal of work, they just turned in and
> "staid" with nothing but their cots and trunks, the first night they
> stuck their candle in the ground, the next they got a chip to fasten it
> on, and the only other furniture they have as yet is a wash basin, and
> an empty box for a seat, and to hear them abuse one another for not
> getting things is too amusing.[22]

Colonel Benjamin F. Scribner, 38th Indiana, moved his family
down from Indiana, settled into a furnished house, and thought he had
the best situation of all:

> My own comfort was not neglected . . . A furnished house,
> vacated by the owners, was within my lines. The keys were brought
> and everything turned over to me for safekeeping. . . . With such
> an establishment, the thought of sending for my wife was suggested,
> and she joined me, bringing two of the younger children and a
> nurse. . . . Other ladies, wives of members of my staff also came.[23]

Letters from these Army of the Cumberland officers and men give
us some insight into their life on April 10, 1863. It was similar to that of
the Army of the Potomac—fairly slow and, in many ways, boring. On
March 30, Hough wrote, "My dearest Mary, I have nothing new to tell
you. I am living the usual camp life, eat sleep drill and study, no signs of
any fighting as yet."[24]

General Beatty, a prolific writer and diarist, wrote on April 8,
reminiscing about the past year's events, comparing the terror of battle
to the boredom of his days in Murfreesboro:

> Six months ago this night, parching with thirst and pinched
> with hunger, we were lying on Chaplin Hills [Perrysburg, Ken-

tucky], thinking over the terrible battle of the afternoon, expecting its renewal in the morning. . . . A little over three months ago we were in the hurry, confusion, anxiety, and suspense of an undecided battle, surrounded by the dead and dying, with the enemy's long line of campfires before us [Stones River]. Since then we have had a quiet time, each succeeding day seeming the dullest.

Rode into town this afternoon; invested twenty five cents in two red apples; spoke with Captain Blair, of Reynold's staff, exchanged nods with W.D.B. of the *Commercial*; saw a saddle horse run away with its rider; returned to camp; entertained Shanks of the *New York Herald,* for ten minutes, drank a glass of wine with Col. Taylor, 15th Kentucky, and soon after dropped off to sleep.

A brass band is now playing, away over on the Lebanon Pike. The pontoniers are singing a psalm, with a view, doubtless, to making the oaths with which they intend to close the night appear more forcible. The signal lights are waving to and fro from the dome of the courthouse. The hungry mules of the Pioneer Corps are making the night hideous with their howls. So, and amid such scenes, the tedious hours pass by.[25]

On April 11, Beatty philosophized about the glory versus the reality of the army, comparing the bleakness of normal army fare to the memories of meals at home:

To the uninitiated, army life is very fascinating. The long marches, nights of picket, and ordeal of battle are so festooned by the imagination of the inexperienced with shoulder straps, glittering blades, music, banners and glory as to be irresistible; but when we sit down to the hard crackers and salt pork, with which the soldier is wont to regale himself, we cannot avoid recurring to the loaded tables and delicious morsels of other days, and are likely at such times to put hard crackers and glory on one side, the good things of home and peace on the other, and owing, probably, to the unsubstantial quality of glory, and the adamantine quality of the crackers, arrive at conclusions not at all favorable to army life.[26]

In an attempt to keep up the "glory" part of the war, parades were held frequently, and sometimes the troops resorted to some trickery to stand out in their performance. First Lieutenant Willie Colter, a Pennsylvania regimental adjutant, was experienced in the ways of making a unit look good:

Friday, 10. In the A.M. had a regimental drill preparatory to the afternoon review. At 3 P.M. formed the line on a cotton field near General Spencer's house. By the aid of the furrows a very good alignment was arrived at. Gen. Rosecrans, however, saw right thru the dodge, and said he, as he passed the right, "Adjutant, you've a very good contrivance for getting a straight line here."[27]

Lieutenant Howe of the 79th Indiana referred to the long three months of camp life after Stones River. On the eighth he wrote in his diary that things were relaxed and that the men entertained themselves in the usual ways: "Men in camp seem in better health and spirits than ever before. Their time, when not on duty, is occupied in healthful amusements such as ball, pitching quoits, tossing cannon balls (!), etc."

Two days later, on April 10, Howe summed up the inertia that seemed to prevail, describing, almost complaining, about the quiet after the fight in December: "Everything has assumed a kind of monotonous domestic way; that is, there is no more excitement about attacks, advances, moving, etc. Still the men are enjoying themselves better than ever and there is a great deal less sickness."[28]

For the many foreign-born soldiers, army life was even harder in this strange new country. John Weissert, a German immigrant in the 8th Michigan Infantry, wrote in German to his wife from Murfreesboro:

Dearest mother, this time I do not know much to write about. I write only because there is nothing to do this afternoon, and my thoughts wander as always to you, in fact they are always with you. Since yesterday we are out of work. Instead we practice a brigade drill from 8–12. Afternoons are free. I do not know what's the matter. Soon the dance will be on again.

Do not worry about me in case there should be another battle. Even if our regiment should be near, we shall not be at the front. My trust is in God! He will guide me safely through all this trouble. But I must confess honestly it looks badly in this country. I wish we were back in Leonberg [near Stuttgart, Germany]. But what can we do.

On the same day, he wrote—in English—to his son Charles: "Charles I send you here a star and straps whare it on yur coath, it is a emblum of universe strength and freedom it is the flage of this Country, it is for what we faiting for, we will stick to that old flage Charle, we can be proud of it."[29]

Angus Waddle remembered the drills as a diversion: "The daily drills, camp guard and picket duty, were just sufficient to relieve the ennui and give zest to camp life and in the evening the dress parades were given with as much attention to detail as though there were thousands of visitors."[30]

Probably a typical day for the Midwestern troops was as described by First Lieutenant John Knight, 7th Iowa Infantry, on April 10:

> Everything here goes on as usual. We are having some beautiful weather and a little more drill than usual. We have Company drill from 7–8 AM, and Battalion drill every afternoon from ½ past three to ½ past 5. Both Regts form as one & drill together, both regiments make one tolerable sized regt. The Ohio Regt. [43d Ohio] is a pretty large one as they are filled up with draft men. We do not have any more word of furloughs yet. The paymaster has not made his appearance yet but we are looking for him every day.[31]

And when not reviewing, drilling, or preparing for drill or review, there was always picket duty. As with most of the other armies, the regiments in the West would go to their outposts for roughly five days at a time, and individual units would provide the actual guard, or picket, in assigned locations.

Captain Jay Caldwell Butler, 101st Ohio, wrote to his mother just after he came off picket duty:

> Yesterday I was out on picket which is a position of no uncommon occurrence of late. As our wing of the army has, for the last two weeks, been continually on the alert, doing a great deal of picket and scouting duty . . . which is necessary to obtain a correct knowledge of the position and movement of the enemy they (the rebs) have recently ventured quite close to our lines in order to obtain provisions and hunt down their conscripts, who are continually seeking to gain our lines.[32]

Mail is a perpetual concern of modern soldiers far from home, and it was no different in 1863. A railroad raid on April 10 in La Vergne, and similar raids before it, affected confidence in sending letters, and particularly money, through the mail system. On the eleventh, Private Bloomfield wrote that the raid worried him some:

> Yesterday one of the trains that left here was captured between here and Laverne. There was one hundred fifty thousand dollars captured. It belonged to one of the brigades in this division. It is afternoon and there has no train arrived yet. I am almost afraid to send

money in this letter. There is always a calm after a storm and they will not be apt to make another dash on this road again for some time.[33]

A frequently voiced complaint came from Alfred Lacey Hough in a letter to his wife dated April 12:

I have yours of April 5th this morning, it made quite a quick trip, and most welcome it is. You say my last was dated March 23rd. I don't see how it is that letters from here are so irregular, it is the complaint of the whole army that letters *from* the army are very slow and frequently miscarry, while letters to the army rarely fail. My last to you, a short one I fear was captured by the Rebs, as they "guerril-laed" a train from here to Nashville last week.[34]

Sixteen-year-old Pvt. George Drake, just out of the hospital in Nashville, wrote to his mother, "I had the fever and ague. I got the butter you sent me, and a little round cake and a small piece of pound cake. The butter is pretty strong. It was just a month a coming."[35] The butter had good reason to be a little strong. German immigrant Private John Weissert, homesick and lonely, lamented, "I was sure I would get a letter today, but unfortunately again I had none, not a single one all month."[36]

General Garfield sounded as did the men of all ranks when it came to letters from home. He complained on April 10:

Yours of the 6th is this moment read. I am greatly distressed that my letters should not reach you. I have received all those you refer to and have answered each of them very soon after they came. In one I sent you the diagram by which you might decipher anything I might write which it would not be prudent to send in the usual manner. . . . In another I sent you a draft of $183+ which I hope is not lost. Besides the letters I have sent several papers with documents sometimes with a few lines in them and sometimes not. I have also sent a large topographical map of this country to Almeda so that you may trace all our movements. . . . I received your letter of the 22nd March [which] was so deeply interesting to me and answered it within an hour of its reception. I very much hope that answer will reach you. The letter, however, was much delayed, having been sent by way of Cairo, and did not reach me till after your next of the 26th came to hand.[37]

The future president had just been appointed General Rosecrans's chief of staff, and he was kept busy with several projects at a time when he was about to become a father. He wrote on April 9 to his wife, Crete (Lucretia), in Ohio:

> There is such a mystery about life in any form that the contemplation of it always fills me with awe. But of incipient life, of life that is to be, with all the grand and fearful possibilities which may attend it, I have no words to tell you what my thoughts were. And then the thought that it is my life, a life which I may never see, that there may be a period of oblivion between the sunset of my own and the morning of that new life . . . I beg you to be happy and cheerful during all the awfully mysterious days through which you will live till the consummation. It is a matter of great regret to me that I cannot be with you and share with you the hopes and thoughts that shall be yours during those sacred days, but you must write to me frequently and fully.[38]

Worse than no mail was the infamous "Dear John" letter. One such letter, doubly devastating because of its reasoning, was the subject of a letter home from a Private David H. Haines, 4th Michigan Cavalry. He was in the hospital from January 1863 to June 5, 1863. While in the hospital he helped another soldier who could not read. In the course of his assistance to this soldier, he noted, the man

> . . . received a letter from his fiance. We went where we were secure from observation & I broke the seal. At the first glance I noticed that everything was not all right. He, however, desired me to read and I did so. The letter was very cold and formal and was to the effect that she desired no longer to be engaged to him and her reasons were that her brothers who were in the rebel army had been captured and died in our prison and that she could never marry one of their murderers as she called him and desired that he would return the ring she had given him with other tokens of love.[39]

Even official channels were disturbed by the uncertainty of the mail. General Garfield expressed concern in an April 12 letter to Secretary of War Stanton, "I should be glad to tell you, once the mails [are] entirely safe, of a plan of mine which is now being put into execution to disturb the equanamity of the rebels in an unexpected place. I hope you will hear from it in the course of a fortnight."[40] He was probably referring to a cavalry raid designed to cut the Atlantic Railroad south of Chattanooga and led by Colonel Abel D. Streight of Illinois.

The health of the Army of the Cumberland appeared to be excellent in the spring of 1863. Although disease had caused thousands of deaths in the first two years of the war, by 1863 the rigors of camp life were accepted and dealt with. Asbury Welsh wrote to his family on March 19: "I have been enjoying pretty good health since I last wrote. The boys in our company are all enjoying good health. The same may be said for the whole army here."[41]

In preparation for the spring offensive, the Army of the Cumberland built a large hospital to accommodate the increased number of patients expected. The Nashville Dispatch reported: "A large hospital—about 700 feet long—is in process of construction here, in the vicinity of the Penitentiary for use of the Army of the Cumberland. When completed it will accommodate an immense number of patients."[42]

And the hospital in Murfreesboro had been getting some attention from Old Rosey, according to Private Bloomfield: "[Rosecrans] has about fifty acres plowed near the convalescent camp for garden. He is going to get the contrabands to raise vegatables for the hospital. He believes in keeping all hands at work on something."[43]

Another diversion was politics. The Midwestern troops in Tennessee seemed more interested in this topic—in particular, the radical Copperhead movement—than their Eastern counterparts. Copperheads were for the most part Northern Democrats who were violently opposed to the war. The soldiers considered these efforts to be treason, pure and simple. They had been through two years of bloody combat, and did not want to hear the politicians saying it hadn't been really necessary. Private Bloomfield put it this way: "You spoke about copper heads One thing they had better keep out of the soldier's clutches. There is no use for them to kick up a muss for this army is for the Union and they cannot make us dis-union."[44]

After the war, Isaac Royce, a lieutenant in the 115th Illinois Volunteer Infantry, remembered the spring fervor of patriotism and the resolutions that came from the troops protesting the disloyalty of their state governments' supporting Copperheads:

It was a time when the army needed encouragement, perhaps the darkest period of the war. In such a time these opponents of everything done by loyal men were busy in the legislatures of Indiana and Illinois trying to secure the passage of resolutions condemning the operations of the government and calling for a cessation of hostilities. It was during our stay in Nashville that these proceedings came to us. The patriotism of the soldiers was most thoroughly aroused. Meetings of the various regiments were held and resolutions adopted, condemning, in the strongest terms the disloyalty thus manifested in the North. The 115th passed them nearly unanimously, though truth requires it to be said that a few voted the other way. The 92nd and 96th Illinois and 84th Indiana gave them a unanimous vote.[45]

Sergeant James M. Sligh, a quartermaster sergeant from Michigan, expressed strong feelings on the issue. "What a miserable old Copperhead traitor Ira Hatch is isn't he?" he fumed. "I saw a notice in a Louisville paper stating that at a democratic meeting of which Ira Hatch was president he said that he was in favor of slavery—and in favor of slavery in Michigan!"[46]

A subject of more than passing interest to both officers and men alike was that of furloughs. While Hooker had devised a system of leaves for his men in Virginia, the Army of the Cumberland was less compassionate. There were furloughs for some, but most men were resigned to their fate, staying in camp. Sergeant Sligh told his mother not to expect him home: "The prospect of coming home this summer looks rather slim I think. If leaves of absence are granted it will be to men that need to go home more than I do, but not to men who want to go home any more than myself."[47]

Some officers, such as Captain James Montgomery of the 33d Ohio, made sure their leave applications got proper attention: "I applied for a 20 day leave again today I took it in person to Genl. Rousseau who is to put it through."[48]

As Rosecrans and his Yankee troops drilled and picketed along the perimeter, a select few had been ordered on a special mission on April 7. The mission was to cut rail lines between Chattanooga and Atlanta. Colonel Abel D. Streight was in command of a provisional brigade originally numbering 1,700 men. The brigade was made up of Streight's 51st Indiana with the 73d Indiana, the 3d Ohio, and the 80th Illinois, all infantry regiments. Streight received his orders from General Garfield in Nashville on April 10 and finally started his expedition on April 26 from Tuscumbia, Alabama. The raid was a Union disaster, thwarted by the Confederacy's finest cavalry, under Brigadier General Nathan Bedford Forrest. The Union infantrymen, mounted on mules, were no match for Forrest, who harried, harassed, and fought Streight until May 3, when the Union forces, exhausted from the fighting, surrendered to the Confederate cavalry. The Union lost almost 1,500 men with their animals and equipment.[49] This was one of the Union's worst cavalry actions of the war.

But as the army rested quietly in its camp on April 10, General Garfield felt it was prepared to move on:

> You have probably seen from the papers that General Rosecrans has chosen me as his chief of staff. I have now been serving in that capacity for nearly two months. During that time we have been steadily at work to prepare this army for its great work, and I am glad to tell that it is now nearly <u>ready</u> to work.[50]

In spite of General Garfield's confidence, the army would not move toward Chattanooga until late in June, two and a half months away.

Even in the shadows of two great armies, life went on in Tennessee as it did in the East. The theater was flourishing in Nashville: on April 10 Mrs. C.H.W. Bend was starring in a play called *Green Bushes,* by Foster and Hamilton, and the military contributed Lieutenant O. D. Kress as leading man. The review the next day declared that the play was excellent. Down the street in the Odd Fellows Hall, the Spragues Minstrels and Comet Band with fifteen "talented performers" were entertaining the citizens of the city and any lucky military men who could get to town.[51] This also was the first anniversary of Nashville's other newspaper, the *Nashville Union.*

The people of Tennessee were coping as best they could, with two major armies facing each other, preparing for their next confrontation.

★

The Union Army of the Cumberland and the Confederate Army of Tennessee met at Chickamauga, Tennessee, in September 1863, and Bragg defeated Rosecrans.

General Rosecrans was replaced by Major General George H. Thomas in October 1863.

Brigadier General Andrew Johnson was in Nashville, Tennessee, as military governor of the state. Elected vice president in 1864, on Lincoln's assassination he became the seventeenth president of the United States on April 15, 1865.

Colonel Benjamin Harrison was in command of the 70th Indiana Infantry in Gallatin, Tennessee, on April 10, 1863. He became the twenty-third president in 1889.

Brigadier General James A. Garfield was in Murfreesboro, Tennessee, as chief of staff of the Army of the Cumberland on April 10, 1863. He became the twentieth president of the United States in March 1881 and was assassinated six months later.

7

★

CONFEDERATES IN TENNESSEE

In today's military, an organizational chart sets forth the various commanders and their responsibilities. If such a chart had existed on April 10, 1863, it would have shown various units and their commanding generals, and who reported to whom. Such charts are very specific and very detailed, but they tend to ignore the personalities of those filling the slots. A chart of the Confederate Army of Tennessee would have been a classic in what was left unsaid.

The top of the chart would show Gen. Joseph E. Johnston as the overall commander of three armies in Tennessee and Louisiana. Subordinate to him were General Braxton Bragg, commanding general of the Army of Tennessee, in Tullahoma, Tennessee, with 50,000 men; Lieutenant General John C. Pemberton, in Jackson, Mississippi, commanding the Department of Mississippi and East Louisiana, with 48,000 men; and Brigadier General W.G.M. Davis and his Department of East Tennessee, in Knoxville, with 14,500 men. General Johnston had almost twice as many men in his several commands as did Lee in Virginia, and his area of responsibility covered eastern Louisiana, Mississippi, Alabama, and east-central Tennessee. On April 10 he faced Grant's Army of the Tennessee (104,000 men), Rosecrans's Army of the Cumberland (82,000 men), and Burnside's Department of the Ohio (22,000 men). To contain these three Union armies he had a total of just over 112,000 effectives.

This was not an assignment that Johnston wanted or had sought. A native of Virginia, Johnston was first commander of the Department of the Potomac (later the Army of Northern Virginia), but was badly wounded in the Peninsular Campaign in 1862 and was replaced by Lee. He was devoted to the Army of Northern Virginia and wanted desperately to get back that command. However, after Lee's successes on the peninsula, Second Bull Run and Fredericksburg, Johnston was not asked to return to the Virginia command when he recovered. Instead, he was given the Western assignment, which he protested and virtually refused. He maintained that it was impossible to guide three separate geographic areas and strategies; he would be duplicating that which should be done by the Confederate government in Richmond.[1] On April 10 he was on a difficult mission in Tullahoma, Tennessee, analyzing Bragg.

Johnston wrote to President Davis on April 10, giving a lengthy statement of his view of the Tennessee situation. He was convinced that Grant was abandoning the Vicksburg campaign and reinforcing Rosecrans; he felt that he would have to evacuate central Tennessee if Grant were to join Rosecrans' Army of the Cumberland. He warned, "If strong re-enforcements were to arrive [for Rosecrans] we could not hold our ground against the Federal army."[2] He put forth two choices: retreat into northern Mississippi or pull back to Chattanooga. But Mississippi was not an option, he maintained:

> It is probable that the country [Mississippi] cannot furnish food for the troops; otherwise I should greatly prefer it. Should the army fall back to Chattanooga to defend East Tennessee, the cavalry must be separated from it to subsist. It is even doubtful if forage for a reasonable baggage train can be found in that district. . . . Our disadvantage in this warfare is, that the enemy can transfer an army from Mississippi to Nashville before we learn that it is in motion, while an equal body of our troops could not make the same movement . . . in less than six weeks. The infantry of Major-General Stevenson's division, ordered from here to Jackson in December, was more than three weeks on the way; its wagons and horses more than a month. The railroads are now in worse condition than they were then.[3]

Besides the military threats of Grant and Rosecrans, he had to supervise a Bragg army in turmoil. Bragg had become immensely unpopular in his camp, had lost the faith of the public, and was now involved in a bitter struggle over his leadership with his two principal subordinates, corps commanders Lieutenant General Leonidas Polk and Lieutenant General William J. Hardee. The conflict had grown so bitter that Hardee had written to President Davis, a cardinal breach of the chain of command, recommending the immediate removal of his boss.[4]

General Bragg was plagued by a hair-trigger temper, a penchant for argument, and a habit of blaming others rather than himself. In an understatement, it could be said that he was short on interpersonal skills. He was a strict disciplinarian; on April 10, the *Cincinnati Daily*

Commercial reported that Bragg shot thirty deserters in a week.[5] He had been chastised in Richmond for his premature victory declaration at Stones River after the first day of the battle, but he seemed to have Johnston's support at the moment.

Bragg's army consisted of two infantry corps. One was led by General Polk, an Episcopal bishop, leading 19,000 men. The second, led by General Hardee, had 15,000 men. In addition, Bragg also had 15,000 cavalry under Major General Earl Van Dorn and Major General Joseph Wheeler. With other troops, his total force numbered 36,000 infantry, 15,500 cavalry, and 2,500 artillerymen, totaling 54,000 men. Bragg had troops spread out from his left wing, under Polk near Shelbyville, and his right wing, at Wartrace under Hardee. Van Dorn had settled in at Spring Hill, Tennessee.

There is an interesting footnote in an April 10 report tabulating troops under Bragg (the report itself showed that from the first to the tenth of April, the army had decreased by 514 men):

> Since the enforcement of the conscript law by officers from this command has been suspended, this army has ceased to increase. Previous to the 1st of April, the recruits and stragglers returning to the army overbalanced the sick sent to the rear. Since the 1st of April, the sick sent to the rear overbalanced the recruits and stragglers returning to the army.[6]

There was much concern over rumors of Union movements at that time, causing Johnston to be worried about placement of his troops. During the week of April 3–11, several reports seemed to indicate that Grant was sending at least part of his force to Rosecrans in Tennessee.[7] Yet at the same time, information from the western side of the Mississippi River reported Grant to be there, heading to the south of Vicksburg.[8] Pemberton telegraphed Johnston on April 3 that Grant's river traffic indicated he was moving toward a consolidation with Rosecrans and that additional troops would be needed in Tennessee. On April 9, Pemberton notified General Samuel Cooper, adjutant and inspector general in Richmond: "Enemy is constantly in motion in all directions."[9] It was not until the fifteenth that Pemberton finally realized that Grant had no intention of abandoning his quest for Vicksburg, and on the seventeenth, he so notified Richmond.

In Richmond, there was little support for the Western Confederates; Virginia was the area that held their attention, and Johnston, Bragg, and Pemberton were left to their own devices. No troops were to be added to the Western theater, due in part to the attitude of Robert E. Lee. He never indicated any desire to reduce his manpower to aid the West. Intending to invade the North again, he wanted every man he could find. In fact, Lee had several times requested that the bulk of Bragg's army be moved to Virginia, with only a holding force left in Tennessee.[10] As a result, Johnston tried to develop a strategy for rapid movement of troops from eastern Tennessee to Bragg, or from Bragg to Pemberton, or any combination thereof. But since sizable forces threatened every theater, and the railroads were not in a condition to provide rapid transit for anyone, there was no immediate solution.[11]

The last piece of Johnston's puzzle was Union Major General Ambrose Burnside. He and his IX Corps had finally arrived in Cincinnati; with his arrival the Department of the Ohio numbered 22,000 men. In hindsight, Johnston needn't have worried: Burnside was in a defensive posture, Rosecrans was in no hurry to move, and only Grant was in motion, seemingly in all directions.

The Army of Tennessee was a study in conflict. Disagreements between Bragg and his subordinates had begun after the Stones River fight in late December, when Bragg ordered a withdrawal from Murfreesboro to Tullahoma, leaving the Federals on the field after the battle. That was not a happy ending for what Bragg had called a victory. His corps commanders, Polk and Hardee, made their unhappiness known, and Bragg finally asked them if he, as their commanding general, still had their confidence. The answer that came back was an emphatic negative; neither his corps commanders nor their subordinate generals had confidence in Bragg. At that point Bragg offered to resign.[12]

President Davis asked Johnston to go to Tullahoma to learn the state of readiness of the army, to decide whether Bragg was fit to continue as commander, and to determine whether or not his officers had enough confidence in Bragg to keep him at his post. Johnston probably suspected that if Bragg were relieved, he, Johnston, would be the logical successor to Bragg's command and he would never get back to his preferred Army of Northern Virginia. So on April 10 Johnston reported to Davis that Bragg was vital to his (Johnston's) command structure and would need to remain:

> On the 19th of March, immediately after reaching this place, I informed the Secretary of War, by telegraph, that General Bragg could not then be sent to Richmond, as he had been ordered, on account of the critical condition of Mrs. Bragg. Being unwell then, I afterward became sick, and am not now able to serve in the field. General Bragg is therefore necessary here.[13]

Bragg did remain, but his two corps commanders still had no confidence in him. A side effect of all this was that Johnston lost much of his support in Richmond, where everyone wanted Bragg out; Johnston's support of Bragg had upset the government's plan to accomplish Bragg's ouster. This made the Western future even more bleak—the need for increased support from Richmond became more critical, and Richmond became more aloof.

In addition to the corps commanders' conflicts with Bragg, Forrest had told Wheeler he would never, under any circumstances, serve under Wheeler again. Then Forrest and Van Dorn had words just before the tenth. All in all, it was not a congenial group of leaders that ran the Confederate show in the West.

TULLAHOMA, TENNESSEE

The men in the camps of the Army of Tennessee were used to the officers' squabbles and their politics; it was none of a soldier's concern. The winter had been as difficult for these men as it had for the Yanks just north of them. In March 1863, Private Benjamin Franklin Jackson of the 33d North Carolina Infantry was miserable and wrote from Tullahoma, "We have tolerable plenty to eat here now but very bad weather. It is snowing here now and when it is not snowing it is raining. It has not missed three days without snowing or raining one."[14] By April 10, the weather had cleared and spring had arrived, but as others had noted in the area, "weather was good, but ground dusty."[15]

Camp life had improved greatly since their arrival in Tullahoma early in January, partly due to ingenuity on the part of the men, but also partly due to the efforts of the commanders. Unlike the Army of Northern Virginia, which was on short rations and was poorly equipped—its men in many cases without clothes and shoes—Bragg's men were reasonably well taken care of. N. C. Hughes, in a biography of Hardee, pointed out, "While the relations between their leaders deteriorated, the strength, training and welfare of the soldiers improved."[16]

Hardee was tough on his men; he controlled their foraging and thievery, and he was a heavy taskmaster. He was especially partial to drill—for his own pleasure, and for his guests, but mostly for his men. He was determined to train his men; drilling taught obedience, teamwork, and precision. The men drilled every day possible during this spring. He personally organized many of the drills and created competitions between units to spark the esprit de corps he was trying to develop. Competitions were held between regiments, between brigades, and between divisions; some of Polk's corps were even challenged to compete.

He trained his troops to load and fire while they were marching, and, to keep track of progress, he had surprise inspections.

Each unit believed it was the best; this was one of the benefits of competitive drill, which brought out the fighting spirit even among their own units. Private John S. Jackman of the 9th Kentucky kept a diary during those days in Tullahoma. The diary began: "Now commenced another siege of inaction. Nothing much to vary one day from another." But Jackman did recall that drilling was a part of that routine, bragging just a little about the brigade: "The boys had a good deal of drilling to do. The brigade at different times was drilled and reviewed in the presence of Genls Breckenridge, Hardee and J. E. Johnston. They all pronounced them the best drilled troops in the army."[17]

For Hardee, it wasn't enough to simply have a review; the review had to be performed in front of a gallery, and that gallery preferably should be female. He became famous in the Army of Tennessee for his reviews and for the great lengths to which he would go to bring out the ladies. Many of the belles of northern Alabama and central Tennessee, encouraged by roving bands of staff officers, made the general happy as they watched the reviews, listened to the deeds of valor cited by commendations, and then returned to party and dance and be serenaded after the parade.[18] Private W. E. Bevens recalled the drills:

> We were in Gen. Hardees Division. We had tents and were comfortable. We drilled 4 hours a day and by way of diversion Gen. Hardee had contests in drilling. We became so expert that we could have made the Virginia cadets ashamed of themselves. Our company was third best and that took good practice. A Louisiana company was ahead of us. It beat us in quickness at "trail arms," "lie down" and "double quick." At walking or running none excelled us at any army maneuver.[19]

One of the largest and longest reviews that spring took place on April 11 in Tullahoma, where General Johnston himself reviewed Bragg's entire army, except for his cavalry. The official report of that day's troop strength for Bragg's infantry showed just over 35,000 men present for duty. The horsemen were off doing other things: Wheeler up north of Nashville, and Van Dorn, camped in Spring Hill, involved in a clash in Franklin.

Judge Advocate Colonel Taylor Beatty mentioned in his diary, "Rode out to a review of Hardee's Corps today—the troops did very well—A great many spectators, especially ladies—for whom Genl.

Hardee has given the entertainment—he has several at his house—and this is the second or third time they have come up from Huntsville."[20]

Captain James L. Cooper of the 20th Tennessee Infantry told in his journal a little about his days in Tullahoma:

> We were kept busy when the weather would admit fortifying, drilling and reviewing. We formed a complete semi-circle of breastworks and redoubts around the place, which we were destined never to use. There was some terrible weather, but as we moved to a better camp and had built chimneys to our tents we did not suffer from it as much as before. Rations were pretty scant, but by stealing and foraging around a little we managed to keep enough on hand to sustain life.[21]

Like Bragg, Hardee was strict in his discipline and harsh in his sentences. Of the thirty deserters reportedly shot by Bragg, probably a number were from Hardee's corps: "Discipline tended to be stern, and corporal punishment and the shooting of deserters were not uncommon. Foraging and the expropriation of farmers' fences and fancies were sharply dealt with."[22] One of Hardee's recruits, J. W. Ward, sounded proud of his unit: "The fact of being in Hardee's corps is sufficient proof that we have to 'Toe the mark.' "[23]

In spite of the stern measures taken against them, desertions, or absences from the army for unauthorized purposes, were still happening at an alarming rate. The total aggregate present and absent of Bragg's army was 94,866.[24] However, actual returns for April 10 show an effective total of all three branches—infantry, artillery, and cavalry—of only 49,401. Had all the men shown up, they would have outnumbered the Federals they faced by more than 10,000. The informality of the Southern soldier had yet to be stifled by any measures taken so far, as was evidenced by an absence rate of almost 50 percent. Desertion often occurred as a result of sickness; a soldier was more likely to go home when he was sick than to trust the proficiency of army medical staff. And when he was recovered, home must have looked much better than a return to the grind of the army.

To prevent some of the disappearances, roll calls were frequent and unexpected. On April 10, Robert M. Holmes of the 24th Mississippi mentioned in his diary the roll calls as well as a number of other items:

> It is not quite so cold as it was yesterday morning, no frost fell during the night. Having but little else to do I seated myself this morning & answered the letter that I received from home on yester-

day. To day we drew rations of bread and bacon also a little salt. In the heat of the day it is quite warm & the wind is blowing very hard. Near night a thin cloud overshaddered the earth which is the case nearly the whole night. A great many news papers are scattered throughout the camps to day but little news can be obtained from them. During the day the roll has been called five times. It is thought this is done to keep the men from going out into the country as it would cause them to be absent from their command perhaps at sometime when the enemy would make an attact & this would cause a great confusion.[25]

While Hardee was training and drilling his men, fifty-seven-year-old General Polk had other interests and concerns. Polk was a unique individual, large, with a commanding presence. He had graduated from West Point in 1827, but almost immediately resigned to join the clergy. He was the bishop of Louisiana in 1861, when he enlisted in the Confederate forces. On April 10 he addressed General Sam Cooper in Richmond, telling the general of his changes in the less than adequate hospital system, which he had rearranged to handle his wounded more efficiently. The new system was described:

> Each corps has its own hospitals, which are devoted exclusively to the use of its own sick. Take the hospitals assigned to my own corps, for example. These are established at Rome and Atlanta, Ga. Every day the sick of my corps, now at Shelbyville, who require hospital treatment are sent down to one or the other of these hospitals. Rations are provided them on the cars, and a surgeon detailed to accompany them. For better security they are placed under the care of an officer, with a detail as a guard, whose duty it is to accompany them to the hospital, to see that they neither escape nor are left by the way, and who turns them over to the commanding officer of the post where the hospital is established. . . . So soon as they are convalescent for light duty, they are put to squad or company drill, for the sake of the excercise and, when competent for field service, they are sent back to their commands in the corps under an officer and a guard, as they came down.[26]

Polk's point was that the hospital was still part of the corps, which could best look after and treat its own. The arrangement also provided that there would be no "escape" from duty through the hospital pipeline. But there was a flaw, which was the point of Polk's message:

But I regret to see then an order has been issued by the Adjutant and Inspector General's Office at Richmond declaring that corps, army and department commanders are excluded from having anything to do with general hospitals and, therefore, all our plans for the benefit of the sick are overthrown at a blow. This order is No. 28, March 12, Paragraph V. I have respectfully to submit that, in my judgment, this is not expedient or wise. It goes back to the old system, which has worked badly, and lost us, by desertion or otherwise, a large number of all who have been sent to our hospitals.[27]

Polk's procedure had been an attempt to plug that hole.

On any given day, there was picketing. Private Robert Holmes, assigned to that duty on April 6, described the assignment:

April 7 We (cos. D & I) now have ordors to have rations cooked and readey to go out on picket guard by one o'clock this evening. At this time or sooner we were into line & marched out to the post. At first both cos. were posted together but very soon the officer of the day came round & we of the 24th were brought back about a half a mile and there posted, this was done to prevent the enemy from capturing both or the whole of the guard, which they could have done if they had known the condition at that post.[28]

Picketing was lonely duty, and it tended to make the men think about being separated from their loved ones. Thomas Wayman Hendricks, 12th Alabama Cavalry, confided to his wife: "Jane you don't know half how bad I want to be at home with you and them, nothing on this earth could afford me half the satisfaction that home and friends there would if I was permitted to go there and stay in peace."[29]

Love was part of a soldier's life, and frequent moves caused some agonizing separations. First Lieutenant Rufus W. Cater had been transferred from his post in Pollard, Alabama, to Tullahoma, and on April 10 he was on a boat en route to Bragg's army. He wrote from Pollard on the seventh, mooning over separation from his love:

My dearest Cousin
How earnest had been my wish that we remain at this place. If I could not see you very often I could hear from you regularly, and there was solace in the thought I was near you. I could anticipate, too, always the pleasure of being with you soon which made me cheerful and resigned to whatever of privation and hardship I have found here. How very fortunate I was to be sent last week to guard

those bridges. Those hours passed with you, oh! they were bright links in the chain of my destiny, brighter, I fear, far brighter than the future will ever weave for me again. Each hour was happier than the one that preceded it, and yet in all of them it seemed my cup was full. But Cousin Fanny, they are gone. Gone forever those golden joyous hours, gone that sweet face to me ever so gentle and so kind. Gone indeed but not to memory lost.[30]

Real love was not always available so sometimes it was enough to have a girl around and a dance or two, according to Private Jackman,

Manchester, the county town of Coffee is a small place on the branch railroad running to McMinnville. At the time we sojourned in its vicinity, the town was very much torn up, both armies having had a turn at the place. The boys, however, found enough society to keep up amusement, and all the winter were flirting with the young ladies. Balls were frequent. I attended two—one at a hotel in town and the other at an unfinished paper mill below town on Duck River. When the latter came off a rain pourd down all night, so no one could go home. At this ball Gus M. & Co. played Bombasto Furioso, a stage having been arranged for the purpose. The boys would defray all expenses, in getting in refreshments Etc. when they would go out to invite the girls the old dames would be informed an abundance of pure coffee would be on hand, when all objections to their girls going to the ball would cease—"You may look for me and my gals to be thar, shore." The boys knew the proper cord to touch to bring the "gals." The "gals" would dance and the old ladies would sip coffee.

Jackman also complimented his own regiment:

The boys conducted themselves in such a manner that they won the esteem of the people. They thought the 9th Kentucky was the best regiment in the army. When the other regiments came up, a great many depredations were committed, that is, hogs killed and so on, but none of the people laid any blame on the 9th.[31]

As the day of April 10 was coming to an end, the army was girding up for the next step, as was the Army of the Cumberland, just to the north in Murfreesboro. Private W. E. Bevens, one of Hardee's infantrymen, summed up the army's condition when he said:

April 23rd real fun began again, but we were alive, active, young, healthy, well-drilled, well-disciplined—in perfect fighting trim.[32]

★

General Leonidas Polk was court-martialed by General Bragg for failure to attack when ordered by Bragg after Chickamauga. He was killed at Pine Mountain, Georgia, in June 1864.

General Bragg was finally relieved by General Johnston in February 1864 and was appointed President Davis's military adviser.

Private Benjamin Franklin Jackson died during the amputation of his leg at the battle of Pickett's Mill in May 1864.

Private Robert M. Holmes was captured at Chickamauga in September 1863 and died in the Union prison at Camp Douglas, Illinois.

Private Thomas Wayman Hendricks was killed in a cavalry charge near Williston, South Carolina, on February 8, 1865.

8

★

EASTERN TENNESSEE
AND KENTUCKY

The Union's Army of the Cumberland and the Confederate Army of Tennessee faced each other across narrow corridors in central Tennessee; however, this was not the case in the eastern part of Tennessee and in Kentucky. In those areas both North and South had troops, but they were not facing each other and were not ready to square off in battle. The Union Department of the Ohio, headquartered in Cincinnati, was the caretaker of Kentucky and parts of Tennessee, while the Department of East Tennessee, in Knoxville, was the Confederate counterpart in those same areas.

THE UNION CAMPS

In the fall of 1862, Major General Ambrose Burnside had been promoted, against his wishes, to command of the Army of the Potomac, and by his own admission he was responsible for the debacle at Fredericksburg during December of that year. He was relieved of that command in January 1863, but agreed to serve as the commander of the Department of the Ohio, far from the scene of his December nightmare. He was modest, and capable, to a degree, but that degree did not include command of critical armies such as the Army of the Potomac.

The Department of the Ohio had recently been strengthened by the arrival of the IX Corps from the Army of the Potomac, with almost 13,000 men. The IX Corps had been traveling since March—from Newport News, Virginia, to Fortress Monroe, Virginia; from there to Baltimore by steamers; and on to Cincinnati on railroad cars. It was a well-traveled corps, having been in North Carolina operations early in the war, then with the Army of the Potomac, and now in Ohio, with Major General J. G. Parke commanding.

On April 10, the IX Corps was just beginning to arrive at its final destination, Camp Dick Robinson, south of Lexington, Kentucky.

George W. Whitman, the younger brother of Walt Whitman, writing to his mother from Paris, Kentucky, gave a few details of the trip—and was also looking for mail:

> As soon as we get to our destination (which I think is not very far from here) I will write you again, and tell you all about the sights I have seen, since we left Newport News, which was on the 26th of March, I have not heard a word from home since I came back to the Regt. but I suppose there must be some letters somewhere on the way to me, I wrote you the night after I got back to Newport News, telling you that we expected to leave there soon, but I suppose you will be surprised to see that we are away down here in old Kaintuck, We are now about 70 miles from Cincinnati Ohio. I like the country here first rate and think likely we will have a good time. I believe there is no large force of Rebs, in this State, but they say, there is a good many small bands of Gurilas that scive around and do considerable mischief. We had a pretty long ride in the cars, having come by Rail all the way from Baltimore but it was not quite as bad as marching, although I got pretty well tired of it . . .[1]

The task of this Union army was to provide garrison troops for Kentucky and central Tennessee, and some rear area protection for Rosecrans's Army of the Cumberland. The Department of the Ohio numbered 22,000, but those troops were scattered over parts of Tennessee, Kentucky, and into Ohio, many serving as train guards. Bowling Green, Kentucky, was the center of activity for many of the train guards, since it was on the Louisville-Nashville rail line; Lebanon, Kentucky, had a set of camps, as did other cities as well. This was not a centralized command but a series of outposts and camps dedicated to protecting the borders and supply lines established by the hard-won victories of the previous two years. The mission of these units was difficult—and more than a little dangerous. The men were constantly on the move, as was witnessed by the recent arrivals; even the department commander, General Burnside, was new.

Private Israel Atkins was in Bowling Green with the 23d Michigan. He wrote home that the 23d was leaving but his health was not good enough for him to travel. He said, "I wish I was able to go with the boys. We are all against the South heart and hand and intend to whip them if it takes our lives. . . . We are whipping the rebbels verry badly everywhere we fight them. We all think the war will end by fall at any rate."[2]

With their constant motion, separation from other units, and the constant threat that Rebel cavalry would appear almost anywhere, these men became lonesome; mail was a highlight. First Lieutenant John C. Buchanan of the 8th Michigan wrote a long and passionate letter on April 12 to his wife, Sophie, from Lebanon, Kentucky, expressing his devotion:

> My Own Dear Wife,
>   It is sabbath day and I am happy to be able to spend the passing hour with the dearest of all my earthly friends the one I love best of all, & indeed to whom I am under the greatest obligation. The days and weeks of absence have not lessened the affection which the little Sophie inspired years ago and which has ever from that period occupied the whole of my heart, poor though the offering be yet it is unreservedly yours. It is not the lightest of my sacrifices to be separated from my dear loving wife & darling boys.[3]

Lieutenant Buchanan was happy on the tenth: he received six letters from his Sophie.

While many of the soldiers, both Confederate and Yankee, wanted to go home, at least one Union officer was going home against his will. Colonel Orlando M. Poe of the 2d Michigan Infantry was relieved of his command. His commission had expired and for unknown reasons he had not received an extension, and so he was replaced by a new colonel. He left for home on the tenth, apparently much to the regret of his men, according to Private Jerome Robbins of Poe's unit:

> One of the most affecting incidents and scenes occurred today in the farewell of Col. Poe from the officers and privates of our regiment. A thorough soldier and disciplinarian and beloved by all. Many were the tears shed and heart pang experienced at the separation. In the farewell address of the Col. he spoke of us in highest terms and spoke with deepest feeling several times he was compelled to stop in his remarks to repress the tears which involuntarily started. Acknowledging his strictness (and which has done so much to discipline the men under him) but humbly asked the forgiveness of any who felt themselves wronged. he left on the one o'clock train amidst the deafening cheers of the soldiers his wife acknowledged the farewell by waving handkerchief, himself his hat.[4]

Poe had led his men through many battles in the Army of the Potomac, most recently the one in Fredericksburg, Virginia. One of the officers of the regiment, Captain Charles B. Haydon, wrote in his diary on the ninth:

It is now believed that we are sure of Humphrey for Col. No one however can tell what may turn up. He is the best man in the Regt. who is elligible to the place. He is not however exactly the man for Col. He is too lax on discipline. There are no better men than the 2nd so long as they know their master. So many devils fresh from hell would not be worse than they if not held with a strong hand.

10th—Col. Poe left us today. It was a pretty serious time and nearly all the officers and men were moist about the eyes when they came to shake hands for the last time. I was very sorry to see him go.[5]

Colonel Poe had been recommended for promotion to brigadier general, but that recommendation expired before it was approved, and he was requested to resign. There appears to be no obvious reason for this action, one of many unexplained military procedures.

While officers may come and go, life in the regiment continues. For those in camp, the routine was always the same: drill and parade, gripe and get paid. Private Robbins observed: "Friday 10th Quite a sultry spring day. Toward evening wind blew quite freely. This A.M. the 12th Ky left for parts unknown supposed to be Nashville [actually it was Bowling Green, Kentucky]. The 18th and 22nd Mich arrived from Danville from which place they started yesterday." Robbins sounded very much the veteran when he added, "It was rather amusing to see their quantity of baggage, to our eyes superfluous."[6]

Wisconsin men were there, too, and they were just as idle, according to a letter written by John F. Brobst, 25th Wisconsin Infantry:

Dan is trying to learn the fiddle. He sawed about two weeks & can't play a tune. . . . Thompson Pratt has got a little nigger to wait on him. He gives him $3.00 a month. He sits in his tent and sends the darky to the cook shanty to get fire to light his pipe and has him sweep out the tent, bring water to wash and drink.[7]

David Millspaugh of the 18th Michigan marched from Danville to Lebanon, Kentucky:

April 10 On the march from Danville to Lebanon As the 22nd [Michigan Regiment] were ahead of us there was a great strife which should get to Lebanon first So our Regt. got up at 2 A.M. and started very still untill we got ahead of the 22nd and passed them about 4 miles from where we encamped got into Lebanon about sunrise we stopped in a field east of the village and I write this sitting on the ground beside a stack of guns . . . We were paid two months pay today to the 1st of February.[8]

Another Wolverine soldier, William Boston, of the 20th Michigan, made brief notes about camp news: "April 10—Our brigade was reviewed yesterday by Gen. Manson. The 18th and 22nd Regt. came here today. They are being paid off and leave tomorrow for Tennessee. . . . Pleasant weather. The boys took possession of a printing office in town and have issued a paper called 'The Union Vidette.' "[9] Unfortunately, no records of the paper survive. Captain Haydon liked the weather during the Manson review: "Weather was fine and the affair went off well."[10]

Captain Alonzo M. Keeler of the 22d Michigan was looking for his paycheck: "All day in expectations of pay . . . Orders to march immediately to Gen. Rosecrans Army Tenn—to be paid in the night tonight."[11]

The Louisville Daily Democrat did some computation and concluded that the 8th Michigan, traveling by foot, water, and rail, had covered 6,000 miles since it was organized on September 23, 1861. It was estimated that 1,000 of those miles had been by foot.[12]

One soldier in the Department of the Ohio was Private Franklin Thompson of the 2d Michigan Infantry, who had enlisted at twenty years of age early in the war—on May 14, 1861. The private had been assigned to various duties, most of them involving nursing at post hospitals. On the tenth, Private Thompson had malaria and was being confined to quarters, but to avoid being sent to a general hospital for treatment, Thompson deserted on April 19 at Lebanon, Kentucky. Only after the desertion was it discovered that Private Thompson was in reality a female. She had successfully kept her secret for almost two years, but she returned home to Detroit to recover her health and once again became Sarah Emma Edmonds. Records confirm that she was present for muster with the 2d Michigan on April 10, 1863, at Camp Dick Robinson, Kentucky, and deserted just nine days later.[13]

As these soldiers maintained their routines and manned their battle stations, their politics were important to them. Copperheads, the so-called Peace Democrats, were viewed with considerable distaste. Lieutenant John C. Buchanan expressed that emotion in an April 12 letter to his wife in Grand Rapids:

Last sabbath I attended the Presbyterian Church. . . . The church is quite wealthy but made up of discordant elements, Union and secesh. Of course, Religion is a secondary consideration. The people are divided on the question, as we might reasonably expect. I think however the union sentiment predominates.

Tell Sis Clara to watch out for Copperheads. I have found none in the south that so richly deserve to have their necks elongated as the Northern traitors. Their day is coming and will be upon them ere they are aware. The appropriation for hemp was a gentle hint.[14]

The subject of Copperheads was also a concern to General Burnside, and the general was in a position to do something about it. As commander of the Department of the Ohio, he had certain powers over his civilian citizenry. While Burnside was settling into Ohio, Congressman Clement L. Vallandigham was continuing to harangue against the war; since Congress had adjourned, he was back in his home state of Ohio. His continual urgings that soldiers desert and that conscripts leave the country, and a host of other traitorous utterings, were distressing to Burnside, who made an effort to quiet him.

On April 10, Burnside composed the first draft of his general order proclaiming that people giving speeches considered "traitorous" or "seditious" would be liable to arrest. The members of the government in Washington knew nothing of his order, which was issued on April 13, 1863; on May 1, they were stunned when, following one of Vallandigham's speeches, Burnside had him arrested and jailed. The congressman was convicted by a military court of expressing sympathy for the enemy and was sentenced to be turned over to the Confederacy.

Later in May, Vallandigham was escorted to General Bragg's lines under a flag of truce, and he was accepted reluctantly by the South. He was not welcomed there, but was able to get passage on a blockade-runner from Wilmington, North Carolina, to Canada. He migrated to Windsor, just across the river from Detroit, where he ran a campaign for governor of Ohio. He won the Democratic nomination but not the election itself, and was lost in political obscurity afterward.

Most of the troops were in camps, writing and drilling, but there was some military action in the department on April 10. The 115th Ohio was reported to have been on a sweep:

The military department of this city heard that rebels were committing outrages in the County of Owen in Kentucky. A squad of about 100 mounted infantry, belonging to the 115th Regiment, stationed at the barracks on Vine Street, between 4th & 5th, in command of Captain Sturgeon, left last week for that region on a scouting excursion. They scoured Owen County, including Warsaw, and Saturday afternoon they returned, having succeeded in capturing 14 prisoners, residents of that county. They will probably be forwarded this morning to Camp Chase.[15]

CONFEDERATE HAPPENINGS

The Confederate Department of East Tennessee had about 14,500 men and was commanded by Brigadier General W.G.M. Davis, who had his headquarters in Knoxville. This army was the equivalent in assignment, if not in numbers, to Burnside's Department of the Ohio. It was to protect the flank of Bragg's army and keep supplies—what supplies there were—moving.

On April 10, General Davis made a suggestion to General Johnston that Davis could place a minimum number of troops in Knoxville and screen them with substantial numbers of cavalry north of the Cumberland River. He reasoned that just a few troops could defend his territory and he could then supply some of his troops to Bragg in Tullahoma. He would keep his infantry by the railroad for rapid movement whenever his cavalry felt a move by the Union was imminent.

The large body of troops we have heretofore maintained in East Tennessee might, with the aid of adequate railroad transportation, be considered part of an army operating in Middle Tennessee. In forty eight hours our force here might, by the use of expedition and with cars sufficient at our command, be thrown into the line at Tullahoma. This would be a safe move if we had, by means of our cavalry force, a security against raids and a guarantee that no advance in large force could be made before the troops could be returned.[16]

General Davis's suggestion was not adopted, probably because of the deteriorating condition of the railroad and the lack of railroad cars, but it was a unique concept, offering his troops to aid others. That was very definitely a reversal of the behavior of most general officers, who usually wanted more men to increase their own commands.

In one of Davis's Confederate camps in London, Tennessee, religion was also a frequent topic in diaries and letters. Joseph Espey, a Georgia Confederate, reported a successful series of revival meetings by an itinerant preacher:

Mr. Warren arrived here he staid with us about three days he seemed to be highly pleased with his visit here he arrived here on Tuesday morning the 31st adult and left on Friday the 3rd inst he staid with us in our cabin The first night he made prar here in the cabin and Wed and Thursday night he preeched at the church in town for the benefit of the soldiers and had large congregations each night and he was highly pleased with the attention and behaviour which they <u>respected</u> him with. I was present each night and I never seen better behaviour and attention any whore.[17]

Not all preachers in Kentucky were as happy with their flocks as was Reverend Warren. In Olmstead, Kentucky, the local circuit-riding preacher, George R. Browder, had his services in Adairville, Kentucky, set for Friday the tenth. He wrote with some sadness, "Went to Adairville not expecting any congregation and was not disappointed. This day was warm & my horse took thumps [hiccups] & I had no good results from this days labor."[18]

Church services helped the loneliness, and writing home helped as well. Confederate John W. Cotton of Alabama wrote on April 11 from Kingston, Tennessee, to his wife and seven children:

Dear wife I take my pen in hand to answer your kind letter which I received yesterday it was a letter I recon you aimed to send by nan gray but capt Slaughter brought it it had a plat of your hair in it that looked very natural but I had a heap rather seen you.
I remain your loving and affectionate husband til death, John W. Cotton.[19]

Cotton signed every letter the same way: "your loving and affectionate husband til death." Cotton was with the 5th Battalion, Hilliard's Legion, Alabama Cavalry. Although his letters were plain and country, they accurately conveyed his thoughts. Earlier he had mentioned that one of his Rebel horsemen was under a different kind of attack: "The body lice bothers him very bad you ort to see him rakeing and scratching and cracking them."[20] In his letter of the eleventh, he showed his concern for the way things might be at home in Coosa County, Alabama:

I wish I could come home and stay a few days til I could see how things were going on but I had rather come to stay but there is no chance to get a furlow now there ant nobody getting furlows but the officers I dont want you to bee uneasy about me I could do very well if I could keep from studying about home it ant worth while for me to tell you how much I study about home but there is one thing that gives me great consolation you have a plenty to live upon and from what I lern there is lots of soldiers wives that has not much to eat if I were to here that you had nothing to eat I should come home at the risk of my life.[21]

Other Confederates roamed the Tennessee countryside and up into eastern Kentucky, stirring up what action they could. One of these was Edward O. Guerrant, and in the mountains near Boonesville, Kentucky, he wrote of forage and hunger:

Thursday 9 April, 1863
Headquarters tonight in the centre of Giltner's (now Pryor's) Regiment at Mr. McClanahan's, who was gone from home as are almost all the men along our line of march. All Union men, bitter, prejudiced and ignorant.
Miss McC. had no husband. Corn, meat and fences vanished from the valley under the administration of 'the boys.' Commissaries had levied upon all the meal and flour at every house and we divide our own abundant stock of starvation and discontent with the poor people of the hills.
All our time, talents and energies are devoted to the procurement of a little corn bread and meat wherewith to sustain life.
Friday 10 April, 1863
A hot, sultry, smokey day. Nothing for breakfast. Like to have lost my bridle.
Very hoarse with cold. Our journey still lay up the Middle Fork of the Ky. river. Up-Up-Up for miles on miles, over fallen trees—gullies—the whole brigade single file, stretching for miles along the winding river.[22]

The brigade was apparently on the march toward Knoxville and General Davis. Guerrant's description dramatized the pillaging of the land by both sides, leaving the women who remained at home to cope as best they could. Guerrant's and Cotton's letters make the desertion problem more understandable, especially for the men from these middle states. Desertion, though, depleted the ranks not only by the absence of the deserter but also by the absence of his pursuer. Joseph Espey, in a letter that was to be delivered by one such pursuer, wrote:

My dear sister it is in haste that I attempt to address you a few lines this morning as I have a chance to send it home by hand. There is three men detailed out of this company to go home after the absentees from this company—Ford Flin and Nelson. They will be at home 4 days. I have not received one letter from you.[23]

Another unit, the 5th Tennessee Cavalry, was scouting in eastern Kentucky as well, roughing it, with their rations provided mostly from the surrounding country. On April 10 they were in Boston, Kentucky, just in from a scout to London. William E. Sloan described some cooking techniques:

Our bread is usually of corn meal, and we mix up a stiff dough and wrap it around the ramrods of our guns, and bake it also before the fire, turning the ramrods continually until the bread is a beautiful brown. We cook our meat in the same manner or on the coals or on a stick drove in the ground in front of the fire. We are not bothered with making coffee or tea as we have neither on hand, though we do sometimes peel some birch bark and make tea of that. Notwithstanding all these hardships we are all having splendid health.[24]

On April 9 Sloan noted, "Move on to Elk Fork (Kentucky)— captured two bushwackers—Bryon Perkins and his son."[25] The Perkinses remain a small footnote in history, with no further word of their fate.

While the soldiers in the field had their privations, this section of the country was struggling with not just the war but also the way to pursue it. Burnside's actions against Vallandigham were an extension of the Union's new policies—waging a war that was rapidly becoming a clash not only against the Confederate armies but, when necessary, against citizens on either side who became too outspoken in their opposition to the war. The next step would be to make this a total war against not just the Confederate armies but the South itself. This policy would include scorched-earth tactics that would bring the war home to the people of the South.

★

Confederate General W.G.M. Davis abruptly resigned on May 6, 1863. Captain Charles B. Haydon was wounded in July 1863 and died of pneumonia in March 1864 after rising to the rank of lieutenant colonel.

David Millspaugh was killed in a ship explosion on his way home after the war.

Because of her desertion, Sarah Emma Edmonds needed a special act of Congress, passed on July 13, 1886, to complete her record of service and receive her pension.

Colonel Orlando Poe reappeared as a regular army captain later in 1863 and finished the war as a brigadier general under General William T. Sherman.

Captain Alonzo Keeler was captured at Chickamauga on September 20, 1863, and was held in prison until March 1, 1865.

Colonel Abel D. Streight was held in Libby Prison until he escaped in February 1864.

9

A FIGHT AT FRANKLIN

The closest the opposing forces came to a full-scale battle on April 10 was in Franklin, Tennessee, and it started early in the morning.

Spring had just arrived in middle Tennessee, and it was a welcome arrival. The winter had been long and cold, and it had been discouraging for the 82,000 Union troops in the Army of the Cumberland and for the 50,000 Confederates in the Army of Tennessee. The Federals had endured not only a bitter winter but also the repeated and successful raids of Confederate cavalry under some of the most daring of the cavalry commanders—Major General Earl Van Dorn, cavalry commander of the Army of Tennessee, and his division commander, Brigadier General Nathan Bedford Forrest. The Confederates had faced the same cold winter and had the rather bitter memory of the battle of Stones River to depress them.

The city of Franklin lies on the Harpeth River, eighteen miles south of Nashville, in a country of rolling hills, meadows, and fields interspersed by groves of evergreens, cedars, and other trees. Franklin was one of the three critical bases of the Army of the Cumberland; the others were Murfreesboro and Nashville. Union troops in Franklin were commanded by Major General Gordon Granger; they formed part of the Union line that protected Nashville.

Granger's forces were on the north side of the Harpeth River; the area included an unfinished fort on a bluff overlooking the town. Fields of fire were clear and provided good observation when the weather was good. Granger had posted the 40th Ohio Infantry Regiment on the south side of the river, on picket, and the rest of the infantry force was positioned on high ground north and east of the city. Brigadier General Absalom Baird's division of 2,880 men held posts designed to control any attack from the south, and Brigadier General Charles Gilbert's division, about 2,310 men, was in camp just behind Granger's headquarters at the fort. Recently there had been just over 6,300 men in town, but

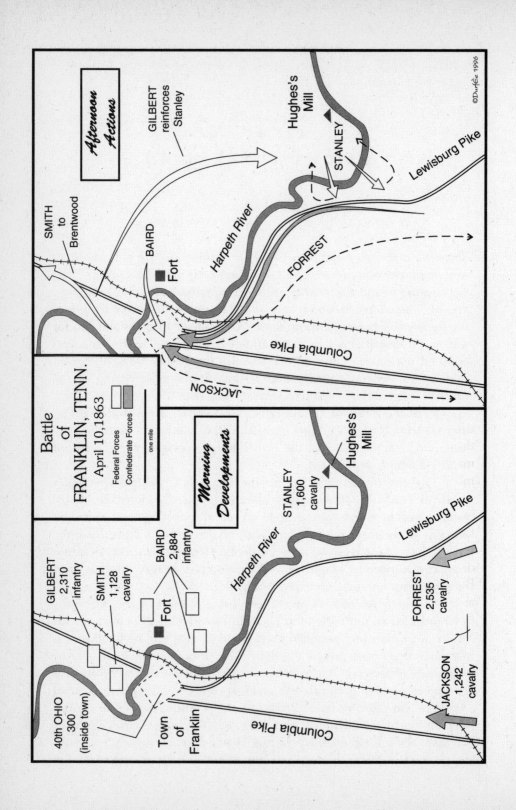

Afternoon Actions

GILBERT reinforces Stanley

Hughes's Mill

STANLEY

Lewisburg Pike

SMITH to Brentwood

BAIRD

Fort

Harpeth River

FORREST

Columbia Pike

JACKSON

Battle of FRANKLIN, TENN.
April 10, 1863

Federal Forces
Confederate Forces

one mile

Morning Developments

STANLEY 1,600 cavalry

Hughes's Mill

GILBERT 2,310 infantry

SMITH 1,128 cavalry

BAIRD 2,884 infantry

Fort

Harpeth River

Lewisburg Pike

FORREST 2,535 cavalry

40th OHIO 300 (inside town)

Town of Franklin

JACKSON 1,242 cavalry

Columbia Pike

on the night of April 9, Major General David S. Stanley's cavalry brigade had arrived from Murfreesboro, 1,600 strong, bringing Granger's total force to almost 8,000 men.[1]

Shortly before April 10, Van Dorn and Forrest had had a disagreement over Forrest's treatment of captured equipment. Both men were fine cavalrymen—daring, courageous, and creative—but both were very sensitive and quick to take offense. After a skirmish at Brentwood in March, the cavalry under Forrest had picked up a large booty of Federal guns and ammunition; on the field, they replaced their own worn-out muzzle-loader rifles with some brand-new Union weapons. After they all rode back to Spring Hill, Van Dorn's quartermaster complained to him that Forrest's men had taken the best equipment for themselves before turning in the rest to the quartermaster. Van Dorn, a West Pointer and a strict disciplinarian, challenged Forrest on the matter. Forrest simply said he thought his men, who had made the capture, had every right to replace worn-out equipment with the better supplies provided by the Union. Van Dorn then raised another thorny issue, asking Forrest if he had released information to the newspapers about cavalry accomplishments at Brentwood. These accounts had given most of the credit for a Confederate success there to Forrest, and Van Dorn was annoyed. Forrest considered the matter an insult; he blew up, and told Van Dorn that he would hold him personally responsible for producing the source of his information. There were some tense moments between the two hot-blooded horsemen, but eventually they shook hands and made up. The incident indicated that there was not always total harmony in the Southern cavalry.[2]

Dawn came early on this dark and windy spring morning, breaking through a haze of dust and mist.[3] It was the signal for the start of a Confederate reconnaissance in force toward Franklin by Van Dorn. In his command, he had two cavalry divisions, 3,100 troopers in all. One division was headed by Forrest, the other by twenty-eight-year-old Brigadier General William H. Jackson. Although young, Jackson was an 1856 West Point graduate and a seasoned cavalry officer. The Confederates rode out of Spring Hill, Van Dorn's headquarters, full of confidence and in high spirits. Possibly, some of their high spirits came from recent rumors that Union forces in Franklin had evacuated the town and the Confederates would be able to renew old friendships in the city—especially with the ladies—once again.[4]

On that dry, hazy morning the air temperature was fifty-four degrees, but with the morning sunshine that figure would rise considerably, punishing those on both sides. A lack of rain had created the dry and dusty conditions; it was so dry, in fact, that nearby Nashville had put into effect a limited rationing of water.[5] These dusty conditions made visibility poor, and Van Dorn's force was well in toward Franklin before it was spotted. Granger acknowledged later that he had been expecting Van Dorn: "For several days previous I had received reports from Murfreesborough and Triune that such an attack would be made by General Van Dorn on the 9th instant."[6]

As they left Spring Hill and headed north to Franklin, the Confederates under Van Dorn took the Columbia–Franklin Pike, the most direct route into the city, until they got a few miles outside the town, still undetected. Then Van Dorn sent Forrest's division east two miles to the Lewisburg Pike, and Van Dorn himself stayed with the main body on the Columbia Road.

Forrest was now on the Lewisburg Pike heading north toward Franklin; Van Dorn, with General Jackson's division, was headed in the same direction on the Columbia Pike. Jackson's troops were led by the 1st Brigade, commanded by Colonel George B. Cosby. Forrest's long slim column was led by Brigadier General Frank C. Armstrong's brigade, and some two miles behind them was Colonel J. W. Starnes, leading Forrest's old brigade. Both Armstrong and Starnes were seasoned, experienced cavalry officers, accustomed to quick decisions and fast-paced action. Next came Colonel J. B. Biffle's 9th Tennessee, followed by four guns of Captain Sam Freeman's battery (the other section was with Armstrong). The Confederates may have believed reports that Franklin had been vacated by Granger's troops; their march was very leisurely, with as much as a mile between regiments.

The action opened at 12:20 P.M., when Jackson's advancing scouts collided with the 40th Ohio pickets on the south side of the Harpeth River. Since visibility was poor, the troops were at close range when Jackson's scouts opened fire. The first unit to reach the town was the 1st Mississippi Cavalry, with the 4th Tennessee Cavalry and the 28th Mississippi Cavalry close behind. According to regimental records, the 28th took by far the most casualties, probably because the Ohioans were surprised by the first charge of the 1st Mississippi but were ready for the 28th.

Private T. F. Jackson of the 1st Mississippi recalled, "Forrest with his command was to go in on the East Pike leading directly into town. He had a Company of Artillery following him to get a position in the rear of the Fort to batter it down. Van Dorn put the 1st Mississippi in to lead the charge, Noxubee Squadron in front. We had orders to charge as soon as we struck the pickets, with a speed to capture them, or go over the breastworks with them."[7]

The Union pickets were surprised, but they managed to return fire until they could reorganize and then pull back to a better defensive position in town. Their two top officers were both out sick that day, so the regiment was being commanded by Captain Charles G. Matchett, the senior officer present. The 40th did a fine job, holding off Jackson's men for almost two hours before being ordered back. They moved companies singly through town, covered by the rest of the regiment, and gradually backed across the Harpeth Bridge, covered by the artillery from the fort. Captain Matchett's report described his withdrawal:

> At this time I caused the men to retire from front to rear by company. This order was executed in admirable style, the front company retiring on double-quick to the rear of the other companies, where they came to the about and deliberately delivered their fire, until they again became the front company, when they again retired as before. In this manner, although exposed to a heavy fire from the enemy, we kept them on a pace less than double-quick until we gained the town, where we took advantage of the houses, yard fences, hedges &c, . . . which we converted into rifle pits, from whence we poured into the enemy's ranks a murderous fire.[8]

The action of the 40th Ohio had bought some time for Granger, who devised a plan to trap the Rebel cavalry. The 1,600 men in General Stanley's relief force were camped some four miles southeast of town at Hughes Mill, in an almost perfect position to flank and cut off all the Confederates. The plan was to send two infantry regiments from Gilbert's division down the river to join Stanley's cavalry. The combined force would then cross the river and attack the rear of the Confederates. Meantime, Granger would order Baird's division to cross the river in town using the pontoon bridge and assault Van Dorn from the front.

As with most battles, few things went as planned. Granger received a frantic dispatch from Brigadier General James D. Morgan, commanding in nearby Brentwood, that Morgan's pickets had been driven in and that Van Dorn was there in force. At that point Granger concluded that even though there were substantial numbers of Confederates to his front, the main attack was probably directed toward Brentwood. He considered the attacks by Van Dorn to be halfhearted and feeble, and this supported Granger's conclusion. He therefore sent his whole cavalry detachment under Brigadier General G. G. Smith to Brentwood, eight miles to the north.

Granger soon realized that Franklin, not Brentwood, was the target, but his cavalry had already left and it was too late to get them back. In his report he disgustedly wrote, "General James D. Morgan's pickets had been driven in only by three or four negroes."[9] Then, before Granger could fully develop his plan to reinforce Stanley, he received word that Stanley was across the river, headed for the Confederates and the gunfire. The order had just gone out to Gilbert to move his regiments to Stanley's aid, so Granger simply told them to get to Hughes Ford as quickly as they could, and he hoped for the best. He also ordered Baird's troops to hurry across the pontoon bridge, and counted on the troops in town to keep Van Dorn occupied. He felt his plan still had possibilities, so he moved his troops as fast as he could.

At this point there was a brief battle between Forrest's artillery, some of which were with Jackson in Franklin, and the guns of the 18th Ohio Artillery, in the fort in Franklin. Jackson's guns were unlimbered and set up by the Carter House in Franklin (a house that would later be enshrined for its part in the big battle of Franklin in November 1864). The Yankee artillery outgunned them substantially, with two large twenty-four-pound siege guns and two three-inch rifles. The bigger guns chased the Rebels out with little effort.

Baird's division was led by the 92d Illinois Infantry; the 92d double-timed across the bridge followed by four other regiments and a battery of artillery. Charles Cort of the 92d recollected later:

> When we got to the pontoon bridge we found the enemy had been closer than we thought. They made a very bold dash. Charged the pickets which were very strong but were repulsed three times, finally broke through and dashed through the town. Five of them, headed by a major, rode to the pontoon bridge, which is within 300 yards of the fort. The guard at the bridge fired, killing three and wounding the other two. The major's horse fell and he was taken prisoner. They must have been drunk!
>
> They tried to plant a battery within ¾ of a mile of the fort when the ol' sieges [guns] opened on them & drove them back. We saw 10 dead rebs and 2 of ours laying on the road. We went out 4 miles in a s.e. direction about dark, got up to our advance. The skirmishers were firing briskly. We filed to the left, formed a line of battle. We could see the bullets striking the road a few rods ahead of us.[10]

Just then the cavalry came onto the field and chased the Rebels back toward Spring Hill, and the infantry was marched back to Franklin. This ended the fighting for most of the Union infantry in Franklin, but not for the cavalry.

The clash in town was noisy and frantic. General Stanley, who was at Hughes's Mill, some distance from the firing, was an impatient man. When he heard the firing of Jackson's scouts and the 40th Ohio's pickets in town, he waited only briefly before he mounted his troops and galloped toward the firing. He crossed the Harpeth River and ran abruptly into parts of Forrest's brigade, strung out along the Lewisburg Pike and dawdling toward Franklin. Ahead of Freeman's artillery, Armstrong's brigade, followed by Starnes, had already passed by Hughes's Mill and was a part of the cavalry then waiting to assault Franklin. But because the Confederate pace was leisurely and its regiments so far apart, as Stanley crossed and headed toward the firing, he ran straight into Freeman's artillerymen, who were at some distance from the regiments in front and behind.

Stanley had crossed the ford and split his command before he surprised Forrest; he sent the 4th U.S. Cavalry by the shortest route to the pike, while the 2d Cavalry Brigade, under Lieutenant Colonel Oliver Robie, took a longer route. The guns that Stanley originally heard were far off, in or just outside Franklin, and none of his troopers had any idea there were Confederates close by. As they pounded toward the fight in Franklin, the 4th U.S. Cavalry crossed a shallow draw. Just as they crested the rise, they saw the guns of Freeman's artillery less than a hundred yards away. At the same time the Southern artillerymen spotted them, and Freeman called to his men to unlimber, load, and fire. Had they another five seconds they might have been able to do it, but the men of the 4th were regulars, from the old professional army; they never wavered, but bore down on the guns. One of the Confederates, James Hammer of the 21st Tennessee Cavalry, wrote home the next day:

> The day before yesterday our Brigade was ordered out with two days' rations and started toward Franklin. They went within about four miles of the town and were surprised by the enemy. The Brigade was marching very quietly along when the enemy suddenly "turned up" and charged our battery. They took the wheels off the guns and threw them in gullies on the side of the road. We had one regiment in the front and one in the rear of the battery, but everything was so unexpected that they could not get into position until the enemy had done considerable damage.[11]

Within seconds of the appearance of the 4th Cavalry the Rebel battery was in chaos. The caisson teams bolted, becoming entangled with each other, and there was much confusion. Over it all, Captain Freeman could be heard shouting, "Stop your firing; my men have surrendered!" And so it was that the captain, thirty-six artillerymen, and four guns were captured by the 4th U.S. Cavalry.[12]

In town, Forrest was worried. He had five regiments moving to his front, artillery had chased his guns out, and Stanley was to his rear, blocking one of his lines of retreat. When he was told of Stanley's appearance, Forrest cried out, "You say he is in Armstrong's rear, do you? Damn him, that's where I've been trying to get him all day! I'll be in his rear directly!"[13] Forrest then broke off his attack in town and headed back down the Lewisburg Pike.

The capture of Freeman's guns was a temporary Yankee victory. The Confederates who were on the road ahead of Freeman, Starnes's brigade, had passed that same area opposite Hughes's Mill some time earlier, and all had been quiet, but when the firing of the 4th Regular Cavalry began, Starnes immediately reversed his course and galloped back. Before they could reach Freeman, Starnes's brigade was hit by the rest of Stanley's Union cavalry, the 3d and 4th Ohio and parts of the 3d Indiana, which slowed down his rescue effort. Starnes drove straight at the Yankee cavalry and sent them back to Hughes's Mill and the safety of the opposite bank of the Harpeth River. Starnes's horse was killed under him; the horse had been given to him only the day before. He also lost an engraved sword, a present from Forrest himself.

As Starnes was fending off the attacks of Stanley's 2d Cavalry Brigade, the 4th had dismounted and began making its way back to the ford. The landscape was covered with fences, making any concerted cavalry charge difficult for either the Federals or the Confederates. Captain James B. McIntyre, commanding the 4th U.S. Cavalry, ordered a dismounted withdrawal back to the ford. He decided it was not possible to take Freeman's four guns back to his camp, so the U.S. troopers did what they could to destroy them, cutting the spokes and spiking the barrels. Then Captain McIntyre released all but thirty-three prisoners and double-timed toward the Mill, firing from the fences wherever possible. He was slowed by the prisoners, and during the withdrawal, two of the prisoners, Captain Freeman and Dr. Skelton, begged the Regulars to let them slow down. At that point, a Federal trooper approached, and both prisoners pleaded with him to let them rest. According to some sources, the trooper pulled his pistol and shot Freeman in the face, killing him, and then shot Skelton through the hand as he held up his arm to protect himself.[14]

There are other versions of the Freeman story, although no formal report was filed by the Confederates on the battle itself. Lieutenant A. L. Huggins, captured with Freeman and the others, reported, "Capt. Freeman was killed after he became a prisoner. The 4th U.S. Regulars were the capturing party, but whether he was killed by them or a stray shot is not known."[15]

One observation was that Freeman was shot by U.S. Sergeant Major Strickland of the 4th U.S. Cavalry. A 7th Pennsylvania Cavalry history confirmed that version, which reported that Freeman was not a prisoner when he was shot:

A short and desperate encounter took place over the guns. Freeman, knowing that Forrest's whole force was at hand, encouraged his men to fight to the last, and when he was completely overpowered, endeavored to retreat with two of his guns. Lt. Pendlebrook with two companies dashed after, and soon overtaking him, demanded his own and the surrender of the guns. Freeman refused, urged his horses on, firing his revolver almost in the face of the lieutenant. At his 3rd shot Sgt. Major Strickland, with a single shot from his revolver, laid him dead on the road . . . Sgt Major Strickland killed Capt. Freeman in a fair fight, and Capt. Freeman's bravery required no false statement, such as made, to perpetuate his memory.[16]

The *Atlanta Southern Confederacy* screamed a conflicting view:

We have met with a reverse. We learn by reliable persons that Gen. Van Dorn, with his cavalry, attacked a heavy force of the enemy near Franklin and was repulsed. Captain Freeman's battery was captured, but retaken after a desperate struggle by our men, in which Freeman was taken prisoner, and—hear it humanity!—was murdered in cold blood!—Murdered after he had been taken prisoner— Murdered for his bravery in fighting for his home. An act so horrible, so hellish, would apal the heart of the wont Bedouin, but the invaders of our soil revel in its blackness.[17]

Dr. Skelton was exchanged soon after his surrender. He noted that he was with Freeman at the time he was killed and swore that the report made to the effect that Freeman had resisted and tried to escape was false and untrue.[18]

General Forrest had been with the lead units; after the battle, he came onto the field to see Freeman's body. "As he came up to the spot where the body of Freeman was discovered, Forrest, deeply agitated, dismounted and took Freeman's hand in his to see if he were really dead. With tears welling from his eyes, and in a voice trembling with emotion, he said, 'Brave man; none braver!' "[19]

The battle was over, but the ripples from it lingered on. Freeman's funeral—on Sunday, April 12, in Spring Hill—was attended by many of Forrest's troopers, including the general himself. The *Atlanta Southern Confederacy* reported:

> His burial took place yesterday at Spring Hill, and was attended by both military and civilians. I noticed General Forrest and Col. Starnes among others in the assembly. Deep sorrow was visible in every face. Even Gen. Forrest—that bronzed warrior, who has gazed unmoved upon the desolation of so many battlefields became a child again, weeping tears of unfeigned grief to see his faithful companion-in-arms, his tower of strength in time of need, fallen so low. Captain Freeman was a model soldier, an excellent gentleman and a true Christian.[20]

The Reverend W. W. Whitsett, who presided at the somber scene, described the emotion of the general: "The next day was Sunday, and I officiated at Freeman's funeral. General Forrest stood at the side of the grave, his tall form bent and swayed by his grief. It was a sight to remember always, the sternest soldier of the army bathed in tears and trembling like an aspen leaf with his pain."[21]

The Union *Nashville Dispatch* report of the battle appeared on April 12: "47 Confederate prisoners were brought into town yesterday evening, said to have been captured near Triune. Among them were Robert Allison and a son of Judge Baxter's. There were rumors of further fighting in the neighborhood of Franklin yesterday but we did not learn any particulars."[22] Lieutenant Nat Baxter and Sergeant R. A. Allison appear on Forrest's report as having been captured in the Franklin fight.

Total casualties were not always easy to determine, and this clash was no exception. Some records do exist, such as Forrest's casualty report; however, the Confederate casualty reports from Jackson's division were never filed, which was not unusual. The Union casualty reports filed by Granger show that his forces had four killed, two severely wounded, two mortally wounded, and nine taken prisoner. Stanley reported six killed, nineteen wounded, and seventeen taken prisoner. Other regimental morning reports listed another man missing and three more wounded. Total Union losses were sixty-three men. Granger's report also indicated that he felt confident that the Rebel losses were at least three hundred. Of the Union wounded, the four in Granger's report all subsequently died of wounds.

Two officers in Stanley's 4th U.S. cavalry died of their wounds.[23]

These two were veteran officers from the old prewar cavalry. Lieutenant Thomas Healy, a native of Ireland, had previously been wounded in Indian fighting in September 1855. Shortly after that he was accidentally shot in the right heel while he was cleaning his Colt pistol, and he was discharged in July 1856 with the bullet still in his foot. His disability certificate said he was totally disabled and was entitled to $8 per month. He never drew any disability funds, but reenlisted on November 1, 1856, as he explained it, "on account of unexpected restoration to health." He died in Franklin on April 23, 1863, at age thirty-three.[24]

The other wounded 4th Cavalry officer was First Lieutenant Thomas W. Simson of New York. Simson had enlisted in the U.S. Army in October 1858 and had been with the 4th Cavalry Regiment for his entire career. His wound incapacitated him to the extent that he never was able to resume duty; he retired from service on February 22, 1865, and on October 26 of that same year he died as a result of his wounds.[25]

Confederate casualties listed in Forrest's report to Van Dorn included five killed, thirty-two wounded, and thirty-three captured; of the wounded, four had mortal wounds. While neither Jackson nor Van Dorn filed reports, service records of the units involved show sixteen killed or died of wounds, twelve wounded, and thirteen captured. These are incomplete records, but they do match closely the totals reported by the 40th Ohio, which was the main target of Jackson's attack. Its report counted seventeen Confederates killed, fourteen wounded, and ten taken prisoner. That would fix the casualty totals at Union 63, Confederate 111. These are probably the most realistic figures available.

Other reports differ, some substantially. Charles A. Cooper's *Chronological & Alphabetical Record of Engagements of the Great Civil War* lists 100 U.S. casualties, 139 Confederate.[26] Benson J. Lossing's *A History of the Civil War* states almost the same—Union, 100 casualties; Confederate, 137.[27] An eyewitness account by Charles E. Cort asserted that up until dark, his unit (40th Ohio) had found 147 dead Rebels;[28] Stanley reported that he had captured and released due to battle conditions 400 to 500 Rebels, undoubtedly a somewhat inflated figure. Frederick H. Dyer's *Compendium* established Union casualties at 59.[29] General Thomas Jordan and J. P. Pryor's *Campaigns of General Forrest* stated: "The loss on the part of the Federals in this fruitless affair is reported by them to be 'less than 100.' The Confederate loss in Forrest's Division was 3 killed, 10 wounded and 30 prisoners, which was scarcely equalled by Jackson's Division."[30]

Newspapers from both North and South used their own estimates, downplaying their own side's losses while exaggerating enemy losses.

The real lesson of statistics, even in small battles, is that accuracy is often sacrificed for drama. This gives cause to suspect any precise figure given for the awesome events such as Gettysburg, Vicksburg, Shiloh, or Spotsylvania. Losses in engagements covering large amounts of time and territory are virtually impossible to report accurately.

In spite of the death and maiming, the day had some lighter moments, as reported by some of the veterans. As Morton's battery of General Jackson's artillery was marching up the Columbia Pike toward Franklin, a messenger came to the battery and asked where he could find Captain Morton. "At the head of the column," he was told. He moved on up the column and asked again, getting the same answer. When he reached the head of the column and saw a slim, beardless youngster, he hesitated and asked again. "I don't want to make a mistake and give this message to the wrong person," he confided. "If I give this order to that boy, Forrest'll give me hell!"[31] The commanding general was only twenty-eight; young leaders were not a rarity in either army.

The Franklin battle was of little consequence. No territory changed hands, and the tactics used by both sides were mediocre at best. But in typical Civil War fashion, the troops themselves performed admirably. The 28th Mississippi was cited by Brigadier General Jackson in General Orders No. 10 for the "gallant and meritorious conduct of the officers and men of the 28th Mississippi Cavalry, First Brigade, in the charge upon Franklin today."[32] The 3d Indiana Cavalry took notice of the behavior of three of its men: General Orders No. 13 of the 3d Battalion, 3d Indiana Cavalry, demoted Sergeant Nickolas Kastner, Company K, for cowardice; Corporal Philip Yackey was promoted to take his place; and Private Magnus became the new corporal.[33]

The senseless killing of Captain Freeman exemplified the pointlessness of the whole engagement. However, although Freeman's death might have been more dramatic, the deaths of Healy, Simson, and the others for no apparent purpose illustrated the futility of many engagements of the Civil War.

★

General Van Dorn was killed by a physician on May 8, 1863, in a love dispute.

Franklin would host a much bloodier battle in November 1864. Five Confederate generals died in that clash.

Union General Stanley received the Medal of Honor for his part in the November 1864 battle of Franklin.

Dr. Colonel J. W. Starnes, who rescued Freeman's guns, was killed at Tullahoma, Tennessee, on June 28, 1863.

Alphonso Charles Webster, a brash and daring—and deceitful—Union captain was executed in Richmond on April 10, 1863, for violating parole. His last words: "I never thought it would come to this."

Soldiers used their gumption and whatever materials they could find to create makeshift homes in their camps. This sketch of the Army of the Potomac's camps in the spring of 1863 show a wagoneer's shanty (top left), a deserted picket hut (top right), and a typical camp scene. *(Library of Congress)*

President Abraham Lincoln, with Major General Joseph "Fighting Joe" Hooker at his right, inspects the Army of the Potomac on Monday, April 6, at Falmouth, Virginia. The reviews continued over the next few days, and the president left to return to Washington on April 10. Though facing political trouble in the capital, Lincoln was warmly received by the troops, mutually boosting morale. *(Library of Congress)*

See Gen. Hooker's letter
April 11th 1863

My opinion is, that just now, with the enemy directly ahead of us, there is no eligible route for us into Richmond; and consequently a question of preference between the Rappahannock route, and the James River route is a contest about nothing. Hence our prime object is the enemies' army in front of us, and is not with, or about, Richmond at all, unless it be incidental to the main object.

What then? The two armies are face to face with a narrow river between them. Our communications are shorter and safer than are those of the enemy. For the same reason, we can, with equal power, fret him now than he can us. I do not think that by raids towards Washington he can derange the Army of the Potomac at all. He has no distant operations which can call any of the Army of the Potomac away; we have such operations which may call him away, at least in part. While he remains intact, I do not think we should take the disadvantage of attacking him in his entrenchments; but we should continually harass and menace him, so that he shall have no leisure, nor safety in sending away detachments. If he weakens himself, then pitch into him.

Notes written by Lincoln aboard the *Carrie Martin* during his return trip to Washington. He cautions General Hooker, "Our primary object now is the enemie's [sic] army . . . not with or about Richmond . . . We should continually harass [Lee] so that he shall know no rest." (*Library of Congress*)

Captain George A. Custer and Brigadier General Alfred Pleasanton on April 10 at Falmouth, Virginia, the headquarters of the Army of the Potomac. *(Library of Congress)*

Elisha H. Rhodes, a first lieutenant in the Army of the Potomac, had recently returned from leave and spent April 10 on picket duty. His diary describes frequent, but not always unfriendly, contact between Yankees and Rebels. *(Robert Hunt Rhodes)*

At top is the home just outside Fredericksburg, Virginia, that was General Lee's headquarters on April 10. Below is General Thomas J. "Stonewall" Jackson's. *(Library of Congress)*

Before he was elected president, James Garfield served as brigadier general in the Army of the Cumberland. He wrote home on April 10 describing the logistics of obtaining supplies and preparing for battle. *(Library of Congress)*

Union Colonel Orlando Poe headed home to Michigan on April 10. Poe had led his men through several battles and had been recommended for promotion to brigadier general, but for unknown reasons his commission was not renewed. *(Library of Congress)*

Lieutenant Nat Baxter, Jr.,
of Freeman's Artillery was one
of about thirty Confederate prisoners
captured on April 10 at the First Battle
of Franklin, Tennessee.

Confederate Major General Joseph Wheeler,
the other "Fighting Joe" and a brilliant
cavalry strategist, led the daring April 10
attack on the Louisville and Nashville
railway line. *(Library of Congress)*

CASUALTY SHEET.

Name, *Frank M. Vanderbaugh*

Rank, *First Lieut*, Company *E.*, Regiment *10th Michigan*

Arm, *Infantry*, State, *Michigan*

Place of casualty, *Near Lavergne Tennessee, in action with Guerrillas.*

Nature of casualty. *Wounded Mortally*

Date of casualty, *April 10th 1863*

FROM WHAT SOURCE THIS INFORMATION WAS OBTAINED.

Report of Killed, Wounded, and Missing of the *10th* Regiment, *Head Quarters 10th Regt M.V.I.* Brigade, Division, Corps, dated *April 10 1863*

Official Reports 1862 & 1863
Army of the Cumberland p. 150
Vol Army Register reports " First Lieut Frank M. Vanderburgh
"Died April 18th 1863 of wounds received in Action."

D. D. Davidson
9—14—'76   Clerk.

The last entry in the service record of First Lieutenant Frank M. Vanderburgh, killed on April 10 defending the Nashville and Chattanooga Railroad against Confederate raiders near Nashville, Tennessee. (*National Archives*)

One of the Union blockhouses protecting the Nashville and Chattanooga Railroad. The Rebels snuck very close to one of these blockhouses and ambushed Vanderburgh and his men, who, believing they were near safety, had relaxed their guard. *(Library of Congress)*

Corydon Foote, a 14-year-old drummer boy with the 10th Michigan, witnessed the April 10 train raid on the Nashville and Chattanooga line. His memoirs, though at times overblown, capture the drama of the raid. *(Corydon Foote)*

Confederate Major General Richard Taylor, son of U.S. president Zachary Taylor, made camp with his men in the Louisiana swamps. A few days later, they would repulse the Union's attack, and Taylor would be cited for outstanding performance. *(Library of Congress)*

On April 10, thousands of Union forces were in Brashear City, Louisiana, preparing to move on Bayou Teche to find food and forage. *(Harper's Weekly)*

On April 10 a Confederate expedition was struggling through the swamps on a mission to salvage guns from the *Barrataria,* a Union ironclad steamer that had run aground and been burned and abandoned three days earlier. *(Harper's Weekly)*

10

TRAIN RAIDS AND
OTHER EXPEDITIONS

The railroads played a critical role in the North; the lines were crucial to the movement and support of the troops. The Union was very fortunate to have excellent railroads and superior railroad management under Brigadier General Herman Haupt and others. By the spring of 1863, the Southern rail system was in a sad state of repair, partly because the South refused to centralize control of the railroads, leaving their maintenance to the states. Manpower was in short supply in the South, and even the slaves weren't always available to work on the railroads.

But the railroads were also vulnerable; as the war moved deeper into the Southern states, the genius and daring of the Confederate cavalry pestered the Union railroad operation on an almost daily basis. During the first two years of the war, both Tennessee and Virginia were almost constant battlegrounds, depleting local supplies in those areas and making the railroads in every sense the Union army's lifeline.

In Tennessee, fortified blockhouses and train guards provided the only protection for the trains. That was not considered first-rate duty. Nor were the forts ideal, according to Theodore Upson of the 10th Michigan, who wrote home on March 10, 1863:

> We are in our stocade. It is a structure perhaps 50′ in dimetre, circular in form, made of logs flattened on two sides set upright in the ground, and the tops which are sharpened project about 8 or 9 feet above the ground, where they are firmly set like posts. There are loop holes for musketry and a small opening covered by a curtain made in the same manner as the main structure. A ditch sourrounds the whole with the dirt thrown against the logs. This would make an excellent defence against Cavelry or Infantry but a few shells would soon knock it to pieces.

Upson also mentioned the dangers of the duty: "Our principal duty is to patrol the Rr. [Memphis and Charleston] for a distance of 2½ miles in either direction, day or night. Our chief danger is that (as has been the case) a bushwacker may slip up and pick off the lonely patrol as he walks his beat. There are so few of us now (so many sick) that we are on duty half of every other night."[1]

In addition to manning these isolated and lonely posts, the army supplied troops to trains to guard against attack by the Rebel cavalry. However, the disadvantage of railroads is that the trains have to go where the tracks lead, and that was often into a Rebel ambush.

THE L & N RAILROAD

On April 10 there were two train raids in middle Tennessee. One was virtually within earshot of the troops in Franklin, although it would have been difficult for any of the Franklin troops to hear anything over the din they were making themselves.

The Army of the Cumberland in Murfreesboro received its supplies from Louisville over the tracks of the L & N (the Louisville and Nashville line), to Nashville, and then down to Murfreesboro on the N & C (the Nashville and Chattanooga line). These lines were fair game for the bold, efficient cavalry under Forrest, Wheeler, Van Dorn, and Brigadier General John Hunt Morgan.

The giant Union Army of the Cumberland and the smaller but impressive Confederate Army of Tennessee had been camped opposite each other just south of Nashville, eighteen miles apart, since January 4.[2] Although the armies had been quiet, their cavalry units had not. The Rebel cavalry had fought repeated engagements against Union outposts such as Franklin, and frequently attacked the supply lines from Louisville to Nashville and Nashville to Murfreesboro. In spite of the impressive lines of Union troops, Confederate cavalry usually controlled the area between Union strongholds.

Major General Joseph Wheeler was one of the Confederate cavalry's best-known leaders. Only twenty-seven, he was nicknamed "Fightin' Joe," just as was the Army of the Potomac's General Hooker. Wheeler was only four years out of West Point, where he had graduated nineteenth out of his twenty-two-man class. Although his class standing was not impressive, he was considered a bright young officer. He had just published a book on cavalry maneuvers that was adopted and distributed by General Joseph Johnston; it was considered the definitive work on the subject. Wheeler had learned in the field, and he had digested the lessons well.

On Friday, April 10, 1863, Wheeler was in charge of two train raids, which he had been planning since April 7. Although he had 6,000 men in his cavalry corps, he needed only a fraction of them to make the two raids. Wheeler decided to take the division led by Colonel J. A. Wharton, numbering about 1,900 men, and 500 troopers under Colonel Basil W. Duke to accompany him and attack the L & N cars, while Lieutenant Colonel S. C. Ferrill and 500 of his best men were to find and destroy the train from Murfreesboro on the N & C line. At dawn on April 10 these men left Liberty, Tennessee, headed for Lebanon, some thirty miles away.

The day was dry, windy, and dusty, but the troopers were all in good spirits as they headed west, looking forward to another go at the railroad and the Yankees. Wheeler's plan was to leave most of his force at the Hermitage, the beautiful plantation home of former president Andrew Jackson, and split the attacking force. As they passed the Hermitage, Wheeler and Wharton, leading the troops of Colonel Thomas Harrison and Colonel Charles C. Crews, turned north toward the Cumberland River and the L & N line; Ferrill and his men turned southwest to Antioch to hit the N & C line, while Colonel Duke was assigned to guard the roads behind the raiders. Passing by the Hermitage was noted by Robert Bunting, chaplain of the 8th Texas Cavalry: "Its warm and dusty and we roll on at a brisk gate right in sight of the sleeping dust of Old Hickory—the place looks beautiful."[3]

These Southerners were in high hopes that they were headed for Kentucky; in that lush land would be food, forage, and easy pickings. They were following the route they had taken on a Kentucky raid the previous fall, so the minute they turned north, Kentucky was uppermost in their minds. That was not to be; their destination was Payne's Landing, ten miles from Nashville on the south bank of the Cumberland. The Cumberland would not be crossed, and Kentucky was just a dream.

Bunting noticed that the advance caused some surprise on the part of the local citizens:

> Onward we moved greatly to the astonishment of the inhabitants, for had one risen from the dead they would scarcely have been more surprised than to see Confederate cavalry on the high way toward Nashville. But their actions plainly declared that they were with us in sentiment. Along the pike we see large wheat fields, and considerable preparation for planting corn.
>
> There is no destruction of fences until within a few miles of the Hermitage where the work is complete for a good distance. But the

citizens have built in places and are trying to raise bread. Although there is scarce anything left to work the land with, for the last Yankee raid swept all the horses for miles.[4]

As they came to the riverbank, General Wheeler posted his artillery battery with its six-pounders, commanded by Lieutenant Arthur Pice, behind some bushes, out of sight. Wheeler had picked this particular spot because it was midway between two Yankee guard posts and near enough to them to see and hear the Union guards. He silently dismounted his two regiments. He had posted segments of the attacking force to his rear to protect his wagon trains, left by the Hermitage turnoff, and ordered part of Colonel Duke's brigade to picket and defend approaches to the Hermitage.[5] All he had to do was wait for the expected train from Louisville.

Early in the morning of April 10, in Bowling Green, Kentucky, Edwin Worden was getting ready to go to work. Worden was a twenty-four-year-old private in Company B, 23d Michigan Infantry Regiment, from East Saginaw, Michigan, and had been in Bowling Green almost from the time he had enlisted in September 1862.[6] His job was to ride the railroad cars on the L & N down to Nashville, then back to Bowling Green on the way to Louisville, guarding against any attacks by the Confederates. On April 10 he was one of twenty-five guards assigned to newly promoted Second Lieutenant Elbridge G. Wellington from St. Johns, Michigan. The duty wasn't too bad, and the dangers were minimal. "You need not be troubled if I should be captured by guerrillas. They were never known to hurt anyone. They simply take all a man has got, parole him and let him go," wrote E. C. Dawes of the 53d Ohio Infantry while he was manning one of the stockade/blockhouses near Nashville.[7]

The train left Louisville at ten o'clock in the morning, pulling eighteen cars, loaded mostly with horses and beef cattle for the troops in Murfreesboro. Some of the new guard cars had been heavily fortified to protect the men, who would be virtually unprotected in most cars. Michigan Private A. S. Bloomfield described the new cars: "On every train there was one car for the guards. They are planked up on the sides and ends with three inch planks with port holes to shoot through. I saw one today that looked like a lamb monitar. It had a wooden turret that is a little higher than the car. It was large enough for one piece of artillery."[8] Unfortunately, Worden's train had no such protection; he rode with the other guards on an open platform car in the middle of the train.

The guards had been alert, but the closer they got to the Nashville fortifications, the more relaxed they became. Worden and his fellow guards were probably looking forward to a few hours in Nashville before catching the return train later that night.

As the train, running slowly, approached Nashville on the north side of the Cumberland, the tracks were at the level of the river. They were passing near a place called Neely's Bend, with a bluff on the right and the river on the left.

Across the wide Cumberland River, at four P.M., Wheeler's waiting was over. The first of Lieutenant Pice's six-pounder shells hit the locomotive dome, the second hit the boiler of the engine, and the train slowly stopped. The din was numbing for the Union guards; even though the Rebels were 300 yards from the train, the cannon fire, fire from the muskets of the dismounted Rebel cavalry, the return fire of the Michigan guard, and the screams of the terrified and wounded animals, combined with the high-pitched shriek of the steam escaping from the engine, made it impossible to hear any orders that might have been given. The fire of the dismounted Confederate horsemen was directed primarily at the train guards, and it chased them back behind the cars. There they fired away at the Rebels for the rest of the brief fight. The Rebels could not cross the river, so they just kept throwing shells into the locomotive, completely destroying it, and into the poor beasts in the cars. The whole affair lasted only from four to four-thirty P.M., with the Rebels firing thirty-five artillery rounds plus the musket fire of the regiments. In all the firing, only one Confederate was wounded—along with two Union guards, one slightly and one severely. The horses and cattle suffered much more, according to Bunting: "In the meantime, the dismounted men pour volley after volley into the cars, wounding and killing the horses and cattle aboard. It seems they were shipping horses for mounted infantry. From the disturbance among the dumb animals great destruction must have been the result."[9]

One of the early artillery shells exploded near Worden and virtually blew off his right arm.[10] The shell also wounded Allen Barnum, another private from Company B, originally from Taymouth, Michigan. He was lucky; he was hit only slightly in the shoulder, and he managed to survive the war.

A blockhouse manned by the men of Company F, 70th Indiana Infantry, was not too far from the train wreck; D. N. Ransdell of that unit recorded in his diary on April 10:

There was great excitement today on account of the rebs firing into a freight train on the banks of the Cumberland River six miles from here. Close to the blockhouse at Mansco Creek where a detachment of Co. F of our Regt is stationed they fired from the opposite side of the river with one battery they completely disabled the engine. Tom Fowler and Joe Adair were near the place when it happened having gone down with the team to take rations to the detachments E & F. But they did not get to witness it. But heard it mighty plain.[11]

N & C RAILROAD

As Wheeler was leading his forces north that morning, the rest of the attackers, under Lieutenant Colonel Ferrill, were headed for another train on the Nashville and Chattanooga tracks. George Turner of Ferrill's Texas Rangers summarized the raid in a letter to his father dated May 5:

> And ten picked men from each company of the [Texas] Rangers and a company of the 11th Texas were sent under the command of Col. Ferrill. We were ordered up at midnight, went out on the Nashville Pike 8 or 10 miles, and turned off through the cedars, passing through and around plantations and fording Stones River we found ourselves on the RR about 7 or 8 miles from Nashville, and in the neighborhood of a large stockade defended by a force of infantry.[12]

As close as they were to the blockhouse, they still were able to sneak down and pry one of the rails loose on a bend in the railroad. As the Texans were preparing their ambush, Union First Lieutenant Frank M. Vanderburgh was relaxing on his detail with forty privates, four noncoms, and his next in command, Lieutenant H. Walter Nichols, riding the cars from Murfreesboro to Nashville. They had shepherded an earlier train down from Nashville and now were coming back to the camp of Company E of the 10th Michigan Volunteer Infantry Regiment. This train had no freight but was carrying passengers back to Nashville, including forty-six Confederate prisoners headed for Union prisons.

Vanderburgh was twenty-four, a native of New York, but recently a resident of Port Huron, Michigan. He had enlisted in December 1861, and had risen from the ranks to first lieutenant in September 1862. He was a quiet, well-liked officer who had been with the guard since January and was very serious about his duties.[13]

At almost exactly four-thirty P.M., the train came into view. As soon as it was close enough, the Texas Rangers let go with their first shot. The round hit the train engine in the boiler, and the engine left the track. The first volley was devastating to the guards, who were riding either on an open platform car or on the tops of the passenger cars.

The guards returned the fire as well as they could; Vanderburgh ordered his forty-five men to jump from the cars and fire away at the Confederates. Ranger George Turner said, "They [the 10th] returned the fire in an instant and jumping out and rallying behind the Cars were about to make us a stubborn fight, when the old Col. ordered a charge and we rushed with a yell, which made them take to an open field. Some of us chased them across it into the woods, killing several in the pursuit."[14]

Vanderburgh reorganized his men behind a cedar fence line, where they held off a pursuing band of Rebels. The lieutenant had been hit in the first volley, a minor wound in the leg, then hit again in the shoulder, but was still standing. Ranger Turner, who was at the fence, went on: "A Yankee officer . . . was getting over the fense. One of the old 11th [Texas Cavalry] was after him and ordered him to surrender but he only replied by hacking at him with his sword, and Texas dropped him in a fense corner with his six shooter.[15]

The Yankee lieutenant, seriously wounded in the stomach, in addition to his other wounds, was now down. Nichols ordered the surviving guards to fall back to the nearest blockhouse, on Mill Creek.

As the Michigan guards retreated, the Rebels faced a scene of much disorder. All shots had been fired at very close range, ten to fifty yards, with devastating effect. There were a number of dead and wounded and more than one hundred passengers to take back to Spring Hill or release. The Confederates, moving with little hesitation, went through the cars gathering everything of value: passengers' personal effects, mail, and an Adams Express Company safe. If Joseph Wheeler's report is believed, the amount in the safe was $30,000 in Federal greenbacks.[16] Other booty was a pistol and equipment that had been presented to General Rosecrans by his officers. Then the Rebels set fire to the train.

After the cars had been completely looted and the passengers relieved of watches, wallets, and valuables, the ladies on the train were helped to nearby homes.

George Turner described the scene:

> The rest of the boys dragged the wounded out of the Cars, secured the prisoners (106) helped out the ladies, two Michagan dames, ripped open the mailbags trunks and boxes, and tumbled out the iron safe of Adams Express and burst it open with rocks. All this was done before one could pass leisurely from one end of the Cars to

the other; we then set fire to the train, trotted off our prisoners, and a couple of the boys gallantly took the Ladies up behind them and carried them to the first house. After getting over their fright, they expressed themselves satisfied with the sudden change in their programme, for two very good reasons, said they, first that they came off without even a bullet hole through their calico and secondly that their curiousity regarding Texas Rangers were satisfied. *viz*—we were white men, good looking, and did things with a *vim*.[17]

Colonel Benjamin F. Scribner, of the 38th Indiana Infantry, later recalled:

My wife had quite an adventure on her way. The railroad at LaVerge was obstructed and the train was attacked by guerillas; they fired into the car windows, scattering the broken glass about, to the consternation of the passengers who filled the cars. Gen. Brannin was on board and called out, "All lie down on the floor!" My wife, huddling together the two children, crouched down between the seats and while shielding them as best she could from the falling fragments of glass, was asked in an excited voice by her 4 year old boy, "Mamma, will they kill us?" The mother replied, "No, my son, God will take care of us." The lad rejoined, "Then why don't He stop the firing?"[18]

In their haste, the raiders missed numerous items. Norwegian Colonel Hans Christian Heg of the 15th Wisconsin sent a letter to his wife:

We have had some excitement here today. The rebels captured the train that went up to Nashville yesterday and took several prisoners and all the money they could find. Christen started on that train for Nashville yesterday & had about $2,000 with him—mostly belonging to himself and Evan & we had great fears he was gone up the spout—but a few minutes ago—we got a telegraph dispatch that he was allright—he was captured but it seems he got away with the money all safe. It took a big load off Evans shoulders.

The next day he wrote:

Christen sent a letter down today from Nashville, giving us an account of his experiences among the rebels . . . He saved his money by putting it in his Boots . . . I saw him the night before he left & told him what he ought to do in a case of that kind. That I had put what money I had at Stones River in my boots and that was all that saved him, I expect.[19]

An article in the *Cincinnati Daily Commercial* indicated that Christen's cash was not all the Confederates missed:

Captain Goodwin, Asst. Provost Marshal General of the Department [of the Cumberland] succeeded in escaping, with all his important papers. Mr. Estbrook, the mail agent, escaped after his clothing had been ransacked and stolen by a chivalrous freebooter. Mr. Shine, cotton speculator of St. Louis, also escaped. Wm. Watt Truesdale, general newspaper agent for this army, was among the captives. Some 30 or 40 sutlers, with large amounts of greenbacks, were among the prisoners, also a nephew of Maj. Gen. Rousseau [Commanding General, 1st Division, XIV Corps], who was returning home with $14,000, intrusted to his care by soldiers, for delivery to their families . . . Col. Hamilton, medical inspector of this department, was among the captives . . . One of the majors of the 1st Middle Tennessee (Stokes) Cavalry, who was captured, was threatened with death as soon as the enemy should reach Lebanon.[20]

The *Nashville Union* also highlighted the raid, reporting, "We regret to learn that Lieutenant Henry of Knoxville, an officer in the 1st Tennessee Cavalry, was killed in the attack on the Murfreesboro train. After being shot he was robbed of $20 and his boots stolen by the Southern Chivalry."[21]

General Wheeler's report concluded:

He [Colonel Ferrill] thinks he killed not less than 100 and wounded a large number. We took about 70 prisoners, including 20 officers, among whom are 2 colonels, 1 major and 3 of General Rosecrans' staff officers. Colonel Ferrill paroled the enlisted men, 1 captain and 7 lieutenants. We brought off the other officers, and about $30,000 in greenbacks, together with a large mail. We also retook 40 of our soldiers, who were on their way to Camp Chase. Colonel Ferrill destroyed the train, and broke up the road and telegraph. Our loss was one man wounded.[22]

Two eyewitness reports stated that two unidentified Confederate officers, prisoners on the train, were also killed in the gunfire during the attack.[23]

As the Rebel cavalrymen were looting, caring for their wounded, taking the ladies to shelter, and burning the train, Lieutenant Nichols and the guard survivors found a blockhouse manned by Company I, 10th Michigan, only a short distance away. The noncom in charge there was an old-timer, forty-year-old Sergeant Thomas Branch, an Irishman who had not only been in the Union army since November 1861 but had served in the British army for almost two years. Actually, he had been promoted to second lieutenant on March 31, 1863, but since the paper-work was still unfinished, he was officially just a sergeant. Lieutenant Nichols and Sergeant Branch, with Branch's fifteen men, headed back to the train wreck just as Ferrill's men were leaving.

Corydon Foote, a fourteen-year-old drummer boy with the 10th Michigan, was on the train with the others from the 10th, just for the ride. His memoirs, written in the third person, relived the scene:

Cord set off on the run to Sergeant Tom's stockade. He raced ahead through the woods, sped by the fury that filled him against the marauders who had shot down Lieutenant Vanderburgh. Sergeant Tom and his men, in search of the firing, were approaching at the double-quick, and Cord was relieved to meet them.

"What's going on down there, Footey," was the sergeant's low-voiced greeting.

"It's guerrillas, sir," Cord told him breathlessly, "a howling mob of 'em! . . ."

"Are you all that got away?"

"No, sir. There's some comin' back with Lieutenant Nicholls. You'll find 'em in a minute, if you keep on. Oh, sir, can't you make 'em go back an' scare off those devil guerrillas the way you did the Johnnies a while ago?"

There was a responsive gleam in Sergeant Tom's eyes.

"Sure I can, boy, as sure as my name's Big Tom." He turned to give instructions to one of his men to go back to the stockade and send the other five men, while he went on to the scene of the attack.

Soon the remnants of those who had escaped from the train led by Lieutenant Nicholls were joined by Sergeant Tom and his men. They made their low voiced plans, scarcely a stone's throw from the blazing train, while they waited for reinforcements from the stock-ade. Cord stayed close to the big Irishman, ready to carry out any order he might be given.

Lieutenant Nicholls and Sergeant Branch decided to separate their forces. Taking advantage of the cover given by the burgeoning foliage, they thought to close in from two sides. The unwary guerrillas, still moving about the flaming train, sorting out plunder and gathering their wounded for departure, would be taken by surprise.

When Sergeant Tom and his men burst upon them with a mighty yelling and firing, and Lieutenant Nicholls and his men appeared no less savagely from another quarter, the guerrillas were routed by the suddenness and violence of the attack. Springing to horse, almost without offering any resistance, they fled wildly along the track and into the woods, leaving their plunder, eight riderless horses and six dead upon the field.[24]

George Turner's Confederate version was less dramatic:

We had just regained our horses when the Infantry from the Stockade came up and poured a volley into us. Taking our Yanks up behind us we galloped out of the way . . . There were large forces of Cavalry near by and we had to work with caution and dispatch, the prisoners were confident of being re-captured, so much so that, after crossing the river and trotting them on foot about 14 miles, one-half of the Officers refused to be paroled.[25]

When the smoke cleared and it was obvious the Rebels were on their way back to their camp, Nichols and Branch began putting out the fires on the train. The wounded were moved to nearby houses, made as comfortable as possible, and treated by an unidentified surgeon.[26] Then they were taken to Nashville General Hospital.

Again, a summary of casualties is made difficult by the variety of reports, official and unofficial. The best compilation would show that five train guards, one Union passenger, and two Confederate prisoners were killed in the attack; three would later die of their wounds, eight others were wounded; and three guards and twelve passengers were captured. Two of the three guards were released without parole at the scene. Wheeler reported one man wounded. Union reports indicated that six Confederates were found dead at the scene, but these bodies could have been the Confederate passengers and Union casualties.

Lieutenant Vanderburgh was taken to Nashville General with the others, but his wounds were mortal. He lived until April 18, giving his father enough time to travel from Port Huron, Michigan, to Nashville to be with his dying son. After young Frank's death, his grieving father took his body back to Port Huron. The congregation attending his memorial service was the largest ever assembled in a Port Huron house of worship. In an eloquent, emotional oration at young Vanderburgh's service, his final moments were dramatically recounted by the Reverend J. S. Hoyt:

> One scene more. A father has gone hundreds of miles to stand by the couch on which lies his wounded patriot son. One fight he has finished. His hand is no more uplifted in war against rebels. With an earnest, and noble, and patriotic and Christian resignation, he is waiting for death, "the last enemy" to strike the final blow . . . During the last hour of his life, he prayed for himself, his friends briefly, but the burden of his prayer was his country. Fervently, most fervently, did our gallant, our noble, our beloved, our honored, our lamented soldier, Frank, pray for our country when, having fallen in her defence, he was passing from earth to heaven. Father of the fallen son! Friends of the beloved companion; this black cloud is arched by a glorious bow. Drop a tear and catch a ray of joy. Ye bend over a patriot, a Christian soldier, whose time of departure had come, who fought a good fight, who finished his course, who kept the faith, whose crowns the Lord, the righteous Judge, will bestow upon him in His own good time.[27]

With so many troops guarding the trains and manning the block-houses along the tracks, it is hard to comprehend how these two raids could have been as successful as they were. Where the captured money went is anyone's guess. One of the raiders lamented the fact that he'd missed the raid—"and my share of the greenbacks."[28]

WAVERLY, TENNESSEE

The countryside in Tennessee and southern Kentucky was the setting for frequent minor skirmishes throughout the war. Both sides were raiding—seeking horses, forage, food, and men to replenish the constant drains the war imposed on them. April 10, 1863, was no exception, even though it was a quiet day by most wartime standards.

One April 10 encounter occurred in Waverly, Tennessee, in the northwestern part of the state. Major Horace J. Blanton had been scouting in that area, rustling horses, conscripting for the Confederates in order to raise a company of Confederate cavalry, and causing more than a little concern for the Union. Partly because of Blanton's successes, General Rosecrans issued an order for all the Tennessee and Kentucky troops to scout their respective territories to find good horses for the Union army. Each of these states had been good country for supplying horses to both sides.

While scouting for horses, the 5th Iowa Cavalry found the elusive Major Blanton in Waverly. The *Cincinnati Daily Commercial* reported, "Last Friday [April 10] a skirmish took place near Waverly, Tennessee, between a party of Federals and rebels in which Major Blandon, 2 captains, a Lt., a surgeon, a Quartermaster and 15 others of the enemy were taken prisoners."[29] The article went on to say that a Captain Wilcox and his Company H of the 5th Iowa Cavalry were out scouting for horses when they were found by a Rebel force led by Major Blanton. Blanton followed Wilcox for a while, but another Union cavalry unit happened on the 5th Iowa; the combined Union units turned on Blanton and captured his party. They were pleased to get Major Blanton, but the report on the Union horses was not so good. The morning report of the 5th Iowa Cavalry, Company M, read, "A skirmish with the enemy while a scout near Waverly, Tenn. 4/10/63. Company returned from scout 4/14—lost five horses on the 10th instant. Said horses give out as a hard scout of 70 miles."[30]

There were no casualties reported by the 5th Iowa, and no injuries to the Confederates, only the capture of the twenty-one recruiters.

FORT DONELSON, TENNESSEE

Another isolated action was reported from Fort Donelson, Tennessee, in the diary of Mrs. Lyon, wife of Colonel William Penn Lyon. She saw five Union gunboats headed down the Cumberland River with supplies, probably for Fort Henry, over on the Tennessee River. They were discovered by a Confederate cavalry unit under Colonel Thomas G. Woodward, who promptly sank the boats with his artillery. As a result, the 13th Wisconsin Infantry, under Colonel Lyon, was ordered out to find Woodward. They had no success, though, and returned to Donelson on the twelfth.[31]

A letter from Colonel Lyon described his efforts to confront the pesky Woodward in Kentucky:

We had a little expedition. One Woodward, a rebel, has a force of about 2,000 men with artillery up the river, harassing boats. We had a force up about 12 miles in the country, and hearing that Woodward was trying to cut it off, I was sent out Sat. A.M to give him a fight. He didn't come, so no fight as usual."[32]

GERMANTOWN, KENTUCKY

A minor skirmish on April 10 near Germantown, Kentucky, was reported in the *Chicago Tribune* on April 18, 1863:

> Lt. Rickertson of the 118th Ohio Regiment, stationed at Demosville, Ky., having received information that a band of rebels were in the habit of holding monthly meetings at Morris's Mills, in Campbell County, left his camp day before yesterday for the purpose of capturing them. He did not find them at Morris's Mills, but 2 miles farther on, near Roushe's house, he captured 2 men belonging to the guerrilla band under "Jim Caldwell." Continuing the pursuit yesterday, Lt. Rickertson encamped within "thirty yards of the rebels without either party having a knowledge of it, and this morning Caldwell's party got the start, Lt. Rickertson, upon hearing of their movement, following in pursuit." The rebels were not overtaken until they reached the vicinity of Germantown, in Mason County, where they were surprised and completely routed. Lieutenant Daniels [D. M.] of the rebel party was killed in the fight that took place, and three others were wounded. Caldwell escaped on a very fleet horse, while his men, except three who were captured, fled to the woods, leaving their horses in the hands of the Nationals.[33]

The *Cincinnati Gazette* of April 13 noted that Lieutenant Daniels had previously been a prisoner of the Yankees at Camp Chase, Maryland.[34] The skirmish was of little note, except to Lieutenant Daniels, who reportedly was killed, and to Private Peter C. Benedum of the 118th Ohio, who, according to several sources, was wounded.[35] Benedum's service record shows nothing about that wound, but the records of Company I show that he was severely wounded in the leg while scouting with Lieutenant Rickertson. Major James W. Caldwell was in command of a company of Brigadier General Benjamin H. Helm's 9th Kentucky Cavalry, doing the usual recruiting and foraging for the Confederates. He escaped from the 118th Ohio on the tenth but was captured in October 1863 in Shelbyville, Tennessee. Records show he was exchanged in October 1864.[36]

No record has been located of a Lieutenant D. M. Daniels in any Kentucky cavalry unit, North or South, but several newspaper sources record his death in that encounter.[37]

OTHER ACTIVITY

Muster rolls of the 118th Ohio show that another Ohioan died on the tenth. Private Wesley McMillen of Company D, returning from a scout, was accidentally shot and killed by pickets of the 15th Indiana Light Artillery near Paris, Kentucky. The twenty-eight-year-old farmer was described as "temperate, married one child, quick temperament, slow disposition." His service record lists him killed on April 16 and present for duty on the tenth; however, regimental musters report him killed on the tenth.[38]

The Official Records show that a Union scout was sent out from La Grange, Tennessee, into northern Mississippi, looking for signs of Rebel activity. The patrol, which took two days, was performed by the 7th Illinois Cavalry, and it took two prisoners.[39] One of the prisoners, James Hoy of Company E, 2d Arkansas Cavalry, had been captured in January by these same cavalrymen and paroled after he took the oath of allegiance. He wasn't so lucky the second time. He was taken to St. Louis, where he became ill, then to a hospital in East Alton, Illinois.[40] The other Confederate captured was Nathan Baldwin, a private in Mitchell's company, Chalmers's 18th Mississippi Regiment. Baldwin was sent north but was exchanged on June 2, 1863.[41] The two captured Rebels reported that Chalmers's regiment was at Hernando, Mississippi, about 600 strong.[42]

Colonel M. K. Lawler commanded an expedition that had been out from Jackson, Tennessee, since April 1. He had about 490 Union troopers from Illinois and western Tennessee; part of their purpose was to distribute circulars urging members of the many Southern guerrilla bands to give up, take the oath of allegiance, and return peacefully to their homes. On the tenth, they were in Bolivar, Kentucky, and arrived back in Jackson on the sixteenth. Colonel Lawler was upset because their horses were of such poor quality that many of them had to be left to die on the march and replaced with captured horses.

All these efforts indicate the fierce competition for men as well as horses; both sides spent a great deal of time and effort trying to find ways to entice the other side to either quit or join up with their foes. Circulars were part of only one strategy. The border states were having their share of problems with surviving in an area where everything was in demand: horses, men, food, and forage; but not the least of all—loyalty.

★

Private Edwin Worden died about midnight on April 10. He was buried in the Nashville National Cemetery, which is bisected by the

L & N railroad. He sleeps forever just a few yards from the railroad he died defending.[43]

Private George Turner was taken sick, discharged, and died in March 1864.

Colonel Heg was mortally wounded at Chickamaugua in September 1863.

Lieutenant John R. Henry, Jr., 1st Tennessee Cavalry, is buried in the Nashville National Cemetery, near Private Edwin Worden, in grave number 231.[44]

James Hoy died in the Federal hospital in East Alton, Illinois, on June 7, 1863, of smallpox.

Major Blanton was captured on the tenth and sent to the first of a series of Union prison camps. He was finally exchanged on March 9, 1864. Right after that he tried again to raise a company, but he never succeeded. He survived the war and took the oath of allegiance on May 16, 1865.[45]

11

THE MISSISSIPPI

GRANT AND VICKSBURG

Other Union departments were resting, fortifying, and gathering strength, but that was not the style of Major General Ulysses S. Grant, who had been working his troops with determination since December. On April 10, Grant was at Young's Point, Louisiana, as commander of the Army of the Tennessee.

Vicksburg, a well-fortified Mississippi city, controlled Mississippi River traffic with its high bluffs and heavy guns. The 200-mile stretch of the winding river from Vicksburg south to Port Hudson was still in Confederate hands. This made Union river passage from Union-held Memphis south to Baton Rouge and New Orleans, both captured from the Confederates in 1862, difficult and dangerous. The South's control of this 200-mile corridor also allowed the passage of supplies and food from the lush areas of the Confederacy west of the Mississippi to the Southern states east of the river. The Union considered Vicksburg to be the key to the closure of this stretch of river; once it fell, Port Hudson would not be far behind. Grant had begun his efforts to take Vicksburg in the fall of 1862, and had still not accomplished it on April 10, 1863.

Commanding general of the Department of the Tennessee, commonly called the Army of the Tennessee, Grant was not yet the hero he was to become in a few short months. In truth, he was considered suspect by the two most powerful men in the U.S. government, President Lincoln and Secretary of War Stanton. Nor was he in the highest favor with his old commander, General Halleck, who was now in Washington, D.C., as general in chief.

Grant had scored impressive successes at Fort Donelson and Fort Henry, but his performance at Shiloh had been disappointing. Rumors continued to surface about Grant's heavy drinking, rumors that were of great concern to the president, but the immediate cause for Lincoln's concern was the failure of all of Grant's efforts to take Vicksburg. In

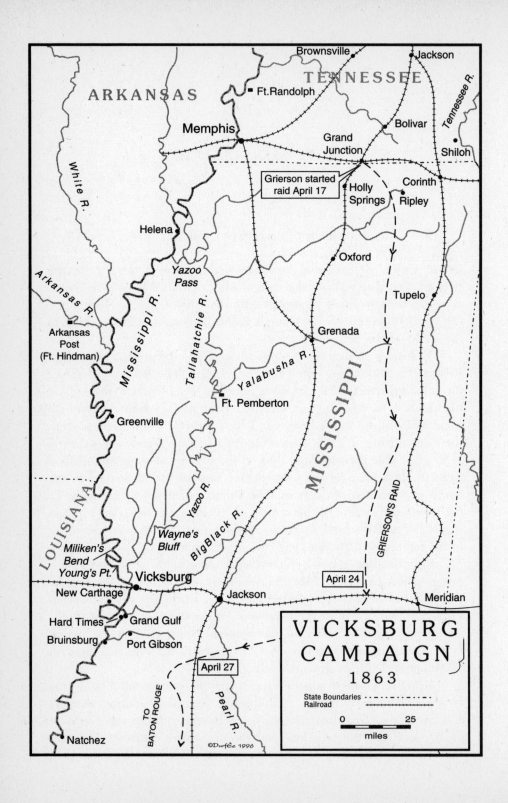

ARKANSAS

TENNESSEE

Brownsville

Jackson

Ft. Randolph

Memphis

Grand
Junction

Bolivar

Shiloh

Tennessee R.

Grierson started
raid April 17

Holly
Springs

Corinth

Ripley

White R.

Helena

Oxford

Tupelo

Yazoo
Pass

Arkansas R.

Arkansas
Post
(Ft. Hindman)

Grenada

Tallahatchie R.

Yalabusha R.

Ft. Pemberton

MISSISSIPPI

Greenville

GRIERSON'S RAID

Yazoo R.

Mississippi R.

LOUISIANA

Wayne's
Bluff

BigBlack R.

Miliken's
Bend
Young's Pt.

April 24

Vicksburg

New Carthage

Jackson

Meridian

Hard Times

Grand Gulf

Bruinsburg

Port Gibson

April 27

TO
BATON
ROUGE

Pearl R.

VICKSBURG
CAMPAIGN
1863

State Boundaries ....
Railroad +++++++++++

0   25

miles

Natchez

©Durfee 1996

April 1863, Lincoln and Stanton were considering Grant's removal. Two senior government officials, Brigadier General Lorenzo Thomas, adjutant general of the army, and Assistant Secretary of War Charles Dana, were in Grant's department on April 10, both for different purposes, but both with orders to size up Grant and decide if he was fit to continue in command. Dana recounted Stanton's instructions:

> Mr. Stanton sent for me to come to Washington. He wanted someone to go to Grant's army, he said, to report daily to him the military proceedings, and to give such information as to enable Mr. Lincoln and himself to settle their minds as to Grant, about whom at that time there were many doubts and against whom there was some complaint.
>
> "Will you go?" Mr. Stanton asked. "Yes," I said. "Very well," he replied. "The ostensible function I shall give you will be that of special commissioner of the War Department to investigate the pay service of the Western armies, but your real duty will be to report to me every day what you see."[1]

Dana arrived at Grant's headquarters in Milliken's Bend, Louisiana, on April 6, ostensibly to check on pay practices in the district, while General Thomas was in the area with a primary purpose of raising black troops to bolster the Union army's manpower needs. When Grant was informed that Dana was coming to spend time with his army, he made sure that Dana was welcomed and was briefed on all military affairs as they developed. Instead of creating antagonism and friction with Dana, he voiced the opinion that Dana's messages to Stanton would greatly relieve him from the odious burden of communications, which he claimed was a chore for him. In short, Grant turned Dana into a staunch supporter who would "sell" Grant's abilities and downplay his shortcomings.

Dana, in his April 9 dispatch to Stanton, described the Grant he saw:

> Grant was an uncommon fellow—the most modest, the most disinterested, and the most honest man I ever knew, with a temper that nothing could disturb, and a judgment that was judicial in its comprehensiveness and wisdom. Not a great man, except morally, not an original or brilliant man, but sincere, thoughtful, deep, and gifted with courage that never faltered. When the time came to risk all, he went in like a simple-hearted, unaffected, unpretending hero, who no ill omens could deject and no triumph unduly exalt.[2]

That was probably Grant's key to success: when the time came to risk all, he was at his best; Dana realized this and reported it clearly.

Because of Lincoln's and Stanton's lack of confidence in Grant, opposition was building on another side. Without Grant's knowledge, Major General John A. McClernand, one of Grant's division commanders, had made a proposition to Lincoln and Stanton in October 1862 that he go back to his home state, Illinois, raise as many as twenty regiments, and form his own special expedition against Vicksburg. McClernand, an old-time Illinois politician, a friend and supporter of Lincoln, had access to the president but no military credentials. Since Grant had been unsuccessful thus far, Lincoln and Stanton saw this proposal as another possibility and gave the required approval, even though Halleck opposed the idea. The orders were kept secret, so Grant knew nothing of the plan. In time, Halleck assigned the troops raised by McClernand to Grant; Grant made McClernand a corps commander (XIII), and Grant retained his total authority. This obviously created some tension between Grant and McClernand.

In addition to his own command problems, Grant was frustrated by Rosecrans in Tennessee and by Major General Nathaniel Banks in New Orleans and Baton Rouge. Grant had communicated freely with both generals, particularly requesting Banks to join him in efforts to open the Mississippi. Grant hoped to have Banks move north from Baton Rouge to draw some attention away from Grant's Army of the Tennessee. Banks, however, chose April 11 to make an expedition up the bayous into western Louisiana. He told Grant that he would be able to supply about 15,000 men, but not until May 10.[3]

Meanwhile, Rosecrans was asking Grant for more troops to help in his standoff with Bragg in Tennessee. Grant sent Brigadier General Grenville Dodge from his XVI Corps to provide screening for Streight's raid later in April, so it was apparent that the Army of the Cumberland would not provide any resources for Grant.

Mrs. Grant was anxious about her husband's situation. When she was in Memphis she heard that General Lorenzo Thomas was coming through to make a decision about General Grant. In early April, Grant asked his wife to travel with the children to his headquarters at Milliken's Bend, and she did so at once. She confided in her memoirs:

I had hardly said "how do you do" before I began to make suggestions, asking the General, "Why do you not move on Vicksburg at once? Do stop digging at this old canal. You know you will never use it. Besides, that is what McClellan has been doing. Move upon Vicksburg and you shall take it." The General was greatly amused and inquired if I too had a plan of action to propose. Of course I had. "Mass your troops in a solid phalanx at a point north of the fortress, rush upon it, and they will be obliged to surrender." He said, smiling, "I am afraid your plan would involve great loss of life and not insure success. Therefore I cannot adopt it. But it is true I will not use the canal. I never expected to, but started it to give the army occupation and to amuse the country until the waters should subside sufficiently to give me a good foothold and then, Mrs. Grant, I will move upon Vicksburg and will take it, too. You need give yourself no further trouble. This will all come out right in good time, and you must not forget that each and every one of my soldiers has a mother, wife, or sweetheart, whose lives are as dear to them as mine is to you. But Vicksburg I will take in good time."[4]

Grant had been active, and certainly creative, in this Vicksburg campaign, but with no success. His first attempt, in December 1862, was to take 40,000 men down the Mississippi Central Railroad into the interior of Mississippi, then have 32,000 men under Major General William T. Sherman go down the Mississippi River simultaneously and attack Chickasaw Bluffs, just north of Vicksburg. The land force heading south along the railroad was stopped by the Confederate cavalry under Forrest; without the support of the land force, Sherman was defeated at Chickasaw Bluffs.

The next effort was to dig a canal across a narrow peninsula in Louisiana, opposite Vicksburg, which would have allowed river traffic to simply bypass the city whether going up or down the river, making the Vicksburg fortifications useless. That effort was frustrated by the river itself, which had been unseasonably high ever since December, and the project was abandoned in March. Next, Grant decided to dig ditches from Duckport, Louisiana, through winding bayous and canals, to come out twenty miles below Vicksburg. One little steamer did get through, but the Federals couldn't get enough water into the ditches to float the larger transports.

An attempt was then made to connect the Mississippi to Lake Providence, in Louisiana; then construct passages through Lake Providence and through the swamps, lakes, and bayous, ending below Vicksburg. This incredible 400-mile project was abandoned in favor of less arduous programs and because Grant became convinced that Vicksburg must be attacked from the east. Although the river itself was high and rains had been excessive from December to April, the water levels in the canals and bayous were not high enough to provide a passable route for Union troops.

There also was an attempt to get inland through Yazoo Pass, then down the Yazoo River for 325 miles, but the Confederates built Fort Pemberton at one of the river bends and sank their own steamer *Star of the West* to block passage. The Union boats had to back up to their starting point, frustrating Grant once again. A Union soldier, Milt Shaw, wrote from one of the transports, the *Von Phul,* on March 10, 1863:

> The report tells us that we go into the Pass [Yazoo] into Moon Lake, thence into Cold water, thence the Tallahatchie, thence into Sunflower into the Yazoo River, by a kind of overland steamboat, mud puddle route unheard of but in the philosophy of modern warfare. Can you imagine the consternation which our advent into this unexplored part of Dahaney will create among bulfrogs & Alligators whose peaceful dreams have hither to been undisturbed since this mass of clay was sent on its voyage around the sun.[5]

The most recent misadventure took place in March 1863, using Rear Admiral David D. Porter's boats and Sherman's troops on Steele Bayou, north of the city. The Union forces were heavily engaged by Confederate marksmen on the riverbank; with heavy vegetation forcing the boats to crawl through the lowlands, the whole expedition almost came to disaster.[6]

On April 10, the last of Grant's efforts was winding down. This was an attempt to dig a canal from the Mississippi to Walnut Bayou. It was never completed.

On April 11, the *Washington Evening Star* published its prognosis:

> The attack on Ft. Pemberton will be renewed. Steele's Division is by this time there. The Yazoo offers the only approach to the rear of Vicksburg and if we fail in taking that fort you may depend on it the siege of Vicksburg will be abandoned. The new canal does not promise to be a success. Important expeditions have been sent out from Grant's army, from which we shall soon have good news.[7]

The newspaper missed it on almost every count.

During the last two maneuvers, Grant had finally decided that a drastic approach was called for; even as the boats and Sherman's troops were limping back, he decided the next try would be down the west side of the river. The Union would cross over below Vicksburg, circle around behind, and cut off Vicksburg completely. That was radical, in military terms, because Grant was also cutting himself off by placing Vicksburg between himself and his supplies. Sherman opposed the plan; he urged a return to Memphis, then moving a massive force south by land directly to Vicksburg, securing all supply lines as it went.[8] Grant viewed Sherman's plan as a retreat and feared that both the government and the nation would look on it as another defeat, so he went ahead with his own plan.[9]

Grant had secretly built several casements and housed several large artillery pieces on the west side of the Mississippi, as close to Vicksburg as they could get. In a letter to his brother written on April 10, Sherman disclosed:

> Mr. Dana is here. He spent a few hours with me yesterday, and I went over with him many of the events of the past year, with the maps and records with which I am well supplied. Indeed, all look to me for maps and facts. Dana remarked to one of Grant's staff incidentally, that he was better pleased with me than he could possibly have expected. In the two days he has been here he has seen an illustration of the truth of my proposition, which has drawn on me such abuse. We have had thousands of men working by night, putting batteries as close up to Vicksburg as possible, secretly, and in opening a channel by which we may in high water reach the river twenty-five miles below Vicksburg. Secrecy was essential, but the papers of Memphis announce the whole fact. I know the Memphis dailies go before daylight each day to Hernando, 25 miles, and are telegraphed to Vicksburg by noon of the same day. Indeed, the day before yesterday we met some Vicksburg officers, who asked that I should come with a flag of truce to discuss a point as to exchange of prisoners, and as we parted, one Major Watts, asked me not to open our batteries last night, as he was going to have a party and did not want to be disturbed.[10]

The fact was, the Confederates knew almost everything about the Union plans and movements, since the disputed ground was still their home territory.

Grant's forces at that time numbered approximately 104,000 men spread over a territory from Memphis down to New Carthage, Louisiana. Major General Steven A. Hurlbut commanded the XVI Corps, based in Memphis, which had about half of Grant's forces, numbering almost 50,000 men. Hurlbut's corps included Dodge's Department of Corinth and other forces in the Department of Jackson, Tennessee.

There was also a division at La Grange, Tennessee; one at Columbus, Kentucky; and the rest of Hurlbut's men in Memphis. While Hurlbut's troops were under Grant's command, the official records do not show them as operating against Vicksburg.[11] But a report dated April 30, 1863, shows that Grant had "Aggregate Present and Absent 73,674," with "Aggregate Present strength of 53,596."[12]

On April 10, part of McClernand's XIII Corps was already down the west side of the Mississippi River at New Carthage, Louisiana, and the rest were about to move down from Milliken's Bend, Louisiana. Major General James B. McPherson's XVII Corps was en route from Lake Providence to Milliken's Bend, and Sherman's XV Corps and Grant's headquarters were at Young's Point, Louisiana, just upriver and across from Vicksburg.

Assistant Secretary Dana's report to Secretary Stanton on April 10 was a positive one. He had spent four days with Grant, Sherman, and Porter, and was pleased with the new movements. In a lengthy and detailed letter, he wrote:

> Everything goes forward encouragingly. . . . The preparations for running the batteries by the gunboats and transports are also nearly completed . . . and that the rest of the squadron, led by Adm. Porter himself, will go down within two days, as the nights are dark and promise to be cloudy. The actual length of the canal and bayou navigation proves to be 37 miles. . . . General Sherman, who I have conversed with at length on the subject, thinks there is no difficulty in opening the passage, but that the line will be a precarious one after the army is thrown across the Mississippi. His preference is for a movement by way of Yazoo Pass, landing the army somewhere in the vicinity of Charleston, and threatening Grenada and Jackson from that point, at the same time as the rich regions of Northern Mississippi is held and the enemy deprived of the supplies derived from the line of the Yazoo and the Sunflower; or he is in favor of moving down by way of Lake Providence to the line of the Tensas and Red Rivers, and by holding that region, sever the rebel connections and shut off their western supplies; but I judge that his mind is now tending to the conclusion of Genl. Grant in favor of crossing, seizing Grand Gulf and operating from that base, and if the new canal should fail he will move his entire force overland to Carthage or thereabouts, run transports enough past batteries to carry them, and provision them by wagons, and by running the batteries afterward. Admiral Porter cordially agrees with the plan now being executed.[13]

It had not taken Dana long to become a firm advocate of the Grant team, and his reports to Stanton were highly complimentary.

Grant's final bayou/canal project, on which he was still working on April 10, was a small one linking Milliken's Bend to the bayou system by a short canal. After April 1, the dry season took water levels to such a low point that the water route would not work. That was not a catastrophe, though; the dry land made overland roads passable, and Grant could move his troops and supply wagons overland to New Carthage instead of relying on the uncertain water routes. Grant later chronicled the difficulties he faced coming into April:

This long, dreary, and, for heavy and continuous rains and high water, unprecedented winter was one of great hardship to all engaged about Vicksburg. The river was higher than its natural banks from Dec. 1862 to the following April. The war had suspended peaceful pursuits in the south, further than the production of army supplies, and in consequence the levees were neglected and broken in many places and the whole country was covered with water. Troops could scarcely find dry ground to pitch their tents. Malarial fever broke out among the men. Measles and small pox also attacked them. The hospital arrangements and medical attendance were so perfect, however, that the loss of life was much less than might have been expected. Visitors to the camps went home with dismal stories to relate; Northern papers came back to the soldiers with these stories exaggerated. Because I would not divulge my ultimate plans to visitors, they pronounced me idle, incompetent and unfit to command men in an emergency, and clamored for my removal. They were not to be satisfied, many of them, with my simple removal, but named who my successor should be. McClernand, Fremont, Hunter and McClellan were all mentioned in that connection. I took no steps to answer these complaints but continued to do my duty, as I understood it, to the best of my ability. Everyone has his superstitions. One of mine is that in positions of great responsibility everyone should do his duty to the best of his ability where assigned by competent authority, without application or the use of influence to change his position.[14]

Outwardly, Grant showed few signs that he was aware of the backbiting that was taking place in many parts of the Union; to all appearances he was oblivious and concerned only with his immediate project.

NAVAL SUPPORT

The Department of the Tennessee had one distinct advantage: it had its own navy. Although Rear Admiral David G. Farragut and his fleet were out of reach in New Orleans, the Mississippi squadron under Admiral Porter (Farragut's stepbrother) had been assigned to Grant's command. They had provided almost all the gunboats, mortarboats, rams, and transports used in all Grant's efforts to date.

Fortunately, the command structure was in harmony under Grant, with the exception of McClernand, who still smarted under the role of corps commander instead of the desired one of expedition commander. The other two corps commanders were General Sherman (XV Corps) and General McPherson (XVII Corps). McPherson was the unsung corps commander in the Department of the Tennessee: capable, loyal to Grant, and an able and dedicated officer. The relationship between Grant and his commanders was, for the most part, congenial and professional. The team of Grant, Porter, and Sherman provided a leadership quality that matched the South's team of Lee, Jackson, and Stuart in Virginia. Although Sherman wrote protesting Grant's new plan, he closed his letter by expressing his cooperation: "Whatever plan of action he [Grant] may adopt will receive from me the same zealous cooperation and energetic support as though conceived by myself."[15]

Porter also expressed some concerns over Grant's bold plan, but in a letter to Secretary of the Navy Gideon Welles he declared, "So confident was I of the ability of General Grant to carry out his plans when he explained them to me that I never hesitated to change my position from above to below Vicksburg."[16]

Porter had been scolded by Secretary Welles for failing to go to Farragut's aid south of Vicksburg and staying with Grant's abortive river and swamp campaigns. Porter replied on the eleventh: "I am sorry the Department is not satisfied with the operations here but you will please remember, sir, that I was ordered to cooperate with the army, and sagacious officers deem these flanking movements of great importance."[17]

Despite Lincoln's and Welles's pressure, Porter was committed to Grant's course and would remain loyal to Grant's programs. This army/navy cooperation was a great advantage for the Union; neither would have had any success in this area without the other. On April 10, Porter was preparing his ships to run the gauntlet past Vicksburg in time to get Grant's men across the Mississippi and in position for the final assault on Vicksburg. Logs were hung from the sides, hay bales were put on the decks, and strengthened panels were placed on the sides, all added in order to deflect the expected shot from the batteries. Porter would leave only eight of his fleet up near the Yazoo Pass; the rest would all go below Vicksburg—with the full knowledge that until Vicksburg fell, there would be no possibility of going back.

As the army sat in its camps, moved along its trails, dug its canals, and prepared for whatever orders the commanding general had in mind, and as Admiral Porter, with his little fleet, was anchored off the Yazoo Pass with gunboats, transports, and rams, awaiting orders to begin the long-awaited campaign, a smaller naval force watched.

THE ELLET MARINE BRIGADE

The Ellet Marine Brigade, commanded by Brigadier General A. W. Ellet, was another Union water force on the Mississippi. This unit had been created to move troops on the Tennessee and Cumberland rivers, as well as on the Mississippi, but it hoped for a more active part in the river war and had, in fact, had a number of successes using its specialty, the ram boats. The ram was an unarmed steamer fitted with an iron prow, which was its main weapon. The rams had sunk a number of Confederate ships on the Mississippi, but in its first real action, the brigade's commander and originator, Colonel Charles A. Ellet, Jr., had been killed; the command then passed to his brother, Alfred W. Ellet. Later it would pass to Alfred's young son, also named Charles Ellet.

It was not a cordial relationship that existed between Porter and the Ellets; Porter felt strongly that there was an awkward command structure, since Ellet was an army officer, and thought this was hampering the navy's efforts. Porter wrote to Welles in Washington on April 11 in response to Navy Department pressures on him in his Vicksburg assignment:

> While it is my desire to carry out the wishes of the Department in relation to all matters connected with operations here, still I must act in accordance with my judgment and a more full knowledge of affairs than the Department could possibly have.
>
> The flanking operations spoken of by the Department have not in any way interfered with any other movements, as the vessels were of a class that could not be sent below without a certain kind of support; that support was not here. I think that the vessels left, and comprising the Ram Fleet, should be turned over entirely to the Navy, to have naval officers on board, and the present officers to be attached to the Marine Brigade or be gotten rid of.

Whatever disaster may happen to those vessels is attached to the Navy, while any success is appropriated by the Ellet Ram Fleet.

I have sent them all up the Tennessee River, where their operations will be mostly confined to land.[18]

On April 8, as the Marine Brigade ram fleet was coaling up on the Ohio River in Cairo, Illinois, getting ready to pick up Colonel Abel Streight in Fort Henry on his way to his ill-fated mission, tragedy struck the rams in a strange incident. As the fleet moved toward Cairo, it tied up on the night of the eighth near New Madrid, Missouri. Two of the ships, the *John Raine* and the *Baltic,* were separated by the coal barge fueling the *Baltic.* Three of the officers were close friends; they had not been together for some time, so the two aboard the *Baltic,* Lieutenants W. H. Sloan and Le Roy Mayne, decided to visit their friend, Lieutenant McCune, on the *Raine.* To get to the *Raine,* Sloan and Mayne had to walk a narrow gangplank to the coal barge, and then walk another narrow plank to cross from the coal barge to the *Raine.*

As they left the *Baltic,* Mayne slipped on the plank and fell between the *Baltic* and the barge. Sloan said that he heard Mayne's head hit the barge, and the current swept the young lieutenant away before a rescue could be made. As they were searching for Mayne, they heard shouts that another man was overboard. When they got back to the ship, they found that Lieutenant McCune had, at almost exactly the same time, left his ship, heading for the *Baltic* to see his old friends, and had slipped and plunged into the river. Neither body was ever recovered; the fleet reached Cairo on the tenth minus these two young officers.[19]

GRANT'S MEN

Many of the men of the Army of the Tennessee were on the move on April 10, but life was still reasonably tranquil for most of the troops, as Private C. W. Gerard of the 83d Ohio Infantry recounted:

Orders came on the 6th for us to move with 6 days rations and we marched back about 10 miles to Walnut Bayou [near Milliken's Bend]. This was a beautiful place and while pretending to dig a canal we really did nothing but enjoy ourselves and eat the planter's hams and shoulders from his smoke house. Yet while here we recruited our health and spirits, and came back new men in body, mind and spirit.[20]

One of Gerard's friends in the 83d, Isaac Jackson, wrote a letter home describing his good life. These men were in the XIII Corps, waiting to be sent down with the rest to New Carthage:

Dear Bro. John   Walnut Bayou, La.
                                                  April 10, 1863

I am very well at present and enjoying myself very much. We have pleasant weather here at present. Last Monday we got orders to move with 6 days rations, 1 day in our haversacks. We could not conjecture what was going on, we thought maybe we were going on a foraging campaign. Or perhaps out to a small town named Richmond about 20 miles from camp, where there are some rebels and there had been some fighting. But neither of these places was our destination. We went about 10 miles out in the country but still near the river (we are only about 1½ miles from the river now) and about 10 miles from camp. So you see how the river twists and turns down here. Our regt is out here digging a canal from the river to Walnut Bayou which is about 1½ miles.

We have a fine time while out here. We don't have to work too hard, the regt is divided into 2 reliefs and work only one hour each and work only 6–8 hours a day. And we have a very pleasant place to come while out here, alongside the bayou on the gently sloping bank which is nice and grassy. We have plenty of rafts which we ride on and, then, the bayou is one of the prettiest places to swim in the world. . . . It gets pretty hot during the day and not a shade tree to be got at, for all the woods are filled with water and we cannot get to it. But still we have very fine weather now, just like our summer back home.[21]

Richmond was a Louisiana village on the route between Milliken's Bend and New Carthage. Troops moved through it periodically, sometimes stopping to set up temporary quarters. On April 10, Surgeon B. F. Stevenson of the 22d Kentucky Infantry (Union) wrote to his wife about the town:

Dear Delia,

I have nothing to write about, absolutely nothing of interest to you. To say that I am in the midst of a beautiful, fertile country, that is suffering all the hardships of war, is only to repeat what you already know.

This village is the seat of Justice of Madison Parish, it is 12 miles

from the river and it is situated in what is called Roundaway Bayou,
which I can only describe by saying:

> *"It runneth north, it runneth south,*
> *It runneth east, it runneth west,*
> *It runneth round the cuckoo nest;"* [22]

Stevenson found the people kind, and he ministered to their needs,
since they had no doctor. He said there was some bitterness, but he
avoided political talk. Another Northern soldier, Private Alfred B. Cree,
also wrote to his wife from Richmond:

> Richmond is a splendid place not verry large but rich men is
> hard to find as in all places where the Feds go as the ladies call them.
> they will tell you mighty quick what they—and what they think.
> One lady told me yesterday we would come back from Vicksburg
> faster than we went; for if twenty of their men would come we
> would all run! I told her she had better bring them on; I asked her
> when her husband went away; She said some time ago and that he
> was a Capt. of a Company in Vicksburg. I told her I supposed we
> would get a chance to see him. [23]

With interludes such as these, the Army of the Tennessee appeared
much like both the Army of the Potomac and the Army of the Cumberland: the troops were in good condition, were in reasonably good health,
and were ready to accomplish their respective missions. The two armies
to the east had been dormant for three months, but Grant had kept his
troops busy with his so-far fruitless engineering projects, and his men
were probably better off for the efforts. Private Isaac Jackson wrote
home again on the twelfth, giving his opinion of the army's condition:

> I am glad that the people at home are arousing to a sense of
> their duty in regard to the traitors at home. The only fault I have to
> find is that they do not treat them as traitors should be treated but
> they are doing much better than they did some time ago. The army
> here are in excellent spirits at present. An army could not be in better
> condition than ours is at present. I think you will hear something
> from us before long. [24]

The *Cincinnati Daily Commercial* commented on the state of things
in Grant's army: "April 10, There is a gleam of good news from Gen.
Grant's department." But it cautioned, "It is not that there has been any

considerable military success, but that the army has become healthy. The soldiers suffered severely during the rainy weather of the winter, but the spring sunshine has enlivened them and they are in good health and high spirits."[25]

The letters written around April 10 were usually optimistic and happy, even with the prospect of battle looming, battle which the soldiers knew would include death for many.

Private John G. Jones, Company G, 23d Wisconsin, reassured his parents:

> Those of us who are left are well and in good spirit, and I think we will be able to stand the weather now. We have been quite busy these last few days. Our Division was reviewed on the 8 and 9th. by General Grant and General Sherman, and General [Andrew Jackson] Smith, and several Brigadier Generals. General Grant himself said that the 23rd. was the best.
>
> We have great fun playing ball every evening, the Col. plays with us . . . Oh, yes, we have drawn new hats to protect us from the sun, extra army hats. We expect a crew of conscripts here soon, they have sent for 300 of them to make up the Regiment. The heat will be enough to kill them.[26]

These soldiers were proud of themselves and their units as they waited for replacements. They were tough old soldiers and they knew it. Private Porter of the 7th Missouri wrote in his journal: "The Soldiers of the Army of the Tennessee were half horse half alligator with a touch of snapping turtle. They could live in the water or out of it as the occasion might require . . . There was a story current about the 7th Missouri that they could catch a hog, take all his bristles and skin off, cook and eat him without leaving the ranks."[27]

Private Walter Flatt, a soldier from Wisconsin serving in an Iowa regiment at Milliken's Bend, was in a somber mood:

> I must try to finish this letter today [April 11] or I may not get another chance for we are to move tomorrow but I dont know where we are going, but I should not wonder mush if the next time you hear from me you will hear of my being in a fight—and you may not hear from me again. We don't know who is to fall but if it should be my lot to be killed it will be hard for you. But let this console you that I died in a good cause and while I have tryed to be faithfull to my country I have been faithfull to my wife and children. Allthough I have been absent from you a year it has only strengthened my love

for my family and I am proud to know that my love is returned with as much warmth as it is given.[28]

Private Flatt referred in his letter to the April 10 orders for the whole Army of the Tennessee to march down the west bank of the Mississippi to New Carthage, Louisiana. McClernand's corps had closed on New Carthage, and the rest were about to leave their old camps near Milliken's Bend. McPherson's corps was coming from Lake Providence and then Young's Point, just below Milliken's Bend, and Sherman would bring up the rear. All troops were to be in New Carthage by the seventeenth; Porter would run the Vicksburg batteries the night of the sixteenth, and Grant would begin his encirclement of the city at that time.

As they marched south these men seemed to have a reasonably good time. The distance from Milliken's Bend to New Carthage was about forty miles, not a particularly long way. The weather was nice, and the countryside provided some unique opportunities for forage. The Illinois boys remembered that march as one of their best:

> The surrounding areas were foraged bare by the advancing regts. and many an Illinois soldier obtained his first look at a genuine southern plantation. Almost everyone of them would come home with stories concerning the daily menu on that march—veal, mutton, poultry and beef—and of the beautiful little family cemetery in the center of Perkins' Plantation.[29]

Private Flatt wrote on the seventeenth, after just arriving in New Carthage:

> We move very often now but our marches are very easy now compared to our marching in Mo. This is very delightfull country and everything looks nice and when I look around and see the natural beauty of every thing I cannot but think what a pity it is that man cannot be at peace with each other when God has so provided for us but unhappily such is not the case.[30]

Although these infantrymen reveled in their travel, Ohio artilleryman Owen J. Hopkins didn't have such a good time. He complained of the high waters and numerous bayous that muddied the roads, making the heavy artillery slip and slide in knee-deep muck, with their wheels buried almost to the hubs in the mire.[31]

While many of the regiments were in motion on the tenth, others waited their turn to move south. One of the principal events of that week was the presence of Brigadier General Lorenzo Thomas, who was just assuming responsibility for raising black regiments under the administration's new policy of including blacks as full-fledged combat troops. It was in this recruiting role that he was visiting the various regiments in Grant's command. It was supposed earlier that he would also report to Lincoln and Stanton on the state of the army around Vicksburg and on Grant's capability to keep his command. It is not evident that he fulfilled this mission of scouting Grant; with Dana watching Grant's every move, it probably wasn't necessary. It is evident that he was carrying out his primary mission with considerable enthusiasm. He was most conspicuous on the eighth, when he reviewed a number of regiments. On that day, General Thomas was making speeches to Brigadier General John McArthur's men, looking for officers to lead two black regiments, and getting good response. One of those in the crowd listening to Thomas's speech was James Newton from Wisconsin. In a letter home dated that day, Newton noted that he was impressed to hear the adjutant general say "that he was authorized by the President to commission all such men selected and that he would just as soon give a commission as Capt. to a private . . ." After Thomas finished, the soldiers wanted to hear from McArthur and set up a cry for him. Private Newton related:

At last he rose and took the stand, when such a cheer as burst forth, I am sure, has not been heard for some time in the entire south. For more than five minutes it was one continued cheer. It gratified him, I know by his looks. He said, "It gratified him to learn that the President had at last settled on policy in regard to this matter; that he, as a soldier, was determined to carry out the views of the government, whatever they were; but that he would always show more alacrity, in the cause when it was in consonance with his own feelings; and such, he felt to be the case now."[32]

Thomas Davis, of the 18th Wisconsin, writing on the tenth from Lake Providence, Louisiana, indicated that Thomas's plea for officers was successful:

Robert Mc and Isaac Newell handed in their names for Subjects for commission but don't know yet whether either will be successful. As for myself I did not make an application for any office. There is plenty of Niggers in this vicinity and I think that two Regts. can be easily raised at this point; Gen. Thos says that Negros that will not make soldiers will be put on the evacuated plantations here and be allowed to cultivate them for their own support.[33]

The effect of the Union's new policy was devastating on newly occupied plantations, as an entry in the diary of plantation owner James Bradley in May 1863 illustrates:

> The immediate effect upon the arrival of Federal troops was the complete demoralization of the Negroes—All work was stopped at once & all discipline thrown aside. Many of the soldiers came on the place and had conversations with the blacks & the result was always greater desecration. They were all elated beyond expression at being told they were free & that they could do as they pleased.[34]

General Thomas's visits prompted even more reviews than usual. Henry Clay Warmoth recorded briefly in his diary:

> Thursday April 9th 1863—Today we Inspected and Reviewed Carrs and Smith Divisions Genl Grant & Staff were out on review.
> Fryday April 10th 1863—Very Warm
> Saturday April 11 1863—Brig. Gen. L. Thomas arrived this morning. Genl McD & Staff called on Him[35]

Edmund Newsome, 14th Wisconsin, observed on April 10: "We're going to have a review today, to see how many it will require to fill up the regiments with conscripts, each state to fill its own regiments."[36]

The adjutant general was still not as important as mail. Mail was all-important to the men of the Army of the Tennessee, as was mentioned in almost every letter. Walter Flatt, who had recently arrived in Louisiana, wrote his wife, "I received one letter from you at Memphis and 3 or 4 since. Some of them was over 2 months old and one was not over a week . . . We ware on the boat 12 daze, but made severl stops on the way [from Saint Louis]."[37] Thomas Davis had a complaint not often heard: too much mail. In a letter to his wife he fretted, "We expect to have General Muster at ten oclock and I have not time to write a long letter though there is no important news since I last wrote. We are kept so busy drilling and guarding that I scarcely have time to answer all the letters I receive."[38]

Captain James Newton, 81st Illinois, wrote on the tenth that he was happy with the mail service: "I rec'd yours of March 24th several days ago."[39] Not bad service, especially in those times and circumstances.

THE CONFEDERATE SITUATION

The city of Vicksburg and the Confederate army felt confident that spring. A large Union army had been held at bay for more than six months; the only real battle had been in December at Chickasaw Bayou, where Sherman, attacking without Grant's planned support, had lost 1,900 men. The Yazoo army/navy expedition had been turned back and the city still had communication and supplies coming in from Jackson, Mississippi.

Confederate General Joseph Johnston was in charge on the east bank of the Mississippi, although on April 10 he was still in Tullahoma, Tennessee, with General Bragg. Lieutenant General John C. Pemberton commanded the forces in the Department of Mississippi and East Louisiana. He had 22,000 men in the defenses in Vicksburg, Major General C. L. Stevenson commanding; 16,000 men under Major General Frank Gardner at Port Hudson; 7,000 at Fort Pemberton, north of Vicksburg on the Yazoo; 2,000 in Columbus, Mississippi; and 1,000 in Panola, Mississippi, for a total of 48,000.[40] Pemberton had lost Van Dorn's cavalry earlier in the year, when Johnston requested their assignment to Bragg in Tennessee; one of Pemberton's frequent complaints was that his cavalry was not adequate for scouting all of Grant's movements.

There was still confusion in the Confederate command on April 10. As early as April 6, Pemberton had observed Porter's boat activity and had assumed that Grant was pulling out after his Yazoo fiasco. He had so notified Johnston, and on the eleventh, he even offered, reluctantly, to send 4,000 men to Bragg. His offer was accompanied by a scout's report indicating that Grant was pulling out, probably going to join Rosecrans in Murfreesboro.[41] This made Johnston uneasy, so he tried to beef up Bragg's forces from places as far away as Mobile.

The speculation about Grant's movements was reinforced by a report from a scouting expedition by the Confederate steamer *Dewdrop,* which had reconnoitered up the Sunflower River as far as the little steamer could go, then sent out scouts in all directions. The report stated:

> The scouts sent to Yazoo Pass saw nothing of the movements of the enemy, but they were informed by General Alcorn, who resides there, that during the 7th, 8th and 9th, six gunboats and 36 trans-

ports, loaded with troops, negroes, horses, wagons, and light artillery, came out through the Pass into the Mississippi River.[42]

The opinion that Grant was retreating was strengthened by most newspapers. The *Vicksburg Daily Whig* reported on the tenth: "There was an unusual quietness among the Yankees across the river yesterday. There was no stir among the troops, and but one arrival at the landing."[43]

On April 14, the Vicksburg paper reported that the Vicksburg assault had virtually ended and that the Union army and navy would soon be on the Tennessee River. Even up in Albany, New York, on the tenth, the *Atlas and Argus* agreed, informing its readers: "Richmond papers report 'The enemy are withdrawing their troops from the Peninsula. Yesterday all tents were struck four large transports have gone up the river loaded with troops. The enemy have cut the levee and turned the water into their old camp ground.' "[44]

The *Chattanooga Daily Rebel* confirmed this: "Vicksburg, 4/10— Nothing new here—2 transports loaded with troops went up today— others are preparing."[45] The Charleston papers announced more specifically: "Western papers state that 20,000 men passed up the river from Vicksburg on the 10th to reinforce Rosecrans."[46] The newspapers surely fostered a feeling of confidence and security. By then Pemberton himself had telegraphed Johnston to say that Grant had given up and pulled back to Memphis.[47]

Confederates such as Colonel J.A.W. Johnson reported that the Rebel army itself was confident and ready for a fight: "The army here is in fine condition, we're almost spiling for a fight. To my mind there is but little prospect of an infantry fight. Gen. Stevenson has one of the finest divisions in the service. He has 4 brigades and can put 12,000 men in a fight tomorrow."[48]

Although many believed that Grant was moving north, not south, the first alert of his move downriver to New Carthage, Louisiana, came in a brief message on the tenth to Brigadier General John S. Bowen, at Grand Gulf, from Pemberton: "Gen. Stevenson telegraphs this morning the enemy captured steamer Clarke at mouth of Red River yesterday; also that picket, on authority of a citizen, reports enemy landing a considerable force at New Carthage. You must allow no boats to go out."[49]

The report was verified by General Bowen. He notified Pemberton later on the tenth: "Col. [F. M.] Cockrell skirmished several hours with the enemy yesterday, driving in their pickets, but failed to draw them over Bayou Vidal. No loss on our side."[50]

Some of the men, however, were aware that something was happening. W. A. Wash, a Tennessee Confederate of Vaughn's brigade, wrote:

> During the 10th and 11th of April the enemy were making moves which we could not exactly comprehend, and evidently not intended for our good.
>
> Many of their transports steamed up the river. Some few, accompanied by iron clads were reconnoitering in the Yazoo River, and some troops were moving back into Louisiana.[51]

In fact, one third of Grant's force was moving past Vicksburg on the west side of the Mississippi south toward New Carthage, another third was on its way there, and soon Sherman would be there, too.

Mainly providing picket coverage for Grand Gulf and Vicksburg, Colonel Cockrell had portions of his Confederate brigade on the west side of the Mississippi in Louisiana. There he found elements of Union General McClernand's XIII Corps on their way from Milliken's Bend. Pemberton had convinced himself that Grant was leaving, yet he was now confronted with a new Union force below Vicksburg on the Louisiana side. Shortly before the tenth, one of the Rebel troopers, Corporal Ephraim McDowell Anderson, recalled:

> Federal forces were already moving down upon this side of the river, and their advance was at New Carthage, only a few miles above. The roll of drums was within hearing distance. Their strength was not accurately ascertained, nor was the design of the movement they were making as yet apparent or obvious . . .
>
> During the stay here, our company was on picket duty most of the time, or reconnoitering the enemy's movements, the situation of their camp, and ascertaining if their advance was in force. This service was mostly discharged in small boats . . . as the country was generally under water.[52]

Corporal Anderson went on to describe a raid that took place on the tenth, or within a day or two of it (no specific date was supplied in the narrative): "This force was bivouacked in the yard and upon the premises of a gentleman whose name was Perkins (Judge John Perkins), a representative in the Confederate Congress . . ."[53] This was the same plantation the Illinois troopers would occupy two days later. Colonel Cockrell heard from some sources that the Yankees were collecting contrabands and holding them in a nearby plantation:

[Col.] Cockrell determined to capture these Negroes, and the picket with them if possible . . . Taking our regiment and a few (other) companies . . . he left camp about three o'clock in the night. His design was to get there, secure his booty, and be off again before the enemy, in such close proximity, would be aroused.

Most of the route lay through a vast sheet of water, covering the surface of both woods and fields, from knee to waist deep, through which the men had to wade, and, at the same time, carefully protect their guns and ammunition.

A somewhat protracted and cautious march brought us about daylight, within sight of the house, when the colonel's dispositions were made so as to capture the parties without delay. The men were ordered not to fire unless attacked from the direction of the camp.

The picket was surrounded and cut off, our men receiving a few shots from it as we advanced. It surrendered immediately, however and was placed under guard. The shots aroused the darkies, who jumped up from their beds, in and around the house, and went yelling in every direction, badly frightened . . . When they found there was no intention to kill them, they became less noisy and clamorous.

The colonel now ordered some of the boys to go upstairs and see if anyone was there. Several of us rushed up the steps, and, upon entering one of the rooms . . . [surprised and captured] a tall, spare, grave looking personage, accompanied by a young athletic . . . Negress . . . It was not long before we discovered that this live and interesting sybarite was the chaplain . . . of an Illinois Cavalry regiment.

This occurrence and the principal actor in it were a source of rare amusement . . . to the pickets we had captured, the men of which . . . belonged to the same regiment as the chaplain.[54]

The humiliated chaplain was probably from the 2d or 3d Illinois Cavalry, judging by the available regimental records.[55]

On the tenth, Confederate Major General Dabney H. Maury, commanding a division under Lieutenant General Pemberton, had just returned to Vicksburg from Fort Pemberton, the outpost north of Vicksburg on the Yazoo River. After the Steele Bayou assault by Sherman had been beaten off in March, Maury had returned to Vicksburg and reviewed Sherman's expedition:

The operations of the enemy were characterized by a great want of energy, but by the usual disregard of the claims of humanity and of the usages of manly warfare; women and unarmed, helpless men were insulted, private dwellings and plantations were destroyed and plundered, the stock stolen or wantonly killed, the fruit trees belted, and every other means taken to gratify the cowardly instincts of base natures.[56]

INSIDE VICKSBURG

While the military struggled to keep up with events, the people of Vicksburg and northern Mississippi were facing the same increasing Union pressure. Grant's noose had been tightening around Vicksburg since January. All of the expeditions down the rivers, and the cavalry raids into the northern interior, had affected life in the city of Vicksburg. One difficulty had been getting mail.

Some Confederates were getting their mail with the help of a pair of enterprising young Rebels who started their own business as mail runners. Absalom Grimes and Bob Louden had been in the Confederate army, but decided they would prefer running mail between the army and the folks back home in Missouri. Grimes explained the intricate arrangements:

> We left the Army at Grand Gulf on March 29. We took things easy this trip, and reached Colonel Selby's, 10 miles northeast of Memphis on April 10. From there Miss Emma Selby took our Kentucky mail to Memphis and there expressed it to Mrs. Nichols, who kept a large hairdressing establishment in Louisville, while she herself proceeded to St Louis on the *Graham* with the Missouri mail. She had made two trips prior to this.[57]

It is not clear how well other mail systems worked, but because of the railroads' poor condition, runners like Grimes and Louden flourished. A note from a Texas officer stationed in Mississippi indicated that he had just received a letter in April 1863 sent him by his wife in July 1862. Even that was better than no mail at all. The newspapers kept the city informed about the war and its events, but individuals could wait for months for news of loved ones. A tragic entry in the diary of Kate Stone, is dramatic evidence:

> April 10
>
> Brother Walter died February 15, 1863 at Cotton Gin, Mississippi. Again has God smitten us, and this last trouble is almost more than we can bear. I can hardly believe that our bright, merry little

Brother Walter has been dead for seven weeks. And we cannot realize that he is gone forevermore. Even peace will not restore him to us at all. It is hard, hard that he should have to go, so full of life and happiness and with such promise of a noble manhood. We were always so proud of our six stalwart boys, and again one is snatched away and we cannot think of them without tears.

For seven long weeks my dear little brother has been sleeping in his lonely grave, far from all who loved him, and we knew it not until a few days ago. Even as I write, I feel his tears on my cheek and see him as I saw him last when I bade him goodby in Vicksburg, reigning in his horse on the summit of the hill and turning with flushed cheeks and tearful eyes to wave me a last farewell. And by the side of this picture is another that has haunted me ever since reading that fateful letter: I see him lying cold and still, dressed in black in his cold black coffin. His slender hands are worn and brown with the toil of his last four months and are crossed on his quiet breast. His handsome clearcut features are glaring cold and white, and the white lids are drawn down over the splendid gray eyes, so easy to fill with tears or brighten with laughter. The smile we know so well is resting on his lips. Happy boy, free from the toil and turmoil of life, safe in the morning of life in a glorious immortality.

It breaks our hearts to think of him sick and dying among strangers, a Negroes face the only familiar one near him . . . "He was riding with the cavalry and felt ill, stayed behind and died next day with his Negro servant Pompey." I hope he did not realize that Death was so near and all he loved so far away. Poor little fellow, he was not used to strangers. He has been surrounded by loved and familiar faces all his short life. He was 18 in December and died in February. He was but a boy and could not stand the hardships of a soldier's life. Four months of it killed him. We have no likeness [picture] of him. He has left only a memory and a name.[58]

Some of the Mississippi plantation owners were giving up. The following ad appeared in the *Daily Mississipian* of Jackson, Mississippi, on April 10:

Creek Bottom Plantation
For Sale
I wish to sell my plantation . . . containing
about 1,000 acres, mostly good creek bottom.
Good dwelling house, negro house, stables, etc. . . . .
Confederate or state money taken.[59]

Miss Mary Loughborough, a 27-year-old who formerly lived in Vicksburg, returned for a visit in April 1863. She described the mood of those who were living through the ordeal and lamented the tragic times:

And soon we see Vicksburg, classic ground forever in America. . . . I had thought, during the first bombardment of Vicksburg, that the town must have been a ruin; yet very little damage has been done, though very few houses are without evidence of the first trial of metal. One, I saw, with a hole through the window; behind one was one of corresponding size through the panel of the door, which happened to be open. The corner of the piano had been taken off, and on through the wall the shot passed; one, also, passed through another house, making a huge gap through the chimney. And yet the inhabitants live in their homes (those who have not lost some loved one) happy and contented, not knowing what moment the house may be rent over their heads by the explosion of a shell.

"Ah!" said I to a friend, "how is it possible you live here?" "After one is accustomed to the change," she answered, "we do not mind it; but becoming accustomed, that is the trial." I was reminded of the poor man in an infected district who was met by a traveler and asked, "How do you live here?" "Sir, we die," was the laconic reply. And this is becoming accustomed. I looked over this beautiful landscape, and in the distance plainly saw the Federal transports lying quietly at their anchorage. Was it a dream? Could I believe that over this smiling scene, in the bright April morning, the blight of civil warfare lay like a pall?—lay over the fearful homesteads—some, even now, jarred by the shock of former conflicts—lay by the hearthstones, making moan in many a bereaved heart looking forward with vague fears to the coming summer.

What soul in the land but has felt and witnessed this grief—unavailing sorrow for the brave and untimely dead? I thought of the letter from the sorrowing one in Iowa, whose son, a prisoner, I had nursed, receiving with the last breath words for the distant, unconscious mother; of her sorrow in writing of him in his distant grave; of her pride in him, her only son. How many in the land could take her hand and weep over a mutual sorrow! And in the hospital wards, men, who still hold the name of Americans, together were talking of battles, prisoners and captors, when each told the other of acts of bravery performed on hostile fields, and took out pictures of innocent babes, little children, and wives, to show each other, all feeling a sympathy and interest in the unknown faces. Verily, war is a species of passionate insanity.[60]

In the hospitals of Vicksburg, death was a relatively common occurrence during the days of their siege. A list of the hospital deaths on April 10, 1863, in Vicksburg reads as follows:[61]

991 Andrew Rodrigen	Co. D 1st Louisiana City Hospital
992 J. G. Murry	Co. E 79th Tennessee City Hospital
993 W. Terry	Co. G 4th Mississippi Hospital no. 3
994 Dennis Murphy	Co. B 11th Louisiana Arty Hospital no. 3
995 Gene Harrison	Co. F 31st Georgia
996 William Taylor	Co. E 80th Tennessee Hospital (Smallpox)
997 William Stewart	Co. B 60th Tennessee City Hospital
998 James Taylor	Co. I 62nd Tennessee City Hospital
No # Infant (Colored)	

In his diary, William Chambers of the 46th Mississippi noted the death of William R. Speed, 46th Mississippi, at the camp hospital on April 10.[62] Soldiers at these facilities, too, probably died alone, far from those who loved them, and the city was really too busy to mourn.

Death was no stranger to the children of Mississippi, with disease prevalent. The *Daily Mississippian* of Jackson reported the spring 1863 deaths in Raymond, Mississippi, of four children of Marmaduke and Levina Shannon. Lucy Shannon died on March 18 at age nine years, ten months; Clara Shannon died on April 6 at age twelve; Arthur Patridge Shannon died on April 8 at age two; and Isabella Howard Shannon died at age seven on April 10. All died of diphtheria; no Shannon children survived.[63]

Even though they were surrounded by tragedy, the people of the city found a brighter side to Vicksburg during these days. Conditions would worsen for them as time went on, but for a while there were still some good times to be had, especially at night, when activity hit its stride. Because of the ever-present military, the men outnumbered the ladies by a large margin. In the evenings the officers would squire the young ladies on buggy rides in the shadows of the forts and batteries of artillery, riding out on the country roads and forgetting for a while the war that surrounded them.[64]

Sometimes they even lightened up enough to play a prank or two on the belles of the day. The *Vicksburg Daily Whig* reported in early April that several young maidens had received enticing invitations for buggy rides from some gallant Confederate officers; however, the men never showed, and the ladies eventually gave up and went home to bed. The disappointed girls found out later that some of the lady rivals were responsible for the bogus invitations.[65] The *Whig* also reported incidents of officers who made promises to young women and were later discovered to be already encumbered by spouses and children back home—an embarrassing and shattering discovery for the women involved.[66]

Romance blossomed in spite of everything. A young Confederate officer, William R. Barry, wrote to his sister from Vicksburg on April 10, confessing that he was in love:

> I have not told you the Cream of it all yet. Oh, it is sweet! I don't think I can tell you I am afraid it will break the charm. I don't care a straw if the Yankees forever and eternally besiege this place. I don't want the war to stop for a long time to come, do you think I am crazy. I believe I am. I expect Maj. Scott will send me to the Asylum yet. . . . The house that we occupy belongs to a Mr. Brooks of this place but he has moved his family out to Brandon to get them out of harms way and if you must know he has a beautiful widowed daughter about sweet twenty one who visited V-burg last week and as a matter of course visited the old homestead. She was so much pleased with our house keeping she asked Mrs. Scott if she had any objections to her occupying her own room and she is now boarding with us. Good bye I am a goner, I hear her in the Parlor thumping the piano.[67]

OUTSIDE THE CITY

In the northern tier of Mississippi counties, Samuel A. Agnew, a circuit-riding preacher, wrote in his diary of the turmoil in the counties just south of Tennessee:

> April 10 This has been another smoky day and a little clouded . . . Understand that within the last 48 hours two mules have been stolen from Uncle Joseph. Some cavalry men who arrested Jno Bishop yesterday as a deserter got one of his mules near Mrs. Billingsleys. Mounted Bishop on it and went off with it. Another was taken out of his lot during last night. He intended to start out today on a search for them . . . A Mr. James Hall was shot by a Mr. McElroy this morning above Kelly's Mill. Hall was a conscriptor and had arrested McElroy's son (a deserter) the night before. Hall was badly hurt; not known whether the wound was mortal. Calvin Irwin was killed at Perryville in October . . . Every member of Salem

congregation under 40 years of age is connected to Richardson's [Confederate] guerrillas.

April 11th Uncle Jos mules are all at home . . . Uncle Joe has not returned yet. Some fear he has been conscripted, as the cavalry have been taking all from 18 to 45.[68]

Reports of atrocities were not commonplace during the war, but occasionally they were reported in the newspapers. The Jackson *Daily Mississippian* reported such an occurrence on April 10:

Some months ago Joshua Hilton, State Senator . . . with two of his nephews and another young man of his neighborhood, was taken prisoner by a company of Yankees while at home attending to his business. They were taken by their captors to one of their military posts in Dent County, where after a short imprisonment they were all deliberately shot except one who managed to escape and tell of the horrible fate of the others. After the men had been shot and their bodies laid on the ground, cold and stiffened in death, the blood-thirsty monsters, in order to make their crime more hideous if possible, actually severed the head from the dead Senator hoisted it upon a pole and planted it by the side of the road.[69]

Newspapers in this war, as in all wars, were inclined to publish such accounts for propaganda purposes, so the accuracy of this one is unknown.

Events such as these, grim as they were, were not uppermost in the minds of the private soldier. His thoughts were more personal. Confederate Private W. A. Stevens of the 46th Alabama, who was north of Vicksburg at Chickasaw, writing home on April 13, expressed the thought uppermost in the minds of most Confederates:

I am a way and canot get back and I no thare is no use in bein down in the mouth a bout it—we just as well laugh as cry though our fare is hard I fear that we will have to fare harder now than we have ben . . . Oh if we cold only have Pease once more and I cold get a home in such a contrey as this if the winter wold not be so raney and the insects so bad in the sumer I think I cold live as happy as a king.[70]

AROUND MEMPHIS

Memphis, one of the Union's most important Mississippi River ports, was the seat of the XVI Corps under General Hurlbut. It was a busy place as it funneled men and goods south to the Vicksburg campaign. Memphis itself was not a bad place to be; it wasn't always as hospitable as the Yankees hoped, but in the midst of debauchery there was culture available, too, according to Lucius W. Barber, a young Illinois volunteer, in his April 10 diary entry:

> In addition to our lyceum, a reading room was established and a small tax of 5 cents a week, for each member, furnished us with all the wholesome reading matter we could digest. A class in bookkeeping was also established; also a sort of normal school for reviewing the common branches of learning. These exercises, with my usual duties, kept my time pretty well occupied and the time glided swiftly and silently by. While we were thus occupied, many were spending the days and nights in the foul atmosphere of the city, frequenting haunts of vice and dissipation. Not satisfied with that, the atmosphere of camp must needs be corrupted with poor degraded women.[71]

Barber, from the 15th Illinois Infantry, wrote again on the fifteenth, bemoaning the state of the city:

> So foul had the morals of the city become that Gen. [Brigadier General James C.] Veatch issued an order expelling 2 boatloads of fallen humanity. Indeed, matters had come to such a pass that a decent lady was ashamed to be seen on the street, and stringent measures had to be resorted to remedy the evil. All the bad passions of the naturally dissipated in our division were brought to light here, and too often were the young and noble drawn into this whirlpool of vice.[72]

Mail was as common a topic in Memphis as elsewhere, both for its absence and for its content. Francis Wayland Dunn, a private in Company A of the 64th Illinois Infantry, was troubled. His brother Ransom, who had been in his company, had died of pneumonia in Corinth in March, and the boys' father, back in Illinois, was taking it very badly. Private Dunn expressed his concern in his diary:

> April 3—Wanted to go to Corinth to express Ransom's knapsack but the train was too late.
> April 6th—Read Fantine in Les Miserables. It is very hard to pass any time and the camp is so lonesome, dreary and tiresome work.

April 8th—A letter came to Ransom

April 9th—No letters from home. I am getting very anxious. Father is so weak and if both are gone then in this present there is nothing earthly to live for nothing but duty.[73]

The following day, April 10, he sounded cheerier but still worried:

Conyer got a letter from father about me. He thought I had been taken on the way from Memphis to Corinth but the train was captured on Sat. and I went on Sun. Father is almost unmaned his writing is nervous and broken. I wish I could go home It is a real sacrifice to give it up In his letter he wanted to know if there was not some way that I could get out of it Get a commission with the understanding that I should resign or some other way. But there is none I could not get out if I was an officer without I was sick and I could hardly get a commission anyway.[74]

On April 10, Sister M., a nun from Saint Agnes Academy in Memphis, wrote a worried letter to General Sherman in Milliken's Bend, looking for reassurances in case the Yankees were not successful in taking Vicksburg. She entreated:

It has been darkly hinted that in the event of Vicksburg's not falling, troops in returning are to be let loose on the town to burn, pillage and destroy life, property and reputation of all who shall then be found here. . . . Let me appeal to your friendship as a man and to your feelings as a father to advise us what course you will pursue in case your own family were so circumstanced. Of course we do not expect information from our friend which would be incompatible with the duty of the general.[75]

There was no answering letter in the file.

At least the weather was good. Outside Memphis, in Corinth, Mississippi, a happy Private George Cadman wrote to his wife from Camp Ohio on April 9:

This seems to be the pleasantest time of the year in this part of the country. It is now spring in all its glory. Flowers are in blossom, birds are singing, and everything seems at peace but man. But the sun is pouring down its rays this afternoon with intense power, and if it were not for a delightful breeze, the heat would be almost unbearable.

On the 7th, the anniversary of the battle of Pittsburg Landing and also of the settlement of Ohio, the troops had a grand time. All the troops around Corinth, fourteen regiments, besides cavalry and artillery, were reviewed and marched into town, where speeches were made with plenty of patriotic demonstrations.[76]

Cadman also enclosed a lengthy poem detailing how he felt about the Copperheads. It wasn't a literary masterpiece, but it expressed the contempt felt by the soldiers toward the movement.

Others were as concerned about their leadership as they were about politics or even camp life. The ranks were ready to fight and willing to suffer any consequences, being almost resigned to chronic mismanagement. Major James H. Goodnow referred to the inept Union leadership in an April 10 letter to his family from Colliersville, Tennessee, where his 12th Indiana Regiment was doing train guard duty:

The armies being nearly even in number in the south west— they [Confederates] may with their generalship beat us after all— This is doubtless the dark side of the subject—but we have nothing to expect from our leaders but blunders and with one or two honorable exceptions our Generals seem only to be in the way of the armies they command.[77]

UNION ACTION IN THE MEMPHIS AREA

The Mississippi River provided other noteworthy incidents on April 10, 1863. Captain William Montague Ferry, 14th Michigan Infantry, was part of the commissary of the 7th Division. He was on board the steamer *Tempest,* running supplies down from Memphis, Tennessee, and Helena, Arkansas. The steamer captain was unhappy about the dangerous trip taking supplies down to Yazoo Pass, where Ferry was to deliver his goods. In a ploy to keep his boat (and himself) out of danger, the *Tempest* captain had two holes drilled in the bottom of the boat. When he arrived in Helena he reported to the port authorities that the boat was sinking and was in no condition to go on. Captain Ferry was suspicious, so he did some sleuthing on his own. The captain, an old Great Lakes seafaring man from Grand Haven, Michigan, knew his way around ships, much to the dismay of the reluctant skipper of the *Tempest.* Ferry found the holes but said nothing at the time. He ordered the pumps manned to keep the boat from sinking any further:

And then had Mr. Captain arrested the next bright morning
before he was out of bed—having had the Carpenter who did the job
<u>first</u> before the Provost Marshall, in whose august presence he made
a clean breast of all the facts and acknowledged that he did the job
<u>by order of the captain</u> to prevent the boat from going down the
pass—walked Mr. Captain (the rebel scoundrel) to the Provost Marshall office and he <u>owned up</u>—Oh, how he begged for mercy! . . .
I am sorry I look so little like a sailor that he should have indulged
the hope of fooling me in regard to any water craft or their peculiar
prerequisites . . . So I am Captain of the steamer just now as well
as Capt. and C.S.[78]

Part of General Hurlbut's job was to garrison much of the surrounding area; his troops were scattered all over the east bank of the
Mississippi. Although the April 30 returns show that he had 50,000 men
present for duty, these were split among a variety of duties and gar-
risons, for Hurlbut was responsible for a substantial territory.

In order to control that much territory, cavalry was a critical factor
in Memphis—as it was in other areas. General Hurlbut had already
committed to sending General Dodge with some 5,000 infantry and
cavalry from the 2d Division, in Corinth, Mississippi, to support the
Streight raid, but Hurlbut was also concerned about the Confederate
force in Panola, Mississippi. This was the Fifth Military District of
Pemberton's Department of Mississippi and East Louisiana, whose cavalry had pestered Memphis-to-Corinth communications for many
weeks. Commander Brigadier General James Chalmers led about 1,000
Mississippi cavalrymen who had been Pemberton's main cavalry, his
eyes and ears as Grant made his many river attempts against Vicksburg.

On April 10, Hurlbut wired Major General B. M. Prentiss, commanding the post in Helena, Arkansas, asking for some help in subdu-
ing Chalmers. Helena formed the western point of a triangle completed
by Memphis and Panola. Hurlbut asked Prentiss to move across the
river and catch Chalmers while Hurlbut came south from Memphis.
Prentiss wired back on the next day, saying he had already sent nine
regiments of infantry, four batteries of artillery, and one company of
cavalry to Grant, and that was all he could spare. So Hurlbut could do
little but look to his own resources.[79] It really didn't matter too much,
since all the activity was in Grant's area, away from the Memphis/
Helena/Panola theater.

Another Union expedition, coming from Greenville, Mississippi,
down Deer Creek, was engaged on April 10. Brigadier General Frederick Steele had been sent by Hurlbut to chase some bothersome Rebels

out of the Deer Creek area. The Confederate cavalry under Colonel Samuel Ferguson was foraging and harassing in the area, and Steele wanted them out. Steele left Greenville, Mississippi, on the seventh with eight regiments and an artillery battery. They found the Confederates about forty-three miles down Deer Creek and had a brief artillery and infantry clash on the ninth; General Steele suffered casualties of one killed and one wounded, then withdrew back toward Greenville.[80]

Rebel Captain E. D. Willett reported on the Confederate part of the action:

On Tuesday April 2nd, Companies "A" and "B" under command of Capt. Willett started for Fish Lake sixty miles up Deer Creek near Greenville. 2nd April marched to Capt. Willis' farm; 3rd April to Thomas' farm; April 4th to Falls' farm; April 5th to Yerger's farm; April 6th to Fish Lake; reported to Maj. Bridges in command of battalion of sharpshooters, 250. Remained there until morning of April 7th, when it was ascertained, that Gen. Steele with 13 regiments, 8 pieces of artillery and 250 cavalry pursued us from Greenville. Col. Ferguson ordered a retreat at 7 o'clock, and we retreated 22 miles to Fall's by dark. Next day fell back to Thomas' where four more companies of 40th [Alabama] came up and three pieces of artillery. There we made a stand and shelled the enemy with seven pieces of cannon, and the enemy, though in superior force, commenced retreating.[81]

Part of Ferguson's command chased Steele's men back, and on the tenth, just short of Greenville, drove in the Union pickets, killing twenty-one-year-old Arnold Conlan of Kane's Company, 15th Illinois Cavalry. Steele was back in Greenville on the tenth, and Confederates were pondering the results of his foray.

In his report dated April 9, Confederate Brigadier General Stephen D. Lee, Ferguson's commander, reported some potential worries:

I have the honor to report my arrival at this point [Willis's place, Upper Deer Creek, eighteen miles above Rolling Fork] last night. Colonel Ferguson halted here to give the Yankees battle, but yesterday evening he discovered that they were falling back rapidly, destroying everything eatable before them, and they are now, or were last night at midnight, 20 miles above this point, at Taylor's place [forty miles above Rolling Fork]. They did not leave a particle of anything for the planters to subsist on, but said they intended to destroy everything this side of Greenville. I have ordered Col. Fergu-

son to follow them with his force, and I will be ready to assist him. It
now becomes a serious matter how troops are to be subsisted above
this point, and the colonel, after discovering further of the movements of the enemy, will be directed to return, at least to this point,
leaving an observing squad near Greenville . . . Their object was, I
think, to destroy provisions. The negroes are in a pretty bad condition, and a larger force of cavalry, say a regiment, is needed here, as
only cavalry can get through the swamps. But it should be borne in
mind that corn will now be scarce, and the general had better delay
till I hear through Colonel Ferguson the extent of their destruction.[82]

The secondary object of Steele's raid was to destroy the crops, the
homes, and the possessions of the Southerners in his path; in this mission he succeeded. Private J. Russell of the 13th Illinois Infantry detailed
the pillaging and burning:

We had marched over one of the richest portions of the State
and when we turned back the work of destruction commenced. Our
route was along Deer Creek and it was very thickly settled by rich
planters. We set fire to their corn cribs cotton-gins and mills, took
their horses mules cattle provisions and many of their negroes . . .
In many instances they had taken their property away to the cane
brakes; but notwithstanding this we got huge quantities of provisions
& other property.[83]

Another skirmish took place on April 10 during the same Steele
expedition in Mississippi. The 76th Ohio and the 4th Iowa Infantry
found some of Ferguson's troops, but neither side reported any casualties, and it was a short-lived affair. Major Charles Dana Miller of the
76th Ohio mentioned the action briefly: "When the Division had
reached Block Bayou, within six miles of Greenville, the rear guard was
fired upon by Rebel cavalry and the infantry again formed in line, but
the enemy again made a hasty retreat. The troops arrived at the boats on
the 10th and bivouacked on the river bank."[84]

GRIERSON'S RAID

On the tenth of April, another cavalry raid was begun that would
partially offset the disastrous ending of Abel Streight's effort. Grant had
requested the raid to divert attention from his west bank movement and
to disrupt as much of the Confederate communications and transportation system as possible. The raiders were to leave almost simultaneously

with the departure of Streight's balky mules, but this second force would have a far better chance for success.

The raid was led by Colonel Benjamin Henry Grierson, a former music teacher from Jacksonville, Illinois, with an almost pathological dislike of horses. Because of a boyhood kick from his pony, Grierson had been badly scarred, both mentally and facially. When he enlisted early in the war and was given a cavalry assignment, he tried every device he could think of to get an infantry commission. He finally resigned himself to the fact that his destiny, and his commission, were tied to cavalry.[85]

His orders came from General Hurlbut in Memphis to Brigadier General W. Sooy Smith, commander of the 6th Division, XVI Corps, at La Grange, Tennessee. The orders were dated April 10, 1863:

> The time for our projected cavalry movement is rapidly approaching. General Dodge, in connection with General Rosecrans, is about to move on Tuscumbia [Streight's raid] . . . As soon as this movement is inaugurated, and the attention of the enemy drawn to that part of our line, your three regiments of cavalry will strike out by way of Pontotoc, breaking off right and left, cutting both roads, destroying the wires, burning provisions, and doing all the mischief they can, while one regiment ranges straight down to Selma or Meridian, breaking the east and west road thoroughly, and sweeping back by Alabama. Rosecrans' cavalry will return through North Alabama, and thus cut the road from Corinth a second time.[86]

On April 13, Hurlbut wired Grierson, home on leave in Jacksonville, Illinois, to return immediately.[87] The raid was on. Grierson's brigade consisted of three regiments: the 6th Illinois, the 7th Illinois, and the 2d Iowa, all cavalry units, about 1,700 men mounted on strong horses, not mules. In addition, Battery K of the 1st Illinois Artillery added six two-pounder guns to the brigade.

The brigade left La Grange, Tennessee, on April 17 and headed originally for Newton Station, Mississippi. However, Grierson decided to split his force; on April 21, he sent Colonel Edward Hatch with his 2d Iowa Cavalry on a separate mission, eastward, then back to La Grange. The idea was to create additional confusion in the Confederates in Mississippi, who would be trying to track both raiding forces. From Newton Station, Grierson and his two Illinois regiments, instead of returning to La Grange, headed southwest through Mississippi, fighting Confederate cavalry on an almost daily basis. The big fight was at Newton Station, where the Yankee cavalry captured two trains and demolished the tracks of the Vicksburg Railroad as a result of a charge led by a dashing Illinois cavalryman, Lieutenant Colonel William Blackburn.[88]

This Union cavalry raid was a huge success, and Grierson received a hero's welcome when he arrived in Baton Rouge fifteen days later. It was obvious he deserved the praise and fame. Grierson summarized what his fifteen days of raiding from La Grange, Tennessee, to Baton Rouge, Louisiana, had accomplished:

> During the expedition we killed and wounded about one hundred of the enemy, captured and paroled over 500 prisoners, many of them officers, destroyed between fifty and sixty miles of railroad and telegraph, captured and destroyed over 3,000 stand of arms, and other army stores and Government property to an immense amount; we also captured 1,000 horses and mules.
>
> Our loss during the entire journey was 3 killed, 7 wounded, 5 left on the route sick; the sergeant major and surgeon of the Seventh Illinois left with Lt. Col. Blackburn, and 9 men missing, supposed to have straggled. We marched over 600 miles in less than sixteen days. The last twenty-eight hours we marched 76 miles, had four engagements with the enemy, and forded the Comite River, which was deep enough to swim many of the horses. During the time the men and horses were without food or rest.[89]

The effect of Grierson's raid was to thoroughly confuse the Confederate forces in Mississippi, taking the pressure off Grant as he moved his troops into position for his next campaign. No mean accomplishment for a music teacher who hated horses.

Grierson's raid illustrated an important part of Grant's strategy: total destruction of anything that would benefit the Confederacy. On April 11, in a message to General Steele, Grant explained his reasoning:

> Rebellion has assumed the shape now that it can only terminate by the complete subjugation of the South or the overthrow of the Government. It is our duty, therefore, to use every means to weaken the enemy, by destroying their means of subsistence, withdrawing their means of cultivating their fields, and in every other way possible.[90]

On April 10, Grant was placing his troops in a position where they would be cut off from their own supply lines and living off the land, destroying what else was left as they moved to encircle Vicksburg. All of the massive movements of Grant's ground forces and Porter's boats were finally directed toward a tactic that was risky but focused. The previous plans had been creative and ingenious, but never as concentrated as this one.

For Confederates, there was an assurance that Vicksburg would be a repeat of what had happened elsewhere in the South. In Charleston, Atlanta, and Virginia, there had been nothing but Confederate success, and the prevailing opinion was that the scenario would not change. Confidence, born of two years of consistent outperformance of Yankee forces, had fostered an aura of invincibility that supported the faith in the "Cause." The impending struggles for Vicksburg and at Gettysburg would be the first significant events that would shatter the myth.

★

General Grant's final plan was successful. Vicksburg was taken, after a forty-seven-day siege, on July 4, 1863.

Grant became the eighteenth president of the United States in 1869.

Porter and Sherman remained lifelong friends and died one day apart in 1891.

Union Major General James McPherson was killed in the battle of Atlanta in July 1864 at the age of thirty-five.

Private W. A. Stevens died in the Johnson Island prison in 1865.

Private John G. Jones was killed in Jackson, Louisiana, on October 5, 1864. He was twenty-one years and four months old.

Kate Stone lost another brother, Coley, just before the war ended.

Lieutenant Colonel William Blackburn was wounded on May 1, 1863, and died shortly after.

John Wayne starred in a 1975 movie version of Grierson's raid, The Horse Soldiers.

12

THE GULF

While General Grant was working his engineering marvels around Vicksburg, he was still firmly attached to the Union, able to move troops and receive supplies through normal routes. Not all departments were so lucky.

The Department of the Gulf, also called the XIX Corps, had one unique feature it did not share with other Yankee departments. Headquartered in New Orleans, it was totally isolated from other Union forces, except by water, and was the farthest from any friendly territory. To the east was Mobile, Alabama; to the north was Port Hudson, Louisiana; and to the west was Texas. Each of these areas was controlled by the Confederates. Only to the south, in the Gulf of Mexico, was there access to a friendly force, the Union navy. The department's isolation was illustrated by the fact that communication between the Department of the Gulf, in New Orleans, and Grant, who was four hundred river miles north of New Orleans, often went through New York.

There were some 34,000 troops in the department. The troops were based in areas around New Orleans and Baton Rouge, and extending to the isolated coastal areas of Ship Island, Mississippi, and Pensacola and Key West, Florida. The department's commanding general was Major General Nathaniel P. Banks, a forty-seven-year-old politician turned general who had replaced the autocratic Major General Ben Butler in October 1862. His was a primarily defensive role, but on April 10 he was in Brashear City, Louisiana, leading an expedition against able Confederate Major General Richard Taylor, son of the twelfth U.S. president, Zachary Taylor, and the commander of the Department of West Louisiana in the Trans-Mississippi Department.

On April 10, 1863, Banks had 7,000 men in the Baton Rouge area and 9,000 men of the 2d Division in the New Orleans sector. Another 3,000 men were spread along the Mississippi-Florida coast. The rest of the army, more than 15,000 men, was moving toward Berwick Bay,

Louisiana, preparing for a move on Bayou Teche in western Louisiana to find food and forage. Two divisions, the 3d, under Brigadier General W. H. Emory, and the 4th, under Brigadier General C. Grover, plus a brigade under Brigadier General Godfrey Weitzel, were ready to begin the offensive on April 11. The Union troops were to move to Brashear City. General Emory and General Weitzel would cross Berwick Bay and frontally attack Taylor's 4,000 Confederate troops; General Grover's division would go by ship, then by flatboats on Grand Lake, and move up the lake to cut off the Confederates.

Banks telegraphed Grant on the tenth:

> We shall move upon the Bayou Teche tomorrow, probably encounter the enemy at Pattersonville and hope to move without delay upon Iberia, destroy the salt works and then to Opelousas. This is the limit proposed. We do not intend to hold any of this country as it weakens our force, but will at once return to Baton Rouge to cooperate with you against Port Hudson. I can easily be there by May 10.[1]

Banks's offensive had one primary goal: to find forage and food. His mission, similar to the one given to Longstreet in Virginia, was to clean out the area so that the North would be supplied and the South would be deprived. To this end his expedition was a success. The fertile lands of the Delta and lower Louisiana were highly productive; as Banks moved to the west, he was able to send back his wagons loaded with the foodstuffs and products of the area. So the 15,000 men Grant had hoped to use at Vicksburg were not available to him. Because Banks's campaign was so successful, he prolonged the expedition, moving farther west, away from Grant. He was fully occupied with his own plan and chose not to get back to rendezvous with Grant. Banks was senior to Grant by date of rank, so he was not subject to Grant's authority.[2]

Most of the Union troops in the commands of Weitzel, Emory, and Grover on April 10 were scattered between New Orleans, Baton Rouge, and Brashear City, but all were moving to Brashear City from their various locations by foot, rail, and wagon. Colonel Thomas Chickering of the 41st Massachussetts entered in his diary:

> On the 28th of March "Grover's Division" to which the 41st was attached, marched from Donaldsville through La Fourche country via Thibadeaux, Terre Bonne & Bayou Boeuf to Brashear, where Divisions of General Emory, Grover, and Weitzel were united under

Major General Banks. Grover's Division left Brashear April 12, 1863.[3]

Another early arrival was Lieutenant Colonel Frank Peck, who, with his 12th Connecticut Volunteers, had moved to a camp just outside Brashear City. He wrote to his mother on March 31, 1863, saying that he was less than enthusiastic about the camp:

There is only a narrow strip of land here between the bayou and the swamp and such a place for mosquitoes is seldom found in this climate. We pitched our tents and slept on the ground. The next morning as we were nibbling our breakfast of hard tack and coffee it began to rain. Somebody looked at his foot and found it in the water. We took warning and raised up. Before we had finished the water had risen so that we had to put our feet on the table and there was not a square foot in the tent not flooded inches deep.[4]

Private Frank M. Flinn, 38th Massachusetts Infantry, recounted the trip to Brashear City:

At 2 o'clock, on the morning of the 9th the reveille woke the sleeping camp. Tents were struck and by 7 o'clock the regiment was on board of the cars bound for the interior of Louisiana [from Algiers, opposite New Orleans]. For eighty miles we rode on platform and baggage cars, through the lowlands of Louisiana. For a long distance we ran through a dense cypress swamp, such a one as we had not seen before. It was like a wall of vegetation, almost, on each side, and through the leaves we could see dark bayous and black pools. Alligators several feet long lay on logs or in the water. Snakes, single or in coils, lay basking in the sun. There were turtles and lizards by the barrel, and the trees were draped with the peculiar southern moss. The road was guarded by the New York and Connecticut Regiments and we did not envy them their pleasant job. A little after noon the train arrived in Brashear City. For fear that the reader may dwell on the idea that Brashear City is a large one, I will say at once that it is not. It consists of a few houses and lots of mud.[5]

The sights and sounds of the swamp areas around New Orleans made powerful impressions on the men; almost all of the regiments were from the northeast coast, and most of the men had never seen anything resembling the exotic scenery of Louisiana. James K. Hosner of the 52d Massachusetts Infantry wrote:

April 10—We have made another move, and are now at "Brashear City," on the emouchure of the Atchafalaya [River]—a city which consists of a wharf and a railroad-depot, and but little besides. My feet rest in the crushed clover, upon which our blankets were spread as we slept last night; and through the opening of the tent, just far enough off to prevent our being swept away by the tail of some enterprising alligator, I see flowing the bayou, with sugar-houses on the opposite shore, and cypresses behind,—the tall dark trees that tell of swamps.[6]

Hosner, a minister, went on to portray not only his visual impression but his emotional impression of the swamps as well:

I have now seen numbers of streams and much country, and am familiar with the strange aspects of a Louisiana landscape. Of course, we know, that, on this globe, water plays the principal part, and land is secondary. As Northerners know nature, however, it is land that is most exulting, bounding, as it does, into hills, standing kingly in mountains; while water, more humble, hides in glens, or flows in submissive rivers before the feet of lordly ranges. Here, however, water bears itself arrogantly—floating sometimes above the level of the soil; sometimes just even with it, as here, where the ripples of the brimful stream threaten the clover-flowers, which are scarcely above them. Meanwhile, a furlong or so in the rear, is the swamp, as ever, close at hand—the traitor in the heart, ready to help the foe outside. Water is thus haughty and encroaching; while land is a poor, cowed, second-fiddle-playing creature—only existing, apparently, that water may have something to pour itself out over and exhibit itself on.[7]

He then critiqued the vegetation:

Then, too, the painful sycophancy of the vegetable kingdom! It owes its whole existence and consequence to land, if anything does; yet here, like a set of false hearted flatterers, trees and weeds go toadying the ruling power. The forests are watery: old trunks robe themselves in moss, counterfeiting the appearance of discolored growths of coral; and, along the brinks of bayous, stout hearted live-oaks even, that ought to be ashamed of themselves, bend almost horizontally over the currents, or indeed, sometimes, as in one case right here in our camp, hold on by the roots, and grow downwards almost, letting the water flow around and over them, just raising their tops above the stream, a rod or two out from shore—all this

fawning and hanging-on, instead of growing straight up, and fling-
ing out their tops like independent and self-respecting growths![8]

Private D. S. Chadbourne of the 22d Maine wrote his father from
Brashear City:

Friday Morning 10th
    This morning the sun has risen clear and it bids fair for a hot
day, we have no stormy nor cloudy weather for nearly a month. I
don't think I have seen a cloud in the sky for two weeks and it is so
hot and sultry about two-thirds of the day. At night it is quite cool
and very heavy dews fall. Also there is a moisture that rises from out
of the ground that would wet two woolen blankets through, but
luckily we have a rubber to spread under us.
    Our regiment is in good condition at this time not hardly any
has been taken sick lately, and the ones that have been sick in Hospital are coming to the regiment almost every day, we have had six
come to our regiment within one week. Our colonel arrived from
Baton Rouge Hospital last night I understand that he is not fit for
duty. Several of the company officers came with him.[9]

Some of the Union troops had already crossed Berwick Bay and on
April 10 were camped in Berwick City. One of these was Private
Ephraim Betts, 114th New York. His diary related the movement of his
unit:

9th April—Pleasant we was ordered to leave camp and went abord
of the Gunboat about 9 AM We did not land the other side of the
Bay till after noon. We formed to march out back and camptd Stade
all night we slept out there—there was fifty five men and one com-
mish officer it was Reynolds. Lieutenant Longwell had command of
the company.
10—Pleasant we lay at Berwick all day & night thare was a good
many troops hear.[10]

These men, Flinn, Hosner, Chadbourne, and Betts, were in separate commands; Flinn and Betts, in the two divisions of Weitzel and
Emory, were destined to cross the Atchafalaya River at Brashear City
and engage Taylor's men near Pattersonville, while the Reverend Hosner and Chadbourne, in Grover's division, were with the troops that
were scheduled to board transports, go up Grand Lake, and disembark

on flatboats near Bayou Teche to cut off Taylor's retreat up the peninsula.

Lieutenant Colonel David Hunter Strother, one of Grover's staff officers, was in high spirits. In his diary, on April 11 he extolled the glories of war:

> The tantara of drums and bugles sounded agreeably to me this morning. War is a business as natural to man as hunting squirrels or tilling the soil. Oh, seraphine philosophers, preachers and poetic politicians, how vain are your theories and futile efforts, and how they evaporate before the great fire of human nature as the dew and mists of morning dry up in the face of the sun. How long are we to permit ourselves to be deceived by ideologists and babblers! Man the peace lover is simply a poltroon and a coward. Roll your drums, flaunt your banners, and advance to the battlefield. War is a joy and glory of our race . . . We embarked men and horses in the steamer *Laurel Hill* and, steaming across the bay, landed at the village and planted our headquarters flag at a private residence at the landing.[11]

Banks's plan was sound; however, the flats needed for getting ashore from the gunboats were not available when Grover arrived at Brashear City, and he was unable to embark until late on the eleventh. He managed to get ashore and inland before Taylor had all of his troops pulled back; however, Taylor still eluded Grover.

As the Union units pulled into their respective positions, they waited for the orders to attack the Southern troops, orders that would come on April 11 and 12.

The U.S. Navy provided another assist to the Union's western campaigns: the gunboats *Clifton, Estrella, St. Marys,* and *Calhoun,* a small flotilla commanded by Lieutenant Commander Cooke, became transports for Grover's troopers. Later in the week these same gunboats would help eliminate the two Confederate ships on Grand Lake, the *Diana* and the ram *Queen of the West,* both of which had been seized from the Union navy earlier in the war.

CONFEDERATES ON THE BAYOU

The Confederates on Bayou Teche were pulling back, keeping just out of the grasp of the two pincers that Banks had devised. The Yankees certainly had the advantage of numbers, almost four to one, but the Confederates knew the territory well and had a primitive fortification at Fort Bisland in Pattersonville, where Taylor found refuge on April 10.

The land there was low and very swampy, with Bayou Teche on one side and a huge spongy morass on the other. The Confederates knew that the Union forces would have to pass through Pattersonville; they intended to hold that area for as long as possible.

Camp, or Fort, Bisland was far from a perfect fortress. Actually, when Taylor's forces arrived they found an incomplete works, not really adequate for any defensive action. Brigadier General Alfred Mouton, one of the first to arrive, reported:

> On reaching Camp Bisland it was ascertained that the line of intrenchments on the east bank of the Teche, corresponding with those on the west bank recently thrown up, had not even been commenced, and by the direction of the major general measures were immediately adopted to complete them. Lt. Mullet and Pvt. Alfred Fusilier, the latter acting on my staff as assistant engineer, were placed in charge late on Friday the 10th. The necessary orders were issued for obtaining hands, and by the most strenuous efforts negroes were collected during the night and the works commenced early on Saturday. From this moment until Monday morning the labor was continued night and day by the troops under my command and the negroes obtained, with only momentary interruptions, occasioned by the artillery fire of the enemy.[12]

Meanwhile, Taylor gathered what few troops he could find in the area, moving them into the fort. Saint Mary's Cannoneers was one such group; on April 10 it arrived at the fort from its normal assignment near the little town of Lecompte, Louisiana. The battery commander, Captain F. O. Forney, reported on April 23:

> Major: I take pleasure, in obedience to your order of this date, to make the following report of the part taken by my company in the engagement which followed the advance of the enemy from Berwick Bay.
> I left camp of instruction at Camp Hunter on the 9th instant, with Lt. Tarelton's section of my battery, stopping below Centerville as ordered to be joined by the two sections of my battery on detached service at Bayou Sale, and on the night of the 10th reached Camp Bisland . . .[13]

Captain Forney's little group of artillerymen had been at Fort Jackson, protecting New Orleans during its attack by Admiral Farragut in April 1862. The other Confederate troops at Fort Jackson had mutinied during Farragut's attack, but these cannoneers had remained faithful to their duty. When the fort surrendered, they were paroled with the officers, exchanged, and had been campaigning with Taylor ever since.[14]

The only mention of fighting in this area on April 10 was Confederate General Taylor's report indicating that Colonel Thomas Green's 5th Texas Mounted Volunteers clashed with advance elements of Union General Weitzel's brigade, with apparently no casualties on either side. The skirmishing accompanied the movement of the scouts of Weitzel's brigade. Colonel Green's Texans furnished the rearguard action all the way back to Fort Bisland. Taylor praised them highly:

> To the military knowledge, intrepidity, and undaunted bravery of Col. T. Green I am greatly indebted for the successful check of the advance of the enemy. From our entrenchments to Opelousas he brought up the rear, faced the enemy at every step, and exhibited energy, zeal and courage unsurpassable by that of any officer in the service.[15]

Colonel Green wasn't the only one cited for outstanding performance. General Taylor was also acknowledged by the commanding general of the Trans-Mississippi Department, Lieutenant General Kirby Smith.

> Headquarters Department Trans-Mississippi
> Alexandria, La. April 23, 1863
>
> General [General S. Cooper in Richmond]:
> I have the honor to inclose a report of General Taylor's recent operations in the Teche and in Western Louisiana. The enemy landed at Berwick Bay a column of at least 18,000 men, thoroughly equipped and prepared for offensive operations. General Taylor's force was not over 4,000.
> The completeness with which the enemy was repulsed in his attacks of the 12th and 13th, the skill and ability with which our little army was extricated from apparently irretrievable destruction on the 14th, the obstinacy with which every foot of ground was contested in the retreat, and the successful saving of our material and stores under circumstances of great difficulty stamps General Taylor as a leader of no ordinary merit.[16]

OTHER UNION TROOPS IN THE GULF COMMAND

Those 15,000 men involved in the Bayou Teche campaign were only a portion of the Union Department of the Gulf; other units of the Gulf command were coping with different assignments as best they could.

In New Orleans, most of the troops were reasonably content. Writing to his sister and brother, Michigan Corporal Charles Henry Moulton indicated that things were not very fair for enlisted personnel:

> I am well and fat as a pork I believe it agrees with me living in this city. We have nothing to do only eat and sleep most of the time—once in awhile we have to get up and dust but we don't care now whether we do much or not the Govt has stopped our extra pay it is very smart in them I would not care if they would only use the officers the same way.[17]

He told how the officers got rations and quarters and made money, then complained, "I am glad Dan is exempt from the draft for God knows I hope he will never have to go soldiering as any man might as well be a dog as an enlisted man in the army our patriotism is getting down thin here the new troops here are deserting like the devil at Baton Rouge."[18] Moulton did make the move from corporal to captain; it is assumed he liked life better as an officer.

Captain Eli A. Griffin of the 6th Michigan Regiment had been on a scout to Ponchatoula, Louisiana, and was just returning to "comfortable" quarters at Camp Sherman, ten miles north of New Orleans. There had been two skirmishes, and the weather had been against them, raining much of the time, so they were glad to be getting back. He wrote on April 9 to a friend back home:

> We have been out longer than expected but will be in our comfortable quarters in a few days at Camp Sherman 10 miles above New Orleans, adjoining Trudeau's Plantation. Old Trudeau and his sons are in the Confed. Army. I have only had my clothes off twice in three weeks or since we left camp slept on the ground the whole time sometime with only a blanket over me . . .
>
> I hope the Conscript Law will do something towards ending this infernal war. It will help some I think at least if we do not succeed soon we may as well quit. But we shall win sure.[19]

Griffin's next letter was to his wife on April 13, from De Sair Station, thirty miles from New Orleans:

I don't think we shall stay here long as it is a terrible place. Swamps and alligators. The boys keep young alligators for pets . . . I went through the Swamp a few days since and its awful. Great snakes and alligators come down to the boat. Dark damp and gloomy and dismal. . . . We get thousands of blackberries here and it makes our fare much better.[20]

In Baton Rouge, Robert W. Torrey, a soldier from Massachusetts, made a diary entry on the ninth, saying simply, "Very hot—the hottest day yet."[21] On the tenth, he added, "I am on company police. Morning, company. Afternoon, company drill from 3:30 until 5 o'clock. No dress parade but roll call as usual. Weather: morning, few clouds; afternoon, cloudy, little broken. The clouds make it a little cooler. Winds, southwest; calm."[22]

Disease was a constant cause for concern with troops in the Department of the Gulf. Captain Jonathan Huntington Johnson, Company D, 15th New Hampshire Volunteers, wrote to his wife on the tenth:

Since I last wrote you I have been quite unwell. I caught cold the night I was on Brigade Officer-of-the-Day, being out so much in the night and this is such a poor climate it is quite sure to make one sick. I am better now, so that I shall be able to do duty today . . . Our Col. and Lt. Col. Blair are very sick now. We have only one field officer for duty and 3 captains, including myself, and 6 lts. for guard duty. Among the soldiers we have seven in the hospital and 8 excused in quarters. The number reporting for duty in my company is 46 privates and non-commissioned. The effective force of the Regt. is about 500 for the 8 companies which are at this place.

I hope that you will not delay any longer in sending your picture, as I wish to see something resembling you very much. I should much rather see the original, but must wait a few months yet. You may rest easy on account of my washer woman, as I have not the least inclination to kiss her or have any likeness of her taken or anything else of that kind. I have not kissed anyone since I left home, and I do not mean to until I return. I wish you to be the first to meet me and receive it.[23]

An unnamed Union soldier recovering from an illness wrote his brother from Camp Banks, near Baton Rouge, on April 11:

I have not done any duty since 3 weeks ago last Thursday. I expect to resume my duties in a day or two. all that ails me is, I am run down, poor appetite, feel weak. the money I received from father was a great blessing to me, did me much good for since then I have been able to buy milk and live on bread and milk. I have a little left which will go for milk.[24]

Lawrence Van Alstyne of the 128th New York Infantry started a diary on April 1, 1863. His regiment was at Camp Parapet, near Baton Rouge. He was in the hospital on April 1, and wrote:

Midnight. I am sitting up to let a tired out nurse get a nap. Holmes died a few minutes ago. He tried to tell me something, but his tongue was so swelled I could not understand what he said. He pulled me clear down to his face and his breath was awful. I pretended to understand, and he settled back as if satisfied and only breathed a few times more. His troubles are over, and those of his old father and mother and his wife and child will begin when the news reaches them. I am glad they did not see the end.

April 3, 1863—Two funerals to-day. We have quite a graveyard started. From all I hear, by talking with soldiers of other regiments, none of them have been as hard hit as the 128th New York. And it all comes from our being stuffed into the hold of the *Arago* a month before we sailed. A big responsibility rests somewhere.

April 7, 1863—Two steamers due and yet no letters. Been loafing around camp so long I feel as if I was an unprofitable servant. But as there is nothing doing I am about as profitable as the rest.

April 8, 1863—The weather is beautiful, everything is growing, I never saw leaves and flowers come so fast.

April 10, 1863—Yesterday I took the place of a nurse who was ailing, and to-day have been with several others to explore the country roundabouts. We came to an orange orchard and found and cut some sprouts for canes. General [Brigadier General Neal] Dow and his staff were riding past, and seeing us, rode full tilt towards us. The general was so busy watching us he never saw a ditch, and into it he went. The horse went down and the general went on his head, landing in the tall grass on all fours. He was not hurt, and after his staff had caught up and helped him on his horse, he came up and said, "To what regiment do you men belong?" Being told, he snapped out, "Report to your quarters at once and don't be seen cutting orange trees again." It is said he roams about like this, driving in any he finds outside, and in other ways making himself unpopular with the boys.[25]

Van Alstyne thought that his regiment suffered heavy losses from disease, but in truth, its losses were only 60 killed in action and 206 men dead of disease. In comparison, the 6th Michigan had 78 men killed in action, but 504 dead of disease.[26] In April 1863 the biggest Union killers were typhoid, diarrhea, and lung disease.[27] For Union soldiers disease proved far deadlier than the fighting.

Disease took its toll, and expiring enlistments took many more. An imminent shortage of troops was an increasing concern to Banks. In a report to Halleck on April 10, his closing paragraph stated:

I respectfully ask attention to a matter that will soon become of great importance to the interests of the Government in this Department. The terms of our nine-months' men begin to expire in May. In August all will have expired. We shall thus lose twenty-two regiments of infantry. . . . Not an hour should be lost in forwarding to this department the men who are to replace the nine-month levies.[28]

Second Lieutenant Henry Warren Howe was aware of the expirations, too, and documented his concern in his diary: "I think Gen. Banks is altogether too cautious and am afraid the 9 months men will go home without firing a gun. It will suit them, for they enlisted for bounty money rather than to fight; also to see the country. I hope all will be conscripted."[29]

One of the enlistees of a nine-months regiment, the 42d Massachusetts Infantry, was Silas Fales, who received a letter from his brother, Henry, dated April 10, 1863: "Business is very good here now. Calvin Plimpton told me he wanted you to come to work for him this spring. Do you think you like soldiering well enough to reenlist after your time is out?"[30] Fales did not reenlist.

Relaxing days were being enjoyed by young Private Henry Graham of the 177th New York:

April 9th, 1863
Went a blackberrying in the afternoon in the hot sun. Gathered about 4 or 5 quarts. Had for supper bread and butter, blackberry sauce and beer. Made a good meal. A mail came and I received one letter from James.

April 10th, Friday. A warm and pleasant day. Had a blackberry pie made from berries I gathered yesterday. Read most of the day in "Pickwick Papers."[31]

Blackberries were favorites of the Midwesterners. A captain in the 6th Michigan, John Corden, observed: "The weather is very pleasant here now just warm enough we have all kinds of vegetables but of course they are very dear. Blackberries are ripe and there are an abundance of them all around us the boys have a great time picking them."[32]

Wilbur Spalding of the 6th Michigan wrote to his wife and children from Camp Sherman, New Orleans, on April 10 (when he wrote the letter he was in camp, but his regiment was on an expedition up to Ponchatoula, Louisiana, chasing rebels and tearing up the railroad bridges):

> I think we are in a pleasant location. . . . The weather is the most beautiful that I ever saw for this time of the year . . . We are all out of money and it is hard work to get enough to get our tobacco . . . the sutler keeps it but asks so much for it we do not get much . . . we can get good tobacco in the city for 75 cents a pd—we could have milk and eggs once in a while if we only had the money to get it with—milk for 10 cts a quart, and eggs for 30 cts a dozen we are just beginning to catch some fish out of the river but they do not seem to like to bite a hook.[33]

GULF AREA CONFEDERATES

Banks's expedition, coupled with Grant's move, was causing considerable uncertainty in Vicksburg. As a result, General Pemberton sent this message to one of his cavalry units on April 10, 1863:

> The major-general commanding directs that you send scouts out around Monticino Bayou toward Baton Rouge and find out if possible what the enemy are about. Be careful, though, not to have them cut off; also instruct your pickets on the river to keep a lookout for all boats passing up or down the river; also at Baton Rouge, and try and discover if the enemy are moving troops down the river.[34]

Confederate Port Hudson, just above Baton Rouge on the Mississippi, had been under Union pressure since about April 1. Private Thomas Rawlings Myers, in the Port Hudson fortress, recalled:

> The siege was begun in dead earnest. The confederates, in prospect of such a siege, had months before prepared elaborate defensive works, well prepared ditches, battery stations at close intervals sup-

plied with heavy and light artillery, magazines and all of the append-
ages of a fortified town or post. General Gardner's force consisted of
not more than 4,500 men of all arms. It would be a long story to
relate all in detail that took place within my observation during this
siege which began about April 1, 1863 and continued uninterruptedly
until July 14th, 1863, when General Gardner surrendered.[35]

Although Myers claims that Gardner had only 4,500 men "of all
arms," official records dated March 30, 1863, show Gardner's forces at
just over 15,000.[36] Myers also sets a date of April 1, 1863, as the beginning of the siege, but other sources place it closer to the end of May
(May 27 to July 9).[37]

Apparently, there was no significant military activity in the area
below Vicksburg on April 10, but several of the Confederate soldiers in
Port Hudson mentioned some minor incidents that day. Confederate
Lieutenant James Taswell Mackey of the 48th Tennessee recorded in his
diary on the tenth: "Several shells were thrown from below the fort,
indicating the presence of the fleet in that quarter."[38]

Daniel Smith of the 1st Alabama Heavy Artillery, also in Port
Hudson, mentioned that on the night of April 10, a raft was set on fire
and drifted downriver. The river patrol put out the fire with no problem.[39]

Private William Y. Dixon entered in his diary:

6th—I was detailed to work at the landing unloading the
steamer 'Star-light,' which had come down Red River with produce
from our army—while I was there the Yankee gunboat 'Hartford'
came down the River, in sight of P.H. & saluted us with bomb shells.

10th—Mr. Godfrey preached in our co.—while he was laying
before us the plan of redemption, the Yanks were hurling at us shells
of Damnation.[40]

SHIPS ON LAKE MAUREPAS

To the north and west of New Orleans, in the Lake Maurepas area, a
Union gunboat, the USS Barrataria, which had been burned and aban-
doned on April 7, lay half scuttled at the mouth of the Amite River.
The Barrataria had been sent up from New Orleans to help the small
Union yacht Corypheus clear Lakes Pontchartrain and Maurepas of any
Rebel boats. The Barrataria, an ironclad steamer, drew too much water
for her duty, so she ran aground her first day on the new assignment.[41]
As usual, the Confederates were anxious to salvage any guns from the

U.S. ships, so they sent out an expedition on the ninth to recover what they could. Colonel J. M. Simonton of the Confederate cavalry reported:

> I ordered Captain Herren [H Company, 1st Mississippi Cavalry] with his and Captain Cochran's companies [Company C, 2d Arkansas Cavalry] of cavalry, to proceed to the wreck of gunboat at mouth of Amite River, to recover guns and other valuables. Captain Herren succeeded in getting a schooner in the Amite River, with which he proceeded to the wreck and placed one gun and a quantity of iron on board and started for the mouth of the Tickfaw, before reaching which he discovered he was being watched by a steamer in Lake Maurepas, and a small party in a yacht was sent out to intercept him. He succeeded in getting into the mouth of the river, and left a portion of his men on board the schooner and went ashore with the balance and placed them in ambush until the party in the yacht passed up the river, when he fired on them, and after a considerable little skirmish succeeded in capturing the entire party (killing one private). Prisoners taken: 1 Adjutant, 6th Michigan, 1 lieutenant, 1 corporal, 1 musician and 4 privates, who are now at this place [Opelousas].[42]

The action described in Simonton's report took place on April 12. That same cannon reappeared as part of the Port Hudson defense and was in the battery manned by Company K of the 1st Alabama.[43]

Away from the actions on Bayou Teche and Lake Maurepas, in Jackson, Mississippi, an event was taking place on April 10, 1863, that was an aftermath of the April 25, 1862 New Orleans surrender. At the time of the surrender, the Confederate commanding general was Major General Mansfield Lovell. The surrender of the city had been a severe blow to the Southerners. The government and many of the citizens blamed Lovell, who had escaped capture by the Union forces, but he insisted he had not been provided with sufficient forces to defend the city. A court of inquiry could be requested by an officer who felt that his conduct was in question. Lovell, who feared that the surrender had tarnished his reputation, called for such a court. The court was convened in Jackson on April 3, 1863, almost a year after Lovell had requested it. It consisted of Major General T. C. Hindman, Major General W. M. Gardner, and Brigadier General T. F. Drayton. Major L. R. Page was the judge advocate and recorder. On April 10, Lovell was testifying.[44]

The only other Gulf region that had any sizable number of Confederate troops was Mobile, Alabama. Major General Simon B. Buckner commanded the Confederate Department of the Gulf, consisting of two divisions. In his Eastern Division, headquartered near Pollard, Alabama, he counted almost 1,000 infantry, 140 artillery, and 400 cavalry. Pollard was northeast of Mobile, at the junction of the Alabama and Pensacola Railroad, coming north out of Pensacola, and the east-west line of the Mobile and Great Northern Railroad, meeting the Pensacola line at Pollard.

In the Western Division of the Department, with its troops scattered around Mobile and south to the Gulf, there were almost 3,000 artillerymen, only 800 infantry, and just over 1,000 cavalry. Buckner's mission was primarily defensive. He had placed his men principally to defend the Mobile harbor; with the continued presence of blockading Union ships in sight of the mouth of the harbor, those troops were on a constant state of alert. The blockade was effective against the town. Just recently there had been a "bread riot" in the city; angry housewives had taken to the streets to protest the prices and supplies available.[45]

On the tenth, nothing of real consequence took place in this area. Buckner's troops had driven off a black regiment on the ninth near Pascagoula, Mississippi, but that had been their first encounter for some weeks. Earlier in the war there had been Union plans to take Mobile, to give the blockading fleet another base, and to tighten the circle around the South, but with the continued efforts against Port Hudson and Vicksburg, and Banks's plan to head west instead of east, there was no immediate plan to take the city.

Admiral Farragut's Union fleet, the Western Gulf Blockading Squadron, was in the Gulf area, too. Farragut had been the hero of New Orleans, capturing the vital Southern city in April 1862 when all other Union efforts seemed to be failing. Since then he had been spending much of his time on the Mississippi River, outside the Confederate fort near Port Hudson. He had periodically run past the batteries to get north of Vicksburg to see Porter. On April 10, four of his boats—the *Switzerland, Albatross, Hartford,* and *Arizona*—were guarding the mouth of the Red River, above Port Hudson. Admiral Farragut had come up the river with the boats and was aboard the *Albatross.* It was Farragut's hope to work with Grant and Porter to close the rivers to Confederate traffic.

In the city of New Orleans itself, life was going on in spite of all the uncertainties of the times. Items of local interest that appeared in the paper were plentiful—and varied:

A nigger sailor was fined $4 for becoming savagely intoxicated. . . .

Mrs. Jones and Mrs. Summers got drunk together. Mrs. Jones was fined $5 and Mrs. Summers was sent to prison for 30 days.

A speech of jealousy was investigated. The court said it was bound to sympathize with the accused under the peculiar circumstances of the case and discharged the fair accused.[46]

According to the New Orleans *Times Picayune* on April 10, 1863 placing a boy in a private school such as the Jefferson Academy for Boys cost $30 for one month, including full board.[47] There was a new and charming vocalist, Minnie Howe, just thirteen years old, who was proclaimed a hit at the Orleans Theatre on Monday.[48] And a note of compassion indicated that the classics were alive and well in New Orleans: "On Monday next there is to be a vocal & instrumental concert at the Opera House under the patronage of the ladies for the benefit of the poor."[49]

This New Orleans–centered island of Yankees in the sea of Confederates was holding its own, and nearing an end to its isolation.

★

Although Banks's Bayou Teche campaign was a success, he lost favor by not aiding Grant. He took Port Hudson on July 9, 1863, five days after Vicksburg's fall.

Confederate Colonel Thomas Green was promoted to brigadier general, but he was killed at Blair's Landing, Louisiana, on April 12, 1864.

Confederate General Alfred Mouton was killed at Sabine Crossroads, Louisiana, on April 8, 1864.

Major General Mansfield Lovell's court of inquiry found him guilty of only two minor infractions in the fall of New Orleans.

General Simon B. Buckner's son, Lieutenant General Simon B. Buckner, Jr., was killed in World War II. He died on Okinawa in 1945.

Lieutenant Colonel Frank Peck died of wounds he received in Winchester, Virginia, on September 20, 1864.

Captain Eli Griffin was killed at the battle of Kenesaw Mountain, Georgia, on June 16, 1864.

Captain Jonathan Huntington Johnson never recovered from his illness; sent home in August, he died on October 13, 1863.

Captain Wilbur Spalding went home on furlough in the fall of 1864, became ill, and died in November.

13

★

THE FAR WEST

It is difficult to summarize April 10 in the Far West; there were no battles for territory, and the farther west the troops, the less concern there was for the war and the more concern there was for the Indians. Virtually everything west of the Mississippi River was considered "the Far West," except for portions of Louisiana where General Grant and General Banks were operating. Troops in the Far West were scattered widely, all the way from the Mississippi River to the Pacific Ocean. The requirements differed significantly for the Union troops in the various areas, and there was no overall strategy for the North. Southern troops were confined mainly to eastern Texas, the Indian Territory (now Oklahoma), Louisiana, and Arkansas, trying to keep supplies flowing to the eastern Confederacy.

UNION FORCES

Early in 1863, Union General Halleck reported on conditions in the Department of Missouri: "[after January 11, 1863] . . . The season was now so far advanced and the roads so impassable that further operations could not be carried on by either party." He expected those conditions to continue until July 15, 1863.[1]

The Union's western states were divided into four departments: the Department of Missouri, covering the present states of Missouri, Oklahoma, Kansas, Nebraska, and Colorado; the Department of New Mexico, with the states of New Mexico and Arizona, and a sliver of Nevada; the Department of the Pacific, including the states of California, Utah, Oregon, Washington, and parts of Idaho and Colorado; and the Department of the Northwest, involving Wisconsin, Iowa, Minnesota, Montana, the Dakotas, and parts of Nebraska.

Most of the Union forces in the Far West were controlled by the Department of Missouri, commanded by Major General Samuel Curtis and headquartered in St. Louis, Missouri. However, many of the Missouri troops were garrison soldiers in St. Louis, Cape Girardeau, and numerous other Missouri towns. All told, Curtis had more than 30,000 men in his department. The Army of the Frontier, with 10,000 men headed by Major General F. J. Herron, was located near Rolla, Missouri, just above the Arkansas border; and the District of Kansas, under Major General James G. Blunt, had 3,000 troops in Fort Leavenworth and in small commands in Colorado, Nebraska, and the Indian Territory.[2] The rest of Curtis's troops were in Missouri on garrison duty.

The Union officers were struggling both with morale and with the Indians. The Cherokee nation was a large part of the Indian Territory; there were continual Union efforts to recruit the Cherokees, as well as the smaller camps of Osages, Crees, Chickasaws, and others. Three Union regiments of Indian soldiers had been organized in 1862, but they all remained in the Cherokee nation, at Fort Gibson; they had been assured they would be used only against forces invading the Indian nation. The 3d Kansas Indian Home Guard Regiment was the most recently formed; the Indian recruits were mainly Confederate Cherokee deserters. There appeared to be little understanding of, or sympathy for, the "White Man's War," so major shifts of loyalty were commonplace as the tides turned, or as incentives were offered.[3]

On March 30, Major General John Schofield was relieved from command of the Army of the Frontier, apparently at his own request. His letter to General Halleck in Washington, dated April 10, 1863, hinted at the politics of the military:

> My Dear General:
>   I thank you for the order sending me to the Army of the Cumberland and for your efforts to secure my promotion. There is a powerful combination of military and political aspirants in this department, whose success requires my removal from any important command here, and sufficiently unscrupulous to resort to any means that might be necessary to accomplish it. . . . I am as willing as anybody to be sacrificed when any good is to be accomplished by it, but do not like to be slaughtered for nothing.[4]

The army had some officers who were difficult to control. An example of this was the case of Colonel William Weer. Originally colonel of the 10th Kansas Infantry, Weer was a very capable field commander, but was known for his predilection for strong drink. During the summer of 1862, he had commanded an expedition into the Indian Territory to recruit and capture some of the Confederate Indians. His force of about 6,000 men, including the 9th Wisconsin under Colonel Frederick Salomon, went deep into Indian country. The expedition was a great success; the Confederate Cherokees were defeated at Locust Grove in the Cherokee nation on July 3, 1862. After that time, Weer had trouble with Salomon, General Blunt, and others. His main problems were drinking and irrational statements. Shortly before April 10, his arrest was being discussed and, at one point, ordered.[5] Whatever the orders may have been, Weer apparently was not arrested at that time; his reports and communications kept coming in to Curtis, Blunt, and Herron.

On April 10, Weer addressed the troops in his division at Forsythe, Missouri. He had been serving as division commander of the 1st Division, Army of the Frontier, since December 31, 1862, when he relieved General Blunt. Private Benjamin F. McIntyre, 19th Iowa Infantry, mentioned Weer and his rambling speech in his diary:

Saturday, April 11th, Forsythe, Missouri,
A pleasant day after a heavy rain last night. An adress from Gen. Herron was read to us tonight. He soon expects big things from us.
We certainly are a mere cypher at this place and lingering out a fruitless destiny.
Col. Weer made a speech to his cavalry on dress parade last night. He seemed to feel pretty good natured and held on the pummil of his saddle as if there was danger of his falling. He refuted charges against him which was that he stated that the 3d Wis. Cavalry were cowards and it was a d———md lie—enough of this however—the whole affair was but the speech and freaks of a drunken man.[6]

The Army of the Frontier's 1st Division, including the 19th Iowa, was down near the Arkansas border; it had received a number of refugees who were anxious to leave the state of Arkansas with its secessionist troops. Private McIntyre's diary entry for April 13 noted: "A considerable number of female refugees came to us today. They have large families of Small children and are certainly objects of pity but we can furnish them with but poor accommodation. Yet we will do for them the best we can and then will eat our diner."[7] It was difficult to tell the real refugees from those planted to learn about the plans of the Northerners.

The Iowa soldiers' stay in Missouri was about to end; on April 22 they were ordered to leave Forsythe and burn it to the ground, which they did.[8] They were to go to Grant's aid in Louisiana, but did not get there until June, almost too late to help.

Private Charles Francis, of Company B, 88th Illinois Infantry, had just arrived in St. Louis and had no immediate concerns about the Rebels. As a newly assigned clerk, he was more involved with the "Tri-Monthly Post Return":

> On 10th of April I arrived at Benton Barracks, near St. Louis and reported to Col. B. L. E. Bonneville, U.S.A., commanding the post. He was another old veteran like unto Morrison [a previous commander of Francis's, described as having been in the Army "40 or 50 years"]. I was immediately detailed by special order to remain at HQ in the nominal capacity of Post Bugler, but in reality my duties were as a clerk in the office of the Post Adjutant.[9]

Francis described the post of Benton Barracks as being situated on Grand Avenue and including the fairgrounds and a large adjoining tract just to the west. Francis was already a seasoned soldier; captured at Stones River, he had come to Saint Louis via Chattanooga, Atlanta, West Point (Georgia), Montgomery (Alabama), Libby Prison, Camp Parole, and Annapolis.[10]

On April 10, the *Nashville Union* reported that an information service was available at the Saint Louis Army Intelligence Office. This office could, and would, supply information about the status—sick, wounded, killed, prisoner, etc.—of any soldier in the Western Department for $2.[11]

CONFEDERATES IN THE FAR WEST

All Confederate forces west of the Mississippi, almost 30,000 men, were in the Department of the Trans-Mississippi, led by Lieutenant General E. Kirby Smith, who was headquartered in Alexandria, Louisiana. The department included the present states of Louisiana (western sections), Arkansas, Oklahoma (Indian Territory), and Texas. Smith had been in command of the department for only one month, having taken over from Lieutenant General Theophilus Holmes, who was now subordinate to him. The department included General Taylor's 4,000 men at Fort Bisland in Louisiana, already engaged with Union General Banks in western Louisiana; the District of Arkansas, under General Holmes at Little Rock, with about 19,000 men; and the Department of Texas, New Mexico, and Arizona, commanded by Major General John Bankhead Magruder, with about 6,000 men scattered throughout Texas.

Holmes's District of Arkansas had four division commanders: Major General Sterling Price, in Little Rock; Brigadier General John S. Marmaduke, in Pocahontas, near the Missouri border; Brigadier General William Steele, in Fort Smith; and Brigadier General Daniel M. Smith, in Pine Bluff, south of Little Rock.

General Marmaduke had positioned his division, with some additional troops, in Pocahontas to facilitate a move into Missouri. Marmaduke was adamant that something should be done to relieve the pressure around Vicksburg and Port Hudson; he asked Holmes for permission to mount a cavalry raid into Union-held Missouri to draw some Union troops away from Mississippi or even possibly Tennessee. The raid was not to start until April 17. Marmaduke began his venture with 5,000 men, but 1,200 were unarmed and 900 were horseless.[12] (This was one of five major cavalry raids that began within a few days of each other in April 1863 in different theaters of the war: for the Union, Stoneman in Virginia, Streight in Alabama, and Grierson in Mississippi; for the Confederates, Marmaduke in Missouri, and generals Jones and Imboden in West Virginia.)

Farther west, General Steele's division, including most of the Indian troops in the Confederacy, was assigned the protection of the Indian Territory. General Smith's division, south in Pine Bluff, was to be used as reserves to support Taylor in Louisiana, if necessary, or to move against Grant.

In the Indian Territory bordered by Union Kansas to the north and Confederate Texas to the south, there had been strong efforts on both sides to recruit Indians. Initially, the Confederacy gained more Indian support than the Union. This was understandable; since the U.S. government had not been particularly fair in its Indian policy, the Indians hoped that a Confederate win would install a government easier for them to deal with.

By April 10, however, there was much discontent among the Indians concerning their treatment by the Confederates. An example of the frustrations of Confederate officers was set forth in a letter from General Steele, commanding general of the Indian Territory, in Fort Smith, Arkansas. His letter, addressed to the powerful Confederate Congressman Louis Wigfall in Richmond and dated April 15, was a lengthy complaint about conditions and problems in his command:

> The Indian country is destitute of everything essential to an
> army, or to the supply of its inhabitants, the crops last year having
> been a complete failure; hence the task of not only furnishing the
> troops with rations, but the indigent loyal Indians with bread,

brought from a distance, thus throwing on the commissariat the necessity of supplying with inadequate means 30,000 or 40,000 natives. This command when I assumed it was destitute of nearly everything . . .

The Indian country is of great importance to us; but it is of more importance to keep the enemy at a distance from the granaries of Texas. Were he to get a foothold in Northern Texas, the dependence of our whole Trans-Mississippi Department for breadstuff would be taken away.[13]

Steele enclosed a letter dated April 12, 1863, from one of the Indians, Lieutenant J. A. Scales, of the 2d Cherokee Regiment, soon to be a delegate to the convention of the Cherokee nation but at that time in the Confederate army. The letter was to Colonel A. P. Adair, commanding the 2d Cherokee Regiment:

The simple truth is we have been very badly treated by the officers of the Confederate States in withholding our pay as soldiers, our clothing and in flooding the country with thousands of dollars of duplicate accounts that today are not worth fifty cents on the dollar, even in Confederate money, to say nothing of the utter failure of the Confederate States to give the protection promised in the treaty, and that at a time when their military pantomime, General Pike, had force enough to defend us. We have been reduced from opulence to penury, driven from our homes, endured cold and hunger, and had our friends murdered by an inexorable foe . . .

Our troops are forced to defend Fort Smith, a filthy sink of corruption and iniquity, inhabited chiefly by a foul, speculating horde, our enemies at heart, who sell the comforts of life to Confederate soldiers at ten prices. It is, doubtless, a point of inestimable military value, especially to Arkansas and Texas. Let Arkansans and Texans defend it.

I am none the less a Southerner, nor is my faith lessened in the least degree in the final success of our cause, neither do I less abhor the negro-fraternizing spirit of abolitionism of the North, but we must confess that Federals treat their perfidious allies better than the Confederate Government, through its officers, has treated its most devoted and loyal Indians. I will not enter the convention [of the Cherokee nation] with that cordial feeling toward the south that I had two years ago. *Quid pro quo* is human nature. Use me well, I love you; abuse me and I don't.[14]

On April 10 there were five regiments and three battalions of Cherokees, Chickasaws, Osages, Choctaws, and Crees wearing the Confederate uniform. One of their regimental commanders, Stand Watie, a Cherokee, became a brigadier general and remained loyal to the South to the end.

The Indians had their problems, and Confederates away from home and family had their own concerns. Captain Elijah P. Petty commanded a company of the 17th Texas Infantry. On April 12 he wrote to his daughter Ella, telling her those things he felt were important for her to know as she grew up. Then he gave his opinion of the military:

> Our army is all here yet no prospect that I see of a move. We are all now pleasantly situated, healthy and of exuberant spirits with itching palms for Yankee scalps praying & hoping for the hour when a chance may send us the oppertunity of giving the rascals a nice thrashing.
>
> I am still in Pine Bluff on Court Martial and the Lord only knows when I will be relieved. I have asked and begged to be relieved but I suppose the authorities think that I can do more good in that capacity than in any other and their will be done not mine. I came to the war to do whatever was required of me and I intend to do so. When my masters say do this I do it and when they [say] abstain from doing that I abstain. I am fearful that I will get so in the habit of obedience to Masters and superiors that I will have to have a Master or Mistress at home and so will have to obey implicitly all the orders and edicts that Ma may issue. Well you know that aint much hardship on me as I have always done so (over the left) and always expect to do so (in a horn). [Both of these old expressions, "over the left (shoulder)" and "in a horn," had a meaning similar to the current slang expression "Not!" indicating that Petty's comments were made facetiously.][15]

Confederate surgeon Junius Bragg was in Little Rock, trying to solve his personal problem. He and his fianceé, Josephine, wanted to get married; he wrote to her on April 9:

> I wrote you a short letter a few days since, as an acknowledgment of the receipt of yours of the last of March . . . I am as anxious to attain the finale of our engagement as you can possibly be.
>
> On the receipt of yours, I went to see Gen. Holmes adjutant he informed me that it would be a "waste of paper" to write out a leave of absence with the expectation of its being approved or granted!

That his orders were plain, explicit and positive on the subject. I suggested to him, that "Just supposing I was going to be married, and was expected home at a certain time, what then?" He laughed and shook his head. I think I can engineer a furlough though, in the course of time, but it will take time to do it.[16]

Lieutenant Colonel James Arthur Lyon Fremantle, an officer of the elite British Coldstream Guards, was a guest of the Southerners in Texas. His diary noted on the ninth: "Colonel Buchel and I slept in Col. Duff's tent, and at night we were serenaded. The officers and men really sang uncommonly well, and they finished with 'God Save the Queen.'"

Fremantle was impressed with the Texans—and amused by them as well. He was traveling for three months in the South, on leave from his regiment in England, purely on a lark. His book, *The Fremantle Diary,* gives little indication of his moral stance toward the war; he was just out for adventure. On April 10 he made some observations about his stay in Brownsville, Texas:

We roused up at daylight, and soon afterwards, Colonel Duff paraded some of his best men, to show off the Texas horsemanship, of which they are very proud.

I saw them lasso cattle, and catch them by the tail at full gallop, and throw them by slewing them around. This is called tailing. They pick small objects off the ground when at full tilt, and, in their peculiar fashion, are beautiful riders; but they confessed to me they could not ride in an English saddle, and Colonel Duff told me they could not jump a fence at all. They were all extremely anxious to hear what I thought of the performance, and their thorough good opinion of themselves was most amusing.

In the evening, a Mr. ——, a Texas Unionist, *renegado,* gave us his sentiments at the Consulate, and drank a good deal of brandy. He finished, however, with a toast,

"Them as wants to fight, let 'em fight—I don't."

The following day Fremantle commented, "I have now become comparatively accustomed and reconciled to the necessity of shaking hands and drinking brandy with everyone."[17]

As Fremantle prepared to leave Texas, so did a new Texas unit. On April 11, 1863, Company E of the 4th Texas Infantry left Waco for the war. John C. West was a member of that unit; his diary for that day had this entry: "Left Waco Tx on the morning of April 11, 1863; bid adieux to my dear little Stark and Mary at home, said goodbye to my sweet wife at the ferry-boat landing (at the foot of bridge street)."[18]

Others were traveling that day. A number of Confederates were being sent from the West to prison camps or exchange points in the East. Three Texans were working their way through the system after being captured at Arkansas Post. One of these three, William Heartsill, had been at Arkansas Post for only three weeks, as part of the 2d Texas Cavalry, when he was captured on January 11, 1863. On April 10 he was headed for Camp Butler, Illinois, then by train from Illinois to Baltimore, by boat to Virginia, and to an exchange at City Point, Virginia, in mid-April. On the tenth he was rolling across Pennsylvania:

> This morning we are dashing through the mountains of Pennsylvania, we pass through Ralston then Trout Run and "here we be" (as a down easter would say,) in the City of Williamsport Penn at 10 o'clk. Here we find plenty of Southern sympathizers; one lady waved a Confederate Flag from the top of a large building. At this place we take the Sunburry and Erie R.R. The first town of any note is Milton, next is Sunburry on the Susquahanna; here we have a little excitement; an old man cheered for "Davis"; another old man ditto for Lincoln, at each other they went; into each other they pitched; the cars rolled on and as far back as we could see the two old Gentlemen were making the white hair fly and the Rebs all yelling for the "Jeff" man.[19]

Private Ben Seaton of the 10th Texas, the second Texan of the three, was also headed back to Dixie at about this time:

> We left thar fer Baltamore on the cars some 950 miles. Saw a grate deal of the old country. Some vary fine land and some vary sorry and at Baltamore we took a steamer fer Forts Munrou. Thar we exchanged boats for City Point—35 miles St James River and then to Petersburg Camp some 16 miles. . . . we have seen a rough time while with the Feds but know we are on Dixie Soil once more. They have fine water in Virginna.[20]

The third Texan on the move was Samuel T. Foster, 24th Texas Cavalry, Dismounted:

> Say between the firt and tenth day of April, we are notified to get ready to go out for exchange, we all have to undergo another

search as we go out— Every man that has a gray blanket has to give it up. If a man has two coats one is taken &c.

We march back to Columbus [Ohio], take the cars headed east; we are put in passenger cars, 2 to each seat, guard at each door, and off we go. Nothing important occurs, and the first place of any note is Pittsburg Pa. black smoky dirty looking place. It looks like coal dust, and smoke was on every thing about Pittsburg . . .

We are now in the great coal region of the U.S. Everything is black—We see great holes in the side of the mountains, where coal is taken out—Our road runs under a great many tunnels along in these mountains—We are on the Pensylvania Central R.R. going from Pittsburg towards Harrisburg—Some fine and wild scenery in these Alegeny Mountains . . .

We arrive in Philadelphia on Sunday evening, and here the crowd threw rocks and brick bats at us—and was about to storm to train, and instead of stopping as usual the train runs in the Depot which was enclosed, the gates shut, and the mob cut off from us.[21]

The Confederates were the enemy in parts of the West, but in other areas Indians were the foe. Actions were few and far apart, but the policies of that era became clear. The Indians were to be punished for any interference with the white settlers and, if need be, eliminated.

From Humboldt, Kansas, still in the Department of Missouri, the 9th Kansas Cavalry reported a foray into lower Kansas; Captain W. Doudna, commanding the expedition, expressed some of the prevailing frustrations and concerns in his April 16 report to General Blunt:

I have the honor to report that, on the 10th day of April, I sent a detachment of my company to the Cottonwood country in search of contraband property. . . . About 40 miles from its mouth, the detachment came up with a herd of about 1,000 head of cattle, in charge of about 40 Delaware and Shawnee Indians. The Indians resisted and the detachment [of 6 men] were unable to take possession of them, the Indians being armed and mounted. . . . I have in herd here or near here about 555 head of cattle, which I have been unable to send to Fort Scott, for the reason that I deem it unsafe to do it without an escort of at least 20 men, for the following reasons: About one week ago a party of bushwhackers made a raid on Lightning Creek, capturing a large amount of stock and committing other depredations; and a few days previous to that a raid was made, I think by the Osage Indians, in the same vicinity, who murdered a very worthy citizen, about sixty years of age, and his son. I am also informed that there is much dissatisfaction among the Osages, and that they are holding secret councils, and have about come to the conclusion that the whites are so divided among themselves that they can make a successful fight against us. . . . Taking all the facts into consideration, I would respectfully suggest the propriety of sending at least two companies more here, not only to protect the citizens from outrages of Indians, but to carry out your orders above referred to, and to protect the Government from depredations in stealing stock by the Indians.[22]

The department was already sending many of its troops to Grant near Vicksburg, so the Kansas captain did not receive his additional cavalry.

On April 11, Nebraska's governor, Alvin Saunders, and E. Creighton, superintendent of the Pacific Telegraph Company, wrote to General Halleck complaining about the removal of troops from Nebraska:

We understand that the Second Nebraska Cavalry has been ordered to cross the Missouri and report at Sioux City [Iowa]. If this order is carried out, it will leave the whole frontier of Nebraska, as well as the emigrants' stage and telegraph to the mountains, unprotected. In our opinion these troops should be left on the west side of the river, at least for the present.[23]

In Colorado, a small detachment of the 3d Colorado Cavalry set out from Colorado City on the morning of April 10 to find a party of Confederate guerrillas. At daylight on the eleventh, it found its quarry. The 3d Colorado killed one man, William Waggle, wounded his companion, John Riley, in the leg, and took William Way prisoner. The official report filed by Lieutenant Colonel George Shoup said he "demanded them three different times to surrender. I did not fire on them until one of them raised his gun on Sgt. Rigsby."[24]

Farther south, in one of the few signs of activity in the Department of New Mexico, Private George Hand, Company G, 1st California Infantry, recorded some post activities in El Paso, Texas:

April 6—Lt. Smith, Sgt. Longwood & 19 privates left for Franklin [Texas] with a lot of Greaser prisoners. Express from Fort West report the horses all recovered 40 Indians killed and as many wounded by a detachment of Cav & one private named Hall wounded. Co. C 5th Inf arrived here today.

April 8—Gov Arry left for Ft. Craig escorted by Corp. Bradley & nine privates, mail arrived this morning.

10th—Wrote to Lou & C A Taylor. Co. E 1st Cav gave a ball.

11th—Charley Kohl with a detachment of Cav Co E arrived Sergt. Fairchild & 9 privates Co E left for the Missouri River Station Videtes. . . . There is to be a grand Mexican show this evening.

12th—The show was a humbug.[25]

THE PACIFIC COMMAND

The Department of the Pacific, commanded by Brigadier General George Wright, covered an area from Colorado west, and from the Canadian border to Mexico. The 4,000 men of this department were the keepers of the peace with the Indians. There were only 1,000 troops in the northwest territories, and fewer than 1,000 in Utah Territory. The remainder were in California, most of them in the San Francisco area, which was headquarters for the department.

In Utah, besides the frequent clashes with Indians, there was considerable friction between the army and the Mormons. The Mormon leader, Brigham Young, had established his colony in the Salt Lake City area in the 1850s, but the group's practices—particularly polygamy—caused open conflict with the U.S. government. As evidence of the continuing problem, a notice concerning Mormons appeared in the *Cincinnati Daily Commercial*: "On April 10 a U.S. Marshal wrote a warrant for the arrest of Brigham Young, for having violated an act of Congress by taking another wife. He responded immediately, and was released on $2,000 bail."[26]

Other evidence was reported by Colonel George S. Evans of the 2d California Cavalry. On April 12, the colonel and his men were attacked by Indians near Pleasant Grove, Utah Territory, a Mormon settlement. The Indians outnumbered the cavalry twenty to one, so the cavalry retired to an adobe house for protection. The Indians tired of firing at the little fortress and finally rode out, taking all of the cavalry's horses, forage, equipment, and everything else in sight. The colonel was outraged:

I enter into detail in mentioning these seemingly unimportant facts, not because I deem them of any importance in themselves, but that they may be taken and considered in connection with the strange but stubborn fact that all this occurred in the town of Pleasant Grove in the face and eyes of a population of several hundred people calling themselves civilized and American citizens—God save the mark! Right in the heart of a Mormon town, where there were perhaps 100 or 150 white men [Mormons], in the broad daylight 75 or 100 savages attack and attempt to murder six American citizens and do carry off mules, harness, and other Government property, and not a hand is lifted to assist or protect them or to prevent the stealing of Government property; but on the contrary they stand around the street corners and on top of their houses and hay-stacks complacently looking on, apparently well pleased at the prospect of six Gentiles [soldiers] being murdered.[27]

Mormons and Indians both seemed to bother the 2d California Cavalry. Colonel William Jones, the commander, filed a report on an April 10 patrol to capture a renegade Indian:

I have the honor to report that on the 9th instant it came to my knowledge that the celebrated war chief Joaquin Jim had arrived from Owen's Valley, and was at a rancheria near the foothills, about seventeen miles east of this camp. On the morning of the 10th I ordered Lt. William L. Knight of Company I, with four men to the place where Joaquim Jim was reported to have been the day before, and capture him and bring him to this camp. . . . When they got to the ranch and were going into the garden the Indian espied them and ran to a deep slough and swam across. Lt. Knight, with his men, rode in the slough, swam their horses across, and after a race of nearly half a mile, during which time he fired five shots from his pistol, three of them taking effect, which effectually stopped his further progress, sending his spirit to the land of his fathers, where he will trouble the white man no more.[28]

This evidently was a premature obituary; a report in the official records dated December 22, 1864, from Fort Churchill, in the Nevada Territory, mentioned Joaquin Jim again:

Further, this chief who is displeased with the whites, is a California Indian (His name is Joaquin Jim). He committed some depredations in California, and when he found out the whites were after him he got away and came among the Owens River Indians to make himself safe. After he got well he encouraged them to make war against the whites before they should concentrate in large numbers.[29]

Another Indian encounter on April 10 was described in a chilling report dated April 24, 1863, from Captain Moses A. McLaughlin, of the same 2d California Cavalry:

> I have the honor to report that in obedience to orders dated Camp Babbitt near Visalia, Cal April 10, 1863, and signed Lt. Col. Wm Jones I left Camp Babbitt on Sunday the 12th . . .
>
> I had the bucks collected together and informed Jose Chico and the citizens who had arrived that they might choose out those who they knew to be friendly. This was soon done. The boys and old men I sent back to the camps, and the others, to the number of 35, for whom noone could vouch, were either shot or sabered. Their only chance for life being their fleetness, but none escaped, though many fought well with knives, sticks, clubs and stones. This extreme punishment, though I regret it, was necessary, and I feel certain a few such examples will soon crush the indians and finish the war in this and adjacent valleys.[30]

Farther north, in the California Humboldt Military District, an expedition set out on April 7 looking for Indians who had murdered one George Bowers. Captain C. D. Douglas, Company F, 2d California Infantry, and commander of Camp Wright, reported:

> I have the honor to report that in consequence of the murder of Mr. George Bowers of Williams Valley (4 miles north of Round Valley) by Indians, I left this post 7th instant with a detachment of 15 men in pursuit of the perpetrators of the murder. I marched in the night into the mountain country they inhabit, so as to conceal my movements from the ever-watchful enemy. Soon after daylight on the morning of the 8th, my indian guide found the trail, which we followed as fast as the snow-storm which was then raging, would permit us to travel. About dark we captured one buck and one squaw who fell behind their party. Soon after their capture I camped under the shelter of large trees, having no tents, as the snow storm was so severe that traveling in the night in such rugged and broken country was found utterly impracticable. I left the camp at daybreak on the morning of the 9th and at 9 AM we found a small camp of the indians we were in pursuit of, who could not keep up with their band. I endeavored to make them all prisoners, but could not, as they would not surrender but fight. I therefore gave the order to fire and the entire party was killed, except for two old squaws who gave themselves up. Six bucks here were killed, not one of the whole party

getting away. I then gave up the pursuit as my men had no rations to go further. [The men returned to Camp Wright on the tenth.][31]

Still in the Humboldt District, another detachment was just coming back from an extended twenty-two-day scout; its report gave further reassurance that the Indians were being dealt with as required:

I have the honor to report the return to Ft. Baker of a detachment of thirty-two men of Co. A, 2nd Inf. Cal. Vol., from a twenty-two day scout under Capt Flynn and Lt Winchill. They had 4 engagements with Indians, all successful. Two of them were fought by Lt Winchill with 15 men. The number of dead indians found was 46, the number killed was no doubt considerably more. Thirty seven squaws and children were brought in as prisoners, of whom only twenty-two have arrived at this post, the remainder having succeeded in escaping on the way.[32]

The only casualty for the 2d California was one man—Private Lynch of Company A—killed.

Colonel Francis Lippitt, 2d California Infantry, commanding the Humboldt District, requested that his men be withdrawn from that district. He explained:

Scouting in this district is exhausting to such a degree that the troops engaged in it must spend a portion of their time in garrison for repose and to recruit their strength, and the mingling of the Humboldt volunteers with the men of my regiment at the same post would be demoralizing and dangerous to the discipline that they have been 18 months acquiring. In consideration of this I hope the department commander will withdraw all the companies of the 2nd Inf. Cal. Vol. from this district, where they are doing so little good, and concentrate them at some point where they may have an opportunity of acquiring regimental discipline and instruction.[33]

His request fell on deaf ears, and the regiment stayed on at the Humboldt post.

There was a change in command in southern California on April 10: Colonel Ferris Forman, 4th California Infantry, assumed control of the District of Southern California and shifted the headquarters of the 4th California Infantry from San Francisco to Camp Drum, near Long Beach. The district had forts near Visalia, California; Yuma, Arizona;

Mojave, New Mexico (on the California–Arizona border); and San Diego, in addition to Fort Drum at Long Beach.

During this period, the actions of most U.S. troops in the Far West region had little impact on the Civil War. Their preoccupation was with their own protection and well-being, not with the war raging in the East.

★

In spite of the governor of Nebraska's protest, the 2d Nebraska Cavalry was assigned to Sioux City (but it continued to operate in Nebraska).

Colonel William Weer was finally arrested and court-martialed on over thirty counts. He was convicted of drunkenness, disobedience, and conduct unbecoming an officer. He was cashiered on August 20, 1864.

Captain Petty was killed almost exactly a year later, April 9, 1864, at the battle of Pleasant Hill, Louisiana.

Surgeon Junius Bragg's efforts prevailed; he was married to Josephine in June 1863.

In July, Colonel Fremantle was with Longstreet's troops at Gettysburg, witnessing the ill-fated Pickett's charge.

PART THREE

★

THE DAY AT SEA

Compared to the numbers of men in the two armies, a relatively small number of men manned the ships that wandered the oceans. At the beginning of the war there was no Confederate navy, and the U.S. Navy had only about 8,000 men scattered throughout the world. By April 10, 1863, there were almost 34,000 men in the Union navy blue, and the Confederates had managed to capture, build, and buy a considerable naval force to oppose the larger number of Union ships.

The Gulf and Vicksburg areas were dependent on navy ships for guns and for transport. The principal Union navy assignment, however, was the blockade, which was becoming increasingly effective.

A recent naval weapon was the ironclad. This class of ship included any vessel that was protected by armor on its sides. These ships were mostly converted steamers, side-wheelers or propeller driven. The new ironclad vessels had been the rage in early war years, but whenever they had been engaged, they proved to be cumbersome and vulnerable. The added weight made them slow and unwieldy. The navy still had great expectations for their use, but their designs in 1863 were inadequate; the ironclads' role diminished after the April 7 Charleston attack, although they found a place in the relative calm of river waters.

Several other naval innovations, or adaptations, were developed during the Civil War. One was the ram, an unarmed steamer with a reinforced prow, designed to do what its name implied: ram opposing ships. Another powerful new tool was the "torpedo." Unlike the self-propelled torpedoes in naval service today, those of the Civil War were similar to mines, only attached to long spars on small boats and detonated under enemy ships. Some were set off electrically from shore. Never fully operational, they were used primarily by Confederates for defensive purposes. The Confederates experimented, with tragic consequences, with a submarine, the *Hunley,* which sank with all hands in its first outing against the Union navy, early in 1864. The Union also had a submarine; it never saw action and sank under tow in April 1863.

14

★

THE NAVIES

Except for Admiral Porter's Mississippi squadron, above Vicksburg, the majority of the Union navy's ships were in the blockading squadrons of the North Atlantic, South Atlantic, eastern Gulf, and western Gulf. The blockade had come into existence in April 1861 when President Lincoln shut off commerce to the seceding states. Early Union navy efforts to intercept blockade-runners were not reassuring, but by April 10, 1863, the ships were in place and the blockade itself was effective. Even though blockade-runners often succeeded in getting through, few foreign ships ventured to run the blockade, and shipping was greatly reduced, causing severe shortages in the South. The blockade had been formed outside almost all of the major Southern ports from Norfolk, Virginia, down the East Coast and around the Gulf of Mexico to Galveston, Texas. Union troops occupied bases in many of these coastal areas, providing additional ports for the blockading fleet. The only eastern Confederate port still open on April 10 was Wilmington, North Carlina; however, Union blockading ships outside the port made commerce risky for any Confederate or foreign ships.

By April 1863, Union coastal bases had been established in Norfolk, Virginia; New Bern, North Carolina; Port Royal, South Carolina; Key West and Pensacola, Florida; and New Orleans, Louisiana. Ships were the only supply lines for these bases, used to support the blockading fleets. While blockading was the navy's principal duty, the fleet also chased blockade-runners over the vast expanse of ocean.

There still was a blockading squadron on the Potomac and the Rappahannock rivers, although its duties and strength had been considerably lessened since McClellan abandoned his peninsula campaign in 1862. In the spring of 1863 the squadron's ships were detailed to keep commerce from taking place along the banks of the rivers. In April there were still theoretically two divisions of the Potomac Squadron on duty in the capital waters; however, the 1st Division, under Commodore

Andrew A. Harwood, with five ships and two mortar schooners, had been sent up to Hooker's army, and two ships had been sent to the North Atlantic Blockading Squadron. The plaintive words of the 2d Division's commander, Lieutenant Commander E. P. McCrea, in his April 15 weekly report, indicated the decline of his assignment. He lamented, "I have no vessels now for any purpose save this one [the *Jacob Bell*], which is the guard ship."[1]

Evidence of the vigilance of Yankee naval forces was noted in the April 10 edition of the *New York Times*:

> Commander Gillis, of the gunboat *Commodore Morris* has done some necessary work up the Ware River [a tributary of the York]. A venemous rebel named Patterson Smith having 20,000 bushels of corn which he was bargaining to the rebel government at Richmond, was visited by Gillis, and furnished with an opportunity of showing that he was as base a liar as a traitor, in reply to questions put to him. The result was that Smith paid Gen. Keyes a visit of compulsion and all the corn on his plantation, excepting 1,500 bushels saved for his family and negroes, together with 2,000 bushels of wheat were burned. Gillis used a force of 100 men in this work and had to fight a large body of rebel cavalry. He used shells in dispersing them, and the bursting of his shells played havoc with the rebels. The plantation of another rebel named Bird was visited by Gillis and 1,000 bushels of wheat and 3,000 bushels of corn consumed—the whole under interruption of rebel cavalry and continuous fighting.[2]

NORTH ATLANTIC BLOCKADING SQUADRON

The most significant navy effort, in numbers of ships involved, was being made by the offshore vessels of the North and South Atlantic Blockading Squadrons. The North Squadron, headed by Acting Rear Admiral Samuel P. Lee, operated out of Hampton Roads, Virginia. In April his squadron was blockading the coasts of Virginia and North Carolina; his flagship, the USS *Minnesota,* was off New Bern, North Carolina, organizing the naval efforts to relieve General Foster's fort in Washington, North Carolina. Lee's squadron had sixty vessels, from tugs to frigates, but their condition varied widely. More than half were in need of repairs or were unfit for service and were hardly worthy of being called naval vessels. Also included were two ironclads, one of which was the *Galena,* described as "used on picket; very dull, speed 4 to 5 knots."[3]

Union General Foster's predicament was considered critical, so

Admiral Lee's fleet made repeated attempts to assist him. On April 1, Lee reported the following ships involved in Foster's support in North Carolina: *Hunchback,* on the Pamlico River; *Seymour,* being repaired; *Hetzel,* in New Bern ("Not worth repairs"); *Lockwood* ("Much needing repairs"); and *Commodore Perry* and *Southfield,* both ferryboats, at Plymouth, North Carolina. Eighteen miles up the Pamlico River, in Washington, were the *Commodore Hull, Louisiana,* and *Ceres* ("Newly repaired and iron screened"[4]). The ships in Washington were separated from the lower fleet, off the mouth of the Pamlico River, by Confederate artillery dug in along the stretch of river below the city.

Logbooks of several of the vessels show activity on the days before and after, as well as on, April 10. The log of the *Ceres* reports on that Friday: "Enemy's batteries opened on the fort outside the town, the battery at Rodman's Point firing occasionally at the fleet; during the afternoon enemy keeping up a continuous fire from Rodman's point and the 32 pounder."[5] The report was signed "John MacDiarmid, Acting Volunteer Lieutenant, Commanding USS *Ceres.*" The days before and after the tenth had similar entries.

Acting Master William G. Saltonstall reported on the activities of the *Commodore Hull* to Commander R. T. Renshaw, senior naval officer:

> Friday, April 10, 1863—Acting Master Josselyn and Acting Ensign Da Camara arrived during the night from the lower fleet, the latter bringing through a small schooner loaded with navy ammunition. Mr. Josselyn started with a similar one, but subsequently returned to the lower gunboats, the wind dying out, and came up in the cutter, bringing some army officers and dispatches. This vessel, though frequently fired at, was not struck. Sent a boat in charge of an acting master's mate down river at night by your orders.[6]

Commander Renshaw, on the *Louisiana,* reported to his senior officer, Commander H. K. Davenport, in Sounds, North Carolina.

> 10th instant, at 8 a.m. four rebel batteries opened fire on our fort and entrenchments, which were promptly answered by the fort and blockhouses. The fire continued for nearly an hour without intermission. Occasional firing from Rodman's and the battery above on the gunboats and town. At midnight Acting Master Josselyn and Acting Ensign Da Camara, of the *Commodore Hull,* arrived from the lower fleet, bringing a schooner laden with naval ammunition.[7]

Admiral Lee was getting continued pressure from other sources for the help of his fleet. On the eleventh, both General Keyes, in command of the Yorktown District in Virginia, and General Peck, in Suffolk, requested gunboat assistance—Keyes because of the attack on Williamsburg and Peck because of Longstreet's massive buildup outside Suffolk. Admiral Lee did what he could, sending several gunboats and two tugs toward Suffolk, but he had few ships left after supporting Foster in Washington, so he could do little to help Keyes. On April 12, Lee wrote to Secretary of the Navy Gideon Welles, describing the pressures in his command and his unhappiness at his inability to help.

> Major-General Keyes telegraphed to me yesterday that our troops toward Williamsburg had been driven by a large force of rebels down toward the mouth of Queen's Creek, and that if a larger force of gunboats was not sent to the York River, even Yorktown itself might fall. At that time the *Commodore Morris* had come to Hampton Roads by my orders to be succeeded by the *Morse*. I at once sent her back with all dispatch to the York River, where she and the *Crusader* now are. This is all the assistance I can render the army in that quarter.
>
> The Department will perceive the embarrassment under which I labor in not being able to answer the calls of the army in the sounds, on the Nansemond, James and York Rivers, for gunboat support to enable it to hold its scattered positions.[8]

The navy had serious problems just keeping its ships afloat. The U.S. gunboat *Miami* ran aground on April 8, but her commander, Robert Townsend, explained that it was not all his fault:

> I sailed at 3 p.m. on the 7th [April] instant, passed through the Slue of Hatteras, and before 10 AM on the 8th got ashore in attempting to cross the Swash at Hatteras Inlet. If the *Miami* drew only the water indicated by her marks (7 feet 9 inches), she should have passed over the Swash with some 9 inches to spare, but—settled as she is amidships—she struck very hard.[9]

He then reported that on the tenth he received some needed assistance: "The tug *Murray* returned from an expedition and also came to our aid. Lightening, heaving, and tugging carried us slowly from point to point, till finally, about 2 p.m. on the 13th, the *Miami* was got over into the deeper water of the sound."[10]

There were irritating problems that went with the responsibility of enforcing the blockade and controlling commerce. Oystermen were one such annoyance. On April 1, Admiral Lee wrote to Gideon Welles, objecting to permits issued by the secretary of the Treasury that allowed several oystermen to fish for their oysters in the Nansemond River, just off the James River. On the tenth, Lee sent the permits back with this message:

> The honorable Secretary of the Treasury is not aware that the one gunboat stationed in the Nansemond to intercept trade and mails from Norfolk, and to prevent the rebels from crossing that river to get in the rear of our outposts at Suffolk, can not keep under observation different oyster boats and parties coming, going, and scattered on different oyster banks in that river.[11]

Admiral Lee settled the matter permanently after General Peck issued a similar permit on April 10 to a certain Edward Bust, giving him permission to carry oysters to Suffolk:

> As that region is infested with smugglers and rebel mail carriers I have found it necessary not only to prohibit the gathering of oysters in the Nansemond but to allow no boats there day or night where such illicit operations can be carried on, and to instruct the guard vessels to recognize no oyster permits after May 1 and until then only in open boats.[12]

One ship that could have made a difference in the sieges of Suffolk and Washington was the Confederate steamer *City of Richmond*. It had been built in Richmond, as an ironclad, to be passed down the James River to run the blockade. After its completion, the difficulty was to get it past the South's own river obstacles, designed to keep out the Union ships. On April 10, the ship was ready to set sail, but politics prevented her from leaving. There had been weeks of haggling over the advisability of opening the obstructions to let it pass. Finally, on April 21, General Robert E. Lee wrote:

> I have just received a letter from Gen. Longstreet dated the 20th, instant, stating that the enemy crossed below Hill's Point on the evening of the 19th; attacked and captured Stribling's Battery at that point operating against the gunboats. He again expressed a desire that the Richmond would only show herself on the James River, and thinks that alone would strengthen his left by 10,000 men. I do not

know that anything can be done by the Navy and only express his wishes.[13]

On April 21 an official position was reached: it would be advisable to wait until the completion of a second ironclad before opening the gates.[14] Robert G. H. Kean, head of the Confederate Bureau of War, confided in his diary: "The Richmond is such a stupid failure, drawing 14' of water so that she cannot get up and down the river even if the obstructions were open to let her pass; and as she can only steam about 3 knots, being worthless as a ram, and her machinery very defective, it is deemed unsafe for her to go down.[15]

SOUTH ATLANTIC BLOCKADING SQUADRON

The South Atlantic Squadron, under Rear Admiral Samuel F. Du Pont, was located outside the bar in Charleston Harbor, South Carolina. Du Pont's squadron blockaded the coasts of the Carolinas and Georgia.

Admiral Du Pont's futile April 7 attack on Charleston had resulted in severe damage to several vessels of his fleet; in addition, the sinking of the ironclad *Keokuk* on April 8 resulted from damage sustained on the seventh. In the attack, there had been a lead force of nine ironclad steamers; of these, one had been sunk and four severely damaged in a period of less than one hour.[16] In spite of this highly unsuccessful iron-clad performance and similar earlier experiences, the navy recently had contracted for twelve light-draft gunboats, similar to the *Monitor,* at a cost of $380,000 each.[17]

The fleet's ships remained outside Charleston for several days, then, on April 10, headed south to Union-held Port Royal, South Carolina, for repairs and refitting. It might have been lucky for them that they left. General Pierre Beauregard, the Confederate commander in Charleston, called a meeting of his officers on April 10 to discuss an attack on the U.S. fleet, lying outside the harbor, since he suspected it was virtually unprotected. His officers agreed that such an attack would give them a chance to try out their new spar-torpedo boats. Beauregard was one of the strong supporters of these boats, and he was waiting for a new one, then being designed. He was so proud of these engines of war that he wrote the following in letters to his two favorite Confederate politicians, Senators R. W. Barnwell and James L. Orr, on April 12: "Have advised a secret expedition which will shake Abolitiondom to foundation if successful. My hopes are strong. I regret much Lee's tor-pedo ram is not finished. It is the greatest invention of the day."[18]

The raid, planned for the twelfth, was never executed because by then Admiral Du Pont had repositioned all the ships—except the *New Ironsides,* which left on the thirteenth.

Despite the large number of Union blockaders, Richmond's *Southern Illustrated News* reported that the steamer *Emma and Anna,* from Nassau, ran through the "great Yankee fleet, Monitors and all" into Charleston on the morning of April 10.[19] Records indicate that she was the only blockade-runner to enter or leave a Confederate port on the tenth.[20]

The navy and the army usually cooperated with each other, but sometimes events caused friction. Such was the case with the army ship *George Washington,* commanded by artilleryman Captain Thomas B. Briggs. The navy's Acting Lt. Edgar Brodhead commanded the navy's USS *E. B. Hale,* a screw steamer, and had been requested to go to the aid of a grounded army ship. The two ships left Beaufort, South Carolina, on April 8 together. En route, the *Hale* ran aground; the *Washington* left to go up the Coosaw River, but returned later that same afternoon. Both ships lay anchored together during the night; at daybreak the *Hale,* which had refloated during the night, left to go back to Beaufort. The *Washington* stayed at anchor until after sunup, when she was attacked and partially sunk by Rebel shore artillery. Captain Briggs then surrendered her.

Brodhead and the *Hale* returned later that day to search for the *George Washington*; he found the wreck of the ship abandoned, burned, and half submerged at the edge of a marsh. It had been reported to Brodhead by those on shore that four wounded men had been left on the *Washington,* but Brodhead's men found only one; he was severely wounded. The other three had been taken off by Confederates; one was already dead and buried. The *Hale* took the wounded soldier to the hospital in Beaufort.

As soon as Brodhead put into Beaufort, army Brigadier General Rufus Saxton, commanding the Beaufort forces, X Corps, immediately confronted Brodhead, charging that the *Hale*'s performance "was a most disgraceful affair."[21] Saxton called for an army court of inquiry, which convened on April 21. On that date the findings were reported to a surprised Admiral Du Pont—no naval personnel had been even aware of the court proceedings. While the report criticized Captain Briggs severely, the court held that:

. . . had the *Hale* remained for orders to move from Captain Briggs, who supposed himself to be in command, the whole affair might have been averted, or the result widely different, and therefore that the destruction of the boat is chargeable to the desertion by the

Hale of her consort, and the surrender of the boat is due to the culpable excitement and lack of presence of mind of Captain Briggs.[22]

Du Pont disagreed with these findings, and replied to Saxton: "You will perceive that Captain Briggs had no knowledge whatever of the nature of such cooperations between the services, in which no officer of the one arm or the other can command both."[23]

Du Pont also wrote to Saxton's superior, Major General David Hunter, saying that the army court proceedings made it mandatory for him to have a naval inquiry as well, since the army court had seriously implicated Lieutenant Brodhead. The findings of the navy court were forwarded to Secretary Welles in Washington and endorsed by Admiral Du Pont: "The finding of the court is 'that the conduct of Acting Lieutenant Edgar Brodhead, commanding the USS *E. B. Hale,* in connection with the loss of the army steamer *George Washington,* is irreproachable, and that no further military proceedings are necessary in this case.' "

Admiral Du Pont added his support of the decision: "I cordially approve of this finding of the court, and fully concur in this complete justification of the conduct of Acting Lieutenant Edgar Brodhead."[24]

The Confederates returned on April 10 to the sunken *George Washington* and were able to salvage one twenty-four-pound cannon and several Enfield rifles, plus some boat equipment.[25] However, the Union troops managed to get one cannon back as well.

One of the Confederate cavalrymen accompanying the artillery unit that attacked the *Washington* was James Barr of the 5th South Carolina Cavalry. In a letter to his family he referred to the attack:

> Pocataglio, S.C. April 12, 1863
>
> Wed. evening about six o'clock we were ordered to Chisholm Island. We were halted near the Island after a hard ride in a canter, but in a fine spirit. I never saw men in a better humor, keen for a fight. We spent the latter part of the night bad as we were halted in an old field and there was a heavy dew and it was cold. We had no blankets and with little fire burning from straw and log we could get. About day artillery opened on the boat. We have taken two prisoners and got one that was killed. He was burned badly. All his clothes were burned off him, balance escaped, some drowned. . . .
>
> We succeeded in getting off with one of the guns, a brass 25 pounder, worth a great deal to us. There were two more on the boat,

the Yankees having taken them off. The day we wanted the other two, the Yankees found us out and commenced shelling us or shelling about the wrecked steamer. At our picket post the shells could be seen coming in too well as they came in a direct course for us. The shells looked beautiful. Solid shot fell in about two hundred yards of us.[26]

James A. Graham, of the 27th North Carolina Infantry, wrote in his diary about his part in the attack:

April 12th, 1863 Coosawhatchie, S.C.
    We had a little fun down here a few days ago. A Yankee gunboat came up the Coosaw River and our battery with 1 or 2 other battery from Pocotaligo were sent down to take it. After firing a few rounds at it the Yankees ran up the white flag, set the boat afire and took to the swamp on the other side of the river. We got 3 prisoners off the burning boat, all of them badly wounded.[27]

South of Beaufort, in Savannah Harbor, the Confederate raider CSS *Atlanta* waited its chance to escape to continue its mission. The surgeon on board was a man named Robert F. Freeman; his report for April 10, 1863, stated in part that he treated eight patients, admitted two, and discharged three. His most serious case appeared to be Boatswain's Mate Edward Price (Price recovered and survived the war):

Hemoptysis: Was taken yesterday p.m. with hemorrhage and spit up 1 or 2 gills of blood, which was stopped by several doses of dry salt. Had repetition of the same last night and this morning, but the quantity of blood lost each time was small. The disease is hereditary—many of his family having died of it. Percussion dull on upper lobe of left lung—Respiratory murmur feeble.[28]

Farther south, the Union South Atlantic blockader *Fernandina* was on Sapelo Island, off the northern coast of Georgia; crew members went ashore on a minor but important mission, according to the surgeon, Ensign Boyer:

4/10/63
    2 of our crew, Scott and Carey, started yesterday after some beef. They returned this morning with 2 head of beef. All hands feel jubilant over the prospect of having fresh beef for the next 2 or 3

days. Paymaster Murray, Ens. Flood and myself took a tramp in the direction of Sampson's plantation. We walked no less than 10 miles and had a pleasant time of it. Killed a moccasin snake.[29]

The senior officers usually faced situations that were a little more serious. One such situation faced by Admiral Du Pont and his blockaders was dealing with foreign vessels. Du Pont received a notice from Gideon Welles on the tenth, reciting the charges of Admiral Sir Alexander Milne, commanding Britain's forces on the coast of North America and in the West Indies. Milne had complained to the British minister of the treatment of English vessels. They had been approached by blockaders and cruisers that fired warning shots across their bows instead of blank cartridges. Welles's reply to Du Pont defended that policy, as he had explained it to the British:

It has been stated in reply that this apparent discourtesy was doubtless in consequence of the great vigilance of our officers in having all their guns shotted while on belligerent duty and from no want of comity; but it would be well, as a rule, to have one small gun loaded with blank cartridge to be used by day as the preparatory signal of warning in accordance with the usage of the sea service. A vessel approaching at night without making the usual signals is not entitled to any of the courtesies of the sea.[30]

EAST GULF BLOCKADING SQUADRON

There were two other blockading squadrons, both in the Gulf of Mexico, guarding the ports from the east coast of Florida to Texas. The East Coast Squadron watched the Florida ports south of St. Augustine and around the coast to just east of Pensacola. The West Gulf Squadron covered all areas west of, and including, Pensacola.

The East Gulf Squadron was commanded by Acting Rear Admiral Theodorus Bailey and had twenty-three ships of various sizes, plus seven tenders. Bailey reported only one bark that was not fit for duty; the rest of his vessels were on station at locations from Jupiter Inlet on the east coast of Florida to Apalachicola on the west coast, including Key West and the Tortugas. Recently there had been some activity from blockade-runners, mostly boats from Nassau and Cuba, in Florida's waters.

On April 6, the USS *Huntsville,* out of Key West, reported the capture of the Confederate sloop *Minnie,* with thirteen bales of cotton, outbound from the Aucilla River on Apalachee Bay and bound for Matanzas, Mexico.[31]

Acting Lieutenant I. B. Baxter of the U.S. bark *Gem of the Sea* reported to Secretary of the Navy Gideon Welles, giving details of the capture of a British schooner, the *Maggie Fulton,* on April 8:

> This morning we were lying at anchor 2 miles from Indian River Inlet, with the wind light from S.E. and weather foggy. At 9 a.m. the fog lifted and we discovered a schooner about 4 miles to the N.E. from us standing to the southward; we fired a gun to bring her to, to which she paid no attention, but kept on her course. I immediately got underway and went in chase of her, as the fog thickened and did not see her again until 3 p.m., when we made her close inshore about 3 miles distant from us, standing to the northward for the inlet. The water being too shoal for us to approach much nearer with the vessel, we lowered our boats and captured her.[32]

The captured cargoes were not significant; however, these boats were typical of the blockade-runners the Union was trying to stop. When the blockade was first installed, the chance that a runner would be caught was one in ten. By 1864 the odds had been lowered to one in three. The short distances from the Bahamas Islands and Cuba to many of Florida's ports made it practical for small boats to attempt these profitable trips.

Besides their sea duties, the navy also scouted in coastal waters, patrolling the rivers and ports. On April 10, a reconnaissance force led by the commander of the USS *Fort Henry* returned to Cedar Key, on the west coast of Florida, after searching some of the rivers in northwestern Florida for blockade-runners and any stockpiles of merchandise coming in or going out. The expedition had been fruitless; the ships returned empty-handed after an eight-day mission. The rivers were shallow and could be navigated only by slow, clumsy boat launches from the *Fort Henry,* the *Sagamore,* and the *St. Lawrence.* The expedition had been hampered by unwieldy boats, bad weather, bad luck, and few Confederates. Its only good luck was that only one seaman had been wounded during the entire eight days. The gulf coast of Florida from Pensacola east was entirely in Confederate hands, so these river sorties were always risky ventures. The Confederates could move faster on land than Union sailors could by sea, and the element of surprise, always hoped for by the navy, was seldom a factor.

The Confederate navy had some presence in the Florida panhandle, but the duty was frustrating. Chattahoochee, Florida, is on the

Georgia-Florida border at the junction of the Chattahoochee and Flint rivers, some seventy miles north of the Gulf of Mexico. A new Confederate steamer, the CSS *Chattahoochee,* was intended to protect the Chattahoochee River from Union moves upriver; however, the barriers across the river many miles below the city of Chattahoochee, which prevented any Union ship's passage, also prevented the *Chattahoochee* herself from getting out to sea. This was a great disappointment, particularly to the junior officers, who craved a little more excitement than the Chattahoochee River appeared to provide.

The ship was reported ready for duty and left Chattahoochee on April 7, headed south on the river to test its engines, its crew, and its guns. Captain John J. Guthrie commanded the crew, which included Lieutenant George W. Gift. Gift wrote to Ellen Augusta Shackelford (later his wife), giving her a complete and critical assessment of the trip:

At Alum Bluff we steamed majestically past the batteries [Fort Preston], not halting to inform the commandant of our business. During the afternoon we fired nine shots down stream and up, three from the rifle, and six from the after 32 pdrs out the stern ports. Which I consider a waste of ammunition as we fired at no mark, and consequently the men were but little instructed. . . . The next morning—Wednesday—we arrived at the first battery six hundred yards from the obstructions by land and four miles by the river. (I never have in my life seen so miserable a place, entirely surrounded on both sides by water, mud and swamp.) The batteries are miserable contrivances, poorly constructed and worse manned and armed.

The soldiers are raw infantry troops under very raw, green unsophisticated officers, who have no confidence in the position, their guns or themselves. . . . As a matter of course our peacock captain made a formal call upon the Commanding Officer, a cross-eyed second Lieutenant and in order to show off in the most consequential manner, concluded to practice at a tree. Thursday was appointed for this display of folly and expenditure of ammunition. The muggins' from the battery came aboard, and Guthrie after much deliberation enunciated his plan for operations, which so disgusted me with his absolute ignorance in regard to the most commonplace matters in the art of gunnery, and use of shells that I lost all interest in an affair that under other circumstances would have filled me with pleasure and excitement, and to cap the climax he spoke of the efficiency of *his* crew—made so by Jim's precepts and my hard work—confound him![33]

The gun drill went well, and the ship went back upriver to Chatta-hoochee, arriving on April 10. Pronounced fit to be a part of the Con-federate navy, the *Chattahoochee* became one of the few Confederate ships in that district.

The junction of the Flint and Chattahoochee rivers was also the site of the old Chattahoochee Federal arsenal, at that time in Confeder-ate hands. Sergeant W. H. Andrews, of the 1st Georgia Regulars, had just arrived at the arsenal with his regiment on April 8. Andrews had no love for his new surroundings:

> The arsenal building is three stories high with a seven-story tower. What a magnificent view could be had if there was anything to look at. But the upper portion of Florida is nothing but pine woods, wire grass and saw palmetto. Nothing to attract the eye. You might go to sleep and while in that condition be moved 100 miles, and when you wake up, you would not know the difference. All of a sameness—how different from Virginia and Maryland. It is certainly God's own country, for it don't look like anyone else would have it.[34]

WEST GULF BLOCKADING SQUADRON

Farther to the west, Rear Admiral David G. Farragut commanded the West Gulf Blockading Squadron. Farragut's fleet numbered more than sixty ships of various sizes, and about ten of them were in some need of repair.[35] These ships were responsible for blockading the coasts of the Confederate states of Alabama, Mississippi, Louisiana, and Texas, not a small assignment when you add the fact that they were trying to break the Confederate hold on the Mississippi River as well.

In joint efforts with his foster brother, Admiral David Porter, Farragut was charged with the task of opening the Mississippi River between Port Hudson and Vicksburg, a stretch still controlled by the South. It was in connection with this duty that on April 10, 1863, he was on his flagship the *Albatross,* outside the mouth of the Red River, above Port Hudson and separated from his fleet by the Confederate batteries at Port Hudson. Earlier in March the *Albatross,* with Farragut on board, and the *Hartford* had run up from New Orleans and were joined by the Marine Brigade ram *Switzerland.* Farragut hoped to open communica-tion with Porter and Grant, who were still above Vicksburg. He also planned to stop any Southern vessels trying to take goods from the west side of the Mississippi into the hard-pressed Confederate states east of the Mississippi. On April 9, the *Hartford* intercepted a Confederate steamer, the *J. D. Clarke,* and captured her, taking three prisoners, a Major Howell and two engineers. On the tenth the *Albatross* went out to salvage the *Clarke*'s machinery, then scuttled her.[36]

The far western end of the blockade was at Galveston, Texas. Confederates retook Galveston on New Year's Day 1863 after several months of Yankee occupation. This effort resulted in a setback for the U.S. Navy, the capture by the Confederates of one of the better U.S. vessels, the USS *Harriet Lane.* The *Lane* was made a part of the Confederate navy, but was trapped in Galveston Harbor, with the blockading Yankee ships watching her from outside the harbor.

There was some good news for the navy off the Texas coast, where the USS *New London* was patrolling outside Sabine Pass, on the Texas-Louisiana border. Lieutenant Commander Abner Read reported to Gideon Welles on April 10:

Sir: I have the honor to report that this morning about 4 o'clock I sent a boat to the light-house [Sabine City] to take a position and make observations as to the strength of the enemy, with the intention, if the report was favorable, to cut out two steamers, lying at the wharf in Sabine City. . . .

About 2 o'clock p.m. a small sloop was seen beating down the Pass, apparently going to the bayou leading near the light-house. She came to anchor at the mouth of the bayou, and those on board got into a skiff with the intention of going ashore. Lieutenant Day [commanding the *New London*'s boat] had placed himself, officers and men, in such a position that when the skiff entered the bayou, he could capture her. The skiff entered the bayou and when within a very few feet he arose from the grass and demanded her surrender, which was complied with without a shot. The prisoners proved to be Captain Charles Fowler, John McLean, pilot, and Edward Lynch, second mate, all of the steamer *Josiah Bell* and one Confederate soldier. Captain Fowler commanded the *Bell* at the capture of the *Morning Light* in January last.[37]

The next day, Commander Read sent another dispatch:

Sir: This morning at 9 o'clock a rebel steamer was seen coming out of the pass. We got ready for action at once and were about to fire upon the enemy when we discovered she bore a flag of truce. I sent a flag to meet it. The object was to make enquiries about Captain Fowler and his men and to send their clothes if they had been taken prisoner by us.[38]

Commander Read's report on the tenth also mentioned other ships:

> Sir: I reported on April 3 the capture of the British schooner
> *Tampico* bound from Sabine Pass to the Belize, with 112 bales
> of cotton. I was informed by the crew of the prize that another
> schooner the *Ben* had run the blockade earlier in the night. Leaving
> Lieutenant-Commander D. A. McDermut (who boarded the prize
> first) to make out the proper papers and put a prize crew on board
> *Tampico,* then to cruise off the Pass until my return, I started imme-
> diately in pursuit, supposing that she was in all probability bound for
> the same destination as the *Tampico.* I stood S. by E. 150 miles; at 6
> o'clock on the morning of the 4th changed course and stood W. 15
> miles, then back towards the Pass, crossing my track out, with the
> hope of falling in with the schooner if my information was correct,
> but without success.
>
> The prisoners we captured to-day inform me that the *Ben,* get-
> ting aground on the night of the 2nd, did not get out until the
> morning of the 3rd, when the *New London* and the *Cayuga* were
> absent in the chase and capture of the *Tampico.*[39]

On April 10, Farragut was also supplying vessels for General
Banks in the Bayou Teche campaign, having sent the *Estrella, Clifton,
Arizona,* and *Calhoun* to protect Banks and also to provide transports for
flanking movements against Confederate General Taylor.

Two of the larger Confederate navy ships, *Diana* and *Queen of the
West,* were rushing to aid General Taylor's forces, hoping to draw the
Union gunboats away from the outnumbered Confederates on land.
(The Confederates had recently captured the Union's *Diana,* and in
February had overwhelmed the Union ram, the *Queen of the West.*
These two ships were on the way toward Fort Bisland but did not
survive the Teche campaign. The *Diana* was blown out of the water by
Union artillery on April 12 and the *Queen* was abandoned as the Rebels
retreated toward Franklin, Louisiana.)

Farragut had boats on Lake Maurepas and Lake Ponchartrain to
control those waters, and had sent two boats to make the landings at
Pascagoula on the ninth. And he still had to oversee the patrolling of the
Confederate coast.

With all of these activities, Admiral Farragut had endured his
share of reverses since the beginning of 1863. The loss of Galveston and
the *Harriet Lane,* the running of the blockade by the CSS *Florida* at
Mobile, and the loss of ships on the Mississippi had all tarnished his

record. Assistant Secretary of the Navy Gustavus V. Fox wrote to Admiral Porter on April 6, expressing dismay at recent events:

> I have been wanting to write to you for some weeks, but have so much to say as to lead me constantly to defer the matter until I have so much on hand that it cannot be communicated in a letter. The Tribune says that the eighty-six years that the Navy has been in existence have not recorded so many disasters as have taken place within the last year.[40]

While Farragut was up the Mississippi and out of touch with his command, Commodore Morris was back in New Orleans, the senior naval officer present. Morris had been left with instructions from Farragut to sell at auction all prize vessels and their cargoes that could not be sent to Key West (Key West was the court of adjudication for prizes). Farragut's worry was that some of the captured cargoes were perishable: "a portion of it is perishing."[41] Fox was certainly not encouraged by Morris's report from New Orleans in Farragut's absence. The report confirmed the loss of the *Diana* to the Confederates; the *Barrataria,* run aground; the *Sachem,* leaky boiler; and the *Colonel Kinsman,* snagged and sunk in Berwick Bay. Coupled with requests for more money, two courts of inquiry, and the poor condition of other parts of his fleet, it was a dismal report.[42]

The Confederate navy in the Gulf had no such trouble with prize ships and cargoes. It had few ships and men available to harass any Union vessels, merchant or navy. On April 10, an order to Confederate Commander W. W. Hunter from the Confederate Navy Department in Richmond dated January 10, 1863, was finally received in Galveston, Texas. So on April 10, Hunter, Confederate commander of naval forces in the western gulf, complied with the three-month-old order and transferred all the men in his command to Lieutenant J. N. Barney, commanding the CSS *Harriet Lane.* "All the men in his command" included one boatswain, one carpenter's mate, and four seamen.[43]

THE REBEL CRUISERS

While the blockading squadrons were patrolling the coasts of the South, other forces of the U.S. Navy were trying to keep the Confederate cruisers from decimating merchant shipping on the Atlantic. The Confederates had been highly successful in slowing down ship movements to and from the North, an effort that had had several side benefits for the Rebel fleet. The threat to Union shipping had driven up both insurance and shipping rates to a point where many shippers were unable or unwilling to meet the high costs involved. The risks also reduced the number of available sailors, many of whom wanted none of the additional perils of being targets of the Confederate raiders. The navy's preoccupation with the blockade made virtually no ships available to escort merchantmen, so there was little protection at sea.

After two years of war, the Southern raiders' successes had caused shipping to decrease dramatically, making prizes for the Confederate raiders increasingly scarce. By April 10, American ship owners were converting their ships to foreign flags or liquidating them at auction. Then Confederate luck began to fail: the neutral nations, Britain and France, tightened their previously loose interpretations of neutrality policies. As a result of these foreign policy changes, Confederate cruisers were often refused ports and provisions where, in the early years, they had been welcomed and feted. This posed great difficulties for Southern captains because the North's blockade and the cruisers' long voyages required them to provision themselves in foreign ports.

The British shipbuilding industry was also under close scrutiny, since it was a violation of English neutrality to build warships for a warring nation such as the Confederacy. All this indicated that the very success of the raiders was threatening further operations.

The original Confederate cruisers had been either captured from the Union navy at the beginning of the war or were built in Southern ports in the early months of the war. Their successes were limited, since the ships were not really designed as raiders. These early ships all suffered from some deficiency, such as speed or maneuverability.

It was still possible to build ships in Britain through devious methods, and the Confederates used these methods to acquire four of their cruisers—the *Alabama,* the *Florida,* the *Georgia,* and later in the war, the *Shenandoah.* The ships were wooden sailing vessels with added steam engines, and were from 500 to 1,040 tons, up to 220 feet long.[44] They were built ostensibly for other nations, but were sold to Confederate agents or sympathizers and converted for war. On April 10, several of these Confederate raiders were in foreign waters, waiting to prey on any American shipping they found.

CSS *ALABAMA*

One of the Confederate captains who became a highly successful raider was Captain Raphael Semmes. In July 1862, a newly built British ship, the *290,* sailed from Britain and rendezvoused with the Confederate supply ship *Agrippina* in the Azores. Semmes, who had been sent from the Bahamas on the *Agrippina,* took command of the *290,* which then set sail as the CSS *Alabama.* Semmes's success was remarkable; by April 10 he had intercepted, bonded, burned, or sunk forty-two merchantmen.[45] On the tenth, he had just arrived at the Brazilian island of Fernando de Noronha, off the coast of Brazil, where he was to receive supplies from the *Agrippina,* captained by Captain Alexander McQueen. Semmes remembered: "The *Agrippina* had not arrived; nor did I ever see her afterward. Captain Bulloch had duly dispatched her, but the worthless old Scotch master made it a point not to find me, and having sold his cargo in some port or other, I have forgotten where, returned to England with a cock-and-bull story to account for his failure."[46]

Next, Semmes wrote disparagingly about the island: "A ship rarely ever touches at the island. There is nothing to invite communication. It is too insignificant for traffic, and has no good harbor, where a ship could repair damages or refit. It is, besides, a penal colony of Brazil, to which it belongs."[47] But in spite of its drawbacks, the island was a rich source of vegetables, fruits, and meats, and so was valuable to Semmes and the crew.

On April 4, Semmes captured the *Louisa Hatch,* loaded with coal, and kept her as a prize instead of burning her. With the disappearance of the *Agrippina,* it was fortunate he had saved the *Hatch,* since her coal provided him with the fuel he badly needed. An accommodating Brazilian governor, Sebastiao Jose Basilio Pyrrho, allowed him to transfer coal at his pleasure. That was a breach of neutrality by Brazil, but was not of importance to the governor, who was glad for Semmes's company. The *Alabama* remained at anchor off Fernando de Noronha until April 22, keeping it out of action and making the shipping lanes safer for American shipping during that twelve-day period.

CSS *FLORIDA*

The CSS *Florida,* another British-built raider, was also constructed in subterfuge. The original hull was named the *Oreto*; it was supposed to be for the Italian government, but was actually being built for Confederate use through a Southerner, James D. Bulloch. The raider was completed and sailed from Liverpool on March 22, 1862, headed for Nassau, where she was outfitted with guns and found her new captain, Lieutenant John Newland Maffitt, an experienced raider.

The British proved inquisitive while the ship was in the Bahamas, and the U.S. counsel pressured Nassau officials to impound the *Oreto.* Officials moved slowly, and even though the Union provided a blockading ship, the USS *Cuyler,* and there were close calls with British officials, the *Oreto* put out to sea quietly on August 8, 1862.

The crew was skimpy, and included young J. Lauren Read, Maffitt's stepson. While they were transferring some provisions near Green Cay in the Bahamas, yellow fever struck the crew. Even as they participated in commissioning ceremonies for the newly named CSS *Florida* on August 17, 1862, crew members were coming down with the dread disease. It riddled the crew, and six members, including young Read, died. Maffitt himself came down with the fever but survived. He eventually headed for Mobile, Alabama.

Four months later, Maffitt, having recovered and having refitted his ship, crept out of Mobile Harbor on a dark and stormy night—to the consternation of Welles, the American press, and the public. The *Florida* had begun its impressive career.

On the twenty-eighth of March, Maffitt captured the Boston bark *Lapwing,* which he decided to use as a tender. He put his men on board as crew, and passed over to the *Florida,* bucket by bucket, the coal from her ample supply. The two ships together captured a New York bark, the *M. J. Colcord,* on the thirtieth, but then were unable to find another prize until April 17. On April 10, the two ships scoured the seas but found nothing, primarily because the *Alabama* had been there before them, taking what prizes were available. The *Florida,* too, was to rendezvous with its tender at the island of Fernando de Noronha in April, and missed seeing the *Alabama* there by only one day.[48]

Maffitt wasn't as lucky as Semmes had been. A new governor had just arrived in Fernando de Noronha, replacing the Rebel-friendly Major Pyrrho, who was removed because he had allowed Semmes to violate neutrality regulations and improve the *Alabama.* The new governor, Colonel Antonio Gomez Leal, had no interest in helping Maffitt, and ordered the *Florida* out after twenty-four hours in port. Maffitt quietly acquiesced in order to keep peace with Brazil.

CSS *GEORGIA*

A new raider, the CSS *Georgia,* was at sea on April 10; just out of Liverpool, England, she was then off the coast of France. The *Georgia,* with an English crew, was met at sea by the Confederate supply ship *Japan* to provide guns and supplies. After the rendezvous, Lieutenant Lewis Maury took command, and the ship was commissioned on April 9. James M. Morgan, a sixteen-year-old junior lieutenant, took part in the commissioning:

We then stood out to sea, where, after we had got safely beyond the three-mile limit, we stopped. Captain Maury called all hands to the mast and read his orders, hoisted the Confederate flag and his pennant, and declared the Confederate States cruiser Georgia to be in commission.

His remarks were greeted with three lusty cheers. He then asked the men who were going with us to step forward and enlist for three years or the war, but, alas, a sea-lawyer had been at work, and not a man came forward.[49]

Although none of the British crew members elected to serve in the Rebel navy, several of the crew members of the *Japan* volunteered, and these men formed the crew of the *Georgia*. Morgan described his new ship:

It was the 9th of April, 1863 when this little friendless ship of only about five hundred and fifty tons started on her long and hazardous cruise. She was as absolutely unfitted for the work as any vessel could conceivably be; she lay low in the water and was very long for her beam; her engines were gear engines, that is, a large wheel fitted with lignum-vitae cogs turned the iron cogs on the shaft, and frequently the wooden cogs would break. . . . Her sail power was insufficient, and, owing to her length, it was impossible to put her about under canvas. She was slow under either sail or steam, or both together.[50]

As the inadequate little craft sailed away from France, leaving the far western French island of Ushant behind, her first day at sea was described by Morgan:

The morning of the 10th of April dawned fair, with light breezes and a comparatively smooth sea, and officers and men set to work fastening to the deck iron traverses for our pivot gun. Then came a most difficult job, shorthanded as we were,—that of mounting the guns on their carriages; and to add to our troubles the sea commenced to rise. With all the most intricate and ingenious tackles our seamanlike first lieutenant could devise, it was an awful strain upon us, as the heavy gun swung back and forth with the roll of the ship. However, by almost superhuman exertions we succeeded in getting the guns into their places on the carriages; then we felt very man-of-warrish indeed.[51]

The log of the ship revealed that on the tenth the crew spotted several sails in the busy channels off France but that they were busy "fitting up the ship." Morgan's assessment was accurate: the *Georgia* had a brief and not very successful career roaming the Atlantic as a raider.

OTHER NAVAL FACTORS

The ports used by the cruisers presented a host of neutrality violations, a constant problem to both sides during the four years of war. Each instance involving a violation on either side meant hours of research, documentation, and, in cases such as the one in Fernando de Noronha, action. Trying to stay neutral perplexed Britain, France, Brazil, Spain, Denmark, and other countries close to the United States. On April 10, several cases were being cited. There was the case of the *Alexandra,* then under construction in Britain; the raiding of the CSS *Alabama;* and other cases were developing.

On April 6, the Danish government in Saint Thomas, West Indies, sent a letter to Admiral Charles Wilkes, senior officer of U.S. vessels in Saint Thomas. This letter was forwarded to Lieutenant Commander Charles E. Fleming, in Admiral Wilkes's absence, on April 10. The lieutenant governor of the island complained that U.S. vessels had used Saint Thomas to prepare to "overhaul and persecute" vessels entering or going out of the harbor. Specifically, the lieutenant governor said that the USS *Wachusett* had slipped her anchor and followed and captured the merchantman *Neptune* as she left Saint Thomas, bringing back to Saint Thomas sixteen sailors as prisoners. On April 11, Commander Fleming of the *Wachusett* wrote back a polite and simple explanation of the event: "It did not occur."[52]

News traveled slowly regarding ships at sea. On April 10, the *New York Times* reported briefly about the fate of the bark *J. P. Ellicott*:

> The bark J.P. Ellicott of Boston laden with stores was captured near St. Thomas by the rebel schooner Retribution on the 10th of January last. A prize crew of five and two prize officers named John Gilbert and Gilbert Hayes were put on board. Soon afterwards the crew took charge of the vessel and put the officers in confinement and returned the vessel to the American consul at St. Thomas. The consul sent the officers and crew to the U.S. Marshall in this city and they arrived yesterday. The officers are held for examination and the crew detained as witnesses. The crew of the prize ship Peterhoff captured while attempting to run the blockade arrived at the Marshall's office yesterday and were detained as witnesses in that case.[53]

The Union navy continued its sea searches and its port investigations with news both good and bad. On the tenth, the USS *Mohican* had come back from a ten-day search in the waters of Cape Verde and surrounding islands off the west coast of Africa. The captain, O. S. Glisson, wrote from the island of Cape Verde on April 11:

> Sir: I have to report to the honorable Secretary of the Navy that I sailed from this port on the 1st day of April on a short cruise to the southward of these islands, after which I stood to the northward, touching at the islands of Brava, Fogo, Saint Vincent, Santa Luzia, Branco, Raza, Saint Nicholas, and returned to this port on the 10th instant, without seeing any suspicious vessels. The health of the officers and crew continues good. In regard to general order relative to correspondence with the Department, I would state that I have no paper on board of the proper dimensions. As soon as I can obtain some I will comply with the regulations.[54]

The news was not as good in a report from the U.S. consul in Matamoras, Mexico, dated April 15. He was frustrated, trying to get some Union ships to put a stop to the privateering that originated from his area. He had asked Farragut for help, but received no response.

> The port of Brazos Santiago has been made a rendezvous for the Texas navy, and one privateer, schooner rigged, sailed from that port on the 13th . . .
> Their [the privateers'] intention is to wait outside and intercept the American vessels that leave this port, of which there are now 13 here.
> It is now impossible for an American vessel to get any freight here, and many of them are being sold.[55]

Better news came on the same date from the U.S. flagship *Lancaster,* lead ship of Union naval forces in the Pacific Squadron. One of its screw sloops, the USS *Narragansett,* had reported on a sweep from Puntarenas, Costa Rica; San Juan and Realejo, Nicaragua; Amapala, Honduras; La Union and Acajutla, El Salvador; and San Jose in Guatemala:

> Commander Stanley represents that there does not seem to be any probability of privateers being fitted out from any of the places he visited against our commerce, although he met a number of

Americans who were traitors to their flag, yet claiming the protection of our Government whenever they anticipated difficulties.[56]

Because of the various time zones in which these ships operated, ships such as the USS *Mohican,* in the Atlantic Squadron in waters off Africa, had watched the first hours of April 10, as it opened the U.S. day, still in the war's first half. The ships of the Pacific Squadron saw the last of April 10 as they sailed in waters off California, little knowing that for all the soldiers, sailors, and citizens on both sides, the next day would usher in the war's second half.

★

Admiral Du Pont was relieved of command on July 5, 1863, and died of disease in June 1865.

Brigadier General Rufus Saxton won the Medal of Honor at Harpers Ferry, but it was not awarded until 1893.

The CSS Chattahoochee *blew up and sank in the Chattahoochee River on May 27, 1863, killing eighteen.*

The CSS Alabama *was sunk by the USS* Kearsarge *off France on June 19, 1864. Semmes survived the war.*

The CSS Florida *was captured in a neutral port in Brazil on October 7, 1864.*

The CSS Georgia *was sold because it was not satisfactory as a raider.*

EPILOGUE

April 10, 1863. The day ended, and the North and South inched toward their meeting at Appomattox, two years away. During the day, 58 Americans were killed, 84 wounded, and 129 captured or missing, a total of 271 casualties on both sides. Death claimed another 143 lives in Union and Confederate hospitals, and probably many more, since Confederate records were incomplete. April 10 was a day of great significance to these men and to their families. The statistics paint one picture of those who were most directly affected by the events of the day. But this picture is a mere recording of facts, and it falls short of showing the scope of the day's meaning.

Other pictures emerge as well. As we read thousands of letters, diaries, and memoirs, my wife, Donna, and I came to know these writers. It was distressing, after becoming acquainted with these people through their personal papers, to learn that they had not survived the war. For us, there was a real sense of loss.

The excerpts in the book represent the many others we were unable to use and give a glimpse into the troubled nation. The pathos of Edgar Jackson's letter from Fredericksburg, the heartbreak of Kate Stone's brother's death in Cotton Gin, Mississippi, the humor of Pliny Brown's fashion comments in Charleston, the enigma of Alphonso Charles Webster's conviction and death in Richmond, and the fervor of Michael Kiener's final plea for his life in Savannah typify the varied events of the day. These, and many others, touched our lives during the many years of putting this effort together.

There is another picture, an unfinished picture that is a puzzle still. How could these men, young and old, swap tobacco and newspapers one day but kill each other, and be prepared to die, the next? Their letters reveal no great hatred of each other, although the newspapers and politicians tried to stir such passion, but they had a sense of commitment to their causes that seldom wavered. In spite of the ease of desertion and the need to go home, there remained a dedication to the "Cause" both North and South. The flag was a symbol to the Northerner, who was more passionate about his flag than about the slavery issue or even about the Save the Union issue. The average Southerner fought to keep the Northern invaders off his land, not to keep slaves. Whatever it was, this dedication was something that burned deeply on both sides. Deeply enough to take the lives of over half a million of the nation's population.

The letters and diaries show a degree of emotion that is both surprising and wonderful. The comments about Lincoln's review, particularly, show the love of the soldiers for the beleaguered president and his genuine concern for them. Here, the eyes seem to be the barometers of the feelings. Lincoln wanted to look into the eyes of his soldiers and they into his; both were awed by what they saw. It is possible that this very personal relationship may be one explanation of the ability of these individuals to withstand two more years of war.

A final picture is of two opposing sides that were so much alike that, merely by reading, it was impossible to determine which side many of the letters represented. Their gripes were the same: mail, drill, food, living conditions, and, most of all, missing their families. With such similarities it seems so tragic that they could wreak such havoc on themselves and on their country. That sort of commitment to an ideal can never fully be explained.

In a different sense, the day was noteworthy as a milestone, a day marking the end of the first half of the war and the beginning of the second half. It would have been of small comfort to the men and women of the North or the South to know that two more years of devastation and death awaited them before it would finally end. The Union would survive, but the cost could never be fully measured in terms of tragedy. The statistics, the events portrayed in the pages of a book, can never transmit, in even the smallest terms, the "last full measure of devotion" that was paid—not just by the dead at Gettysburg but by all the peoples of the North and the South through those 1,458 days of history.

APPENDIX A

★

CASUALTIES, APRIL 10, 1863

EXECUTIONS

Captain Alphonso C. Webster, 1st Loudoun Independent Rangers (Union), in Richmond, Virginia

Private Michael Kiener, 1st Georgia Sharpshooters (Confederate), in Savannah, Georgia

DEEP CREEK, VIRGINIA TRAIN WRECK

Captain Isaac B. Bowditch, Commissary of Vermont, killed

Unknown train engineer, killed

GLOUCESTER POINT, VIRGINIA

Captain Robert Tomlin, Godwin's cavalry, wounded (Confederate)

One unknown, killed (Union)

Four unknown wounded (Union)

FOLLY ISLAND

Private John McDonald, 100th New York Infantry, captured (Union)

Corporal Charles Sabine, 100th New York Infantry, died of wounds (Union)

EDISTO ISLAND

Sergeant Townsend Mikell, Stono Scouts, captured (Confederate)

R. E. Seabrook, Stono Scouts, captured (Confederate)

J. J. Wescoat, Stono Scouts, captured (Confederate)

A. C. Lee, Stono Scouts, captured (Confederate)

W. S. Murray, Stono Scouts, captured (Confederate)

W. B. Whaley, Stono Scouts, captured (Confederate)

F. M. Bailey, Stono Scouts, captured (Confederate)

Joseph Eddings, Stono Scouts, captured (Confederate)

W. G. Baynard, Stono Scouts, captured (Confederate)

Acting Ensign Rhoades, USS *Kingfisher,* wounded (Union)

Total casualties all units, all engagements, 271

FRANKLIN, TENNESSEE

Confederate

Private W. W. Caperton, Company B, 28th Mississippi Cavalry, killed

Private Albert G Keyes, Company B, 28th Mississippi Cavalry, died of wounds

Junior Second Lieutenant Samuel J. Lepley, Company B, 28th Mississippi Cavalry, died of wounds (5/1/63)

Private S. T. Moorman, Company B, 28th Mississippi Cavalry, killed

Private James Pentecost, Company B, 28th Mississippi Cavalry, killed

Captain Croom Bellamy, Company C, 28th Mississippi Cavalry, killed

Corporal T. H. Christian, Company C, 28th Mississippi Cavalry, killed

Private James W. Jelks, Company D, 28th Mississippi Cavalry, died of wounds (4/16/63)

Private E. S. Fraser, Company D, 28th Mississippi Cavalry, died of wounds (4/18/63)

Private M. C. McCoy, Company D, 28th Mississippi Cavalry, killed

Private Joseph R. Moseley, Company D, 28th Mississippi Cavalry, killed

Private William D. Russell, Company F, 28th Mississippi Cavalry, died of wounds (5/6/63)

Second Lieutenant Samuel F. Billingsley, Company G, 28th Mississippi Cavalry, killed

Private Thomas H. Mulholland, Company G, 28th Mississippi Cavalry, killed

Private G. M. Sandifer, Company G, 28th Mississippi Cavalry, died of wounds (5/21/63)

Private Joseph Barr, Company G, 28th Mississippi Cavalry, killed

Private E. H. Whitley, Company H, 28th Mississippi Cavalry, died of wounds (5/20/63)

Private Florence Leary, Company A, 28th Mississippi Cavalry, wounded

Private Quinton T. Barclay, Company B, 28th Mississippi Cavalry, wounded

Private Jesse Biddel, Company B, 28th Mississippi Cavalry, wounded

Lieutenant F. P. Campbell, Company B, 28th Mississippi Cavalry, wounded (lost hand)

Ordnance Sergeant Hernandez D. Money, Company B, 28th Mississippi Cavalry, wounded and captured

Private A. D. Ponder, Company C, 28th Mississippi Cavalry, wounded

Private C. F. Tupper, Company D, 28th Mississippi Cavalry, wounded and captured

Private C. Vicery, Company D, 28th Mississippi Cavalry, wounded and captured

Private John Weiss, Company D, 28th Mississippi Cavalry, wounded

Private J. C. Lawton, Company E, 28th Mississippi Cavalry, wounded and captured

Major Edward P. Jones, Company F, 28th Mississippi Cavalry, wounded and captured

Private B. G. Lindsay, Company F, 28th Mississippi Cavalry, wounded

Private A. G. Lott, Company H, 28th Mississippi Cavalry, wounded

Private Patrick Walsh, Company K, 28th Mississippi Cavalry, wounded

Private F. M. Sorrell, Company A, 28th Mississippi Cavalry, captured

Private Marcus D. L. Franklin, Company D, 28th Mississippi Cavalry, wounded and captured

* Private Elias Bennett, Company E, 28th Mississippi Cavalry, captured

Corporal G. B. Galey, Company E, 28th Mississippi Cavalry, captured

* Private E. E. Morris, Company E, 28th Mississippi Cavalry, captured

* Private Joshua Wilkinson, Company E, 28th Mississippi Cavalry, captured

* Private William Yarborough, Company E, 28th Mississippi Cavalry, captured

* Private R. M. Sledge, Company F, 28th Mississippi Cavalry, captured

* Private R. J. Scott, Company F, 28th Mississippi Cavalry, captured

Private T. H. Huffman, Company K, 28th Mississippi Cavalry, captured

Second Lieutenant G. Johnson, Company A, 1st Tennessee Cavalry, wounded severely in thigh

Corporal Thomas Fruland, Company I, 1st Tennessee Cavalry, killed

Sergeant G. J. Christy, Company A, 1st Tennessee Cavalry, wounded slightly

Private W. B. Green, Company A, 1st Tennessee Cavalry, wounded severely in leg

Private G. A. Brewer, Company A, 1st Tennessee Cavalry, wounded slightly

Private D. Stein, Company I, 4th Mississippi Cavalry, wounded slightly

Private C. Richardson, Sanders's battalion, wounded slightly

Private R. Vandiver, Company D, 3d Arkansas Cavalry, wounded slightly

Sergeant Hogan, Company E, 3d Arkansas Cavalry, wounded slightly

Private J. Waller, Company H, 3d Arkansas Cavalry, wounded mortally

Sergeant Major Wm. Nolen, 3d Arkansas Cavalry, wounded slightly

Private I. I. Thompson, Polk's company, wounded slightly

Surgeon D. Pryor, 1st Brigade, captured

Quartermaster Clerk Adolphus Burnside, captured

Private B. J. Ameryton, Company A, 3d Tennessee Cavalry, wounded slightly

Sergeant I. W. Morse, Company B, 3d Tennessee Cavalry, captured

Private B. C. Carter, Company C, 3d Tennessee Cavalry, wounded mortally

Corporal J. W. Fisher, Company D, 3d Tennessee Cavalry, wounded severely in thigh

Private Jas. Newton, Company F, 3d Tennessee Cavalry, killed

Private John Crunk, Company F, 3rd Tennessee Cavalry, wounded through the chest

Private Thos. Harper, Company G, 3d Tennessee Cavalry, wounded mortally

Private Harden Bell, Company G, 3rd Tennessee Cavalry, captured

* Horses killed

Private Wm. Whitworth, Company K, 3d Tennessee Cavalry, wounded
  slightly
Private John Gibson, Company C, 9th Tennessee Cavalry, wounded slightly
Captain L. D. Kirk, Company D, 9th Tennessee Cavalry, wounded slightly
Private J. D. Bayhill, Company D, 9th Tennessee Cavalry, wounded seriously
Private Gideon Hicks, Company F, 9th Tennessee Cavalry, killed
Private Thomas Kidd, Company H, 9th Tennessee Cavalry, killed
Private R. W. Vincen, Company H, 9th Tennessee Cavalry, wounded
  severely
Private Sam Sharp, Company H, 9th Tennessee Cavalry, wounded severely
Private James Baker, Company H, 9th Tennessee Cavalry, wounded mortally
Private G. W. Gordon, Company B, 3d Tennessee Cavalry, wounded
Private Harry C. Lyle, Company B, 3d Tennessee Cavalry, wounded
Private Andrew J. Lyle, Company B, 3d Tennessee Cavalry, wounded
Private H. H. Mackbee, Company B, 3d Tennessee Cavalry, wounded
Captain Samuel Freeman, Freeman's battery, killed
Lieutenant A. L. Huggins, Freeman's battery, captured
Sergeant Nat Baxter, Freeman's battery, captured
Sergeant R. A. Allison, Freeman's battery, captured
Private H. Skelton, Freeman's battery, captured
Private John F. Allen, Freeman's battery, captured
Private J. R. Ashley, Freeman's battery, captured
Private O. V. Anderson, Freeman's battery, captured
Private Jansen F. Cowan, Freeman's battery, captured
Private Payton F. Carr, Freeman's battery, captured
Private Samuel Duke, Freeman's battery, captured
Private John C. Goodnow, Freeman's battery, captured
Private W. T. Haggard, Freeman's battery, captured
Private J. Pink Hamilton, Freeman's battery, captured
Private Wiley Jean, Freeman's battery, captured
Private J. A. Mulloy, Freeman's battery, captured
Private J. T. McCauley, Freeman's battery, captured
Private Wm. McDaniel, Freeman's battery, captured
Private James J. Neeley, Freeman's battery, captured
Private Wm. J. Neld, Freeman's battery, captured
Private Wm. Rowland, Freeman's battery, captured
Private T. I. Scott, Freeman's battery, captured
Private A. J. Spickland, Freeman's battery, captured
Private H. H. Sugg, Freeman's battery, captured
Private W. E. Turley, Freeman's battery, captured
Private F. H. Twitty, Freeman's battery, captured
Private James F. Wallace, Freeman's battery, captured
Private And. J. Wright, Freeman's battery, captured
Private Russ H. Wright, Freeman's battery, captured
Private John Wyatt, Freeman's battery, captured

Private R. J. Rinton, Freeman's battery, wounded
Sergeant W. H. Redman, Forrest escort, wounded severely
Private W. W. Hastings, Forrest escort, wounded severely
Private John Prius, Forrest escort, wounded slightly
Private I. S. McFarland, Forrest escort, wounded

Union

Ordnance Sergeant Wilson Burrows, Company A, 40th Ohio Infantry, killed
Private Washington D. Link, Company C, 40th Ohio Infantry, killed
Private Thomas Huntington, Company C, 40th Ohio Infantry, killed
Private Alpheus Babb, Company B, 40th Ohio Infantry, died of wounds
Private Samuel I. Morrow, Company B, 40th Ohio Infantry, died of wounds (5/6/63)
Private John Brady, Company C, 40th Ohio Infantry, died of wounds (4/16/63)
Private Martin Woolheather, Company C, 40th Ohio Infantry, died of wounds
Private Oscar Duvall, Company A, 40th Ohio Infantry, captured
Private Samuel Hubbard, Company A, 40th Ohio Infantry, captured
Private Wilson Olney, Company A, 40th Ohio Infantry, captured
Private Albert Williams, Company A, 40th Ohio Infantry, captured
Private Elwood Hale, Company B, 40th Ohio Infantry, captured
Private John V. Fleming, Company B, 40th Ohio Infantry, captured
Sergeant Jesse N. Oren, Company B, 40th Ohio Infantry, captured
Private Wallace Bennett, Company C, 40th Ohio Infantry, captured
Private Michael Madigan, Company C, 40th Ohio Infantry, captured
Private Adam Suverly, Company C, 40th Ohio Infantry, captured
Private Louis Moss, 3d Ohio Cavalry, wounded
Private Peter Donovan, Company G, 3d Indiana Cavalry, died of wounds (4/18/63)
Private B. Donovan, Company C, 4th Indiana Cavalry, wounded
Private J. O. Hill, Company L, 7th Pennsylvania Cavalry, wounded
Private J. Jones, Company L, 9th Pennsylvania Cavalry, wounded
Unknown, 2d East Tennessee Cavalry, killed
Private H. Smith, Granger's Messenger, wounded
Second Lieutenant Thomas Healy, Company D, 4th U.S. Cavalry, died of wounds (4/23/63)
First Lieutenant Thomas W. Simson, Company B, 4th U.S. Cavalry, died of wounds (10/26/65)
Private Charles M. Cowarder, Company D, 4th U.S. Cavalry, killed
Private William Bennigan, Company K, 4th U.S. Cavalry, killed
Private Nathan Wright, Company M, 4th U.S. Cavalry, killed
Private Frederick Hensinger, Company D, 4th U.S. Cavalry, died of wounds (4/15/63)
Sergeant William Martin, Company A, 4th U.S. Cavalry, captured

Farrier Timothy Mulderoney, Company C, 4th U.S. Cavalry, captured
Private Michael Maroney, Company D, 4th U.S. Cavalry, wounded
Private Jacob McCormick, Company D, 4th U.S. Cavalry, wounded
Private John Miller, Company D, 4th U.S. Cavalry, wounded
Private Michael Quinn, Company D, 4th U.S. Cavalry, wounded
Private Alexander Martin, Company D, 4th U.S. Cavalry, captured
Private Andrew Bunn, Company D, 4th U.S. Cavalry, captured
Private Hibbard C. Daniels, Company D, 4th U.S. Cavalry, captured
Private John C. Perry, Company G, 4th U.S. Cavalry, wounded and
    captured
Private Ambrose Whetsel, Company G, 4th U.S. Cavalry, captured
Private Lawrence Siebert, Company G, 4th U.S. Cavalry, captured
Sergeant Robert W. Thompson, Company K, 4th U.S. Cavalry, captured
Sergeant John Kerwan, Company K, 4th U.S. Cavalry, captured
Farrier Edward Shoerling, Company K, 4th U.S. Cavalry, captured
Farrier Kimball, Company K, 4th U.S. Cavalry, captured
Private A. Rippen, Company K, 4th U.S. Cavalry, captured
Private Smith, Company K, 4th U.S. Cavalry, captured
Corporal John Dean, Company M, 4th U.S. Cavalry, captured
Private William Sanders, Company M, 4th U.S. Cavalry, captured
Unknown, Granger's escort, wounded
Unknown, 4th Ohio Cavalry, killed
Six unknown, 2d East Tennessee Cavalry, wounded
Two unknown, 3d Indiana Cavalry, wounded
Three unknown, 4th Ohio Cavalry, wounded

ANTIOCH, TENNESSEE
First Lieutenant Frank M. Vanderburgh, Company E, 10th Michigan
    Infantry, died of wounds (4/18/63)
Private George W. Bartlett, Company E, 10th Michigan Infantry, killed
Sergeant James Chapman, Company E, 10th Michigan Infantry, died of
    wounds (4/14/63)
Private William Jones, Company E, 10th Michigan Infantry, killed
Private James Murphy, Company E, 10th Michigan Infantry, died of wounds
    (4/12/63)
Private Frank Tacy, Company E, 10th Michigan Infantry, killed
Private Freeman Young, Company E, 10th Michigan Infantry, killed
Private J. M. Carrington, Company E, 10th Michigan Infantry, wounded
Private Patrick Lane, Company E, 10th Michigan Infantry, wounded
Private Robert Peake, Company E, 10th Michigan Infantry, wounded
Private John Harris, Company E, 10th Michigan Infantry, wounded
Private Peter O'Neill, Company E, 10th Michigan Infantry, captured
Private Urias Peck, Company E, 10th Michigan Infantry, wounded
Private Benjamin Wallace, Company H, 10th Michigan Infantry, killed
Private John Lashbrook, Company H, 10th Michigan Infantry, wounded

Private David Henry, Company H, 10th Michigan Infantry, wounded
Private Wm. G. Harris, Company H, 10th Michigan Infantry, captured
Private Miron M. Hungerford, Company H, 10th Michigan Infantry, captured
Colonel Wood, 16th Indiana, train passenger, captured
Colonel George P. Buell, 58th Indiana, train passenger, captured
Major Cliff, 1st Middle Tennessee Cavalry, train passenger, captured
Surgeon Hurxthal, 11th Michigan, train passenger, captured
Surgeon Andrew Duey, 11th Michigan, train passenger, captured
Captain Newberry, 11th Michigan, train passenger, captured
Lieutenant John H. Johnson, 11th Michigan, train passenger, captured
Lieutenant Chas. J. Fox, 21st Michigan, train passenger, captured
Lieutenant J. B. Hunt, 10th Michigan, train passenger, captured
Captain Monk, 10th Michigan, train passenger, captured
Captain Warren, Quartermaster, train passenger, captured
Captain Maple, Commissary, train passenger, captured
Lieutenant Spencer, Ordnance, train passenger, captured
Unknown Confederate train passenger, killed
Unknown Confederate train passenger, killed
Lieutenant John R. Henry, Jr., 1st Tennessee Cavalry (Union), killed

NEELY'S BEND, TENNESSEE
Private Edwin Worden, Company B, 23d Michigan Infantry, killed
Private Allen Barnum, Company B, 23d Michigan Infantry, wounded
Unknown, Pikes Pattery (Confederate), wounded

WAVERLY, TENNESSEE
Major Horace J. Blanton, Recruiting, captured
Twenty unknown recruits (Confederate), captured

GERMANTOWN, KENTUCKY
Lieutenant M. B. Daniels, 2d Kentucky Cavalry (Confederate), killed
Private Jeff. McGrew, 2d Kentucky Cavalry (Confederate), captured
Unknown, 2d Kentucky Cavalry (Confederate), wounded
Unknown, 2d Kentucky Cavalry (Confederate), captured
Private Peter A. Benedum, Company I, 118th Ohio Infantry (Union), wounded

DEER CREEK, MISSISSIPPI
Private Arnold Conlan, 15th Illinois Cavalry (Union), killed

NORTHERN MISSISSIPPI
Private James Hoy, Company E, 2d Arkansas Cavalry (Confederate), captured

Private Nathan Baldwin, Mitchell's company, 18th Mississippi (Confederate), captured

SABINE PASS, TEXAS

Navy Captain Charles Fowler, steamer *Josiah Bell* (Confederate), captured
Navy Pilot John McLean, steamer *Josiah Bell* (Confederate), captured
Second Mate Edward Lynch, steamer *Josiah Bell* (Confederate), captured
Unknown Confederate soldier, captured

APPENDIX B

UNIT LOSSES, APRIL 10, 1863

UNION

Unit	Killed & DOW	WIA	MIA	Units Engaged Total
FRANKLIN, TENNESSEE				
40th Ohio	7		10	17
3d Ohio Cav.		1		1
4th Ohio Cav.	1	3		4
1st Ohio Arty.				0
18th Ind. Btry.				1
7th Pa. Cav.		1		7
2d. E. Tenn. Cav.	1	6		0
1st Mid. Tenn. Cav.				0
78th Illinois				3
3d Indiana Cav.	1	2		1
4th Indiana Cav.		1		27
4th U.S. Cav.	6	4	17	1
9th Pa. Cav.		1		1
Misc. Troops		1		
Total Franklin	16	20	27	63
ANTIOCH, TENNESSEE				
10th Michigan	8	8	15	31
Other	1			1
Total Antioch	9	8	15	32
NEELY'S BEND, TENNESSEE				
23d Michigan	1	1		2
WAVERLY, TENNESSEE				
5th Iowa Cav.				0
GERMANTOWN, KENTUCKY				
118th Ohio			1	1
DEER CREEK, MISSISSIPPI				
15th Ill. Cav.	1			1

CONFEDERATE

Unit	Killed & DOW	WIA	MIA	Total
3d Arkansas			2	2
4th Mississippi		4		4
1st Tennessee	1	5		6
Sanders's Bn.		1		1
Escort (Polk's)		1		1
4th Tennessee	1	6	2	9
9th Tennessee	2	6		8
3d. Tenn. Co. B		4		4
Freeman's Battery	1	1	29	31
Forrest's Escort		4		4
1st Mississippi				0
28th Mississippi	17	14	10	41
	22	46	43	111
8th Texas Cav.				0
11th Texas Cav.				0
Passengers	2			2
Pike's Battery		1		1
Col. Crew's Brigade				0
Blanton Irregulars			21	21
2d Kentucky Cav.	1	3	5	9
Ferguson Cav.				0

BLACK BAYOU, MISSISSIPPI					Ferguson Cav.				0
4th Iowa				0					
76th Ohio				0					
FOLLY ISLAND, SOUTH CAROLINA					21st South Carolina				0
100th N.Y.	1	1		2					
1st N.Y. Marine Arty.				0					
GLOUCESTER POINT, VIRGINIA					Godwin Cav.			1	1
4th Delaware	1			1					
169th Pennsylvania	2	2		4					
2d Mass. Cav.				0					
BERWICK BAY, LOUISIANA					Terry's 5th Texas				0
1st La. Cav.				0					
2d Mass. Cav.				0					
1st U.S. Arty.				0					
SABINE PASS, TEXAS					Navy Officers			4	4
USS *New London*				0					
EDISTO ISLAND, SOUTH CAROLINA					3d. S.C. Scouts			9	9
USS *Kingfisher*		1		1					
DEEP CREEK, VIRGINIA					None				
Train Crew			2	2					
EXECUTIONS									
Richmond			1	1	Savannah, Georgia	1	2	2	1
NORTHERN MISSISSIPPI SCOUT									
Totals	32	32	46	110		26	51	84	161

Total Union	32	32	46	110
Total Confederate	26	51	84	161
Grand Total Casualties	58	84	130	271

The above figures were taken from Official Records of the War of the Rebellion, Series I and II; Official Naval Records of the War of the Rebellion, Series I; various regimental casualty and morning reports; U.S. Register of Deaths 1863.

APPENDIX C

★

UNION HOSPITAL DEATHS APRIL 10, 1863

NAME	UNIT	CAUSE	STATE
John McSole	Co. F, 9th Connecticut	Typhoid	Conn.
J. Se D Otis	Co. K, 14th Connecticut	Gunshot wound	Conn.
	State Deaths 2		
Judson Rittner	Co. B, 25th Iowa	Typhoid	Iowa
Robert Moore	Co. B, 33d Iowa	Unknown	Iowa
Beau Wm. Ninehouse	Co. B, 37th Iowa	Diarrhea	Iowa
M. S. Taylor	Co. C, 36th Iowa	Pneumonia	Iowa
John P. Fitch	Co. E, 27th Iowa	Pneumonia	Iowa
Aaron H. Goffrey	Co. G, 34th Iowa	Brain fever	Iowa
P. A. Scott	Co. I, 3d Iowa Cav.	Smallpox	Iowa
Hennycut Hose	Co. K, 30th Iowa	Diarrhea	Iowa
Calvin Lemonds	Co. M, 36th Iowa	Diarrhea	Iowa
	State Deaths 9		
Andrew Salden	Co. A, 89th Illinois	Brain fever	Ill.
Arnold Conlan	Co. B, 15th Illinois Cav.	Killed in action	Ill.
Chester P. Harsh	Co. B, 19th Illinois Inf.	Typhoid	Ill.
Thomas Walsh	Co. C, 19th Illinois Inf.	Died of wounds	Ill.
J. C. Downing	Co. D, 114th Illinois	Pneumonia	Ill.
Lewis Fleming	Co. D, 119th Illinois	Erysipelas	Ill.
James W. Fletcher	Co. D, 81st Illinois	Diarrhea	Ill.
Michael Blessing	Co. E, 93d Illinois	Malaria	Ill.
Henry Goudy	Co. G, 87th Illinois	Hepatitis	Ill.
W. R. Fry	Co. I, 113th Illinois	Pneumonia	Ill.
Judson Thomson	Co. I, 127th Illinois	Diarrhea	Ill.
James W. Gregory	Co. K, 134th Illinois	Pneumonia	Ill.
J. Y. Johnson	Co. K, 34th Illinois	Pneumonia	Ill.

NAME	UNIT	CAUSE	STATE
And. J. Clark	Co. K, 97th Illinois Inf.	Diarrhea	Ill.
Thomas H. Clark	Co. K, 97th Illinois Inf.	Disability	Ill.

State Deaths 15

Isaac B. Kirk	21st Indiana	Typhoid	Ind.
Benjamin F. Long	3d Indiana Cav.	Diarrhea	Ind.
George Thompson	85th Indiana Inf.	Unknown	Ind.
Joseph K. Vanatter	Co. A, 54th Indiana	Remit. fever	Ind.
George W. Hoit	Co. A, 69th Indiana	Diarrhea	Ind.
Thomas Bubble	Co. B, 69th Indiana	Diarrhea	Ind.
John Pike	Co. C, 16th Indiana	Diarrhea	Ind.
John Divelbiss	Co. C, 34th Indiana	Diarrhea	Ind.
William Moore	Co. D, 69th Indiana	Diarrhea	Ind.
Jefferson Moorehead	Co. D, 99th Indiana	Peritonitis	Ind.
Wm. L. Clark	Co. E, 38th Indiana	Diarrhea	Ind.
Benjamin Webb	Co. I, 38th Indiana	Gunshot	Ind.
Joseph Hemphill	Co. I, 63d Indiana	Typhoid	Ind.
Benjamin Bright	Co. I, 69th Indiana	Remit. fever	Ind.
Swan Johnson	Co. I, 75th Indiana	Pneumonia	Ind.
Marion P. Light	Co. I, 85th Indiana	Typhoid	Ind.
William Miller	Co. K, 69th Indiana	Serufuld	Ind.
Lafayette Mosier	Co. K, 81st Indiana	Pneumonia	Ind.

State Deaths 18

Jared Sloane	Co. D, 39th Kentucky	Typhoid	Ky.
Thomas J. Martz	Co. D, 5th Kentucky	Bowel obstruction	Ky.
Benjamin Copps	Co. E, 17th Kentucky	Diarrhea	Ky.
David D. Kidwell	Co. E, 7th Kentucky	Typhoid	Ky.
James Sollards	Co. G, 39th Kentucky Inf.	Typhoid	Ky.
John Charles	Co. H, 39th Kentucky	Typhoid	Ky.
John W. White	Co. H, 3d Kentucky	Unknown	Ky.
William Parsons	Co. K, 39th Kentucky	Pneumonia	Ky.
Joseph P. Lumer	Co. B, 24th Kentucky	Unknown	Ky.

State Deaths 9

Robert Ware	44th Massachusetts	Double pneumonia	Mass.
G. W. Knight	Co. E, 53d Mass	Typhoid	Mass.

State Deaths 2

Chas. A. Parkman	Co. A, 26th Maine	Typhoid	Maine
Robert Welch	Co. B, 12th Maine	Diarrhea	Maine

NAME	UNIT	CAUSE	STATE
David P. Little	Co. C, 22nd Maine	Smallpox	Maine
Samuel McCollum	Co. H, 24th Maine	Diphtheria	Maine

State Deaths 4

William Jones	10th Michigan	Killed in action	Mich.
Martin Green	8th Mich. Cav.	Typhoid	Mich.
Edwin Worden	Co. B, 23d Michigan	Killed in action	Mich.
Frank Tacy	Co. E, 10th Michigan	Killed in action	Mich.
George Bartlett	Co. E, 10th Michigan	Killed in action	Mich.
Truman Young	Co. E, 10th Michigan	Killed in action	Mich.
Benjamin Wallace	Co. H, 10th Michigan Inf.	Killed in action	Mich.
Josiah Barber	Co. H, 6th Michigan	Bronchitis	Mich.
Timothy Spillman	Co. I, 19th Michigan	Typhoid	Mich.
Thomas Punningham	Co. G, 26th Michigan	Pneumonia	Mich.

State Deaths 10

Robert Fuller	Co. A, 3d Missouri	Typhoid	Mo.
William Fleener	Co. C, 35th Missouri	Scurvy	Mo.
McCartney Harrison	Co. F, 32d Missouri	Diarrhea	Mo.
Eldridge Benedict	Co. F, 5th Missouri Cav.	Typhoid	Mo.
Jacob F. Lang	Co. K, 33d Missouri	Pneumonia	Mo.

State Deaths 5

Charles G. Hall	Co. C, 3d New Hampshire	Apoplexy	N.H.

State Deaths 1

G. W. Holt	Co. A, 20th New Jersey	Smallpox	N.J.
Peter Eckman	Co. C, 10th New Jersey Inf.	Smallpox	N.J.
Charles Kemp	Co. D, 12th New Jersey	Typhoid	N.J.
George Goodwin	Co. D, 23d New Jersey	Lung inflammation	N.J.
Jonothan Goodsoe	Co. G, 27th New Jersey	Brain inflammation	N.J.
Samuel Schooley	Co. H, 23d New Jersey	Pneumonia	N.J.
L. W. James	Co. I, 24th New Jersey	Typhoid	N.J.
D. Woods	Co. K, 22nd New Jersey	Pythsis	N.J.

State Deaths 8

E. A. Deacon	10th New York Arty.	Typhoid	N.Y.
David Whittier	10th New York Arty.	Typhoid pneumonia	N.Y.
T. J. Harrigan	Co. A, 147th New York	Typhoid	N.Y.
Albert Feathercamp	Co. C, 59th New York	Unknown	N.Y.
Andrew Quick	Co. D, 6th N.Y. Arty.	Typhoid	N.Y.

NAME	UNIT	CAUSE	STATE
Henry Wilcox	Co. G, 150th New York	Lung inflammation	N.Y.
Chas. Knickerbocker	Co. H, 176th New York	Marasmus	N.Y.
James Ormson	Co. H, 5th N.Y. Arty.	Delirium tremens	N.Y.
Henry Youeles	Co. I, 130th New York	Pneumonia	N.Y.
Thomas J. Moore	Co. K, 126th New York	Ulcers	N.Y.

State Deaths 10

Wesley McMillen	118th Ohio	Shot by pickets	Ohio
Abraham Behm	114th Ohio	Diarrhea	Ohio
Edward C. Loyd	116th Ohio	Chorea	Ohio
Thomas Wigdom	121st Ohio	Measles	Ohio
William Yates	21st Ohio	Typhoid	Ohio
Gustav Kahle	37th Ohio	Typho Mal	Ohio
John Brady	40th Ohio	Died of wounds	Ohio
Thomas Huntington	40th Ohio	Killed in action	Ohio
Washington D. Link	40th Ohio	Killed in action	Ohio
Wilson Burroughs	40th Ohio	Killed in action	Ohio
Eli Bailey	40th Ohio	Pneumonia	Ohio
Martin Wetheither	40th Ohio Inf.	Died of wounds	Ohio
George Wagoner	49th Ohio	Typhoid	Ohio
Charles T. Jenkins	4th Ohio	Unknown	Ohio
William Flint	50th Ohio	Diarrhea	Ohio
F. W. Wheelbarger	56th Ohio	Diarrhea	Ohio
Austin Edgington	63d Ohio	Diarrhea	Ohio
Henry White	71st Ohio	Rubeola	Ohio
Robert Miller	77th Ohio	Diarrhea	Ohio
James Palmer	7th Ohio Cavalry	Typhoid	Ohio
H. A. Sprague	92nd Ohio	Typhoid	Ohio
Basel Rodgers	Unknown	Typhoid	Ohio

State Deaths 22

Simson B. Clayton	114th Pa. Inf.	Typhoid	Pa.
J. Wiley	150th Pa. Inf.	Smallpox	Pa.
George Turner	5th Pa. Cav.	Diarrhea	Pa.
James Young	71st Pa. Inf.	Periconditis	Pa.

State Deaths 4

John R. Henry, Jr.	1st Tennessee Cav.	Killed in action	Tenn.

State Deaths 1

Alphonso C. Webster	1st Loudon Co. Rangers	Executed	Va.

State Deaths 1

NAME	UNIT	CAUSE	STATE
H. W. Eastman	8th Vermont Inf.	Diphtheria	Vt.
Isaac B. Bowditch	Vermont	Rail accident	Vt.

State Deaths 2

NAME	UNIT	CAUSE	STATE
Thomas Loring	34th Wisconsin	Delirium tremens	Wis.
Kanna Patterson	Co. A, 15th Wisconsin Inf.	Gunshot wound	Wis.
Orrin Judkins	Co. B, 23d Wisconsin	Diarrhea	Wis.

State Deaths 3

NAME	UNIT	CAUSE	OTHER SERVICES
John Hurley	1st Bn, 18th U.S. Infantry	Unknown	U.S.
Charles M. Cowarder	4th U.S. Cav.	Killed in action	U.S.
Thomas Healey	Co. D, 4th U.S. Cav.	Killed in action	U.S.
William Bennigan	Co. K, 4th U.S. Cav.	Killed in action	U.S.
Franklin Peterson	Co. K, 4th U.S. Cav.	Typhoid	U.S.
Nathan Wright	Co. M, 4th U.S. Cav.	Killed in action	U.S.
Samuel Smith	Co. I, 3d U.S. Cav.	Pyemia	U.S.
William H. Finnegan	Co. K, 4th U.S. Cav.	Killed in action	U.S.

Regular Army Deaths 8

George W. Fouty	Steamer *St. Clair*	Wounds

Navy Deaths 1

Total Hospital Deaths 135

NOTES

List of Abbreviations

The following abbreviations are used in the notes for frequently used depositories:

AR   National Archives, Washington, D.C.

BUR   Burton Historical Collection, Detroit Public Library, Detroit, Michigan

CHS   Chicago Historical Society, Chicago, Illinois

CM   Eleanor S. Brockenbrough Library, Museum of the Confederacy, Richmond, Virginia

GRPL   Grand Rapids Public Library, Grand Rapids, Michigan

LC   Manuscript Division, Library of Congress, Washington, D.C.

LSU   Special Collections, Hill Library, Louisiana State University, Baton Rouge, Louisiana

MDAH   Mississippi Department of Archives and History, Manuscript Collections, Jackson, Mississippi

MHC   Michigan Historical Collections, Bentley Historical Library, University of Michigan, Ann Arbor, Michigan

MSU   University Archives and Historical Collections, Michigan State University, East Lansing, Michigan

NL   Newberry Library, Chicago, Illinois

NYSL   New York State Library, Albany, New York

SHC   Southern Historical Collections, Wilson Library, University of North Carolina at Chapel Hill, North Carolina

USAMHI   United States Army Military History Institute, Carlisle, Pennsylvania (CWTIC: Civil War Times Illustrated Collection; HCWRTC: Harrisburg Civil War Round Table Collection)

INTRODUCTION: AT THE MIDPOINT

1. Delphy Carlin to Abraham Lincoln, 10 April 1863, Lincoln Papers, LC.

2. Frederick Phisterer, *Statistical Record of the Armies of the United States,* Campaigns of the Civil War Series (New York: Blue and Gray Press, n.d.), p. 215.

3. Ibid., p. 214.

4. Ibid., p. 70.

5. Surgeon General's Office, *Medical and Surgical History of the Civil War* (Wilmington, N.C.: Broadfoot Publishing Co., 1990), p. 70.

6. Page Smith, *Trial by Fire: A People's History of the Civil War and Reconstruction* (New York: McGraw Hill, 1982), p. 429.

7. George Templeton Strong, *The Diary of George Templeton Strong* (New York: Macmillan Co., 1952), p. 264.

8. Mark Mayo Boatner III, *Civil War Dictionary* (New York: McKay Publishing Co., 1959), p. 367.

9. James Ford Rhodes, *History of the Civil War* (New York: Macmillan Co., 1917), p. 175.

10. Ibid., p. 201.

11. Strong, *Diary,* p. 311.

12. James D. Richardson, *Messages and Papers of the Presidents,* 9 vols. (Bureau of National Literature and Art, 1904), 6:164.

13. *Nashville Union,* 10 April 1863.

14. Allan Nevins, *The War for the Union*, 3 vols. (New York: Charles Scribner and Sons, 1960), p. 367.

15. Boatner, *Civil War Dictionary,* p. 613.

16. Frederick H. Dyer, *A Compendium of the War of the Rebellion,* 3 pts. (New York: Thomas Yoseloff, 1959), III:1100.

17. Adjutant General's Office Report, AR.

18. E. W. Locke, *"We Must Not Fall Back Anymore": Three Years in Camp and Hospital* (Boston: G. D. Russell and Co., 1870).

19. Civil War Centennial Commission, *Facts About the Civil War* (Washington, D.C.: Civil War Centennial Commission, 1959), p. 9.

20. Phisterer, *Statistical Record,* p. 215.

21. *The War of the Rebellion: A Compilation of the Official Records of the Union and Confederate Armies,* various vols. (Washington, D.C.: Government Printing Office, 1889–1900) (hereafter cited as *ORs).*

22. E. B. Long, *The Civil War Day by Day* (New York: Doubleday and Co., 1971), p. 336.

23. Country Beautiful, *Civil War: The Years Asunder* (Waukesha, Wis.: Country Beautiful, 1973), p. 140.

24. *ORs,* Series I, 18:485.

25. Shelby Foote, *The Civil War*, 3 vols. (New York: Random House, 1963), 2: p. 163.

26. *Weekly Jr. Register,* Franklin, La., 9 April 1863.

27. *Richmond Dispatch,* 10 April 1863.

28. Boatner, *Civil War Dictionary,* p. 169.

29. Nevins, *The War for the Union,* p. 2:423.

30. *Richmond Dispatch,* 11 April 1863.
31. Franklin Lafayette Riley, *Grandfather's Journal: Company B, 16th Mississippi* (Dayton, Ohio: Morningside, 1988), p. 131.
32. *Rockingham Register and Virginia Advertiser,* 24 April 1863.

1: THE CAPITALS

1. Allan Nevins, *The War for the Union,* 3 vols. (New York: Charles Scribner and Sons, 1960), p. 2:203.
2. Ibid., p. 202.
3. Carl Sandburg, *Abraham Lincoln, the War Years, 4* vols. (Harcourt, Brace and Co., 1939), 2:208–9.
4. Edwin Haven to family, 12 April 1863, MSU.
5. James Harvey Kidd, *Personal Recollections of a Cavalryman: With Custer's Michigan Cavalry Brigade in the Civil War* (Ionia, Mich.: Sentinel Print Co., 1908), p. 101.
6. Levi W. Baker, *9th Massachusetts Battery,* (n.p.: Lakeview Press, 1888), p. 49.
7. Charles H. Moulton, *Ft. Lyons to Harpers Ferry* (Shippensburg, Pa.: White Mane Publishing Co., 1987), p. 93.
8. General Halleck to General Heintzelman, General Samuel P. Heintzelman Papers, LC.
9. Harry F. Jackson, *Back Home in Oneida* (Syracuse, N.Y.: Syracuse University Press, 1965), pp. 66–67.
10. Sandburg, *Abraham Lincoln,* 2:213.
11. Adam Gurowski Diary, 10 April 1863, BUR.
12. Frederick W. Seward, *Seward at Washington* (New York: Derby and Miller, 1891), p. 160.
13. Stephen Vincent Benét, *John Brown's Body* (New York: Holt, Rinehart and Winston, 1969), pp. 212–13.
14. Sandburg, *Abraham Lincoln,* 2:272.
15. Stephen Vincent Benét Report, Lincoln Papers, LC.
16. Margaret Leech, *Reveille in Washington* (New York: Harper and Brothers, 1941), p. 260.
17. Ibid., p. 261.
18. *Washington Evening Star,* 10 April 1863.
19. Ibid.
20. Martin Samuel, Jr., *The Road to Glory* (Guild Press of Indiana, 1991), p. 167.
21. Shelby Foote, *The Civil War,* 3 vols. (New York: Random House, 1963), 2:162.
22. Josiah Gorgas Journal, SHC.
23. Sallie Putnam, *Richmond During the War* (New York: G. W. Carleton, 1867).
24. Foote, *The Civil War,* 2: p. 105.
25. David Crenshaw Barrows to overseer, 12 April 1863, SHC.

26. Mary Chesnut, *Diary From Dixie* (New York: D. Appleton and Co., 1905).

27. Foote, *The Civil War,* 2: p. 648.

28. *Journal of the Congress of the Confederate States of America, 1861–1865,* 3:272–76.

29. Rembert W. Patrick, *Jefferson Davis and his Cabinet* (Baton Rouge, La.: LSU Press, 1944).

30. *Richmond Dispatch,* 10 April 1863.

31. Sarah Elizabeth Mercer Diary, 9 April 1863, Mercer Family Papers, SHC.

32. B. N. Clements to John Huston, 10 April 1863, LC.

33. Briscoe Goodhart, *History of the Loudon County Rangers* (Washington, D.C.: Press of McGill and Wallace, 1896), p. 28.

34. Ibid.

35. Ibid., p. 206.

36. Ibid., p. 207.

37. *Richmond Daily Sentinel,* 27 March 1863.

38. Elizabeth Van Lew Journal, New York City Library.

39. Confederate Records, AR.

40. *ORs,* Series II, 5:862.

41. *Richmond Daily Dispatch,* 11 April 1863.

42. *ORs,* Series IV, 2:477.

2: MR. LINCOLN'S ARMY

1. Carl Sandburg, *Abraham Lincoln, the War Years,* 4 vols. (Harcourt, Brace and Co., 1939), 2:100.

2. Clifford Dowdey, *The Land They Fought For: The Story of the South as the Confederacy* (Garden City, N.Y.: Doubleday, 1955), p. 248.

3. General Oliver O. Howard, *Autobiography of Gen. O. O. Howard* (New York: Baker and Taylor Co., 1908), p. 348.

4. Bruce Catton, *Glory Road* (Garden City, N.Y.: Doubleday and Co., 1952), p. 170.

5. *ORs,* Series I, vol. 25, pt. 2, p. 180.

6. James Ford Rhodes, *History of the Civil War* (New York: Macmillan Co., 1917), p. 210.

7. *ORs,* Series I, vol. 51, pt. 1, p. 1000.

8. Ibid.

9. Noah Brooks, *Washington in Lincoln's Time,* ed. H. Mitgang (New York: Rinehart, 1951), p. 51.

10. Major T. A. Meysenberg, *Military Order of the Loyal Legion,* p. 296.

11. Julia Butterfield, ed., *A Biographical Memorial of General Daniel Butterfield* (New York: Grafton Press, 1904), p. 161.

12. Ibid.

13. Ira Seymour Dodd, *The Song of the Rappahannock* (New York: Dodd, Mead and Co., 1898), pp. 138–42.

14. Butterfield, *General Daniel Butterfield,* pp. 159–61.

15. Brooks, *Washington in Lincoln's Time,* p. 54.

16. Princess Felix Salm-Salm, *Ten Years of My Life* (New York: R. Worthington, 1877), p. 44.

17. Arthur L. Van Vleck Diary, SHC.

18. Alonzo A. Quint, *The Potomac and the Rapidan* (Boston: Crosby and Nichols, 1864), p. 67.

19. Rice C. Bull, *Soldiering: The Civil War Diary of Rice C. Bull, 123rd New York Volunteer Infantry* (San Rafael, Calif.: Presidio Press, 1977), p. 33.

20. Henry Henney Diary, 10 April 1863, CWTIC, USAMHI.

21. John West Haley, *The Rebel Yell and the Yankee Hurrah,* ed. Ruth Silliker (Camden, Maine: Down East Books, 1985), p. 75.

22. Edwin O. Wentworth to his family, 7 April 1863, Wentworth Papers, LC.

23. Marsena Rudolph Patrick, *Inside Lincoln's Army* (New York: Thomas Yoseloff, 1964), p. 232.

24. Jacob H. Cole, *Under Five Commanders* (Paterson, N.J.: News Printing Co., 1906), p. 12.

25. Shelby Foote, *The Civil War,* 3 vols. (New York: Random House, 1963), 2:236.

26. George Gordon Meade, *Life and Letters of George Gordon Meade* (New York: Charles Scribner's Sons, 1913), p. 363.

27. Sandburg, *Abraham Lincoln,* 2:87.

28. Foote, *The Civil War,* 2: p. 236.

29. Stephen B. Oates, *With Malice Toward None: The Life of Abraham Lincoln* (New York: Harper and Row, 1977), p. 346.

30. Ibid., p. 347.

31. George T. Stevens, *3 Years in the 6th Corps* (Alexandria, Va.: Time-Life Books, 1984), p. 187.

32. Butterfield, *General Daniel Butterfield,* p. 159.

33. Ibid.

34. Foote, *The Civil War,* 2: p. 234.

35. John Gibbon, *Personal Recollections of the War* (New York: G. P. Putnam's Sons, 1928), p. 110.

36. *New York Times,* 10 April 1863.

37. Samuel Wheelock Fiske, *Mr. Dunn Browne's Experiences in the Army* (Boston: Nichols and Noyes, 1866), p. 133.

38. Horatio Rogers, *Personal Narrative* (Rhode Island Soldiers and Sailors Historical Society, 1880–1881), pp. 6–7.

39. Sandburg, *Abraham Lincoln,* 1 vol. ed., p. 360.

40. S. Fiske, *Dunn Browne's Experiences,* p. 137.

41. J. N. Favill, *Diary of a Young Officer* (Chicago: R. R. Donnelly and Sons Co., 1909), p. 225.

42. S. Fiske, *Dunn Browne's Experiences,* p. 140.

43. Wilbur Fisk, *Hard Marching Every Day: Civil War Letters of Pvt. Wilbur Fisk* (Lawrence, Kans.: University Press of Kansas, 1992), p. 62.

44. Henry N. Blake, *Three Years in the Army of the Potomac* (Boston: Lee and Shepherd, 1865), p. 166.

45. Ibid.
46. Robert Hunt Rhodes ed., *All for the Union* (Lincoln, R.I.: A. Mowbray, 1985), pp. 102–3.
47. Edwin Wentworth to his wife, 7 April 1863, LC.
48. Sergeant William K. Haines Diary, 10 April 1863, LC.
49. S. Fiske, *Dunn Browne's Experiences,* p. 141.
50. Ibid., p. 133.
51. W. Fisk, pp. 58–59.
52. John Reuben Thompson, "Music in Camp," in *Poems and Songs of the Civil War,* ed. Lois Hill (New York: Gramercy Books, 1990), pp. 52–53.

3: GENERAL LEE'S ARMY

1. Berry Benson, *Berry Benson's Civil War Book,* ed. Susan Williams Benson (Athens, Ga.: University of Georgia Press, 1962), p. 34.
2. Jedediah Hotchkiss, *Make Me a Map of the Valley* (Dallas: Southern Methodist University Press, 1973), p. 127.
3. Douglas Southall Freeman, *Lee,* abridged 1 vol. ed. (New York: Charles Scribner's Sons, 1961), p. 286.
4. Clifford Dowdey, *Lee* (Boston: Little, Brown and Co., 1965), p. 381.
5. *ORs,* Series I, vol. 25, pt. 2, p. 687.
6. Ibid., p. 697.
7. Ibid.
8. Ibid., p. 725.
9. Ibid., p. 696.
10. Ibid., p. 180.
11. William Willis Blackford, *War Years with Jeb Stuart* (New York: Charles Scribner's Sons, 1945), p. 203.
12. *ORs,* Series I, vol. 25, pt. 2, p. 713.
13. Edward A. Moore, *The Story of a Cannoneer* (Lynchburg, Va.: J. P. Bell Co., 1911), pp. 174–75.
14. Benson, *Civil War Book,* p. 34.
15. James M. Gaston to his wife, 10 April 1863, James McFadden Gaston Papers, SHC.
16. Thomas Ruffin to his father, 11 April 1863, Thomas Ruffin Papers, SHC.
17. Charles R. Chewning, *Journal of Charles R. Chewning* (Spotsylvania, Va.: R. B. Armstrong, 1986), p. 13.
18. James M. Gaston to his wife, 10 April 1863, SHC.
19. Edmund Dewitt Patterson, *Yankee Rebel* (Chapel Hill: University of North Carolina Press, 1966), p. 97.
20. Leonidas A. Torrence to his mother, 12 April 1863, Leonidas C. Glenn Papers, SHC.
21. Franklin Lafayette Riley, *Grandfather's Journal,* ed. Austin Dobbins (Dayton, Ohio: Morningside Press, 1988), p. 130.
22. Benson, *Civil War Book,* p. 34.

23. William Andrew Fletcher, *Rebel Private, Front and Rear* (Austin, Tex.: University of Texas Press, 1954), pp. 52–53.

24. John H. Worsham, *One of Jackson's Foot Cavalry* (New York: Neale Publishing Co., 1912), p. 156.

25. Ibid., pp. 155–56.

26. Dr. Elias Davis to his wife, Gussie, 10 April 1863, SHC.

27. James Harvey Wood, *The War: "Stonewall" Jackson, His Campaign & Battles* (Gaithersburg, Md.: Butternut Press, 1984), pp. 112–13.

28. Worsham, *Jackson's Foot Cavalry,* p. 156.

29. Ibid.

30. John Paris to Reverend W. H. Wills, 9 April 1863, Wills Correspondence, SHC.

31. Samuel A. Firebaugh Diary, 9 April 1863, SHC.

32. Riley, *Grandfather's Journal,* p. 129.

33. Edgar Allan Jackson, "Letters of Edgar Allan Jackson," pamphlet (n.p.) p. 21.

34. Ibid.

35. J. Russell Reaver, "Letters of Joel Blake," in *Apalachee,* (Tallahassee Historical Society, 1962), 5:11–12.

36. Riley, *Grandfather's Journal,* p. 129.

37. James I. Robertson, Jr., *The Stonewall Brigade* (Baton Rouge: Louisiana State University Press, 1963), p. 183.

38. Patterson, *Yankee Rebel,* p. 97.

4: LONGSTREET'S INDEPENDENT COMMAND

1. Douglas Southall Freeman, *Lee,* abridged 1 vol. ed. (New York: Charles Scribner's Sons, 1961), p. 286.

2. General Moxley Sorrell, *Recollections of a Confederate Staff Officer* (New York: Neale Publishing Co., 1905), p. 153.

3. Mark Mayo Boatner, III, *Civil War Dictionary* (New York: McKay Publishing Co., 1959), p. 490.

4. Samuel G. French, *"Two Wars"* (Nashville, Tenn.: Confederate Veteran, 1901).

5. *ORs,* Series I, vol. 18, pp. 574, 675.

6. Freeman, *Lee,* p. 286.

7. *ORs,* Series I, vol. 18, p. 282.

8. J. Thomas Petty Diary, 10 April 1863, CM.

9. H. C. Kendrick to his family, 25 April 1863, SHC.

10. John Henry Lewis, *Recollections from 1860–1865* (Washington, D.C.: Peale and Co., 1895), pp. 60–61.

11. James Longstreet, *From Manassas to Appomattox* (New York: J. B. Lippincott, 1896), p. 325.

12. Ibid., p. 326.

13. Dr. James R. Boulware Diary, 10 April 1863, Personal Papers Collection, Archives Research Services, The Library of Virginia, Richmond.

14. David Emmons Johnston, *The Story of a Confederate Boy in the Civil War* (Bloomington, Ind.: Indiana University Press, 1959), p. 183.

15. W. H. Morgan, *Personal Reminiscences of the War of 1861–1865.* (Lynchburg, Va.: J. P. Bell Co., 1911), pp. 159–60.

16. David E. Cronin, *Evolution of a Life* (New York: S. W. Green's Sons, 1884), p. 177.

17. *ORs,* Series I, vol. 18, p. 275.

18. George B. Abdill, *Civil War Railroads* (Seattle: Superior Publishing Co., 1961), p. 83.

19. *Shreveport Weekly News,* 27 April 1863, p. 6.

20. Charles F. Johnson, *The Long Roll* (East Aurora, N.Y.: Roycrofters, 1911), p. 227.

21. Ibid., p. 228.

22. Charles Spencer Diary, 10 April 1863, SHC.

23. Cronin, *Evolution,* p. 172.

24. George Pickett, *Soldier of the South* (Richmond, Va.: Books for Libraries, 1928), p. 36.

25. M. J. Clark, "Reminiscences," in *Confederate Veteran Magazine,* 40 vols. (Wendall, N.C.: Broadfoot's Bookmark, 1986) 19:225.

26. Mrs. Virginia Clay, *A Belle of the Fifties* (New York: Doubleday, Page and Co., 1905), p. 199.

27. Walter Harrison, *Pickett's Men: A Fragment of War History* (New York: D. Van Nostrand, 1870), p. 74.

28. John Edward Dooley, *A Confederate Soldier: His War Journal* (Washington, D.C.: Georgetown University Press, 1945), pp. 88–89.

29. Elizabeth Curtis Wallace, *Glencoe Diary* (Chesapeake, Va.: Norfolk County Historical Society of Virginia, n.d.), p. 25.

30. *ORs,* p. 283.

31. John Dyer, *The Gallant Hood* (New York: Bobbs Merrill, 1950), p. 167.

32. *27th Massachusetts Infantry Regiment History,* p. 169.

33. John Jasper Wyeth, *Leaves from a Diary Written while Serving in Co. E 44th Mass.* (Boston: L. F. Lawrence and Co., 1878), p. 48.

34. James B. Gardner, ed., *Forty Fourth Massachusetts Infantry Record of Service* (Boston: Private Printing, 1887), pp. 177–78.

35. John Lee Holt, *I Wrote You Word* (Lynchburg, Va.: H. E. Howard, 1993), pp. 128–29.

36. Annie Blackwell Sparrow, "Reminiscences," typescript, George H. and Laura E. Brown Library, Washington, N.C., pp. 11–12.

37. *ORs,* p. 217.

38. *27th Massachusetts Infantry Regiment History,* p. 177.

39. Ibid.

40. *3rd New York Volunteer Artillery,* p. 164.

41. *Appleton's Annual Cyclopedia,* 42 vols. (New York: D. Appleton and Co., 1903), 3:702–3.

42. Zenas T. Haines, *Letters from the 44th Regt, MVM* (Boston: Printed at Herald Job Office, 1863).

43. John G. Barrett, *The Civil War in North Carolina* (Chapel Hill, N.C.: University of North Carolina Press, 1963), p. 158.

44. *3rd New York Artillery,* p. 169.

45. *27th Massachusetts Regiment History,* p. 178.

46. Haines, *Letters,* 10 April 1863.

47. G. S. Williams to his parents, 10 April 1863, SHC.

48. Wyeth, *Leaves,* p. 45.

49. *27th Massachusetts Regiment History,* p. 173.

50. Wyeth, *Leaves,* p. 47.

51. Haines, *Letters,* 9 April 1863.

52. G. S. Williams to his parents, 10 April 1863, SHC.

53. Alexander Smith Webb to his mother, 8 April 1863, SHC.

54. R. A. Shotwell Papers, 12 April 1863, BUR.

55. *ORs,* p. 591.

56. Ibid., p. 593.

57. Ibid., pp. 247–48.

58. Ibid.

59. Ibid., p. 249.

60. Thomas Kirwan, *Memorial History of the 17th Massachusetts Volunteer Infantry* (Salem, Mass.: Salem Press, 1911), pp. 173–75.

61. W. J. Baker to his wife, 11 April 1863, Blanche Baker Papers, SHC.

62. George Phifer Erwin to his father, 12 April 1863, SHC.

63. George Whitaker Wills to his sister Lucy Cary Wills, 12 April 1863, SHC.

64. Ibid.

65. Lamotte Davendorf Letter, 25 April 1863, NYSL.

66. Kirwan, *Memorial History,* p. 175.

67. G. S. Williams, 10 April 1863, SHC.

68. *ORs,* p. 594.

69. A. S. Bickmore to Cleveland Abbe, 10 April 1863, Cleveland Abbe Papers, LC.

70. Stephen Blanding, *Recollections of a Sailor Boy* (Providence, R.I.: E. A. Johnson, 1886), p. 239.

71. Ibid.

72. *Official Records of the Union and Confederate Navies in the War of the Rebellion* (Washington, D.C.: Government Printing Office, 1894–1922), Series I, vol. 8, pp. 663–64 (hereafter cited as *Navy ORs).*

73. Ibid.

74. Blanding, *Recollections,* pp. 234–35.

75. *ORs,* p. 968.

76. Benjamin Robert Fleet, *Green Mount* (Lexington, Ky.: University of Kentucky Press, 1962), pp. 218–21.

77. *ORs,* p. 261.

78. Ibid.

79. D. J. Godwin Service Record, AR.
80. *Richmond Enquirer,* 10 April 1863.
81. *Richmond Dispatch,* 13 April 1863.
82. Lyman S. Foster to his family, 12 April 1863, Foster Family Papers, Civil War Miscellaneous Collection, USAMHI.
83. *ORs,* p. 341.
84. *Yorktown Cavalier,* 14 April 1863.
85. *ORs,* p. 591.

5: WHERE IT ALL BEGAN

 1. George B. Davis et al., *Official Military Atlas of the Civil War* (New York: Gramercy Books, 1983; originally published Washington, D.C.: Government Printing Office, 1891–95), plate IV, 1.
 2. J. Thomas Scharf, *The Confederate States Navy,* (N.Y.: Rogers and Sherwood, 1887) p. 758.
 3. Daniel J. Carrison, *The Navy from Wood to Steel* (New York: Watts, 1965), p. 110.
 4. *ORs,* Series I, 14:893.
 5. Gideon Welles, *Diary of Gideon Welles* (Boston: Houghton Mifflin Co., 1911), p. 263.
 6. Ibid.
 7. *ORs,* p. 437.
 8. Ibid., p. 440.
 9. Ibid., p. 437.
10. Ibid., p. 438.
11. Ibid.
12. M. H. Fitzgerald Diary, 10 April 1863, Fitzgerald Family Papers, MHC.
13. B. S. De Forest, *Random Sketches and Wandering Thoughts* (Albany, N.Y.: Avery Herrick, Publisher, 1966), p. 49.
14. John Hay, *Lincoln and the War, in Diaries and Letters of John Hay,* ed. Tyler Dennett (New York: Dodd Mead, 1939), p. 59.
15. General David Hunter to President Lincoln, 10 April 1863, Abraham Lincoln Papers, LC.
16. *Southern Illustrated News,* 18 April 1863.
17. Ibid.
18. John B. Jones, *A Rebel War Clerk's Diary* (New York: Old Hickory Bookshop, 1935).
19. Annie J. Jones to Cadwallader Jones, 10 April 1863, Cadwallader Jones Papers, SHC.
20. Pliny Brown to Edward Porter Alexander, 10 April 1863, Edward Porter Alexander Correspondence, SHC.
21. *ORs,* pp. 893–97.
22. Mary Chesnut, *Diary from Dixie* (New York: D. Appleton, 1905), p. 436.
23. Emma E. Holmes Diary, 10 April 1863, SHC.
24. Pliny Brown Letter, 10 April 1863, SHC.

25. Emma Holmes Diary, SHC.

26. Josiah Gorgas Journal, 12 April 1863, SHC.

27. *Charleston Daily Courier,* 13 April 1863.

28. Charles D. Sabine to his brother, 15 February 1863, Pension Records, AR.

29. *Charleston Daily Courier,* 13 April 1863.

30. *ORs,* pp. 284–85.

31. Adjutant General's Office Report, Sec. 4234 BAGOEB73, 15 May 1863, AR.

32. *Navy ORs,* Series I, 14:121–22.

33. Captain Percival Drayton, *Naval Letters* (New York: n.p., 1906).

34. *Charleston Daily Courier,* 11 April 1863.

35. *ORs,* p. 697.

36. Ibid., pp. 712–13.

37. Ibid., pp. 940–41.

38. Various Confederate personnel records, AR.

39. Thomas Wentworth Higginson, *Army Life in a Black Regiment* (Alexandria, Va.: Time-Life Books, 1982), p. 134.

40. Susie King Taylor, *A Black Woman's Civil War Memories* (New York: M. Wiener Publishers, 1988), p. 58.

41. *ORs,* p. 447.

42. James Henry Gooding, *On the Altar of Freedom: A Black Soldier's Civil War Letters from the Front* (Amherst: University of Massachusetts Press, 1911), p. 11.

43. Michael Kiener Personnel Records (Confederate), AR.

6: THE ARMY OF THE CUMBERLAND

1. James A. Garfield, *The Wild Life of the Army: Civil War Letters of James A. Garfield* (East Lansing, Mich.: Michigan State University Press, 1964), p. 256.

2. Philip H. Sheridan, *Personal Memoirs* (New York: C. L. Webster and Co., 1888), p. 259.

3. Captain Ephraim A. Wilson, *Memoirs of the War* (Cleveland: W. M. Boyne Printing Co., 1893), p. 174.

4. John Beatty, *Memoirs of a Volunteer,* ed. Harvey S. Ford (New York: W. W. Norton and Co., Inc., 1946), p. 184.

5. A. S. Bloomfield to his sister, 11 April 1863, Bloomfield Letters, LC.

6. *Nashville Union,* 11 April 1863.

7. Ezekiel Ennis Service Record, AR.

8. Beatty, *Memoirs,* p. 187.

9. James M. Sligh to his mother, 12 April 1863, Sligh Family Papers, MHC.

10. Asbury Welsh to his father, John Welsh, 29 March 1863, Frakes Family Private Papers, Chicago.

11. James H. M. Montgomery to his family, 10 April 1863, Montgomery Family Papers, LC.

12. Daniel Waite Howe, *Civil War Times* (Indianapolis: Bowen-Merrill Co., 1902), 10 April 1863.

13. Charles C. Hood Diary, 10 April 1863, Charles Crook Hood Collection, LC.

14. Eugene H. Bronson to Ed. P. Flanders, 2 June 1863, E. P. Flanders Papers, MHC.

15. A. S. Bloomfield to his sister, 27 April 1863, Bloomfield Letters, LC.

16. Ibid.

17. Asbury P. Welsh to his father, 19 March 1863, Frakes Family Private Papers, Chicago.

18. Angus L. Waddle, *Three Years with the Armies of the Ohio and the Cumberland* (Chillicothe, Ohio: Scioto Gazette Book and Job Office, 1889), p. 46.

19. Henry A. Buck to Helen A. Buck, 1 April 1863, Buck Manuscripts, BUR.

20. Beatty, *Memoirs,* p. 184.

21. A. S. Bloomfield to his sister, 27 April 1863, Bloomfield Letters, LC.

22. Alfred Lacey Hough, *Soldier in the West: Civil War Letters of Alfred Lacey Hough* (Philadelphia: University of Pennsylvania Press, 1957), p. 89.

23. Benjamin F. Scribner, "How Soldiers Are Made," p. 103, NYSL.

24. Hough, *Soldier in the West,* p. 89.

25. Beatty, *Memoirs,* p. 185.

26. Ibid., p. 187.

27. Susanne Colton Wilson, comp., *Column South, with the 15th Pennsylvania Cavalry* (Flagstaff, Ariz.: J. F. Colton and Co., 1960), p. 34.

28. Howe, *Civil War Times,* 8 April 1863.

29. John Weissert to his wife, 10 April 1863, MHC.

30. Waddle, *Three Years,* p. 46.

31. John Knight, *Civil War Letters of John Knight,* comp. Lucy Brown (Oak Park, Ill.: Lucy Brown 1940).

32. Jay Caldwell Butler, *Letters Home* (Binghamton, N.Y.: privately printed, 1930), p. 48.

33. A. S. Bloomfield to his sister, 10 April 1863, Bloomfield Letters, LC.

34. Hough, *Soldier in the West,* p. 90.

35. George Drake, *The Mail Goes Through: Civil War Letters of George Drake,* ed. Julia A. Drake (San Angelo, Tex.: Anchor Publishing Co., 1964), 11 April 1863.

36. Weissert Letter, 10 April 1863, MHC.

37. Garfield, *Civil War Letters,* p. 255.

38. Ibid., p. 254.

39. David Haines Letter, Haines Papers, BUR.

40. Garfield, *Civil War Letters,* p. 257.

41. Welsh Letter, 19 March 1863, Frakes Family Private Papers, Chicago.

42. *Nashville Dispatch,* 10 April 1863.

43. Bloomfield Letter, 27 April 1863, LC.

44. Bloomfield Letter, 11 April 1863, LC.

45. Isaac Henry Clay Royce, *History of 115th Regiment Illinois Volunteer Infantry* (Terra Haute, Ind.: Isaac H. C. Royce, 1900), p. 56.
46. James M. Sligh to his mother, 12 April 1863, Sligh Family Papers, MHC.
47. Ibid.
48. James H. M. Montgomery Diary, 10 April 1863, Montgomery Family Papers, LC.
49. *ORs,* Series I, 23:294.
50. Garfield, *Civil War Letters,* p. 256.
51. *Nashville Dispatch,* 10–11 April 1863.

7: CONFEDERATES IN TENNESSEE
 1. Shelby Foote, *The Civil War, 3* vols. (New York: Random House, 1963), 2:172–75.
 2. *ORs,* Series I, vol. 23, pt. 2, p. 745.
 3. Ibid.
 4. Ibid., pp. 170–71.
 5. *Cincinnati Daily Commercial,* 10 April 1863.
 6. *ORs,* p. 749.
 7. *ORs,* Series I, vol. 24, pt. 3, pp. 719–33.
 8. Ibid., p. 731.
 9. *ORs,* Series I, vol. 23, pt. 3, p. 730.
10. Ibid.
11. Thomas L. Connelly, *Autumn of Glory* (Baton Rouge: Louisiana State University Press, 1965), p. 98.
12. Ibid., p. 172.
13. *ORs,* Series I, vol. 23, pt. 3, p. 745.
14. Alto Loftin Jackson, ed. *So Mourns the Dove: Letters of Benjamin Franklin Jackson* (New York: Exposition Press, 1965), p. 50.
15. Colonel Taylor Beatty Diary, 10 April 1863, SHC.
16. Nathaniel C. Hughes, Jr., *General William J. Hardee, Old Reliable* (Baton Rouge: Louisiana State University Press, 1965), pp. 150–51.
17. John S. Jackman Journal, 23 April 1863, LC.
18. Ibid.
19. W. E. Bevens, *Reminiscences of a Private* (Newport, Ark.: self-published, 1913), p. 38.
20. Colonel Taylor Beatty Diary, 10 April 1863, SHC.
21. Captain James Lyton Cooper, "Memoirs," in *Tennessee Historical Quarterly* 15, June 1956.
22. Hughes, *General William J. Hardee,* p. 151.
23. Ibid.
24. *ORs,* p. 749.
25. Robert Masten Holmes, *Kemper County Rebel: The Civil War Diary of Robert Masten Holmes* (Jackson: University and College Press of Mississippi, 1973), p. 83.
26. *ORs,* p. 747.

27. Ibid.
28. Holmes, *Kemper County Rebel,* pp. 80–81.
29. Thomas Wayman Hendricks, *Cherished Letters of Thomas Wayman Hendricks* (Birmingham, Ala.: Birmingham Publishing Co., 1947), 13 April 1863.
30. Rufus W. Cater to his cousin Fanny, 7 April 1863, Rufus Cater Papers, LC.
31. John S. Jackman Journal, 23 April 1863, LC.
32. Bevens, *Reminiscences,* p. 38.

8: EASTERN TENNESSEE AND KENTUCKY

1. George Washington Whitman, *Civil War Letters of George Washington Whitman,* ed. Jerome M. Loving (Durham, N.C.: Duke University Press, 1975), pp. 90, 91.
2. Israel Atkins to his mother and father, 13 April 1863, Israel Atkins Papers, MSU.
3. Lieutenant John C. Buchanan to his wife, Sophie, 10 April 1863, Buchanan Letters, GRPL.
4. Jerome J. Robbins Diary, 11 April 1863, MHC.
5. Charles B. Haydon Diary, 9 April 1863, MHC.
6. Jerome J. Robbins Diary, 10 April 1863, MHC.
7. John F. Brobst, *Well Mary—Civil War Letters of a Wisconsin Volunteer,* ed. Margaret Brobst Roth (Madison: University of Wisconsin Press, 1960), p. 66.
8. David Millspaugh Diary, 10 April 1863, MHC.
9. William Boston Diary, 10 April 1863, MHC.
10. Charles Haydon Diary, 10 April 1863, MHC.
11. Alonzo M. Keeler Diary, 10 April 1863, MHC.
12. *Louisville Daily Democrat,* 11 April 1863.
13. Franklin Thompson Service Record, AR.
14. Lieutenant John C. Buchanan to his wife, Sophie, 12 April 1863, Buchanan Letters, GRPL.
15. *Cincinnati Daily Commercial,* 13 April 1863.
16. *ORs,* Series I, 23:747.
17. Joseph Espey to his sister Margaret Espey, 10 April 1863, SHC.
18. George Richard Browder, *The Heavens Are Weeping: Diaries of George Richard Browder* (Grand Rapids, Mich.: Zondervan Publishing Co., 1987), p. 149.
19. John Cotton, *Yours Till Death* (Tuscaloosa, Ala.: University of Alabama Press, 1951), p. 59.
20. Ibid., p. 58.
21. Ibid., p. 60.
22. Edward Owings Guerrant Diary, 9–10 April 1863, SHC.
23. Joseph Espey to his sister, 10 April 1863, SHC.
24. William E. Sloan Diary, 31 March 1863, Tennessee State Archives, Nashville.

25. William E. Sloan Diary, 9 April 1863, Tennessee State Archives, Nashville.

9: A FIGHT AT FRANKLIN

1. *ORs,* Series I, vol. 23, pt. 1, pp. 222–24.
2. Ibid., pp. 155–57.
3. *Nashville Dispatch,* 12 April 1863.
4. *A Soldier's Honor: Major General Earl Van Dorn by his Comrades* (New York: Abbey Press, 1902),
5. *Nashville Union,* 11 April 1863.
6. *ORs,* p. 222.
7. T. F. Jackson Memoirs, Manuscript Collection, Mississippi Department of Archives and History, Jackson.
8. *ORs,* p. 229.
9. Ibid., p. 226.
10. Charles Edwin Cort, *Dear Friends: The Civil War Letters and Diary of Charles E. Cort* (Helyn W. Tomlinson, 1962), pp. 2–3.
11. Annette Tapert, ed., *The Brothers' War: Civil War Letters to Their Loved Ones from the Blue and Gray* (New York: Times Books, 1988), p. 135.
12. E. L. Drake, *Annals of the Army of Tennessee* (Nashville: A. D. Haynes, 1878), p. 23.
13. Andrew N. Lytle, *Bedford Forrest and His Critter Company* (New York: Minton, Balch and Co., 1931), p. 148.
14. John W. Morton, *Artillery of Nathan Bedford Forrest's Cavalry* (Nashville: M. E. Church South, Smith and Lamar, agents, 1909), p. 88.
15. Robert Selph Henry, *First with the Most Forrest* (New York: Bobbs Merrill, 1944), p. 798.
16. J. G. Vale, *Minty and the Cavalry* (Harrisburg, Pa.: Edwin K. Meyers, 1886), pp. 146–47.
17. *Atlanta Southern Confederacy,* 16 April 1863.
18. John A. Wyeth, *That Devil Forrest* (N.Y.: Harper and Brothers, 1959), p. 163.
19. Ibid., p. 163.
20. *Atlanta Southern Confederacy,* 22 April 1863.
21. Lytle, *Bedford Forrest,* p. 149.
22. *Nashville Dispatch,* 12 April 1863.
23. Lt. Thomas Healy and Lt. Thomas Simson Service Records, AR.
24. Healey Service Record, AR.
25. Francis B. Heitman, *Historical Register & Dictionary of the United States Army, 2* vols. (Washington, D.C.: Government Printing Office, 1903), 2:413.
26. Charles R. Cooper, *Chronological and Alphabetical Record of the Engagements of the Great Civil War* (Milwaukee, Wis.: Gaxton Press, 1904).
27. Benson J. Lossing, *A History of the Civil War* (New York: War Memorial Association, 1902), p. 224.
28. Cort, *Civil War Letters,* p. 4.

29. Frederick H. Dyer, *A Compendium of the War of the Rebellion,* 3 pts. (New York: Thomas Yoseloff, 1959), II:589.

30. General Thomas Jordan and J. P. Pryor, *Campaigns of General Forrest* (Cincinnati: J. P. Miller Co., 1868).

31. Morton, *Artillery of Forrest's Cavalry,* p. 89.

32. *ORs,* Series I, vol. 52, pt. 2, p. 455.

33. Regimental Records, AR.

10: TRAIN RAIDS AND OTHER EXPEDITIONS

1. Theodore F. Upson, *With Sherman to the Sea: Letters and Diaries of Theodore F. Upson* (Baton Rouge: LSU Press, 1943), pp. 94, 95.

2. J. W. DuBose, *Gen. Joseph Wheeler and the Army of Tennessee* (New York: Neale Pub. Co., 1912), p. 159.

3. Robert Franklin Bunting to *Tri Weekly Telegraph,* 24 July 1863, Robert F. Bunting Papers, The Center for American History, University of Texas of Austin.

4. Robert Franklin Bunting Diary, 10 April 1863, University of Texas at Austin.

5. *ORs,* Series I, vol. 23, p. 219.

6. Edwin Worden Service Record, AR.

7. Ephraim C. Dawes Diary, Ephraim C. Dawes Papers, NL.

8. A. S. Bloomfield to his sister, 27 April 1863, LC.

9. Robert Franklin Bunting to *Tri Weekly Telegraph,* 24 July 1863, University of Texas at Austin.

10. John Robertson, *Michigan in the War* (Lansing: W. S. George and Co., 1882), p. 430.

11. D. M. Ransdell Diary, 10 April 1863, SHC.

12. Frank Batchelor and George Turner, *Batchelor-Turner Letters,* an. H.J.H. Rugeley (Austin, Tex.: Printed by Steck Co., 1961, Copyrighted by H.J.H. R.), p. 48.

13. Francis Vanderburgh Service Record, AR.

14. Batchelor and Turner, *Letters,* p. 48.

15. Ibid.

16. *ORs,* p. 219.

17. Batchelor and Turner, *Letters,* p. 48.

18. Benjamin F. Scribner, *How Soldiers Were Made* (New Albany, Ind.: n.p., 1887), p. 103.

19. Colonel Hans Christian Heg, *Civil War Letters* (Norwegian American Historical Association, 1936), 11 April 1863.

20. *Cincinnati Daily Commercial,* 15 April 1863.

21. *Nashville Union,* 14 April 1863.

22. *ORs,* p. 219.

23. Batchelor and Turner, *Letters,* pp. 48–49; *Nashville Dispatch,* 14 April 1863.

24. Corydon Edward Foote, *With Sherman to the Sea* (New York: John Day Co., 1960), pp. 94–95.

25. Batchelor and Turner, *Letters,* pp. 48–49.

26. *ORs,* p. 218.

27. Rev. J. S. Hoyt, Francis Vanderburgh Funeral Oration, 3 May 1863, BUR.

28. Leonidas Giles, *Terry's Texas Rangers* (Austin, Tex.: Pemberton Press, 1967), p. 22.

29. *Cincinnati Daily Commercial,* 15 April 1863.

30. Company M 5th Iowa Cavalry Records, AR.

31. Mrs. William Lyon Diary, 10 April 1863; Colonel William Penn Lyon, "Reminiscences of the Civil War," NYSL.

32. Colonel William Penn Lyon, 13 April 1863, NYSL.

33. *Chicago Tribune,* 18 April 1863.

34. *Cincinnati Gazette,* 13 April 1863.

35. 118th Ohio Infantry Regimental Records, AR.

36. James W. Caldwell Service Record, AR.

37. *Chicago Tribune,* 18 April 1863; *Cincinnati Gazette,* 13 April 1863.

38. Wesley McMillen Service Record, AR; Regimental Muster, 118th Ohio Infantry, AR.

39. *ORs,* Series I, vol. XXIV, pt. 1, p. 515.

40. James Hoy Service Record, AR.

41. Nathan Baldwin Service Record, AR.

42. *ORs,* Series I, vol. 24, pt. 1, pp. 516–17.

43. National Cemetery Records, Nashville.

44. U.S. Quartermaster's Department, *Roll of Honor,* (Washington, D.C.: Government Printing Office, 1868) 12:165.

45. Horace J. Blanton Service Record, AR.

11: THE MISSISSIPPI

1. Charles A. Dana, *Recollections of the Civil War* (New York: Appleton and Co., 1898), p. 20.

2. *ORs,* Series I, vol. 24, pt. 1, p. 77.

3. Ibid., pp. 182–83.

4. Julia Dent Grant, *The Personal Memoirs of Julia Dent Grant* (New York: Putnam, [1975]), p. 111.

5. Milt Shaw to Alf Giagne, 10 March 1863.

6. Mark Mayo Boatner, III, *Civil War Dictionary* (New York: McKay Publishing Co., 1959), pp. 871–73.

7. *Washington Evening Star,* 11 April 1863.

8. *ORs,* Series I, vol. 24, pt. 3, pp. 179–80.

9. John Fiske, *The Mississippi Valley in the Civil War* (Boston: Houghton Mifflin Co., 1900), pp. 226–27.

10. William T. Sherman to his brother, 10 April 1963, General William Tecumseh Sherman, LC.

11. *ORs,* p. 249.

12. Ibid.

13. Dana to Stanton, 10 April 1863, Lincoln Papers, LC.

14. Ulysess S. Grant, *Personal Memoirs* (New York: Da Capo Press, Inc., Plenum Publishing Corp., 1982), p. 458.
15. *ORs,* p. 180.
16. *Navy ORs,* Series I, vol. 24, p. 280.
17. Ibid., p. 541.
18. Ibid.
19. Warren D. Crandall, *History of the Ram Fleet* (St. Louis, Mo.: privately printed, 1907), pp. 271–72.
20. C. W. Gerard, *A Diary, the Eighty-third Ohio Volunteer Infantry in the War,* (n.p., n.d.).
21. Isaac Jackson, *Some of the Boys: Civil War Letters of Isaac Jackson* (Carbondale: Southern Illinois University Press, 1960), p. 23.
22. B. F. Stevenson, *Letters from the Army* (Cincinnati: Robert Clarke and Co., 1886), 10 April 1863.
23. Alfred B. Cree to his wife, 14 April 1863, LSU.
24. Jackson, *Civil War Letters,* p. 24.
25. *Cincinnati Daily Commercial,* 10 April 1863.
26. John Griffith Jones to his parents, 11 April 1863, John Griffith Jones Correspondence, LC.
27. "Porter's Private Journal," David Dixon Porter Papers, LC, pp. 561–62.
28. Walter Flatt, "Man's Home," Typescript letters to his wife and children, 10 April 1863.
29. Victor Hicken, *Illinois in the War* (Urbana: University of Illinois Press, 1966), p. 94.
30. Flatt, "Man's Home," 17 April 1863.
31. Owen Johnston Hopkins, *Under the Flag of the Nation: Diaries and Letters of a Yankee Volunteer in the Civil War* (Columbus: Ohio State University Press, 1961), p. 50.
32. James K. Newton, *A Wisconsin Boy in Dixie: Selected Letters,* (Madison: University of Wisconsin Press, 1961), p. 15.
33. Thomas Davis to his wife, 10 April 1863, MSU.
34. James Bradley Diary, May 1863, James E. Bradley Family Papers, LSU.
35. Henry Clay Warmoth Diary, 9–11 April 1863, SHC.
36. Edmund Newsome, *Experiences in the War of the Great Rebellion* (Carbondale, Ill.: E. Newsome, 1879), 10 April 1863.
37. Flatt, "Man's Home," 10 April 1863.
38. Thomas Davis Letter, 10 April 1863, MSU.
39. Newton, *Selected Letters,* p. 15.
40. *ORs,* Series I, vol. 24, pt. 3, pp. 702–6.
41. Ibid., p. 734.
42. Ibid., p. 763.
43. *Vicksburg Daily Whig,* 10 April 1863.
44. *Albany Atlas and Argus,* 10 April 1863.
45. *Chattanooga Daily Rebel,* 10 April 1863.
46. *Charleston Daily Courier,* 14 April 1863.

47. *ORs,* Series I, vol. 24, pt. 3, p. 731.
48. Colonel J.A.W. Johnson, quoted in *Atlanta Southern Confederacy,* 10 April 1863.
49. *ORs,* p. 731.
50. Ibid.
51. W. A. Wash, *Camp, Field and Prison Life* (St. Louis, Mo.: Southwestern Book and Publishing Co., 1870), p. 24.
52. Richard Wheeler, *Siege of Vicksburg* (New York: Crowell, 1978), p. 102.
53. Ibid., p. 101.
54. Ibid., p. 103.
55. Federick H. Dyer, *A Compendium of the War of the Rebellion, 3* pts. (New York: Thomas Yoseloff, 1959), III:1021–23.
56. *ORs,* Series I, vol. 24, pt. 2, p. 420.
57. Absalom Grimes, *Confederate Mail Runner* (New Haven, Conn.: Yale University Press, 1926), pp. 119–20.
58. Kate Stone, *Brockenburn: The Journal of Kate Stone* (Baton Rouge: Louisiana State University Press, 1955), pp. 186–87.
59. *Daily Mississippian,* (Jackson, Miss.) 10 April 1863.
60. Mary W. Loughborough, *My Cave Life in Vicksburg* (Spartanburg, S.C.: Reprint Co., 1976), pp. 11–13.
61. Fisher Funeral Home Original Records, 10 April 1863, Vicksburg Historical Museum.
62. Sergeant William P. Chambers, *My Journal* (Mississippi Historical Society, 1925), p. 261.
63. *Daily Mississippian,* 12 April 1863.
64. Peter F. Walker, *Vicksburg: A People at War, 1860–1865* (Chapel Hill: University of North Carolina Press, 1960), p. 150.
65. *Vicksburg Daily Whig,* 4 April 1863.
66. Ibid.
67. William R. Barry to his sister, 10 April 1863, MDAH.
68. Samuel Andrew Agnew Diary, 10 April 1863, SHC.
69. *Daily Mississippian,* 10 April 1863.
70. Chattahoochee Valley Historical Society, *War Was the Place: A Centennial Collection of Confederate Letters* (Atlanta, Ga.: Chattahoochee Valley Historical Society, 1961), pp. 86–87.
71. Lucius W. Barber, *Army Memoirs of Lucius Barber, Co. D, 15th Illinois Volunteer Infantry* (Chicago: J.M.W. Jones Stationery and Printing Co., 1865), p. 35.
72. Ibid.
73. Francis Wayland Dunn Diary, 3–9 April 1863, Francis Wayland Dunn Papers, MHC.
74. Ibid., 10 April 1863.
75. Sister M. to General Sherman, 10 April 1863, Sherman Papers, LC.
76. George Cadman to his wife, 9 April 1863, SHC.
77. James H. Goodnow to his family, 10 April 1863, MHC.

78. William M. Ferry to his wife, 12 April 1863, William Montague Ferry Papers, MHC.

79. *ORs,* pp. 184, 187.

80. W. L. Ritter, "Third Maryland Battery on the Mississippi in 1863," Southern Historical Society Papers (Millwood, N.Y.: Kraus Reprint Co., 1977), 7:247.

81. Elbert D. Willett, *History of Co. B, 40th Alabama Regiment C.S.A.* (Anniston, Ala.: Printed by Norwood, 1902), pp. 30–31.

82. *ORs,* p. 505.

83. J. Russell to his friends, 17 April 1863, LSU.

84. Charles Dana Miller, "A Narrative of the Service of Brevet Major Charles Dana Miller," Typescript, Vero Beach Public Library, Vero Beach, Florida.

85. D. Alexander Brown, *Grierson's Raid* (Urbana: University of Illinois Press, 1962), pp. 23–24.

86. *ORs,* Series I, vol. 24, pt. 3, p. 185.

87. Ibid.

88. Brown, *Grierson's Raid,* pp. 107–111.

89. *ORs,* pp. 528–29.

90. Ibid., pp. 186–87.

12: THE GULF

1. *ORs,* Series I, vol. 24, pt. 3, p. 182.

2. Frederick Phisterer, *Statistical Record of the Armies of the United States,* Campaigns of the Civil War Series (New York: Blue and Gray Press, n.d.), p. 251.

3. Thomas Chickering, *Imprints—A Diary of Thomas Chickering* (Boston: J. E. Farwell and Co., 1863), p. 8.

4. Lieutenant Colonel Frank Henry Peck to his mother, 31 March 1863, Montgomery Family Papers, LC.

5. Frank M. Flinn, *Campaigning with Banks and Sheridan* (Boston: W. B. Clarke and Co., 1889), p. 29.

6. James K. Hosner, *The Color-Guard* (Boston: Walker, Wise and Co., 1864), p. 120.

7. Ibid., p. 122.

8. Ibid.

9. D. S. Chadbourne to his father, 9 April 1863, LSU.

10. Ephraim Betts Diary, 9–10 April 1863, LSU.

11. David Hunter Strother, *A Virginia Yankee in the Civil War,* ed. Cecil D. Eby, Jr. (Chapel Hill: University of North Carolina Press, 1961), pp. 166–67.

12. *ORs,* Series I, vol. 15, pp. 396–97.

13. *ORs,* Series I, vol. 53, p. 465.

14. Charles L. Dufour, *The Night the War Was Lost* (Garden City, N.Y.: Doubleday and Co., 1960), p. 326.

15. *ORs,* Series I, vol. 15, p. 399.

16. Ibid., p. 386.
17. Charles Henry Moulton to his brother and sister, 9 April 1863, MHC.
18. Ibid.
19. Eli A. Griffin to John Woodruff, 9 April 1863, MHC.
20. Eli A. Griffin to his wife, 13 April 1863, MHC.
21. Rodney Webster Torrey Diary, 9 April 1863, NYSL.
22. Ibid., 10 April 1863, NYSL.
23. Jonathan Huntington Johnson, *Letters and Diaries of Jonathan Huntington Johnson,* collected and compiled by his grandson, Alden Chase Brett (A. C. Brett, 1961), 10 April 1863.
24. Anonymous Letter, 11 April 1863, Miscellaneous Civil War Collection, LSU.
25. Lawrence Van Alstyne, *Diary of an Enlisted Man* (New Haven, Conn.: Tuttle, Morehouse and Taylor Co., 1910), pp. 94–97.
26. Frederick H. Dyer, *A Compendium of the War of the Rebellion, 3* pts. (New York: Thomas Yoseloff, 1959), 3: p. 1284.
27. Surgeon General's Office, *Medical and Surgical History of the Civil War, 15* vols. (Wilmington, N.C.: Broadfoot Pub. Co.), 1:297.
28. *ORs,* p. 294.
29. Henry Warren Howe, *Passage from the Life of Henry Warren Howe* (Lowell, Mass.: Courier-Citizen Co., Printers, 1899), 14 April 1863.
30. Henry E. Fales to his brother Silas, 10 April 1863, LC.
31. Henry Graham Memoir 1862–63, 9–10 April 1863, LC.
32. John Corden to his wife, 12 April 1863, MHC.
33. Wilbur Spalding to his wife and children, 10 April 1863, MHC.
34. *ORs,* p. 1039.
35. Thomas Rawlings Myers, "Memoirs," Tennessee State Archives, Nashville.
36. *ORs,* Series I, vol. 24, pt. 3, p. 702.
37. Phisterer, *Statistical Record,* p. 138.
38. Lieutenant James Taswell Mackey Diary, 10 April 1863, CM.
39. Daniel P. Smith, *History of Co. K, First Alabama Regiment* (Gaithersburg, Md.: Butternut Press, 1984), p. 56.
40. William Y. Dixon Diary, 6, 10 April 1863, William F. Dixon Papers, LSU.
41. *Navy ORs,* Series I, vol. 20, p. 131.
42. *ORs,* Series I, vol. 15, p. 400.
43. Smith, *History of Co. K,* p. 56.
44. Dufour, *The Night the War Was Lost,* pp. 346–48.
45. Shelby Foote, *The Civil War, 3* vols. (New York: Random House, 1963), 2:164.
46. *New Orleans Times Picayune,* 10 April 1863.
47. Ibid.
48. Ibid.
49. Ibid.

13: THE FAR WEST

1. *ORs,* Series I, vol. 22, pt. 1, p. 9.
2. Ibid., pt. 2, pp. 187–88.
3. W. Craig Gaines, *The Confederate Cherokees: John Drew's Regiment of Mounted Rifles* (Baton Rouge: Louisiana State University Press, 1963), p. 111.
4. *ORs,* Series I, vol. 22, pt. 2, p. 209.
5. Ibid., p. 208.
6. Benjamin F. McIntyre, *Federals on the Frontier: Diary of Benjamin McIntyre,* ed. Nannie M. Tilley (Austin: University of Texas Press, 1963), p. 136.
7. Ibid., p. 137.
8. Michael Fellman, *Inside War: The Guerrilla Conflict in Missouri During the Civil War* (New York: Oxford University Press, 1989), p. 79.
9. Charles Lewis Francis, *Narrative of a Private Soldier in the Volunteer Army* (Brooklyn, N.Y.: William Jenkins, 1879), 10 April 1863.
10. Ibid.
11. *Nashville Union,* 10 April 1863.
12. General Clement Anselm Evans, ed., *Confederate Military History, 12* vols. (Atlanta: Confederate Publishing Co., 1899), 12:131.
13. *ORs,* Series I, vol. 22, pt. 1, pp. 820–21.
14. Ibid., p. 822.
15. Elijah Parsons Petty, *Journey to Pleasant Hill: Civil War Letters of Captain Elijah P. Petty* (San Antonio: University of Texas, 1982) pp. 167–68.
16. Junius Newport Bragg, *Letters of a Confederate Surgeon* (Camden, Ark.: Hurley Co., 1960), 9 April 1863.
17. Lieutenant Colonel James A. Fremantle, *The Fremantle Diary,* ed. Walter Lord (Boston: Little, Brown and Co., 1954), 9 April 1863.
18. John Camden West, *A Texan in Search of a Fight: Being the Diary and Letters of John Camden West* (Waco, Tex.: Texian Press, 1969), p. 7.
19. William W. Heartsill, *1491 days in the Confederate Army,* ed. Bell I. Wiley (Jackson, Tenn.: McCowat-Mercer Press, 1954), p. 119.
20. Benjamin M. Seaton, *The Bugle Softly Blows: Confederate Diary of Benjamin M. Seaton* (Waco, Tex.: Texian Press, 1965), p. 32.
21. Samuel T. Foster, *One of Cleburne's Command* (Austin: University of Texas Press, 1954), pp. 34–35.
22. *ORs,* p. 221.
23. Ibid., p. 211.
24. Ibid., p. 249.
25. George O. Hand Diary, 10 April 1863, LC.
26. *Cincinnati Daily Commercial,* 13 April 1863.
27. *ORs,* Series I, vol. 50, pt. 1, p. 206.
28. Ibid., p. 393.
29. Ibid., p. 1113.
30. Ibid., p. 209.
31. Ibid., p. 203.

32. Ibid., p. 188.
33. Ibid., p. 454.

14: THE NAVIES

1. *Navy ORs,* Series I, vol. 5, p. 258.
2. *New York Times,* 10 April 1863.
3. *Navy ORs,* Series I, vol. 8, pp. 699–700.
4. Ibid.
5. Ibid., p. 682.
6. Ibid., p. 694.
7. Ibid., p. 682.
8. Ibid., p. 715.
9. Ibid., p. 666.
10. Ibid.
11. Ibid., p. 700.
12. *ORs,* Series I, vol. 18, p. 595.
13. Ibid., p. 1009.
14. Ibid.
15. Robert G. H. Kean, *Inside the Confederate Government: Diary of Robert G. H. Kean, Head of the Bureau of War* (New York: Oxford University Press, 1957), p. 52.
16. *Navy ORs,* Series I, vol. 14, pp. 6, 7.
17. *New York Daily Tribune,* 10 April 1863.
18. *ORs,* vol. 14, p. 898.
19. *Southern Illustrated News,* 18 April 1863.
20. Stephen R. Wise, *Lifeline of the Confederacy* (Columbia: University of South Carolina Press, 1988), p. 252.
21. *Navy ORs,* pp. 116–17.
22. Ibid., p. 118.
23. Ibid., p. 119.
24. Ibid., p. 121.
25. *ORs,* Series I, vol. 14, p. 283.
26. James Michael Barr to his family, 12 April 1863, CM.
27. "James A. Graham Papers," *James Sprunt Historical Studies,* (Chapel Hill: University of North Carolina Press, 1928), vol. 20, no. 2, 12 April 1863.
28. CSS *Atlanta* Medical Log, 10 April 1863, LC.
29. Surgeon Boyer Diary, 10 April 1863, CHS.
30. *Navy ORs,* pp. 122–23.
31. *Navy ORs,* Series I, vol. 17, p. 411.
32. Ibid.
33. George W. Gift to Ellen Augusta Shackleford, 11 April 1863, Ellen Gift Collection, SHC.
34. W. H. Andrews, *Footprints of a Regiment: A Recollection of the First Georgia Regulars* (Atlanta: Longstreet Press, 1992), p. 114.
35. *Navy ORs,* Series I, vol. 20, p. 282.

36. Ibid., pp. 765–66.
37. Ibid., p. 128.
38. Ibid., p. 130.
39. Ibid., p. 129.
40. Ibid., Series I, vol. 24, p. 533.
41. Ibid., p. 133.
42. *Navy ORs,* Series I, vol. 20, p. 132.
43. Ibid., pp. 814–15.
44. John M. Taylor, *Confederate Raider* (Washington, D.C.: Brassey's, 1994), p. 105.
45. Chester G. Hearn, *Gray Raiders of the Sea* (Camden, Maine: International Marine Publishing, 1992), p. 314.
46. Raphael Semmes, *Memoirs of Service Afloat* (New York: Blue and Gray Press, 1987), p. 595.
47. Ibid., p. 597.
48. Hearn, *Gray Raiders,* pp. 79–80.
49. James M. Morgan, *Recollections of a Rebel Reefer* (Boston: Houghton Mifflin Co., 1917), p. 116.
50. Ibid., pp. 116–17.
51. Ibid.
52. *Navy ORs,* Series I, vol. 2, pp. 149–50.
53. *New York Times,* 10 April 1863.
54. *Navy ORs,* p. 155.
55. Ibid., p. 158.
56. Ibid., p. 156.

SELECTED BIBLIOGRAPHY

The following references have been selected from thousands of books and manuscripts examined during several years of research. Many other sources provided important clues, even though they are not listed. The four published works used most frequently are:

War of the Rebellion: Official Records of the Union and Confederate Armies (ORs). 128 vols., Washington, D.C.: 1880–1901.

Official Records of the Union and Confederate Navies in the War of the Rebellion (Navy ORs). 30 vols., Washington, D.C.: 1896–1927.

Frederick H. Dyer. *A Compendium of the War of the Rebellion* 3 parts New York: Thomas Yoseloff, 1959.

Mark Mayo Boatner III. *The Civil War Dictionary.* New York: David McKay Co., 1959.

These books were indispensable in writing this book.

PRIMARY SOURCES

Manuscript Letters, Diaries, and Memoirs

1. National Archives, Washington, D.C.: Pension and Service Records of George W. Bartlett, Horace J. Blanton, Thomas Branch, Thomas Briggs, James Caldwell, James Chapman, Ezekiel Ennis, Samuel Freeman, D. J. Godwin, Thomas Healy, James M. Henry, James Hoy, William Jones, Charles Sabine, Thomas Simson, Abel Streight, Franklin Thompson, Frank Tocy, Robert Tomlin, Francis Vanderburg, Benjamin Wallace, Robert Ware, Alphonso C. Webster, James Welsh, Edwin Worden, and Freeman Young.

2. Burton Historical Collection, Detroit Public Library, Detroit, Michigan: Henry A. Buck, Letters; Adam Gurowski, Diary; David H. Haines, Letters; William Rush, Diary; Charles H. Salter, Letter, Duffield Papers; R. A. Shotwell, Papers.

3. Chicago Historical Society, Chicago, Illinois: John J. Ballard, "Diary of a Confederate"; George Dodd Carrington, Diary; Dr. Samuel Willard, Case Record Book.

4. Eleanor S. Brockenbrough Library, Museum of the Confederacy, Richmond, Virginia: James Barr, Letters; William Kennedy Estes, Diary; E. G.

Halloway, Diary; James Taswell Mackey, Diary; Lieutenant W. L. Maury, Log of CSS *Georgia;* Lawson Morrissett, Diary; J. Thomas Petty, Diary; Kate Mason Rowland, Collection; Cornelius D. Walker, Diary.

5. Library of Congress: Cleveland Abbe, Papers; Alston Family Papers; Orra Bailey, Papers; J. Benjamin, Diary (Confederate Collection); A. S. Bloomfield, Letters; William H. Bradbury, Papers; Rufus Cater, Papers; General Joshua Chamberlain, Papers; B. N. Clements, Papers; Charles Calvin Enslow, Letterbook; General Charles Ewing, Papers; Henry Graham, "Memoir 1862–63"; Sergeant William Haines, Diary; Isaac Hallock, Papers; George O. Hand, Diary; General Samuel Peter Heintzelman, Papers; General Ethan Allan Hitchcock, Papers; Lyman C. Holford, Papers; Joseph Holt, Papers; Charles Crook Hood, Collection; Jedediah Hotchkiss, Collection; John S. Jackman, Journal; John Griffith Jones, Correspondence; General Joseph W. Keifer, Papers; Mary Lorrain Greenhow Lee, Diary; Abraham Lincoln Papers; John Wesley Marshall, Diary; Captain James H. Montgomery, Diary, Montgomery Family Papers; General Marsena Rudolph Patrick, Diary; David Pease, Collection; Admiral David Dixon Porter, Papers; Charles Welling Reed, Papers; David A. Rice, Collection; Edmund Ruffin, Diary; W. C. Shackleford, Letter; General Philip Henry Sheridan, Papers; General William Tecumseh Sherman, Papers; George Boyd Smith, Papers; Bela Taylor St. John, Papers; Edward McMasters Stanton, Papers; Charles O. Terry, Papers; Gilbert Thompson, Memoir; George Alfred Trenholm, Papers; Edwin Oberlin Wentworth, Papers; E. Willis, Letterbook (Confederate Collection); Charles H. Woodwell, Diary; Henry Stevens Wylie, Diary; USS *Cayuga,* Log.

6. Special Collections, Hill Library, Louisiana State University, Baton Rouge, Louisiana: Charles B. Allaire, Letters; Anonymous Letter, Miscellaneous Civil War Collection; Ephraim Betts, Diaries; James E. Bradley, Family Papers; D. S. Chadbourne, Letters; Alfred B. Cree, Letter; William Y. Dixon, Papers; J. Russell, Letters.

7. Michigan Historical Collections, Bentley Historical Library, University of Michigan, Ann Arbor, Michigan: William Boston, Diary; Eugene H. Bronson, Letter; E. P. Flanders, Papers; John Corden, Letters; Francis Wayland Dunn, Papers; William Montague Ferry, Papers; Claudius Grand, Diary, Fitzgerald Family Papers; Eli A. Griffin, Letters; Charles B. Haydon, Diary; Alonzo Keeler, Diary; David Millspaugh, Diary; Charles Henry Moulton, Papers; Jerome Robbins, Diary; Sligh Family Papers; Wilbur Spalding, Papers; John Weissert, Letters.

8. University Archives and Historical Collections, Michigan State University, East Lansing, Michigan: Israel Atkins, Papers; James Brandish, Papers; Thomas Davis, Papers; Othniel Gooding, Papers; Edwin Havens, Papers; John C. McClain, Diary.

9. Mississippi Department of Archives and History, Manuscript Collection, Jackson, Mississippi: William R. Barry, Letters; Samuel F. Billingsley, Service Record; T. F. Jackson, "Memoir."

10. Newberry Library, Chicago, Illinois: E. C. Dawes, Diary; Thomas Parish Murphy, Papers (typescript).

11. New York State Library, Albany, New York: Albert N. Ames, Papers; Waters Whipple Braman, "War of the Rebellion"; Philip Corell, Papers; Colonel John Simpson Crocker, Papers; Lamotte K. Davendorf, Papers; Stafford Godfrey, Diary; John W. Hays, Papers; William Penn Lyon, Diary; Benjamin F. Scribner, "How Soldiers Are Made." Rodney Webster Torrey, Diary.

12. Southern Historical Collections, Wilson Library, University of North Carolina at Chapel Hill, North Carolina: Samuel Andrew Agnew, Diary; James W. Albright, Diary; Edward Porter Alexander, Correspondence; Blanche Baker, Papers; George Beall Balch, Letterbook; David Cranshaw Barrows, Papers; Isaac Basset, Diary; Colonel Taylor Beatty, Diary; Catherine Barbara Brown, Diary; Lucy Wood Butler, Papers; George O. Cadman, Correspondence; William Calder, Papers; Thomas Lanier Clingman, Papers; D. Coleman, Diary; Dr. Elias Davis, Papers; Lacy Drury, Papers; George Phifer Erwin, Letters; Joseph Espy, Letters; Samuel A. Firebaugh Diary; James McFadden Gaston, Papers; Ellen Gift Collection; Leonidas C. Glenn, Papers; Josiah Gorgas, Papers; Duff Green, Correspondence; Thomas Jefferson Green, Papers; James Hervey Greenlee, Diary; John Berkley Grimball, Diary; Edward Owen Guerrant, Diary; William Robert Gwaltney, Diary; Eli Spinks Hamilton, Papers; George Hanvey, Papers; Edward J. Harden, Papers; Major George Washington Finley Harper, Diary; David Golightly Harris, Journal; Christopher Hollowell, Papers; Emma E. Holmes, Diary; Thomas J. Jennings, Papers; Cadwallader Jones, Papers; H. C. Kendrick, Correspondence; Francis Milton Kennedy, Diary; Levert Family Papers; George William Logan, Papers; Henry Armand London, Papers; John Newland Maffit, Papers; James Mallory, Farm Journal; James Washington Matthews, Diary; George A. Mercer, Diary; Oliver E. Mercer, Papers; William Letcher Mitchell, Papers; Jacob Pearch/John Paris, Diary; Thomas Ruffin, Papers; Charles Spencer, Diary; Samuel Spencer, Papers; Ruffin Thomson, Papers; Arthur L. Van Vleck, Diary; Henry Clay Warmouth, Diary; Wayside Home, Union Point, Georgia, Register; Alexander Smith Webb, Papers; Edmund Jones Williams, Letters; G. S. Williams, Papers; Henry Willis Williams, Correspondence; George W. Wills, Letters.

13. Tennessee State Library and Archives, Nashville, Tennessee: Thomas Rawling Myers, Memoirs; I. N. Rainey, "Experiences in the Confederate Army"; William E. Sloan, Diary.

14. United States Army Military History Institute, Carlisle, Pennsylvania
   a. Civil War Times Illustrated Collection: William H. Brown, "Reminiscences"; Richard F. Eddins, Correspondence; John E. Hart, Correspondence; Henry Henny, Diary and Letters.
   b. Harrisburg Civil War Round Table Collection: Jared L. Ainsworth, "With the New York Dragoons"; A. Billig, Letter (William W. Geety Papers); Gregory A. Caco, Collection; Andrew G. Curtin, Collection; W. R. Eddington, "Memoir April 2, 1842–July 25, 1934"; McCahan Family, "History of the 9th Pennsylvania Cavalry"; David Nichol, Let-

ters; Robert W. Rodgers, "Diary—100th Pennsylvania Infantry Regiment."

c. Civil War Miscellaneous: Henry S. Carroll Papers; Foster Family Papers.

15. Miscellaneous

George H. and Laura E. Brown Library, Washington, North Carolina: Annie Blackwell Sparrow, "Reminiscences"; Henry Jesse Sumner, "Civil War Diary." Frakes Family Private Papers, Chicago, Illinois: Welsh Letters. Public Library, Grand Rapids, Michigan: John C. Buchanan, Letters. Horney Family Collection, Chicago, Illinois: G.W.H. Kemper, Diaries. McCain Library and Archives, University of Southern Mississippi, Hattiesburg, Mississippi: Service Records of Mississippi Regiments. New York City Library: Elizabeth Van Lew, Journal. Historical Museum, Vicksburg, Mississippi: Fisher Funeral Home Records. Center for American History, University of Texas at Austin: Robert F. Bunting, Papers. Virginia State Library and Archives, Richmond, Virginia: John R. Bagley, Letters; Dr. James R. Boulware, Diary; Elizabeth Van Lew, "Memoirs."

Printed Letters, Diaries, and Memoirs

Andrews, W. H. *Footprints of a Regiment: A Recollection of the First Georgia Regulars.* Atlanta: Longstreet Press, 1992.

Barber, Lucius W. *Army Memoirs of Lucius Barber, Co. D, 15th Illinois Volunteer Infantry.* Chicago: J.M.W. Jones Stationery and Printing Co., 1865.

Batchelor, Frank and George Turner. *Batchelor-Turner Letters.* an. H.J.H. Rugeley. Austin, Tex.: Printed by Steck Co. Copyrighted by H.J.H.R., 1961.

Beatty, John. *Memoirs of a Volunteer.* Edited by Harvey S. Ford. New York: W. W. Norton and Co., 1946.

Benson, Berry. *Berry Benson's Civil War Book.* Athens: University of Georgia Press, 1962.

Blake, Henry N. *Three Years in the Army of the Potomac.* Boston: Lee and Shepherd, 1865.

Blanding, Stephen. *Recollections of a Sailor Boy.* Providence, R.I.: E. A. Johnson and Co., 1886.

Bull, Rice C. *Soldiering: The Civil War Diary of Rice C. Bull, 123rd New York Volunteer Infantry.* San Rafael, Calif.: Presidio Press, 1977.

Chattahoochee Valley Historical Society. *War Was the Place: A Centennial Collection of Confederate Letters.* Atlanta, Ga.: Chattahoochee Valley Historical Society, 1961.

Chesnut, Mary. *Diary from Dixie.* New York: D. Appleton and Co., 1905.

Cort, Charles Edwin. *Dear Friends: The Civil War Letters & Diary of Charles E. Cort.* Helyn W. Tomlinson, 1962.

Cotton, John. *Yours Till Death.* University, Ala.: University of Alabama Press, 1951.

Dana, Charles A. *Recollections of the Civil War*. New York: Appleton and Co., 1898.

De Forest, B. S. *Random Sketches and Wandering Thoughts*. Albany, N.Y.: Avery Herrick, Publisher, 1966.

Dooley, Captain John Edward. *A Confederate Soldier: His Journal*. Washington: Georgetown University Press, 1945.

Drake, George. *The Mail Goes Through: Civil War Letters of George Drake*. San Angelo, Tex.: Anchor Pub. Co., 1964.

Drayton, Captain Percival. *Naval Letters*. New York: n.p., 1906.

Favill, J. M. *Diary of a Young Officer*. Chicago: R. R. Donnelly and Sons, 1909.

Fiske, Samuel Wheelock. *Mr. Dunn Brown's Experiences in the Army*. Boston: Nichols and Noyes, 1866.

Fisk, Wilbur. *Hard Marching Every Day: Civil War Letters of Pvt. Wilbur Fisk*. Edited by Emil and Ruth Rosenblatt. Lawrence, Kans.: University Press of Kansas, 1992.

Fleet, Benjamin Robert. *Green Mount*. Lexington, Ky.: University of Kentucky Press, 1962.

Fletcher, William Andrew. *Rebel Private—Front and Rear*. Austin: University of Texas Press, 1954.

Flinn, Frank M. *Campaigning with Banks and Sheridan*. Boston: W. B. Clarke and Co., 1889.

Foote, Corydon. *With Sherman to the Sea*. New York: John Day Co., 1960.

Foster, Samuel T. *One of Cleburne's Command*. Austin: University of Texas Press, 1954.

Fremantle, James A. L. *The Fremantle Diary*. Edited by Walter Lord. Boston: Little, Brown and Co., 1954.

Garfield, James A. *The Wild Life of the Army: Civil War Letters*. East Lansing: Michigan State University Press, 1964.

Gerard, C. W. *A Diary: The Eighty-third Ohio Volunteer Infantry in the War*. (n.p., n.d.)

Gibbon, John. *Personal Recollections of the War*. New York: G. P. Putnam's Sons, 1928.

Gooding, James Henry. *On the Altar of Freedom: A Black Soldier's Civil War Letters from the Front*. Amherst: University of Massachusetts Press, 1911.

Grant, Julia Dent. *The Personal Memoirs of Julia Dent Grant*. New York: Putnam, [1975].

Grant, Ullysses S. *Personal Memoirs*. New York: Da Capo Press, Inc., Plenum Publishing Corp., 1982.

Grimes, Abasalom. *Confederate Mail Runner*. Edited by M. M. Quaife. New Haven, Conn.: Yale University Press, 1926.

Haines, Zenas T. *Letters from the 44th Regiment Massachusetts Volunteer Infantry*. Boston: Herald Job Office, 1863.

Hall, James E. *Diary of a Confederate Soldier*. n.p., 1961.

Haskell, John Cheves. *Haskell's Memoirs*. New York: G. P. Putnam's Sons, 1960.

Hay, John. *Diaries and Letters of John Hay.* Edited by Tyler Dennett. New York: Dodd, Mead, 1939.

Heartsill, William Williston. *Fourteen Hundred and 91 Days in the Confederate Army.* Edited by Bell Irvin Wiley. Jackson, Tenn.: McCowat-Mercer Press, 1953.

Heg, Hans Christian. *Civil War Letters of Col. Hans Christian Heg.* n.p.: Norwegian American Historical Association, 1936.

Holmes, Robert Masten. *Kemper County Rebel: the Civil War Diary of Robert Masten Holmes, C.S.A.* ed. Frank Allen Dennis. Jackson: University and College Press of Mississippi, 1973.

Hough, Alfred Lacey. *Soldier in the West: Civil War Letters of Alfred Lacey Hough.* Philadelphia: University of Pennsylvania Press, 1957.

Howe, Daniel Waite. *Civil War Times.* Indianapolis: Bowen-Merrill Co., 1902.

Jackson, Alto Loftin, ed. *So Mourns the Dove.* New York: Exposition Press, 1965.

Jackson, Edgar Allan. "Letters of Edgar Allan Jackson." (n.p. n.d.)

Jackson, Isaac. *Some of the Boys: Civil War Letters of Isaac Jackson.* Carbondale: Southern Illinois University Press, 1960.

Jones, Jenkin Lloyd. *An Artilleryman's Diary.* Madison, Wis.: Wisconsin Historical Commission, 1914.

Jones, John B. *A Rebel War Clerk's Diary.* New York: Old Hickory Bookshop, 1935.

Larson, James. *Sergeant Larson, 4th Cavalry.* San Antonio, Tex.: Southern Literary Institute, 1935.

Livermore, Mary A. *My Story of the War.* Hartford, Conn.: A. D. Worthington and Co., 1889.

Locke, E. W. *"We Must Not Fall Back Anymore": 3 Years in Camp and Hospital.* Boston: G. D. Russell and Co., 1870.

Loughborough, Mary W. *My Cave Life in Vicksburg, with Letters of Trial and Travel.* Spartanburg, S.C.: Reprint Co., 1976.

Lyon, Colonel William Penn. *Reminiscences of Civil War.* San Jose, Calif.: Muirson and Wright, 1907.

Mathis, Ray, ed. *In the Land of the Living: Wartime Letters by Confederates.* Troy, Ala.: Troy State University Press, 1981.

McIntyre, Benjamin. *Federals on the Frontier: Diary of Benjamin McIntyre,* ed. Nannie M. Tilley. Austin, Tex.: University of Texas Press, 1963.

Morgan, James M. *Recollections of a Rebel Reefer.* Boston: Houghton Mifflin Co., 1917.

Newton, James K. *A Wisconsin Boy in Dixie (Selected Letters).* Madison: University of Wisconsin Press, 1961.

Nugent, William Lewis. *My Dear Nellie: The Civil War Letters of William L. Nugent.* Jackson: University Press of Mississippi, 1977.

Petty, Elijah Parsons. *Journey to Pleasant Hill: Civil War Letters of Captain Petty.* San Antonio: University of Texas, n.d.

Pickett, George. *Soldier of the South*. Richmond, Va.: Books for Libraries Press, 1928.

Riley, Franklin Lafayette. *Grandfather's Journal: Company B, 16th Mississippi*. Dayton, Ohio: Morningside, 1988.

Salm-Salm, Princess Felix (Agnes LeClerc). *Ten Years of My Life*. New York: R. Worthington, 1877.

Seymour, William J. *The Civil War Memoirs of Captain William J. Seymour*. Baton Rouge: Louisiana State University Press, 1991.

Sheridan, General Philip Henry. *Personal Memoirs of P. H. Sheridan, General, U.S. Army*. New York: C. L. Webster and Co., 1888.

Sherman, General William Tecumseh. *Home Letters of General Sherman*. Edited by M. A. DeWolfe Howe. New York: Scribner's Sons, 1909.

Sorrel, General G. Moxley. *Recollections of a Confederate State Officer*. New York: Neale Publishing Co., 1905.

Stevens, George T. *Three Years in the 6th Corps*. Alexandria, Va.: Time-Life Books, 1984.

Stevenson, Surgeon B. F. *Letters from the Army*. Cincinnati: Robert Clarke and Co., 1886.

Stone, Kate. *Brokenburn: The Journal of Kate Stone*. Baton Rouge: Louisiana State University Press, 1955.

Strong, George Templeton. *The Diary of George Templeton Strong*. New York: Macmillan, 1952.

Strother, David Hunt. *A Virginia Yankee in the Civil War*. Edited by Cecil D. Eby, Jr. Chapel Hill: University of North Carolina Press, 1961.

Tappert, Annette. *The Brother's War: Civil War Letters to their Loved Ones*. New York: Times Books, 1988.

Taylor, Susie King. *A Black Woman's Civil War Memories*. New York: M. Wiener, 1988.

Upson, Theodore F. *With Sherman to the Sea: Letters and Diaries of T. F. Upson*. Baton Rouge: Louisiana State University Press, 1943.

Van Alstyne, Lawrence. *Diary of an Enlisted Man*. New Haven, Conn.: Tuttle, Morehouse and Taylor, 1910.

Waddle, Angus L. *Three Years with the Armies of the Ohio and Cumberland*. Chillicothe, Ohio: Scioto Gazette Book and Job Office, 1889.

Wash, Captain W. A. *Camp, Field and Prison Life*. St. Louis, Mo.: Southwestern Book and Publishing, 1870.

Welles, Gideon. *Diary of Gideon Welles*. Boston: Houghton Mifflin Co., 1911.

White, Oliver. *Service in the Marine Artillery*. Toulon, Ill.: n.p., 1863.

Whitman, George Washington. *Civil War Letters of G. W. Whitman*. Edited by Jerome M. Loving. Durham, N.C.: Duke University Press, 1975.

William, General Alpheus S. *From the Cannon's Mouth*. Detroit: Wayne State University Press, 1959.

Wilson, Captain Ephraim A. *Memoirs of the War*. Cleveland: W. M. Bayne Printing Co., 1893.

Worsham, John H. *One of Jackson's Foot Cavalry.* New York: Neale Publishing Co., 1912.

Wyeth, John Jasper. *Leaves from a Diary Written While Serving in Co. E 44th Mass.* Boston: L. F. Lawrence and Co., 1878.

Newspapers

Albany (N.Y.) *Atlas and Argus; Atlanta Southern Confederacy; Charleston* (S.C.) *Daily Courier; Chattanooga Daily Rebel; Cincinnati Daily Commercial; Confederate Veteran* (Richmond); *Daily Messenger* (Washington, N.C.); *Daily Mississippian* (Jackson, Miss.); *Daily National Intelligencer* (Washington, D.C.); *Daily Richmond Examiner; Daily True Delta* (New Orleans); *Detroit Advertiser and Tribune; Detroit Free Press; Frederick* (Md.) *Examiner; Living Age* (Boston); *Louisville* (Ky.) *Daily Democrat; Nashville Daily Union; Nashville Dispatch; New Orleans Times-Picayune; New York Daily Tribune; New York Times; Richmond Daily Sentinel; Richmond Dispatch; Richmond Whig; Rockingham* (Va.) *Register; Virginia Advertiser; Shreveport* (La.) *Weekly News; Southern Illustrated News* (Richmond); *Vicksburg* (Miss.) *Daily Whig; Washington* (D.C.) *Evening Star; Watertown* (N.Y.) *Daily News; Weekly Junior Register* (Franklin, La.); *Weekly Savannah* (Ga.) *Republican.*

SECONDARY SOURCES

Regimental Histories

Anders, Leslie. *The Eighteenth Missouri.* Indianapolis: Bobbs-Merrill Company, n.d.

Andrews, W. H. *Footprints of a Regiment (1st Georgia Regulars M Co).* Atlanta: Longstreet Press, 1992.

Baker, Levi W. *Ninth Massachusetts Battery.* Boston: Lakeview Press, 1888.

Beach, Surgeon John N. *History of the 40th Ohio Volunteer Infantry.* London, Ohio: Shepherd and Craig, Printers, 1884.

Carter, William R. *History of 1st Tennessee Cavalry (Union).* Knoxville: Gant-Ogden Co., 1902.

Collins, Lieutenant R. M. *Chapters from Unwritten History in the War Between the States.* St. Louis: Nixon-Jones, 1893.

Crandall, Warren D. *History of the Ram Fleet.* St. Louis: privately printed, 1907.

Divine, John. *35th Battalion Virginia Cavalry.* Lynchburg, Va.: H. E. Howard, 1985.

Duke, Basil W. *History of Morgan's Cavalry.* Bloomington: Indiana University Press, 1960.

Gaines, W. Craig. *The Confederate Cherokees: J. Drew's Regiment of Mounted Rifles.* Baton Rouge: Louisiana State University Press, 1989.

Gardner, James B., ed. *Forty-Fourth Massachusetts Infantry: Record of Service.* Boston: Cambridge University Press, 1887.

Giles, Leonidas Banton. *Terry's Texas Rangers.* Austin, Tex.: Pemberton Press, 1967.

Goodheart, Briscoe. *History of the Loudoun County Rangers.* Washington, D.C.: Press of McGill and Wallace, 1896.

Hall, Henry. *Cayuga in the Field, a Record of the 19th New York Volunteers etc.* Auburn, N.Y.: Truair, Smith and Co., 1873.

Hannaford, E. *Sixth Regiment Ohio Volunteer Infantry.* Cincinnati: Hannaford, 1868.

Hewes, F. W. *History of the . . . 10th Michigan Volunteer Infantry.* Detroit: John Slaters Printing, 1864.

Higginson, Thomas Wentworth. *Army Life in a Black Regiment.* Alexandria, Va.: Time-Life Books, 1982.

Hinkley, Julian W. *Service with the Third (Wisconsin Infantry).* Wisconsin History Commission, 1912.

Hosner, James K. *The Color Guard.* Boston: W. B. Clarke and Co., 1889.

Kirwan, Thomas. *Memorial History of the 17th Regiment Massachusetts Volunteer Infantry.* Salem, Mass.: Salem Press Co., 1911.

Myers, Frank. *The Comanches: A History of White's Battalion, Virginia Cavalry.* Marietta, Ga.: Continental Book Co., 1956.

Rhodes, Robert Hunt, ed. *All for the Union: History of the 2nd Rhode Island Volunteer Infantry in the Civil War.* Lincoln, R.I.: A Mowbray, 1985.

Ritter, W. L. "Third Maryland Battery on the Mississippi in 1863," *Southern Historical Society Papers.* Millwood, N.Y.: Krauss Reprint Co., 1977.

Robertson, James T. *Stonewall Brigade.* Baton Rouge: Louisiana State University Press, 1963.

Royce, Isaac Henry Clay. *History of the 115th Regiment Illinois Volunteer Infantry.* Terra Haute, Ind.: Isaac H. C. Royce, 1900.

Sipes, William B. *History of the 7th Pennsylvania Cavalry.* Pottsville, Pa.: Miners Journal Print, 1905.

Smith, Daniel P. *History of Company K, First Alabama Regiment.* Gaithersburg, Md.: Butternut Press, 1984.

Sykes, Edward Turner. *Walthall's Brigade: A Cursory Sketch with Personal Experiences.* n.p., 1916.

Willett, Captain Elbert D. *History of Co. B 40th Alabama Regiment C.S.A.* Anniston, Ala.: Norwood, 1902.

Wilson, Suzanne Colton, comp. *Column South with the 15th Pennsylvania Cavalry.* Edited by Colton and Smith. Flagstaff, Ariz.: J. F. Colton and Co., 1960.

Gardner, J. B. *Record of Service: Forty-fourth Massachusetts Infantry.* Boston: privately printed, 1887.

————. *Vermont Volunteers, Revised Roster.* Montpelier, Vt.: Press of the Watchman, 1892.

Government Sources

California Adjutant General. *Records of California Troops.* Sacramento: State Office, 1890.

Civil War Centennial Commission. *Facts About the Civil War.* Washington, D.C.: Civil War Centennial Commission, 1959.

Confederate States Congress. *Journal of the Congress of the Confederate States of America 1861.* Richmond, Va.: 1863.

Davis, George B., et al., *Official Military Atlas of the Civil War.* New York: Grammercy Books, 1983. Originally published Washington, D.C.: Government Printing Office, 1903.

Heitman, Francis B. *Historical Register and Dictionary of the United States Army.* 2 vols. Washington, D.C.: Government Printing Office, 1903.

Lindsley, John B. *Military Annals of Tennessee.* Nashville: n.p., 1886.

Michigan Adjutant General. *Annual Report of the State of Michigan for the Year 1863.* Lansing, Mich.: John A. Kerr and Co., 1864.

Richardson, James D. *Messages and Papers of the Presidents,* vol. 6, *1861–1869.* Bureau of National Literature and Art, 1904.

Surgeon General's Office. *Medical and Surgical History of the Civil War.* 15 vols. Wilmington, N.C.: Broadfoot, 1990.

Tennessee Adjutant General. *Report on the State of Tennessee.* Nashville: n.p., 1866.

U.S. Quartermaster's Department. *Roll of Honor.* 27 vols. Washington, D.C.: Government Printing Office, 1868.

Books

Abdill, George B. *Civil War Railroads.* Seattle: Superior Publishing Co., 1961.

Appleton's Annual Cyclopedia. New York: D. Appleton and Co., 1903.

Barrett, John G. *The Civil War in North Carolina.* Chapel Hill: University of North Carolina Press, 1963.

Benét, Stephen Vincent. *John Brown's Body.* New York: Holt, Rinehart and Winston, 1969.

Brooks, Noah. *Washington in Lincoln's Time.* New York: Rinehart, 1958.

Brown, Brigadier General George H., comp. *Record of Service of Michigan Volunteers in the Civil War.* Kalamazoo, Mich.: Ihling Bros. and Everard, n.d.

Brown, D. Alexander. *Grierson's Raid.* Urbana: University of Illinois Press, 1962.

Butterfield, Julia L., ed. *A Biographical Memorial of General Daniel Butterfield.* New York: Grafton Press, 1904.

Catton, Bruce. *Glory Road.* Garden City, N.Y.: Doubleday and Co., 1952.

Catton, Bruce. *Mr. Lincoln's Army.* Garden City, N.Y.: Doubleday and Co., 1951.

Chambers, Lenoir. *Stonewall Jackson.* New York: William Morrow and Co., 1959.

Cooper, Charles R. *Chronological and Alphabetical Records of the Engagements of the Great Civil War.* Milwaukee: Gaxton Press, 1904.

Dowdey, Clifford. *Lee.* Boston: Little, Brown and Co., 1965.

DuBose, John W. *General Joseph Wheeler and the Army of Tennessee.* New York: Neale Publishing Co., 1912.

Dufour, Charles L. *The Night the War Was Lost.* Garden City, N.Y.: Doubleday, 1960.

Dyer, John. *The Gallant Hood.* New York: Bobbs Merrill, 1950.

Foote, Shelby. *The Civil War.* 3 vols. New York: Random House, 1963.

Freeman, Douglas Southall. *Lee.* New York: Charles Scribner and Sons, 1961.

Henry, Robert Selph. *First with the Most Forrest.* New York: Bobbs-Merrill, 1944.

Hill, Lois, ed. *Poems and Songs of the Civil War.* New York: Grammercy Books, 1990.

Hitchcock, Benjamin W. *Hitchcock's Chronological Record of the American Civil War.* New York: Benjamin W. Hitchcock, 1866.

Horn, Stanley F. *Army of the Tennessee.* New York: Bobbs-Merrill, 1941.

Hughes, Nathaniel C. *General William J. Hardee: Old Reliable.* Baton Rouge: Louisiana State University Press, 1965.

Ingersoll, L. D. *Iowa and the Rebellion.* Philadelphia: J. B. Lippincott and Co., 1866.

Jordan, General Thomas, and Pryor, J. P. *Campaigns of General Forrest and of Forrest's Cavalry.* Cincinnati: J. P. Miller Co., 1868.

Leech, Margaret. *Reveille in Washington.* New York: Harper and Brothers, 1941.

Livermore, Thomas. *Numbers and Losses in the Civil War.* New York: Houghton Mifflin and Co., 1900.

Long, E. B. *Civil War Day by Day.* New York: Doubleday and Co., 1971.

Longstreet, James. *From Manassas to Appomattox.* New York: J. B. Lippincott, 1896.

Lonn, Ella. *Desertion During the Civil War.* New York: Century Co. (American Historical Association), 1928.

Lossing, Benson J. *A History of the Civil War.* New York: War Memorial Association, 1912.

Lytle, Andrew N. *Bedford Forrest and His Critter Company.* New York: Minton, Balch and Co., 1931.

McPherson, James. *Battle Cry of Freedom: The Era of the Civil War.* New York: Oxford University Press, 1988.

Miller, Francis Trevelyan, ed. *Photographic History of the Civil War.* 10 vols. New York: Review of Reviews Co., 1911.

Moore, Frank. *Rebellion Record.* New York: Putnam, 1863.

Morton, John W. *Artillery of Nathan Bedford Forrest's Cavalry.* Nashville: Publishing House of ME Church South, 1909.

Nevins, Allan. *The War for the Union.* 3 vols. New York: Charles Scribner and Sons, 1960.

Phisterer, Frederick. *Statistical Record of the Armies of the United States.* Campaigns of the Civil War Series. New York: Blue and Gray Press, n.d.

Putnam, Sallie A. B. *Richmond During the War.* New York: G. W. Carleton, 1867.

Quint, Alonzo H. *The Potomac and the Rapidan.* Boston: Crosby and Nichols, 1864.

Rhodes, James Ford. *History of the Civil War.* New York: Macmillan Co., 1917.

Ripley, Warren. *Artillery and Ammunition of the Civil War*. New York: Promontory Press, 1970.

Robertson, John. *Michigan in the War*. Lansing, Mich.: W. S. George and Co., 1882.

Sandburg, Carl. *Abraham Lincoln, the War Years*. New York: Harcourt, Brace and Co., 1939.

Smith, Page. *Trial by Fire: A People's History of the Civil War and Reconstruction*. New York: McGraw-Hill, 1982.

Taylor, John M. *Confederate Raider*. Washington, D.C.: Brassey's, 1994.

Taylor, Richard. *Destruction and Reconstruction*. New York: D. Appleton and Co., 1879.

Walker, Peter F. *Vicksburg—a People at War, 1860–1865*. Chapel Hill: University of North Carolina Press, 1960.

Wheeler, Richard. *Siege of Vicksburg*. New York: Crowell, 1978.

Wise, Stephen R. *Lifeline of the Confederacy: Blockade Running During the Civil War*. Columbia: University of South Carolina Press, 1988.

Woodbury, Augustus. *Major General Ambrose Burnside and the 9th Army Corps*. Sidney S. Rider and Brother, 1867.

Wyeth, John A. *That Devil Forrest*. New York: Harper Brothers, 1959.

———. *Calendar of the Civil War*. Boston: Rockwell and Churchill, 1890.

INDEX